international
review of
social history

Special Issue 24

Conquerors, Employers and Arbiters: States and Shifts in Labour Relations, 1500–2000

Edited by Karin Hofmeester, Gijs Kessler, and Christine Moll-Murata

Published by the Press Syndicate of the University of Cambridge
The Pitt Building, Trumpington Street, Cambridge, CB2 1RP
1 Liberty Plaza, Floor 20, New York, NY 10006, USA
10 Stamford Road, Oakleigh, Melbourne 3166, Australia

© Internationaal Instituut voor Sociale Geschiedenis

*A catalogue record for this book is available
from the British Library*

Library of Congress Cataloguing-in-Publication Data applied for

ISBN 9781316642528 (paperback)

Printed in the UK by Bell & Bain Ltd, Glasgow, UK.

CONTENTS

Conquerors, Employers and Arbiters: States and Shifts in Labour Relations, 1500–2000

Edited by
Karin Hofmeester, Gijs Kessler, and Christine Moll-Murata

IRSH 61 (2016), Special Issue, pp. 1–26 doi:10.1017/S0020859016000523
© 2016 Internationaal Instituut voor Sociale Geschiedenis

Conquerors, Employers, and Arbiters: States and Shifts in Labour Relations 1500–2000, Introduction

KARIN HOFMEESTER, GIJS KESSLER, and
CHRISTINE MOLL-MURATA

International Institute of Social History
Cruquiusweg 31, 1019 AT Amsterdam, The Netherlands

E-mail: kho@iisg.nl

ABSTRACT: The introductory article to this volume offers an analytical framework for the capacities in which states have historically affected labour relations. The framework captures the full range of possible manifestations of state power, including early states, empires, regional authorities, and city states. It distinguishes between the state as a direct actor or participant, carrying out tasks deemed essential for its functioning, and the state as an arbiter, redistributor, or regulator. As conquerors or employers, states are confronted with a basic dilemma: how to extract and allocate the labour resources required to accomplish state tasks. Borrowing from Charles Tilly, the two broad categories of capital and coercion are used as a heuristic device to bring order to the ways in which states have solved this dilemma. Contrary to Tilly's trajectories of state formation, states' reliance on capital or coercion is subject to a great degree of flexibility, both over time and across space. In their capacities as mediators and regulators, modern states came to have an even more profound impact on labour relations, as state building moved away from the single focus on organizing the extraction of resources to a wider mission of fostering welfare, economic development, and human capital formation.

INTRODUCTION

This volume owes its existence to the Global Collaboratory on the History of Labour Relations, a long-standing effort uniting labour historians across the globe in an attempt to trace and explain historical shifts in labour relations over a timeframe roughly coinciding with the rise and subsequent development of capitalism (1500–2000).[1] Labour relations are understood as the full range of vertical and horizontal social relations under which work

---

1. The Global Collaboratory on the History of Labour Relations is based at the International Institute of Social History, Amsterdam, and financed by the Gerda Henkel Stiftung (Dusseldorf), the Netherlands Organisation for Scientific Research (NWO), and the International Institute of Social History. See https://collab.iisg.nl/web/LabourRelations/, last accessed 20 May 2016.

is performed, starting from a basic subdivision in society between those who are not expected or who are unable to work (the young, the elderly, and the infirm) as well as the unemployed, and those who work, whether part-time or full-time, outside the home or at home, in self-employment, or as wage earners, in slavery, or as employers.[2] The first phase of this project (2007–2012) consisted of data mining and brought together data on labour relations on the basis of a shared taxonomy (see the appendix to this introduction for the taxonomy and the definitions of the various labour relations) in five benchmark years (1500, 1650, 1800, 1900, 2000) for a wide range of countries across Europe, Asia, Africa, and the Americas.[3]

The second phase of the project seeks explanations for shifts in labour relations as well as for the possible patterns observed therein. Causes and consequences of shifts in labour relations are explored by looking in depth at possible explanatory factors in a series of dedicated workshops in order to subsequently combine the insights this produces into proper multi-causal explanations. The central question that interests us here is under what conditions shifts take place, how these impacted the way work was valued and compensated, and what the consequences were for the level of inequality in society.[4]

The first workshop in this series examined the role of the state in effecting shifts in labour relations; the results are reported in the present Special Issue.[5] The reason that we started our investigation based on the state is that the state emerged from our fact finding as the single most visible factor inducing shifts in labour relations, such as the emergence of the second serfdom in seventeenth-century Muscovy, the rise of military labour through mercenary armies and navies, conquest and subjugation, colonial exploitation, and the mass resort to convict labour and forced labour in twentieth-century

---

2. Karin Hofmeester *et al.*, "The Global Collaboratory on the History of Labour Relations, 1500–2000: Background, Set-Up, Taxonomy, and Applications", available at http://hdl.handle.net/10622/4OGRAD, last accessed 17 June 2016.

3. For the data, please refer to https://collab.iisg.nl/web/labourrelations/results, as retrieved on 20 May 2016. For Africa, a sixth cross section for 1950 has been included in the data-mining programme.

4. Leo Lucassen, "Working Together: New Directions in Global Labour History", *Journal of Global History*, 11:1 (2016), pp. 66–87.

5. The workshop "Political Change as a Determinant of Shifting Labour Relations" took place on 6–7 February 2014 at the International Institute of Social History in Amsterdam. The editors of this Special Issue would like to thank Maarten Prak for his help and advice in convening this workshop, and all participants for their contributions, whether reworked into articles and included in this Special Issue, or expressed during presentations (i.e. of the work of Andrea Caracausi, William Guanglin Liu, and Alessandro Stanziani). We are grateful, too, for the comments by the discussants Maarten Prak, Ewout Frankema, and Anna Meeuwisse, which have found their way into the thoughts underlying this introduction. The editors would like to express their thanks to our English-language editor, Chris Gordon, and to the cartographer, Annelieke Vries-Baaijens, for their committed and reliable work on the articles presented here.

totalitarian societies. Other examples of state intervention in labour relations are the abolition of slavery, regulation of child and women's labour, labour legislation, and, in a more recent past, the introduction of welfare states exempting part of the population from the need to work in order to support oneself. The articles in this volume look at shifts in labour relations in a wide diversity of periods and places, ranging from the sixteenth-century silver mines of Potosí in the Andes to late twentieth-century Sweden, and from seventeenth-century Dzungharia to early twentieth-century colonial Mozambique.

In this Special Issue, we use the term "state", a widely accepted term or concept in the various debates on state formation, even though the term "polity" more adequately captures the range of possible manifestations of state power, including early states, empires, and, at the meso and micro levels (including neighbourhoods and their governments), regional authorities and city states. Our use of the term "state" should not be read as a sign of an uncritical and straightforward identification of the state as a single-level actor, with one single and coherent policy. State-society relations, the role of supranational polities as well as the role of social agency in shaping, resisting, deflecting, and modifying state action, are taken on board wherever possible in the articles in this volume, also leaving room for unintended consequences of state policies.

STATE FORMATION: RESOURCE EXTRACTION AND GOVERNANCE

The principal analytical framework for our findings is provided by the scholarship on state formation. Our understanding of states is both organizational and instrumental. To start with, a definition of the organizational element: states consist of institutions and personnel that determine political relations radiating to and from a centre. They cover a territorially demarcated area over which they exercise power to make binding rules and, in doing so, they are backed up by organized physical force.[6] The more instrumental definition of states is more difficult to give, since definitions of state functions are often determined by political theories and thus can be contradictory; moreover, state functions differ over time and space. However, an indispensable activity of any state is the extraction of the resources, in cash, kind, or manpower, needed to exercise power and determine political relations. Centralizing power, enforcing a monopoly on the use of coercion, and extracting the resources allowing rulers to achieve these first two goals are the basic steps in state formation.

---

6. This definition is based on Michael Mann, *The Sources of Social Power. Volume 2: The Rise of Classes and Nation-States, 1760–1914* (New York, 2012), pp. 54–56.

In addition, state formation can also include the development of infrastructure, education, and social security systems. However, the occurrence of these forms of state formation varies widely over time and space. Before we address a reasoned selection of the extensive literature on state formation, it is necessary to identify the relevance of the different aspects of state formation for labour relations, so we can connect these to the shifts in labour relations that can be historically observed.

Firstly, it is necessary to distinguish between the state as a direct actor or participant, carrying out tasks deemed essential for its functioning, and the state as an arbiter, redistributor, or regulator. As a direct actor, the state influences labour relations as an employer – initially, above all, as a military employer – as well as in its capacity as a conqueror, effecting existing and possibly imposing new labour relations on conquered societies. For want of a better term, this also includes the "employment" of forced labour and conscript labour. As an arbiter, redistributor, or regulator, the state acts to steer other social forces in directions deemed to be beneficial either for the functioning of the state itself, or to political and ideological agendas espoused by the state. These two capacities of the state are not strictly separated, but intertwined, and have existed side by side throughout trajectories of state formation, although, over time, the importance of the state as an arbiter and regulator has undeniably increased.

It has been argued in response to our categorization that if the state participates in the labour market, it is not, and cannot be, a purely impartial arbiter or redistributor, because as an employer it must live up to the obligations and regulations it imposes, including, for example, possible restrictions on the use of forced or tributary labour, and this can affect policymaking. Also, states can be dominated by and act in the interests of certain social groups or classes and will therefore often tend to take sides.[7] Some of the authors of this Special Issue stress this point more strongly than others.

In constructing the analytical framework for this volume, and the workshop that preceded it, we were inspired by the work of Charles Tilly on early modern European state-formation processes. In his seminal work on the relationship between war-making and state-building,[8] he argues that European rulers, locked in geopolitical competition, were continuously confronted with the need to raise the means and extract the resources to wage their increasingly costly wars. This constituted the main driving force behind the processes of state formation as they played out in early modern Europe. Rulers needed to mobilize more and more resources to fund their wars and built increasingly elaborate extraction apparatuses, which eventually developed into the states we know today.

---

7. We would like to thank Marcel van der Linden for this remark.
8. Charles Tilly, *Coercion, Capital, and European States, AD 990–1990* (Cambridge, MA, 1990).

Tilly distinguished between three principal trajectories along this path, and it was particularly this aspect of his work that inspired us, because it fitted so well with the patterns observed in the articles presented in this Special Issue. Even though Tilly's ideas have been criticized for being modelled too narrowly on the experience of early modern Europe, we have found them to be a very useful heuristic instrument in all times and places to analyse the methods used by states to extract resources and to determine labour relations. Firstly, there was the capital-intensive trajectory, followed by early city states such as Venice and, later, by the Dutch Republic, which could easily tap the significant commercial wealth generated within the territories under their rule, and relied on taxation to fill their coffers and recruit labour for their armies and navies.[9] On the opposite side of the spectrum were the northern and eastern European states, such as Sweden and Russia, further away from important trade routes and commercial wealth and therefore with little choice other than to rely on coercion and the forceful extraction of resources to raise the means for war, developing bulky state apparatuses in the process. In contrast to Venice and the Dutch Republic, labour was less easily recruited on the market, and this caused a tendency to rely on tributary labour. In the long run, however, the most successful proved to be the capitalized-coercion trajectory, which combined the forceful extraction of resources with the incorporation of capitalists in the state structure through the granting of privileges, thereby enabling the ruler to constantly tap this wealth to enlarge state capacity. Such states, like England and France, won out because they could amass taxes on a much larger scale than city states like Venice and use these financial means to build large armies and navies, bringing them out on top in the perpetual interstate competition over power.

Crucial in the process of state formation in Europe, Tilly argues, was that states needed legitimacy in order to place fiscal and other obligations on the population, and this resulted in a constant process of bargaining with the population over the extraction of resources. In this process, European states granted rights and privileges and made concessions to individuals and groups of citizens who controlled the resources to be extracted. As states attempted to ever broaden their tax base, this eventually lay at the root of the democratization processes of the late nineteenth and early twentieth centuries.

Critics of Tilly's interpretation scheme point to its limitation both in time and in space. To start with the first, Michael Mann states that Tilly's theory is

---

9. In his book, Tilly uses the term capital in a very broad sense. Though for some early societies it is better to speak of compensation rather than capital, for clarity's sake we chose to stick with Tilly's classical capital-coercion dichotomy.

too military driven and thus applies mainly to earlier periods, when the principal activity of many states was indeed war-making.[10] In the second half of the nineteenth and in the twentieth century, most European states, at least internally, expanded civilian activities, by building infrastructures, national education systems, and welfare systems. All these are state-formation processes that cannot be explained in terms of war-making. Here, according to Mann, other aspects of civil society play a role, such as religion, secular ideologies, and other sets of norms and values he calls ideological sources of power.[11] This is also where Marcel van der Linden's suggestion to add culture to capital and coercion as causes of state formation comes in.[12] As we will see in the articles in the second half of this volume, which focus on the state as arbiter and moderator, ideology comes to the fore as a major motivational force in state action, more explicitly so than where states act primarily in their capacities as conqueror or employer.

Secondly, Tilly's work has also come in for criticism because it insufficiently accounts for non-European patterns of state formation, in particular in parts of the world where war-making was less important for state formation.[13] Literature focusing on state-society relations as part of state formation in non-Western countries shows how societies could often challenge processes of state formation and – in the case of former colonies – transformation. Pre-colonial forms of state formation were crucial in these processes.[14] As regards taxation, it has been pointed out that not all forms of taxation are conducive to democratization or the granting of rights. When states can raise sufficient resources by taxing lightly, for example, as the Chinese state did throughout many centuries of its history, they can actually get away with no or

10. Michael Mann, "Review of Coercion, Capital and European States, A.D. 990–1990", *American Journal of Sociology*, 96:5 (1991), pp. 1260–1261, 1260. For a review of Tilly's complete oeuvre, see Marcel van der Linden, "Charles Tilly's Historical Sociology", *International Review of Social History*, 54:2 (2009), pp. 237–274; for his remarks on state functions see p. 266.

11. For Mann's general ideas about the four sources of power – ideological, economic, military, and political – see Michael Mann, *The Sources of Social Power. Volume 1: A History of Power from the Beginning to AD 1760* (New York, 1988), pp. 22–32. For the role of ideology in building welfare states, see *idem*, *The Sources of Social Power. Volume 3: Global Empires and Revolution, 1890–1945* (New York, 2012), ch. 9.

12. Van der Linden, "Charles Tilly's Historical Sociology", p. 271.

13. Mann, *The Sources of Social Power. Volume 2*, p. x.

14. Karen Barkey and Sunita Parikh, "Comparative Perspectives on the State", *Annual Review of Sociology*, 17 (1991), pp. 523–549; Christian Krohn-Hansen and Knut G. Nustad, "Introduction", in Christian Krohn-Hansen and Knut G. Nustad (eds), *State Formation: Anthropological Perspectives* (London, 2005), pp. 3–26, 7–8; Georg Sørensen, "War and State-Making: Why Doesn't it Work in the Third World?", *Security Dialogue*, 32:3 (2001), pp. 341–354; Brian D. Taylor and Roxana Botea, "Tilly Tally: War-Making and State-Making in the Contemporary Third World", *International Studies Review*, 10:1 (2008), pp. 27–56; Wolfgang Reinhard, *Geschichte der Staatsgewalt. Eine vergleichende Verfassungsgeschichte Europas von den Anfängen bis zur Gegenwart* (Munich, 1999), pp. 480–508.

very little bargaining at all.[15] Also, Tilly's interpretation was based too much on the experience of early national states and later nation states, ignoring the experience of other state formations, such as empires, the importance of which in world history has recently been underlined.[16] Indeed, recent work by Roy Bin Wong has revealed a significantly different modus operandi of the late imperial Chinese state in resource extraction and governance, which poignantly underlines the fact that state formation in Asia is still an understudied phenomenon, notwithstanding a growing body of literature that sets the stage both on colonial and post-colonial Asian states as well as on Asian states that were never colonized.[17]

15. R. Bin Wong, "Taxation and Good Governance in China, 1500–1914", in Bartolomé Yun-Casalilla and Patrick Karl O'Brien (eds), *The Rise of Fiscal States: A Global History, 1500–1914* (New York, 2012), pp. 353–377; Marjolein 't Hart, *Waarom belastingen goed zijn voor democratie. Staatsvorming en politieke cultuur in wereldhistorisch perspectief* (Amsterdam, 2014); Peer Vries, *State, Economy and the Great Divergence: Great Britain and China, 1680s–1850s* (London, 2015).

16. Alessandro Stanziani, *Bâtisseurs d'empires. Russie, Chine et Inde à la croisée des mondes, XVe-XIXe siècle* (Paris, 2012); Jane Burbank and Frederick Cooper, *Empires in World History: Power and the Politics of Difference* (Princeton, NJ, 2010).

17. R. Bin Wong, "The Political Economy of Agrarian Empire and its Modern Legacy", in Timothy Brook and Gregory Blue (eds), *China and Historical Capitalism: Genealogies of Sinological Knowledge* (New York, 1999), pp. 210–245; *idem*, "China before Capitalism", in Larry Neal and Jeffrey G. Williamson (eds), *The Cambridge History of Capitalism. Volume 1: The Rise of Capitalism: From Ancient Origins to 1848* (Cambridge, 2014), pp. 125–164, 143–149. For examples of publications on state formation in Asia, see Hamza Alavi, "The State in Post-Colonial Societies: Pakistan and Bangladesh", *New Left Review*, 74 (1972), pp. 59–80; Sabyasachi Bhattacharya, *The Colonial State: Theory and Practice* (Delhi, 2016); Wenkai He, *Paths Toward the Modern Fiscal State: England, Japan, and China* (Cambridge [etc.], 2013). For state formation in Africa, see Lisa Anderson, *The State and Social Transformation in Tunisia and Libya, 1830–1980* (Princeton, NJ, 2014); *idem*, "The State in the Middle East and North Africa", *Comparative Politics*, 20:1 (1988), pp. 1–18; Jean-François Bayart, *The State in Africa: The Politics of the Belly* (London [etc.], 1993); *idem*, *L'Etat au Cameroun* (Paris, 1979); Colin Leys, "The 'Overdeveloped' Post-Colonial State: A Re-evaluation", *Review of African Political Economy*, 5 (1976), pp. 39–48; John Lonsdale, "States and Social Processes in Africa: A Historiographical Survey", *African Studies Review*, 24:2/3 (1981), pp. 139–225; *idem*, "The Growth and Transformation of the Colonial State in Kenya, 1929–52", Staff Seminar Paper 17, University of Nairobi: Department of History (1980); *idem*, "The Emergence of African Nations: A Historiographical Analysis", *African Affairs*, 67:266 (1968), pp. 11–28; John Lonsdale and Bruce Berman, "Coping with the Contradictions: The Development of the Colonial State in Kenya 1895–1914", *The Journal of African History*, 20:4 (1979), pp. 487–505; John Lonsdale, "The Conquest State of Kenya", in J.A. de Moor and H.L. Wesseling (eds), *Imperialism and War: Essays on Colonial Wars in Asia and Africa* (Leiden, 1989), pp. 87–120; John Lonsdale, "State and Markets in Colonial Kenya: Two Studies in Ambiguity", in Elisabeth Linnebuhr (ed.), *Transition and Continuity of Identity in East Africa and Beyond: In Memoriam David Miller* (Bayreuth, 1989), pp. 303–320; Donald S. Rothchild and Noami Chazan, *The Precarious Balance: State and Society in Africa* (Boulder, 1988); F. Stark, "Theories of Contemporary State Formation in Africa: A Reassessment", *Journal of Modern African Studies*, 24:2 (1986), pp. 335–347. For Latin America, see Fernando Coronil, *The Magical State: Nature, Money, and Modernity in Venezuela* (Chicago, IL, 1997); Fernando Lopez-Alves, *State Formation and Democracy in Latin America, 1810–1900* (Durham, NC, [etc.], 2000); Oscar Oszlak, "The Historical Formation of the State in Latin America: Some

The global aspect of state formation and state activities forms part of recent literature on the different capacities and modalities of states in fostering economic development, and in particular in creating the institutions conducive to economic development.[18] Of particular interest to us here is the attention paid to this issue within the framework of the Great Divergence debate on the origins of the differential development of Asia and Europe. Crucially, the early modern Chinese state appears to have operated on fundamentally different principles from its European counterparts in its political economy and economic policies.[19] Whereas European states concentrated their efforts on stimulating economic development, creating the conditions, often monopolies, for merchants and capitalists to generate wealth that could subsequently be taxed, the late imperial Chinese state aimed in many ways to create a level playing field, acting against concentrations of wealth and power and relying on a fiscal policy of relatively light taxation of as large a number of peasant producers as possible.[20]

THE STATE AND LABOUR RELATIONS

Considering labour relations, our approach starts with the state in its capacity as a direct participant, as conqueror, or employer facing the question how to mobilize and allocate the labour power and resources required to carry out the civil and military tasks deemed essential for its functioning. In our view, this involves a choice between two principal options: (1) to impose taxes in money or kind and to use the resources accumulated in this way to pay people to perform the tasks to be fulfilled, whether military, civil, or auxiliary (i.e. capital); or (2) to mobilize the people, resources, and equipment to carry out these tasks by imposing direct labour obligations (i.e. coercion). States can choose to follow either option with their own people and institutions, or can decide to outsource these activities and co-opt other people, groups of people, or even states, to carry out these tasks, granting them privileges, autonomy within larger state

Theoretical and Methodological Guidelines for Its Study", *Latin American Research Review*, 16:2 (1981), pp. 3–32, Alfred Stepan, *State and Society: Peru in Comparative Perspective* (Princeton, NJ, 1978); Vincent C. Peloso and Barbara Tenenbaum (eds), *Liberals, Politics, and Power: State Formation in Nineteenth-Century Latin America* (Athens, GA, [etc.], 1996); Laurence Whitehead, "State Organization in Latin America Since 1930", in Leslie Bethell (ed.), *The Cambridge History of Latin America*, Volume VI, Part 2 (Cambridge, 1994), pp. 3–98.

18. On the relationship between institutions and economic growth, see Douglass C. North and Robert Paul Thomas, *The Rise of the Western World: A New Economic History* (Cambridge, 1973); Sebastián Galiani and Itai Sened (eds), *Institutions, Property Rights, and Economic Growth: The Legacy of Douglass North* (Cambridge, 2014).

19. Jean-Laurent Rosenthal and Roy Bin Wong, *Before and Beyond Divergence: The Politics of Economic Change in China and Europe* (Cambridge, MA, 2011).

20. R. Bin Wong, "The Political Economy of Agrarian Empire"; *idem*, "China before Capitalism".

structures, powers of supervision, or subjugation over others, for example. In this introduction, we rely on the dichotomy between capital and coercion to bring some order to the wide variety of policies deployed by states to carry out their core tasks. Of course, the two options are not mutually exclusive, and practically all states rely, to some extent, on both of these options, but the mix between them varies both among states and over time. Moreover, larger states, and particularly empires, can rely on coercion in one area, or in relation to certain groups, on taxation in another, and opt to outsource and co-opt these tasks in one area and act themselves in another.[21]

In sum, the research agenda for the contributions to this Special Issue was to provide an analysis of empirical cases of shifts in labour relations where the state intervened in one way or another. The following sections contain the findings of the individual articles and contributions to the workshop. They show how the three options of acquisition and disposal of labour power were handled by states across the globe, in different times and different settings. At the end of this introduction, we will provide an interpretation of these cases in the framework of the explanatory matrix of state activities and the typology of the roles of states as conquerors, employers, and arbiters.

THE STATE AS CONQUEROR: THE CHOICE BETWEEN COERCION AND CAPITAL

Due to their monopoly on the means of violence, states as direct participants of the labour market have strong means of determining labour relations. This applies particularly to imperial states in the phases of conquest, when they strive to enlarge their territory. Yet, not all states choose coercion to recruit labour. The articles and contributions considered in this introduction look at China from the Song to the Qing (tenth to nineteenth centuries) as well as Russia in the seventeenth and eighteenth centuries, and the Spanish colonial empire from the sixteenth to the eighteenth centuries. By contrast, Venice, as a city state, is an excellent example of the option to recruit by capital and co-optation.

In her article "Tributary Labour Relations in China During the Ming-Qing Transition (Seventeenth to Eighteenth Centuries)", Christine Moll-Murata focuses on the Chinese state in the period of transition from the Ming (1368–1644) to the Qing dynasty (1644–1911). The conquest of the empire by the Manchu changed the "physiology" of the Chinese state in several important respects. The Manchu dynasty brought along its own system of social-military organization based on banners – groups of hereditary military households comprising both warriors and their families and servants. Before the conquest

---

21. Such combined approaches have been identified as typical of empires. See Burbank and Cooper, *Empires in World History*; Sven Beckert, *Empire of Cotton: A Global History* (New York, 2014).

of China these banners had been engaged in self-sufficient farming in peace-time, but were paid by the state in times of war. After the conquest of the empire, they protected the court and key strategic towns and were freed from all other obligations but its military ones, for which they were permanently remunerated in silver and grain. This system combined elements of coercion (labour service) and capital (remuneration), not only in goods, but also in privileges, and a great deal of autonomy was granted to the bannermen. Apart from relying on the banners, the Qing dynasty also deployed a professional army of paid Han Chinese soldiers – the Green Standard Army. This reliance on capital, rather than coercion in military organization, marked a departure from the corvée principles on which Ming-era military mobilization had been based, and Moll-Murata attributes this change also to the influx of silver during that period.

At the workshop, these findings were placed in a long-term perspective in a paper by William Guanglin Liu.[22] Looking at military wages and remuneration over a period from the early Song dynasty (960–1279) to the Ming (1368–1644), Liu presented a picture of a Chinese state switching back and forth between reliance on capital and coercion in its task of footing and maintaining an army. Before the Song, military organization relied on land-based, hereditary military households, but monetization and commer-cialization during the Tang-Song transition in the tenth century resulted in the introduction of indirect taxation and a shift towards military recruitment based on direct employment and remuneration in cash. This system was reversed again, however, due to the impact of the Mongol conquest (1200–1279), which put military organization back on a demonetized footing under the Yuan dynasty (1279–1368). This practice was continued under the subsequent Ming dynasty, based on military settlements of soldier-farmers, who fulfilled military duties and contributed grain to state reserves. The main cause of this change was the end of the commercialization of the Song period, which left the early Ming dynasty unable to mobilize a mercenary army as their predecessors had done, and they therefore chose to rely on the hereditary military household system, which could function independently of monetized state finance. In conjunction, Guanglin Liu's and Moll-Murata's findings draw our attention to the degree of commercialization and particularly monetization of an economy as a crucial variable in determining outcomes of the capital-coercion choice that states face.

This is also powerfully illustrated by Dmitry Khitrov's article, "Tributary Labour in the Russian Empire in the Eighteenth Century: Factors in Development". The late eighteenth-century system of tributary labour

22. William Guanglin Liu, "Patterns of Imperial China's State Employments and Changes in Real Wages: A Long-Term Perspective", paper presented at the workshop "Political Change as a Determinant of Shifting Labour Relations".

obligations in the Russian empire formed an essential element of the system of military mobilization on which the Russian state had based its impressive territorial expansion from the sixteenth century onwards. Against the larger background of serfdom in the Russian heartland, Khitrov focuses on two groups performing tributary labour duties in the southern and eastern border provinces of the Russian state. These were the military service class, who performed military duties in exchange for allotments of land, and state peasants assigned to work in industries that were of strategic military significance for the Russian state.

The military service class consisted of various military settlers, Cossacks, and co-opted non-Russian groups, who had in common that, in exchange for land, they carried military service obligations in the southern and eastern border areas of Russian expansion. The tributary labour obligations of the state peasants assigned to certain industries were also an essentially non-monetary system of labour mobilization. The two cases studied by Khitrov therefore provide further evidence of what has been described as Russia's quintessential model of war-making and war-related resource mobilization that developed in a low-capital environment, relying on non-monetary instruments such as conscription, military settlement, grain deliveries, and land allotments in exchange for service.[23]

The Russian case compares in an interesting way with that of the city state of Venice, a typical example of the capital-intensive trajectories of state formation. As Andrea Caracausi showed in his paper presented at the workshop, Venice relied largely on monetary means of mobilizing military labour for its fleet, primarily by paying patricians to actually carry out the operation of the ships, but also in recruiting the skilled labour for the Arsenal, where its galleys were built. Shipbuilders at the Arsenal were assured of a wage, even if there was no work, thus achieving the same effect of avoiding the market in the supply of strategic labour as in Russia, but by monetary, rather than coercive means. It should be noted, though, that for actually rowing the galleys the Venetian fleet also made ample use of the forced labour of prisoners of war, which serves to underscore that practically all states, to some extent, combine coercion and capital in achieving their aims.[24]

The articles by Raquel Gil Montero and Paula Zagalsky, "Colonial Organization of Mine Labour in Charcas (Present-Day Bolivia) and Its Consequences (Sixteenth to the Seventeenth Centuries)", and Rossana Barragán Romano, "Dynamics of Continuity and Change: Shifts in Labour

---

23. Alessandro Stanziani, "Warfare, Labor and the Expansion of Muscovy", paper presented at the workshop "Political Change as a Determinant of Shifting Labour Relations".

24. Andrea Caracausi, "Working for the State in the Republic of Venice in the 16th and 17th Centuries", paper presented at the workshop "Political Change as a Determinant of Shifting Labour Relations".

Relations in the Potosí Mines (1680–1812)", focus on labour relations in the Andean silver mines, discovered by the Spanish conquerors in the 1540s. When Viceroy Toledo was in office (1569–1581) he re-established and drastically changed a pre-Hispanic tributary system, the *mita*. Toledo transformed this system into a state-organized and enforced draft of coerced labour to ensure a continuous supply of labour to the Potosí silver mines. Communities of indigenous people had to send tributaries as *mitayos* to the mines. *Mita* work was done in weekly turns. Having done their turn, the *mitayos* could spend their "free" time as hired workers in the mines (as *mingas*). Having returned home after a period of corvée, they worked under reciprocal labour relations on their own land or that of their communities, thus combining various types of labour relations over the year. Some of the natives preferred to work for Spanish landowners, rather than be subjected to the extremely harsh labour obligations of the *mita*. The royal officials accepted this if the landowners paid the tribute that the *mitayos* owed the state. Thus, the coercion-intensive trajectory of the Spanish colonial state also relied on the co-optation of local authorities and Spanish individuals and on outsourcing part of the extractive activities to them.

Rossana Barragán focuses on the subsequent periods of silver mining and refining in Potosí. In the seventeenth century, production in the silver mines decreased. Consequently, the *mita* changed from corvée labour to a payment in cash, to be paid to the mine and refining-mill operators. The trajectory followed by the Spanish state was still coercive, but now capital had replaced labour. When, in the 1730s, mining activities were re-intensified, some *mitayos* started to combine the unfree labour they had to perform during their "turn" with self-employed ore refining, working as so-called *kajchas*. As Barragán explains the *mitayos*, *mingas*, and *kajchas* were often one and the same person, who combined a wide variety of labour relations varying from unfree tributary to free wage work to self-employment.

Startled by this new development, the mine operators asked the Spanish Crown for a new allocation of labour under the *mita*. Barragán shows how lengthy discussions brought to the surface differences in interests and views regarding the desirability of coerced labour in favour of one specific interest group: the Spanish mine operators. These differences manifested themselves among the different levels of state administration in Potosí, Lima, Seville, and Madrid. It would take the Napoleonic occupation of Spain and the establishment of a National Assembly to abolish the *mita*. Here, a state-led system of coerced labour was finally abolished by a representative body installed by the French occupying state, mirroring the development of shifts in labour relations through the state as conqueror, only this time in the metropolis.

In his contribution "The Labour Recruitment of Local Inhabitants as *Rōmusha* in Japanese-Occupied South East Asia", Takuma Melber analyses a relatively short period compared with the other articles. The political change in focus was more one of the ruler than of the system, since Japanese colonial rule directly replaced that of the Dutch. In order to build the necessary infrastructure in the South East Asian territories, the Japanese governors first hired workers. When workers failed to commit themselves in sufficient numbers, coercion was applied. The corresponding shift in labour relations was thus, mainly, from hired labour for non-market institutions to slavery. This article points out that during the immediate pre-war situation and during the war itself, the Japanese occupation caused South East Asian economies to become isolated from the world market. This resulted in unemployment and a shift by peasant smallholders away from cash crops to food production. When recruitment was coerced, those who had to join the infrastructural projects worked as tributary slaves. Those who could avoid forced labour by committing themselves to paramilitary work can be regarded as doing obligatory work for the polity. They could thus be employed side by side on the same project, and being able to opt for the less coerced mode could, literally, make a difference between life and death.

Lest the impression arise that the choice between coercion or capital and between performing the activities oneself or outsourcing them was something related only to early periods of state formation, many more modern states came to face the same issues in colonial contexts, and often chose approaches based on coercion, even if, at the same time, these very same states had come to rely on taxation and capital-intensive methods in the metropolis. To some extent, in colonial contexts they came to face a challenge similar to that of the early modern period, i.e. how to extract resources from societies with a low degree of monetization and commercialization. Colonial authorities, particularly in sub-Saharan Africa, were often caught in a low-income cycle: to be able to invest in infrastructure, they needed customs revenues, which could be obtained only through some form of commercialization, for which it was necessary to invest in infrastructure, etc. To break this deadlock, they resorted to forced labour and corvée labour, either for commercial agriculture or for infrastructural work.[25]

THE STATE AS DIRECT AND INDIRECT EMPLOYER

Direct as well as indirect, i.e. outsourced, employment in the service of the state in periods after consolidation of power often caused changes in labour relations, as various articles in this Special Issue show. In her

---

25. Marlous van Waijenburg, "Financing the African Colonial State: The Revenue Imperative and Forced Labour", *African Economic History Working Paper*, 20 (2015).

contribution "Political Changes and Shifts in Labour Relations in Mozambique, 1820s–1920s", Filipa Ribeiro da Silva shows how the Portuguese state, forced by the supranational power of the Conference of Berlin (1884–1885), had to occupy the colonial territories over which it wanted to gain rights. The Portuguese decided to employ an instrument they had used more often during their colonial history: outsourcing. Since the sixteenth century, various forms of outsourcing were in place: there was the *Prazos da Coroa*, a system of land tenure that had taken the form of chieftaincies in Mozambique; mining, agriculture, and trade was developed through outsourcing; but also, management of trade routes between Mozambique and Goa and in the Atlantic had been under private management. However, by the end of the nineteenth century, the newly gained areas of central and northern Mozambique that had been outsourced to two main companies chartered by the state were vaster than any area ever before. Moreover, the companies were authorized to issue their own regulations, their own currency, and establish their own police force. Not only the scale and the state-like functions of these companies were unprecedented; for the first time, private enterprises were encouraged to subjugate African leaders, enrol the African population and, thus, recruit, allocate, and control labour in the African continent itself. Sometimes, this co-optation of African leaders was voluntary, sometimes coerced. To give this change a legal basis and a moral justification, a new labour code was established that determined that all men "fit to work" had the moral obligation to do so and that through work Africans could "civilize themselves".

In the areas commanded by the companies, labour relations that used to be predominantly reciprocal and tributary, with a small share of free and unfree (often slave) labour for the market, became more commodified, as the companies forced men into (often unfree forms of) wage labour and women into reciprocal, subsistence labour.

In her article "Grammar of Difference? The Dutch Colonial State, Labour Policies, and Social Norms on Work and Gender, c.1800–1940", Elise van Nederveen Meerkerk explores similarities and dissimilarities between the efforts of the Dutch state in the Netherlands and the Netherlands Indies during the first half of the nineteenth century to enhance the industriousness of the population. Whereas in the Netherlands, these efforts served primarily to combat poverty, through the establishment of peat colonies where people on poor relief had to work, in the Netherlands Indies, the Cultivation System, established in 1830, was an instrument to increase the surplus generated by the colonial economy. This difference notwithstanding, the peat colonies in the Netherlands and the Cultivation System in the Netherlands Indies shared a common emphasis on industriousness as the key to advancement, and were indeed conceived and implemented by one and the same person, General Johannes van den Bosch (1780–1844). The Cultivation

System relied principally on coercion to enhance the industriousness of Javanese peasants, requiring them to set aside part of their land to produce cash crops such as coffee, sugar, and indigo for the Dutch authorities. In practice, the work in the Dutch peat colonies also came to resemble tributary labour, from 1859 onwards solely for the Dutch state as owner of the colonies.

Fernando Mendiola's article "The Role of Unfree Labour in Capitalist Development: Spain and Its Empire, Nineteenth to the Twenty-First Centuries" looks at the continuity of unfree labour in spite of political change.[26] The phases under observation here are the late Spanish colonial empire, and the periods of liberal parliamentarism, civil war, Fascist dictatorship, and parliamentary democracy up until the present.

The cases considered include slavery on Cuban sugar plantations and – in more limited scope – on the island of Bioko (Fernando Pó) off the coast of Equatorial Guinea; prison labour, obligatory labour in infrastructure, and military service; the prisoners of war in the Spanish concentration camps until 1945; and the recent indentured migrant labour working either in Spain or abroad in subcontracting companies. Overall, Mendiola notes that – within the ensemble unfree labour relations – slavery played a central role in the periods of the liberal revolution and the colonial empire, whereas during the period of liberal parliamentarism we see a shift to tributary labour for the state. These forms of unfree labour prevailed in the colonies, whereas in the metropolis unfree labour diminished until the period of civil war and fascist dictatorship. The Spanish state condoned slavery in the nineteenth century, but actively promoted convict labour, with varying degrees of legitimization. In his analysis, Mendiola argues that unfree labour served the purpose of capital accumulation, and that private enterprises and the state profited in various ways from these labour obligations.

Erdem Kabadayı's contribution "Working for the State in the Urban Economies of Ankara, Bursa, and Salonica: From Empire to Nation State, 1840s–1940s" examines public service employment at the city level in the mid-nineteenth century Ottoman empire and in the nation states of Turkey and Greece, which emerged after the disintegration of the empire and the accompanying population exchanges of the 1920s. His findings are based on a comparison of three cities, of which two are in modern-day Turkey (Bursa, Ankara) and one in Greece (Salonica). As public service employment in the mid-nineteenth century was organized to a large extent at the

---

26. This article was originally offered to the *International Review of Social History* as an independent contribution. Since the author used the taxonomy of the Collaboratory in its analysis, the editors of this Special Issue were glad to include it in this volume, for which it forms an interesting counterpoint. This is because, unlike the workshop participants, who studied political change as an explanation of changing labour relations, Mendiola looks at the continuity of unfree labour in spite of political change.

neighbourhood level, he finds that the degree of ethnic and religious seg-regation between neighbourhoods in these cities had a strong impact on the religious and ethnic profile of public service sector employment. In cities with a high degree of segregation, like Salonica, or, to a lesser extent, Bursa, non-Muslims were well represented, whereas in Ankara, where the degree of segregation was much lower, Muslims clearly enjoyed comparative advantages in entering public service employment, something that Kabadayı relates to the dominant position of Islam in what was, officially, a multi-ethnic empire. After the population exchanges of the 1920s and the emergence of the nation states of Greece and Turkey, public service employment in the three cities came to reflect the ethnic and religious profile of the respective countries in a more direct manner.

These examples, as well as the other cases from the literature, can provide us with some clues as to the regularities and the issues involved in the choice between the various options the state had: to choose the capital or coercive trajectory (or a combination of both) and to perform the extractive activities with its own personnel and organizations, or to outsource them. To start with, it is obvious that the degree of monetization of a society plays a crucial role: although taxes can be, and often are, levied in kind, a low degree of commercialization and monetization generally appears to enhance the attractiveness of resorting to mobilization and the coercive extraction of labour and other resources, something already emphasized by Tilly as well.[27] Or, perhaps, this causality should be framed somewhat differently: monetization and commercialization allow for resource extraction based on taxation which would not otherwise have belonged to the range of possible options. The difference is one that revolves around assumptions on the expected pattern – do states resort to coercion when they cannot tax, or do states resort to coercion by default unless there happens to be an opportunity to tax? Certainly, from our modern point of view, we tend generally to expect taxation to be the default behaviour and coercion the *explanandum*, but the resort to coercion almost across the board in colonial situations by states relying on taxation in the metropolis does cast some doubt on such assumptions.

A second observation is that war and war-like situations tend to favour the use of coercion in recruiting and allocating labour to accomplish state tasks. This is true not only for military and military-auxiliary labour, where it is easier to explain, but also for infrastructural and industrial work not directly related to the military effort, as we see in Melber's contribution on the *Rōmusha* in the Japanese empire during World War II, and as Mendiola has documented for the Spanish Civil War. Examples of war-like situations in which the same mechanisms appear to be at play outside of the scope of

---

27. Tilly, *Coercion, Capital, and European States*, p. 88.

this volume include Soviet industrialization in the 1930s[28] as well as colonial contexts of subjugation of one nation by another.

THE STATE AS ARBITER AND MEDIATOR

Over time, in many Western states the capacity of the state as arbiter, mediator, and provider of social protection became more important, while military conquest receded. Paralleling the vast increase in the reach of the state within society, which involved more direct government employment, state-building moved away from the single focus on organizing the extraction of resources to a much wider mission, geared towards fostering welfare and economic development as well as human capital formation. The rise of complex legal systems, higher levels of education, and the availability of communication and information technologies enabled the state to enhance its roles. Intertwined with these efforts were what we have referred to as "labour ideologies", i.e. belief systems, norms and values as well as ideals and aspirations relating to work and labour relations and informing policy choices.[29] These can be religiously, politically, or ethnically inspired, or, as is more often the case in today's world, derived from economic theory or interpretations thereof. What is essential to the issues we are looking at in this volume is that these "ideologies" shape policymaking; indeed, they underlie some of the basic tenets of contemporaneous social systems, as in the case of the modern welfare state, based on the idea that certain sections of the population ought, by common effort, to be relieved of the necessity to work.

As Elise van Nederveen Meerkerk shows in her contribution to this volume, poor relief in the early nineteenth-century Netherlands was still based on the formula "who does not work, shall not eat", as epitomized by the peat colonies founded by Johannes van den Bosch. But, in the course of the century, labour ideologies changed. The idea of the male breadwinner gained foothold, and child and women's labour protection laws increasingly aimed to exclude women from the labour process and encourage an exclusive role for women in household work. Although postulated as universal values, attitudes and policies towards women's labour in the colonies differed – indeed, Javanese women were seen as industrious and their contribution to the work of the household in farming and, notably, cash-crop farming as essential within the framework of the Cultivation System. Only much later, in the early twentieth century, did some of the ideas long in vigour in the metropolis, trickle down to the colonial context,

28. Oleg V. Khlevniuk, "Prinuditel'nyi trud v ekonomike SSSR, 1929–1941 gody", *Svobodnaia Mysl'*, 3 (1992), pp. 73–84.
29. Karin Hofmeester and Christine Moll-Murata (eds), *The Joy and Pain of Work: Global Attitudes and Valuations, 1500–1650* (*Special Issue 19, International Review of Social History, 56, 2011*) (Cambridge, 2012).

but they never really came to have an impact on female labour participation, as economic considerations continued to have the upper hand in policy decisions. Borrowing a term from Stoler and Cooper, Van Nederveen Meerkerk refers to a "Grammar of Difference", combining different norms in metropole and periphery regarding one and the same issue and leading to different labour relations for women in both areas.

Religiously inspired labour ideologies appear to have caused the gender-specific patterns of public service employment as described by Erdem Kabadayı for the 1920s urban centres of Bursa and Ankara in the newly born Turkish republic. The influence of Islam minimalized female public service employment, and indeed all employment in these three cities, particularly if compared to the cities of Salonica and Athens in the recently created Greek national state. A further example of gendered labour ideologies is provided by Takuma Melber, who refers to opinions raised in Japan during World War II that resisted the replacement of men in factories by women until it became absolutely imperative due to the erosion of the industrial workforce by military mobilization, because it conflicted with existing ideals of women as mothers and souls of the household.

During the second half of the twentieth century, the role of the state in shaping labour relations became even greater. Not only did the state evolve to become one of the largest employers in any society, in both western and eastern Europe it also built up a welfare state that exonerated a substantial part of the population from the duty to work, particularly through the introduction of retirement pensions and general, obligatory schooling.[30] In western Europe this was complemented by unemployment benefits for those involuntarily left out of the labour market, and in eastern Europe by policies of ensuring (and requiring) full employment for people of working age.[31]

The contributions by Max Koch, "The Role of the State in Employment and Welfare Regulation: Sweden in the European Context", and Raquel Varela, "State Policies Towards Precarious Work: Employment and Unemployment in Contemporary Portugal", trace the development of the welfare state in Sweden and Portugal and the labour ideologies that accompanied it. Over time, a shift can be observed from "targeted" social welfare to a more universal approach and then back again as neo-liberal policies of deregulation and flexibilization started to spread from the 1990s. Koch's contribution takes up the conceptualization of the state's functions as employer and arbiter for

---

30. Reinhard, *Geschichte der Staatsgewalt*, pp. 398–403; Béla Tomka, *Welfare in East and West: Hungarian Social Security in an International Comparison, 1918–1990* (Berlin, 2004); A. McAuley, "The Welfare State in the USSR", in Thomas Wilson and Dorothy Wilson (eds), *The State and Social Welfare: The Objectives of Policy* (London, 1991), pp. 191–213.

31. Paul R. Gregory and Robert C. Stuart, *Soviet Economic Structure and Performance* (New York, 1990), pp. 268–269.

twentieth-century Sweden and compares the Social Democratic period from the 1940s to the 1990s with the subsequent more deregulatory phase after Sweden joined the European Union in 1995. In a detailed view of the perspective of arbitration, he sees the state as "an object of agency of the sociopolitical coalition that creates and recreates it" and as an actor, "structured *and* structuring at the same time". As such, he points to the three related fields of activity of capitalist states: ensuring property rights through legislation and adjudication, redistribution by taxation and welfare administration, and arbitration by temporarily harmonizing conflicting group interests and creating consensus. In the particular setting of Sweden's relatively late membership of the EU, while policy designs and ideas emerged from new supranational agents and institutions and the accumulation of capital increasingly became a transnational process, the state remained important as a participant and actor in international regulation. Internally, in the deregulatory process, state actions towards the labour force became less visible, since much disciplining, regulating, and supporting was imparted to the "entrepreneurial employee", which, as Max Koch perceptively remarks, resulted in a much improved "economy of power" compared with the earlier period of Social Democratic and top-down state impact, when collectively organized and class-aware workers prevailed.

Raquel Varela's contribution focuses on the same period as that of Max Koch. Both countries joined the European Union at a relatively late stage (Portugal in 1986, Sweden in 1995), and the basic socioeconomic conditions were similar, though standards of living were higher in Sweden. But while Max Koch more directly links up with EU participation and supranational policy ideals and ideas, Raquel Varela concentrates on the implementation of labour policies that practically reinstated the ideal of the "right to work" instituted in the Portuguese constitution after the Carnation Revolution in 1974. She argues that in attenuating the effects of labour precarity and unemployment, the state acted as a direct participant in the labour market, functioning as both employer and mediator. In her view, welfare policies intended to address social inequalities and to promote reintegration into the labour market led instead to increased job insecurity and were closely related to the deregulation of employment. Moreover, deregulation did not imply less, but increased state intervention in the economy, since, for instance, there has been no reduction in the state's role as a direct employer – in fact, the number of people employed by the state has increased. In Varela's view, the state actively promoted a policy of cushioning the effects of deregulation, with the aim of maintaining the competitiveness of the Portuguese economy.

SHIFTS IN LABOUR RELATIONS AND THE STATE

What have we learned from the investigations in this issue into the role of the state as a causal factor in effecting historical shifts in labour relations? Firstly, relative to the "physiology" of states, we have found that trajectories of state formation matter. Particularly for states on a coercion-intensive trajectory, the link between state action and shifts in labour relations is evident, for example in early modern Muscovy and Russia, where geopolitical competition and forward expansion was accompanied by the emergence of, and increase in, tributary labour relations. Similarly, along the capital-intensive trajectory, state formation and the military recruitment it entails has been a factor in the rise of military labour markets, and therefore shifts to commodified labour relations. The best example here is, probably, the Dutch Republic, which attracted sailors to man its fleet from a hinterland far beyond its own borders.[32]

It has also become clear from the contributions to this volume that there is by no means a one-to-one relationship to trajectories of state formation and the reliance on capital or coercion in mobilizing the resources and recruiting the labour required to carry out the tasks deemed essential for the functioning of the state. In fact, most states relied on a mix of capital and coercion, of monetary and coercive-administrative means, to accomplish their tasks. They also often outsourced part of their resource-extractive activities, thereby relying heavily on the instrument of co-optation. Particularly in the border areas of the larger land-based territorial empires, such as China's and Russia's, or rapidly expanding overseas empires, such as Spain's in the early modern period or Portugal's in the late nineteenth century, co-optation was a formidable instrument to deal with the constant challenge of neighbouring nomadic and semi-nomadic polities. In fact, more than anything, states appear surprisingly rational in choosing between capital and coercion and between outsourcing and co-optation or performing the activities themselves. States also appear to be flexible, switching between instruments over time, depending on the circumstances of the period and the challenges faced. The best-documented example here is that of the Chinese empire, which, in the course of the second millennium AD, switched back and forth several times between reliance on capital and coercion in military recruitment.

This should serve as a powerful reminder that there is no such thing as a fixed trajectory over time in the shifts in labour relations as effected by state formation. This is important because, on the face of it, shifts in labour relations appear to provide evidence of such a unilinear trajectory

32. This was argued by Filipa Ribeiro da Silva in a further presentation to the workshop "Political Change as a Determinant of Shifting Labour Relations" entitled "The Role of State in the 'Recruitment' of Free and Unfree Labor during European Expansion: Insights from the Portuguese and Dutch Cases". See also Jelle van Lottum and Jan Lucassen, "Six Cross-Sections of the Dutch Maritime Labour Market: A Preliminary Reconstruction and Its Implications (1610–1850)", in Richard Gorski (ed.), *Maritime Labour: Contributions to the History of Work at Sea, 1500–2000* (Amsterdam, 2007), pp. 13–42.

over time, from unfree to free labour. On the basis of our findings in this volume, we argue that this appearance is the manifestation of a causal link for which we have found evidence, i.e. between the degree of monetization of a society and the likelihood that states choose to rely on monetary instruments, rather than tributary obligations, to mobilize resources and labour. As most societies for which we have evidence have moved in the direction of greater monetization over the past 500 years or so, this tends to factor out tributary solutions over time, creating the appearance of a trend towards free rather than unfree labour. Crucial evidence to the contrary, though, is provided by that of the Chinese state during the transition from the Song to the Yuan, as well as by the readiness of colonial states, heavily reliant on capital in the metropolis, to resort to the use of coercion and tributary labour obligations in the periphery when confronted with societies with a low degree of monetization.

This brings us to the state in its capacity of a conqueror. We have found the state, in this role, to have been a causal factor in effecting shifts in labour relations. As conquerors, states can adapt existing forms of labour relations, as Spain did with the *mita* in Charcas. They can impose their own models, which can involve abrupt shifts in labour relations, as in the case of the Manchu conquest of China and the introduction of the banner system that accompanied it, or, vice versa, the incorporation of nomadic tribes into the Russian empire and the ensuing imposition of tributary labour relations. But we have also seen how states impose models other than their own. Some of the colonial states, for example, relied on capital at home and coercion in the colonies, like the Portuguese and the Spanish in Mozambique and Charcas, respectively. The imposition of the Cultivation System in the Netherlands Indies by the Dutch colonial state, as described by Van Nederveen Meerkerk, represented a shift in labour relations as part of such a two-tier model of state policy. A shift, moreover, that had repercussions not only in the periphery, but also in the centre itself, as the surplus generated by the exploitative Cultivation System in the colonies accommodated the rise of the male breadwinner model, relegating women to the sphere of domestic labour. In a similar vein, but with the opposite effect, conquest by the Japanese empire during World War II resulted in women joining the labour force in Japan to replace the men who had been mobilized into the army. Thus, conquest involves shifts in labour relations not only in the conquered territories, but also often, although not necessarily so, in the heartlands of the states concerned.

As states expand their reach, their impact on labour relations also increases, both in their capacity as arbiters or mediators, and as direct participants. To start with the latter, over time, states have become the single most important, and in some cases only, employer, and this makes them major "trendsetters" in labour relations, monopolizing certain sectors of the labour market and determining levels of remuneration and contractual standards. Most importantly, though, states have come to deeply affect labour relations in their roles of arbiters, legislators, and mediators. The example of the Ottoman empire and its ideology of Turkification and Islamification, leading to a drastically changed ethno-religious and gender makeup of the public sector, shows how the state as employer – even if it were a crumbling empire – could heavily influence labour relations. Modern states are driven in this respect by a powerful mixture of considerations related to their need to carry out the tasks essential for their functioning and the labour ideologies inspiring the models they aspire to implement. Such labour ideologies have been responsible for some of the most far-reaching shifts in labour relations seen over the past 200 years, notably the rise of the welfare state, based on the fundamental premise that a certain part of the population ought, by common effort, to be set free of the obligation to work, because of its inability to work, as a reward for past efforts, or in order to allow them to acquire the necessary skills to effectively participate in the labour process in the future.

A final development that also ought to be seen as the expression of certain labour ideologies is that states increasingly submit themselves to the arbitration or regulation of supranational bodies, whether within the framework of structures such as the European Union or as members of organizations such as the United Nations or the International Labour Organization. In her contribution to this volume, Elise van Nederveen Meerkerk describes how, in the 1920s, the International Labour Organization put increasing pressure on the Dutch colonial state to introduce labour protection for women and children in the colonies. Finally, in their contributions to this volume Max Koch and Raquel Varela link deregulation within the framework of the European Union to a shift in labour relations that has played out in Europe over the past two decades, away from a system based primarily on employment, collective bargaining, and inclusive social welfare to a more entrepreneurial model based on self-employment, individual risk-aversion schemes, and a concomitant greater "precarity" in labour relations. What should be stressed, though, is that this rise and subsequent decline of the welfare state is a largely Western story. For many states in the Global South economic development, providing social security and support, and labour regulation and protection are still very much goals to be achieved and policies to be implemented.

APPENDIX: TAXONOMY AND DEFINITIONS OF LABOUR RELATIONS OF THE GLOBAL COLLABORATORY ON THE HISTORY OF LABOUR RELATIONS

Since all articles in this volume refer to the core analytical tool of the Global Collaboratory on the History of Labour Relations, for the convenience of the reader we present here the entire taxonomy with the essential definitions. For an unabridged version of the definitions, including examples and methodological guidelines, see Karin Hofmeester *et al.*, "The Global Collaboratory on the History of Labour Relations, 1500–2000: Background, Set-Up, Taxonomy, and Applications", available at http://hdl.handle.net/10622/4OGRAD, last accessed 17 June 2016.

Definitions of Labour Relations

Non-working:

1. *Cannot work or cannot be expected to work*: those who cannot work, because they are too young (≤6 years), too old (≥75 years),[33] disabled, or are studying.
2. *Affluent*: those who are so prosperous that they do not need to work for a living (rentiers, etc.), and consequently actually do not work.
3. *Unemployed*: those wanting to work but who cannot find employment.

Working:
Reciprocal labour:

Persons who provide labour for other members of the same household and/or community.

4a. *Leading household producers*: heads of (mostly) self-sufficient households (these include family-based and non-kin-based forms).
4b. *Household kin producers*: subordinate kin, including spouses (men and women) and children of the above heads of households, who perform productive work for that household.
5. *Household kin non-producers*: subordinate kin, including spouses (men and women) and children of heads of households, who perform reproductive work for the household.
6. *Reciprocal household servants and slaves*: subordinate non-kin (men, women, and children) contributing to the maintenance of (mostly) self-sufficient households.

---

33. These minimum and maximum ages are culturally determined. The age brackets chosen will always be indicated in the database and explained in the methodological paper.

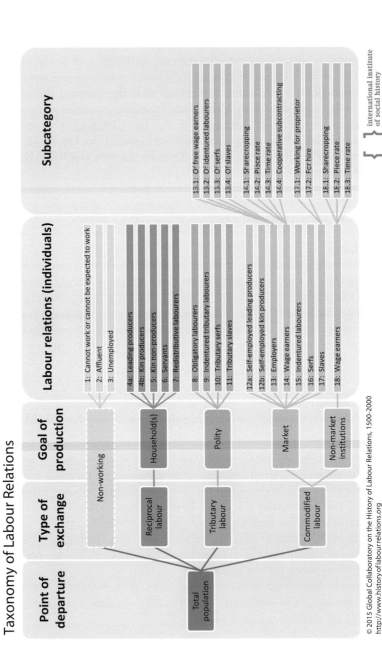

Figure 1. Taxonomy of Labour Relations.

7. *Community-based redistributive labourers*: persons who perform tasks for the local community in exchange for communally provided remuneration in kind.

Tributary labour:

Persons who are obliged to work for the polity (often the state, though it could also be a feudal or religious authority).

8. *Obligatory labourers*: those who have to work for the polity, and are remunerated mainly in kind.
9. *Indentured tributary labourers*: those contracted to work as unfree labourers for the polity for a specific period of time to pay off a debt or fine to that same polity.
10. *Tributary serfs*: those working for the polity because they are bound to its soil and bound to provide specified tasks.
11. *Tributary slaves*: those who are owned by and work for the polity indefinitely.

Commodified labour:

Work done on the basis of market exchange in which labour is "commodified", i.e. where the worker or the products of his work are sold.

For the market, private employment:

12a. *Self-employed leading producers*: those who produce goods or services for the market with fewer than three employees, possibly in cooperation with
12b. *Self-employed kin producers*: household members including spouses and children who work together with self-employed leading producers who produce for the market.
13. *Employers*: those who produce goods or services for market institutions by employing more than three labourers.
    13.1 Employers who employ free wage earners.
    13.2 Employers who employ indentured labourers.
    13.3 Employers who employ serfs.
    13.4 Employers who employ slaves.
14. *Market wage earners*: wage earners (including the temporarily unemployed) who produce commodities or services for the market in exchange mainly for monetary remuneration.
    14.1 Sharecropping wage earners: remuneration is a fixed share of total output.
    14.2 Piece-rate wage earners: remuneration at piece rates.
    14.3 Time-rate wage earners: remuneration at time rates.
    14.4 Cooperative subcontracting workers at piece rates.

15. *Indentured labourers for the market*: those contracted to work as unfree labourers for an employer for a specific period of time to pay off a private debt.
16. *Serfs working for the market*: those bound to the soil and bound to provide specified tasks.
17. *Slaves who produce for the market*: those owned by their employers (masters).
    17.1   Slaves working directly for their proprietor.
    17.2   Slaves for hire.

For non-market institutions:
18. *Wage earners employed by non-market institutions* (that may or may not produce for the market), such as the state, state-owned companies, the Church, or production cooperatives.
    18.1   Sharecropping wage earners.
    18.2   Piece-rate wage earners: remuneration at piece rates.
    18.3   Time-rate wage earners: remuneration at time rates.

IRSH 61 (2016), Special Issue, pp. 27–48 doi:10.1017/S0020859016000432
© 2016 Internationaal Instituut voor Sociale Geschiedenis

Tributary Labour Relations in China During the Ming-Qing Transition (Seventeenth to Eighteenth Centuries)

Christine Moll-Murata

Faculty of East Asian Studies, Ruhr-Universität Bochum Universitätsstrasse 150, 44780 Bochum, Germany

E-mail: Christine.Moll-Murata@ruhr-uni-bochum.de

Abstract: This study analyses the shifts in labour relations due to state intervention, first during the conquest of the Ming empire between 1600 and 1644 by its Manchurian contenders, and thereafter until about 1780, as the Manchurian Qing dynasty established itself and drove the Chinese empire to its greatest expansion. The main focus lies on the socio-military formation of the Eight Banners, the institution that, for about 200 years, epitomized the domination of the Chinese empire by a small elite group of about two per cent of the population. These findings will be contextualized in the larger setting of labour relations of the early and mid-Qing, when state intervention occurred in the form of arbitration in labour conflicts, but also, in a much more aggressive manner, in the decimation of the Qing rulers' Dzungharian rivals. In the framework of Charles Tilly's paradigm of capital versus coercion, while both are present in the Chinese case, the capital-oriented path seems more distinct.

INTRODUCTION

States in the role of conquerors can and do resort to conscription, forced labour, and resettlement of their own subjects, and act as slave raiders and downright subjugators towards people of the areas conquered. The state can act as employer towards old and new subjects; and it can, as a redistributor, enforce labour services as taxation in kind, or the necessity to work in order to be able to pay taxes and fulfil their obligations towards the polities. Lastly, states provide legislation and adjudication and thus act as arbiter. This paper aims to present the Chinese state in the transition from the Ming to the Qing dynasties in all of those roles that impacted on the ways in which people were expected to extract, produce, and render service for themselves and their families, for private employers, and for the sector under direct dynastic control.

The present study will portray three salient points of political impact on labour relations: the formation of the Manchu Banners in the period roughly 1600 to 1650; the increase in unfree labour relations in the form of bond service in Central and Southern China, a process that continued between 1500 and 1650 and gradually waned in the eighteenth century; and finally, the most negative way a conquering state can influence labour relations: by annihilation or expulsion of a population from its territory, as demonstrated in the case of the Dzunghars in the 1750s and 1760s. This is where shifts in labour relations due to political activity can be shown most clearly. Numerically, these three processes involved a comparatively small segment of the population. The much greater part experienced, if anything, changes due to reasons that hinged on market mechanisms and especially on demography. The relatively peaceful period after the consolidation of the Qing dynasty in 1683 and, consequently, the population growth in the eighteenth century can be considered an achievement of Qing political rule that prepared the ground for changes in labour relations from more self-sufficient to more market-related forms. Yet, since this impact on labour relations was quite indirect, and ran counter to the professed Qing ideal of a calmly self-sufficient, rural populace, it will be treated here as a backdrop to more direct government and polity intervention in the three samples discussed. This evidence will be set into the capital-coercion para-digm outlined by Charles Tilly. Although this dichotomy was intended mainly as an explanatory tool for an interpretation of European historical experiences, Tilly also applied it to China, drawing on G. William Skinner's analysis of administrative and economic centres.[1] Tilly transposed Skinner's insights to his own framework by identifying the administrative centres as belonging to the realm of top-down coercion, while the markets and economic centres arose from the bottom-up and largely self-regulatory activities of local elites and merchants.[2] Yet, Skinner's and, as a consequence, Tilly's evidence was based largely on the eighteenth and nineteenth cen-turies, when the interplay of coercive means and capital incentives differed from those during the period of dynastic decline in the Ming and the rise of the Qing studied in this article.

HISTORICAL BACKGROUND

The Manchus, who established the Qing dynasty and ruled China from 1644 to 1911, were a confederation of several groups who defined themselves as the descendants of the Jurchen, an earlier North Asian confederation that had once conquered North China in the twelfth century. Important steps in the formation of Manchu identity and political power were the unification of

1. Charles Tilly, *Coercion, Capital, and European States, AD 990–1990* (Cambridge, MA, 1990), pp. 127–130. G. William Skinner, *The City in Late Imperial China* (Stanford, CA, 1977), pp. 222–224, 275–351.
2. Tilly, *Coercion, Capital, and European States*, pp. 127–130.

several Jurchen tribes by Nurhaci (1559–1626), who declared himself their leader (*khan*) around 1600, and the grouping of these people first into smaller units, the companies (*niru*), which, in turn, were subordinated to larger divisions, the banners (*gusa*).[3] The original Jurchen population was meant to be entirely included in those banners, thus breaking or superseding their previous affiliations to clans or tribes. Banners were socio-military units, in the sense that entire households belonged to them – not only fighting men, although the designations for these units are military.[4] At the end of the formative phase (until c.1615) the banners consisted of about 60,000 households.[5] In 1616, due to the increase in the number of people who belonged or were forced to affiliate, four more banners were added. Around 1642, the largest groups of non-Jurchens who had been incorporated into the banners, i.e. Han Chinese (the so-called Chinese armies or "Chinese-martial" *hanjun*) and Mongols, were separated from the Manchus, so that there actually existed twenty-four banners, organized along lines of ethnic affiliation.[6]

In later conquests, companies of members of further ethnic groups, such as the Russians from the defeated border fort of Albazin on the Amur, Dzunghars who had capitulated, and Muslims from Turkestan, were added to the banners. The Jurchen under Nurhaci conquered the Liaodong region to the east of the Liao River (1621–1626), where conflicts with the Han Chinese arose. Several policies to appease and accommodate the Chinese were applied both by Nurhaci and his successor Hong Taiji (1592–1643). Since these strategies pertain to labour relations, they will be discussed separately.

To mention just the landmark years of the Jurchen expansion into China, the ethnic self-designation "Manchu" was chosen in 1635, the dynasty was named Qing ("the pure"), and a Chinese-style capital with government institutions was established at Shenyang in 1636.[7] At least since about 1618, when Nurhaci declared war on the Ming, it had been the ambition of Jurchen/Manchu rulers and their Chinese councillors to force the Ming to

---

3. Gertraude Roth, "The Manchu-Chinese Relationship, 1618–1636", in Jonathan D. Spence and John E. Wills, Jr. (eds), *From Ming to Ch'ing: Conquest, Region, and Continuity in Seventeenth-Century China* (New Haven, CT, [etc.], 1979), pp. 1–38, 6.

4. As Gijs Kessler pointed out to me, there is a similarity here with Russian estates, which might have a military foundation but which included entire households as well. The same was true for the "military households" of the Ming dynasty who had been assigned this specific, hereditary obligation at the beginning of the Ming. The difference with the Qing is that the Jurchen/Manchu included (or at least intended to include) their entire population and that of the other conquered ethnic groups.

5. Roth, "Manchu-Chinese Relationship", pp. 6 and 44f., endnote 2, suggests a figure of 200 companies of 300 households each.

6. Pamela Kyle Crossley, *The Manchus* (Oxford, 1997), p. 207.

7. *Ibid.*, pp. 78–79. Mark C. Elliott, *The Manchu Way: The Eight Banners and Ethnic Identity in Late Imperial China* (Stanford, CA, 2001), pp. 70–71.

accept Manchu dominance in the Manchurian home territory. In the course of a bloody conquest, Central and Southern China was first allotted as a kind of feudal territory to three military leaders affiliated with Chinese-martial banners. However, when these aspired to exclusive rule over all China, their fiefs were seized from them. The conquest of Taiwan and its incorporation into the Qing empire in 1683 marked the point of consolidation of Qing rule over China. From then on, until the mid-eighteenth century, expansionary wars were waged especially on the northern and western periphery. Among these, the struggle against the Dzunghars, a Mongolian confederation that wanted to establish an empire of its own, peaked in the 1750s and 1760s and resulted in a high death toll.[8]

LABOUR RELATIONS IN THE FORMATIVE PROCESS OF THE MANCHU ETHNIC GROUP: JURCHENS BEFORE THE INTRODUCTION OF THE BANNERS

For the Jurchen/Manchu[9] people and the conquered Han Chinese, Mongolians, and Dzunghars, among many others, the expansion of the Qing brought about complex changes in social relationships – not least in labour relations.

As Crossley remarked, at the outset a *khan* was a "keeper of slaves"; regardless of their language, customs, or habitat, these slaves owed him total service and received protection and symbolic or real familiarity in return.[10] In this sense, the Jurchen population was expected to pledge allegiance to Nurhaci and, as such, to become formally his subjects in the sense of "servants" or even "slaves". In theory, this would imply labour relations of the obligatory labour kind. For the entire population this type of "slavery" was formal rather than factual,[11] but real slavery in the sense of treating people as saleable commodities also occurred in Jurchen society.

Traditionally, the Jurchens lived in a combination of economic pursuits including hunting, fishing, plant gathering (especially ginseng), animal breeding (especially horses), and, since around 1500, increasingly also agriculture, which can be characterized as semi-nomadic or "limited nomadism".[12] To be precise, three distinct zones of tribal activities can be defined. The "Wild Jurchens" in the north on the Amur and Ussuri rivers

---

8. For recent accounts of the Dzungharian wars, see Peter Perdue, *China Marches West: The Qing Conquest of Central Eurasia* (Cambridge, MA, 2005), and James Millward, *Eurasian Crossroads: A History of Xinjiang* (New York, 2007).

9. The self-designation before 1635 was Jurchen, thereafter Manchu. In this article, the ethnonym Jurchen/Manchu is applied for the transitional period.

10. Crossley, *The Manchus*, p. 54.

11. *Ibid.*, p. 72.

12. Elliott, *The Manchu Way*, p. 48; Crossley, *The Manchus*, p. 40.

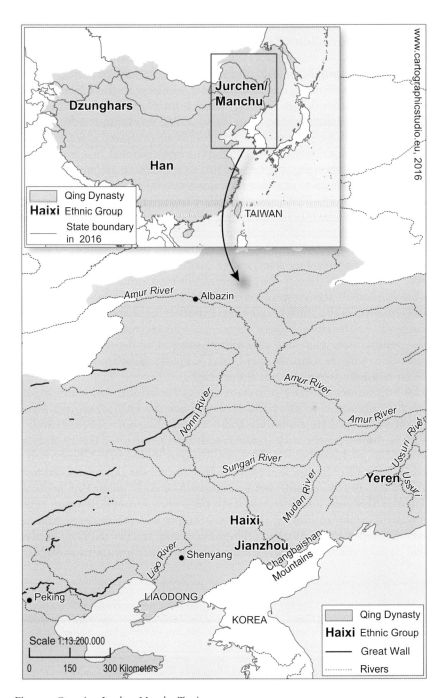

Figure 1. Overview Jurchen-Manchu Territory.

were mainly hunters and fishers, with additional pig-raising and non- or half-sedentary agriculture. The Haixi Jurchens east of the Nonni River and in the Sungari River region experienced the strongest Mongolian influence, practised agriculture in the east, and raised cattle in the west. The Jianzhou Jurchen in the south, on the Mudan River and next to the Changbaishan Mountains, bordering on Korea, were hunters and fishers, gathered freshwater pearls and ginseng roots, farmed, and produced textiles.

Material exchange with the Chinese had been organized since the early fifteenth century. Tribute to the Ming court was delivered in a system that foresaw that neighbouring peoples who had accepted Ming domination were to present particular natural products at certain intervals. They would receive gifts in return, often more valuable than those they had brought, and were allowed to trade along their itinerary. In the course of the fifteenth century, some of the Jurchen tributary missions appeared in the Ming capital in numbers bordering 800 or 900, or even 1,000.[13] This led to restrictions on the number of people entitled to engage in tribute trade, and to conflicts among those who wished to make the journey and enjoy the benefits of this type of trade.[14]

Established in the early fifteenth century by the Chinese authorities, horse markets in the border region were another form of material exchange. Moreover, Jurchen local products were sold and exchanged for Chinese tea, silk, cotton, rice, salt, and agricultural tools. Unofficial trade was also conducted with Korean, Mongol, and Chinese merchants,[15] mostly to obtain weapons, ironware, and copper cash.

Elliott outlines a three-tier system of social relations, with elites (*irgen*) directly responsible to the tribal leaders, later the *khan*; semi-free *Jušen*, who were obliged to submit tax and perform obligatory work, including military duties, for the tribal leaders; and unfree serfs or slaves, who were dependants of household heads (*aha*, *booi*, or *booi aha*).[16] There was a certain ethnic fluidity in the system in that not all the *Jušen* (and certainly not all the unfree group) were Jurchens/Manchus; they also included Chinese, Mongols, and Koreans. Both the upper and middle strata could own serfs or slaves. During the early Ming, it was the enslaved captives taken during warfare on the Jurchen-Ming and Jurchen-Korean borders who mostly performed the agricultural work in the Jurchen villages.[17]

13. Morris Rossabi, "The Ming and Inner Asia", in Denis Twitchett and Frederick W. Mote (eds), *The Cambridge History of China, Volume 8, Part 2: The Ming Dynasty 1368–1644* (Cambridge, 1998), p. 268, mentions fifty trade missions from the Jurchen to Peking in 1436, some of which comprised between 3,000 and 4,000 participants.
14. Gertraude Roth Li, "State Building before 1644", in Willard J. Peterson (ed.), *The Cambridge History of China, Volume 9, Part 1: The Ch'ing Empire to 1800* (Cambridge, 2002), p. 22.
15. Elliott, *The Manchu Way*, p. 50.
16. *Ibid.*, p. 51.
17. Roth Li, "State Building before 1644", p. 21.

The slave owners could dispose of them as they wished, resell and even kill them.[18] This points to a linkage of military engagement for raiding and acquisition of manpower, and the predominant delegation of agricultural activities to the captives, at least in the earlier phases of the polity. Although scholarly opinions about the exact period of transition to an economy based on stronger engagement in agriculture vary, the annexation in 1621 of the Liaodong area is most often considered a starting point for a system of agriculture supervised by the banners, where ordinary banner people would work in the fields.[19] Jurchen households typically consisted of five to seven members, and, in addition, a number of slaves who were not relatives, but people from other ethnic groups. Before the formation of the banners, the households would form units that hunted and gathered food together, and in the case of warfare they were grouped into larger temporary companies. After the introduction of the banners these sometimes very small communities were placed under a unified command that could eliminate previous loyalties and impose new ones.[20]

According to Roth Li's perceptive analysis, the border and tribute trade caused a clearer division between wealthy and poor people within the Jurchen tribes, especially in southern Manchuria, where more trading opportunities could be realized than in the north, where group hunting was still the major economic activity. With wealth, the political aspirations of group leaders became more evident, as did internal competition and warfare. It is highly plausible that in the course of the sixteenth century Jurchen merchants desired a stronger administration that could guarantee the security of their transactions.[21] This trend may well have led to the rivalry among Jurchen leaders, the emergence of Nurhaci, and the institution of the banners, which cut through previous tribal affiliations and connections among the Jurchen.

Before the introduction of the banners shortly after 1600, Jurchen labour relations can be characterized, in the terms of the Collaboratory, as reciprocal and tributary, with the first traces of commodification. For the reciprocal type of labour, labour relations 4a (leading household producers), 4b (household kin producers), and 5 (household kin non-producers) applied to the Jurchen hunters, fishers, and gatherers. The sources are not quite clear as to whether the produce traded at the markets and on the tribute missions was sold and bought by specialized merchants; at any rate, a certain degree of commodified labour (labour relations 12a, self-employed leading producers, and 12b,

18. *Ibid.*, p. 39.
19. Liu Xiaomeng, *Manzu buluo yu guojia* [The Manchurian Tribe and State] (Beijing, 2007), pp. 207, 215.
20. Roth Li, "State Building before 1644", p. 21.
21. *Ibid.*, p. 24.

self-employed kin producers) can be assumed.[22] The enslaved agricultural workers mentioned above correspond to labour relation 6 (reciprocal household servants and slaves), which is defined as "subordinate non-kin (men, women, and children) contributing to the maintenance of self-sufficient households".[23]

LABOUR RELATIONS AMONG THE JURCHENS AFTER THE INTRODUCTION OF THE BANNERS (c.1600)

The banners formed the basic socio-military unit of the Jurchen people under the rule of Nurhaci and his successors. As to why this type of organization was introduced, the historiography points as a rule to the concentration of power in the person of Nurhaci. The new units gradually superseded the traditional smaller tribal or clan communities. Historical records of the foundation of Manchu rule do not spell out a clear causality of why the companies (and later the banners) were established, but it gives the context, "[Nurhaci] assembled the growing masses of adherents and grouped them into companies of 300 people [...] earlier, when our people went on warfare or on a hunt, it was not calculated how many participants there were, but they all set out following their tribe or fortified settlement".[24] According to this narrative, companies and banners were formed to optimize and professionalize military and hunting operations and to homogenize manpower into equal units. At the same time, like the previous clans and villages, they encompassed the entire population, including women, children, and dependants, and were permanent structures rather than hunting or raiding parties that dispersed after the spoils had been divided. Especially after the establishments of the first banners, the "adherents" – not all of them of their own volition – also encompassed subjugated Chinese, Mongolians, and Koreans, as well as Jurchen groups from the northernmost periphery that had been out of reach earlier, but now partly came into the expansionary orbit of Nurhaci and his followers. The number of people involved is estimated at about 100,000 taxed males before 1615, a figure that rose to at least several hundreds of thousands

---

22. Karin Hofmeester *et al.*, "The Global Collaboratory on the History of Labour Relations, 1500–2000: Background, Set-Up, Taxonomy, and Applications", paper submitted to the conference "Big Questions, Big Data", IISH, 4–5 November 2015, pp. 17–20, available at http://hdl.handle.net/10622/4OGRAD, last accessed 1 December 2015.
23. *Ibid.*, p. 18.
24. *Huang Qing kaiguo fanglüe* [Operational Plans for the Foundation of the August Qing, 1786], comp. by Agui *et al.*, reprint ed. *Zhongguo fanglüe congshu*, vol. 7 (Taipei, 1968), ch. 3, pp. 49ff., translated by Erich Hauer, *Die Gründung des Mandschurischen Kaiserreiches* (Berlin, 1926), p. 34.

during the phase of western expansion between 1616 and 1625.[25] This is generally held to be the entire population.

After the banners were introduced, the middle strata (*Jušen*) formed their core. Basically, they were agricultural producers whose land was taxed, as well as hunters and gatherers. In peacetime, they essentially supported themselves and their households, working for a subsistence living and for the market. When taking part in campaigns, they were supported by the polity, especially in the period of Hong Taiji's dominance (1626–1643).[26] This support came in the form of grain stipends, the so-called "walking grain provisions" (*xingliang*). The labour relations of the active fighters belong to the tributary mode, labour relation 8 (obligatory labourers: those who have to work for the polity). When not campaigning, the banner people relied on traditional ways of supporting themselves and their families, and on war booty.[27]

The time span between 1618 and 1636 saw initiatives to make the Jurchens and the Chinese under their control adapt to each other, and this pertained, too, to labour relations. After a relatively relaxed relationship in the 1610s, when both parties viewed the other as more or less equal,[28] the situation following the first attempts of the Manchus to conquer Liaodong in 1618 grew tenser. Integrationist and separationist moves on the part of Jurchen rulers followed, and the Chinese rebelled. In the integrationist phase, Nurhaci ordered that in some regions Jurchen conquerors should live together with the Chinese in their households, on equal terms.[29] This policy was resented by the Chinese, and after a series of rebellions and the (alleged?) poisoning of resident Jurchens the Chinese were reorganized and distributed to Manchu officials in a status resembling slavery.[30] Nurhaci's successor Hong Taiji, a usurper in need of Chinese support, placed the Chinese who had surrendered to his rule under their own officials, had them registered, and aimed at realizing equality between the Chinese and Jurchens.[31]

Under Nurhaci, an effort was also made to attract Han Chinese people from the region west of the Liao River to settle in the newly conquered Liaodong, promising them a life as "free and equal landowners", stressing that "All will equally be the khan's subjects and will live and work the fields

25. Zhang Jiasheng, *Baqi shilun* [Ten Essays on the Eight Banners] (Shenyang, 2008), p. 94.
26. Crossley, *The Manchus*, p. 82.
27. Elliott, *The Manchu Way*, p. 192.
28. Roth, "Manchu-Chinese Relationship", p. 6.
29. *Ibid.*, p. 14.
30. *Ibid.*, p. 20. According to Roth, *tokso* implies "imperial grants of cultivated land and people" – to the Jurchen headmen. In this sense, the people were conceived of as a commodity.
31. *Ibid.*, pp. 13, 21. The *tokso* were eliminated thereafter. Roth refers to a statement by Hong Taiji to the effect that, before 1625, the Chinese were all slaves to the Manchus – possibly trying to present himself as their liberator.

on an equal basis."[32] Yet, in the process of conquest in Liaodong, there is clear evidence that some of the Chinese previously living there were enslaved, with a gradation from downright chattels (*aha*) to bondservants (*booi niyalma*). Roth points out that originally slaves were people captured in battle, but a document from 1624 also reveals a case in Liaodong where households with property of less than a certain amount of grain were enslaved, while those who possessed more were set free.[33]

Until the Manchu established themselves as an imperial dynasty in Peking, large numbers of non-Manchu people were made soldiers for the conquerors, as a hereditary obligation. After the conquest, some of them rose to senior positions in the civilian ranks. This distinctive new rank and new type of labour relation emerged largely due to the fact that the ruling group of Manchus needed the administrative and linguistic skills of the Chinese and occasionally other non-Chinese people to govern China.

The period between Nurhaci's rise around 1600 and the conquest of the Ming territory in 1644 thus brought about changes in tributary labour relations due to socio-political change in the organization of the banner people and their dependants. It was made possible by the Jurchen/Manchu appropriation of power due to military superiority and the ensuing prerogatives for recruiting unfree labour, first in a region considered peripheral by the Ming, and eventually in North China south of the Great Wall.

CHANGES IN LABOUR RELATIONS AFTER THE MANCHU CONQUEST OF CHINA

After the conquest of Peking, and subsequently of all of China, bannermen garrisons were established in the capital and in most provincial capitals. In these garrisons, the bannermen households, including their retainers (slaves and bondservants), received stipends and were thus no longer producers, but instead rendered hereditary military service. In the terminology of the Collaboratory, this still corresponds to tributary labour of type 8 (those who have to work for the polity), but with the difference that this was now remunerated on a permanent basis. The payment for the bannermen in the garrisons was mainly monetized, being paid monthly in silver, and in addition grain allowances were given in kind.[34] The banner people were also granted land in the newly conquered territories, to be tilled by dependants (bondservants or slaves). Yet, banner people as a rule opted not to till the land personally, but to sell it in order to pay for

32. *Ibid.*, p. 9 and endnote 7.
33. *Ibid.*, p. 12.
34. The state-organized transport of grain, especially rice, from the producing areas in central and southern China to the capital Peking was another kind of tributary – or quasi tributary – occupation in the public-service sector that was peculiar to the Chinese tax administration system.

other expenses.[35] Since, due to fertility, the number of banner people and their dependants south of the Great Wall kept rising, to a degree the government could not afford, several campaigns were started to repatriate banner people to Manchuria. The idea was to have them earn their own living, opening up land for agriculture, but this was not greatly successful.

Research on the social history of the banners has also offered further estimates of their numbers and the level of state revenue necessary for their upkeep. Elliott quotes a figure of between 300,000 and 500,000 adult males, excluding bondservants, in the Eight Banners at the time of conquest (1644), with about forty-three per cent being Manchu, twenty-two per cent Mongol, and thirty-five per cent Chinese.[36] For the early eighteenth century this might have risen to between 850,000 and 1.6 million bannermen. Including women, children, and bondservants, this may have added up to between 2.6 million and 4.9 million people. At this time, about half of the active bannermen were employed in Peking to guard the capital, while twenty per cent were employed in Manchuria and thirty per cent in the garrisons in China proper and on the borders.[37] The ratio of active bannermen to dependants (family members, bondservants, and slaves) varied from garrison to garrison, with highs of ten and lows of five dependants to one salaried bannerman.[38] In the terms of the Collaboratory, by no means all people in the banners worked in tributary labour relations. On the contrary, the labour relations of family members and bondservants were reciprocal; bondservants and slaves belonged to labour relation 6 (reciprocal household servants and slaves: subordinate non-kin), and the family members of banner people and of the bondservants and slaves who did not work as servants themselves belonged to labour relation 5 (household kin non-producers) and 1 (non-working) (for the children and elderly).

Moreover, tributary labourers for the polity did not only imply military labour for defence. The maidservants in the palaces, for instance, were drafted from the banners and worked between the ages of fifteen and twenty-five or thirty. This corresponds to labour relation 8 (those who have to work for the polity). Moreover, the palace in Peking had a certain number of positions for daily workers in casual jobs in palace or garrison maintenance (*sula*). The workers recruited as *sula* belonged to the banners and bondservant companies, and thus had a status that should have entitled them to receive lifelong state support for their subsistence. Yet if, in addition, they took on daily maintenance work in return for modest remuneration, this can be understood as commodified work since this type of work offered scope for extra income when funds were not sufficient to feed the worker and his family. For the palace institution employing these

---

35. Elliott, *The Manchu Way*, p. 314.
36. *Ibid.*, p. 117.
37. *Ibid.*
38. *Ibid.*, pp. 117–118, 120–121.

workers, the Imperial Household Department (Neiwufu), this arrangement allowed for flexibility in the event of immediate need, for major ceremonies for instance. Since there was a – restricted – market for labour of this type, it could be argued that this was of labour relation type 18.3 (wage earners employed by non-market institutions, time rate payment).[39] Outside the palace precincts, another group of workers for the banners were those who laboured on the imperial agricultural estates. The historiography refers to about 11,000 worker positions engaged on these domains in the vicinity of the capital, where grains, cash crops, fruit, and vegetables were grown, cattle were raised, and horses bred. More worked on estates in Manchuria. Their personal status was either one that resembled serfdom (labour relation 10), since they were forbidden to leave the estates, and the commitment was hereditary. These workers, mostly captives and convicts, owned no means of production. Other farmers had commended themselves to the imperial house, but retained the right to self-management and even to sublet their land. They had to pay rent and provide particular services in addition, such as gathering certain mushrooms, herbs, or ginseng. Yet, whereas the Imperial Household Department demanded mainly labour service from the serf-like workers, the main exigency from the farmers who had commended themselves, and who as a rule oversaw the performance of the others, was payment in silver rather than their labour in agriculture. The overseers were registered as bondservants and at least theoretically forbidden to return to their previous status as ordinary citizens.[40]

Military campaigns were frequent during the expansionary phase. When not on campaign, the bannermen in their garrisons who were entitled to receive a stipend were supposed to guard the garrison and maintain their military preparedness. Formal collective drills were assigned in two three-month periods per year, and for the rest of the time soldiers were expected to train their skills, especially by bow-shooting from horseback, and by hunting, which was deemed the most befitting occupation (except warfare) for a bannerman.[41] In addition, banner people were entitled to a large share of lucrative military and civilian administrative positions.

39. Evelyn S. Rawski, *The Last Emperors: A Social History of Qing Imperial Institutions* (Berkeley, CA, [etc.], 1998), pp. 168–172.

40. Qi Meiqin, *Qingdai neiwufu* [The Imperial Household Department in the Qing Dynasty] (Beijing, 1998), pp. 195–196.

41. The regulations of the Eight Banners, *Baqi tongzhi*, do not specify how to distribute the prey. Clearly, the hunting activities after the garrisons were installed were not in the first place intended to secure a livelihood, but to train for warfare and to maintain the lifestyle of their ancestors. Li Jingrui and Tie Nan, "Manzu weichang de youlai ji qi lishi zuoyong" [The Origins of the Manchurian Battle and its Function in History], *Manzu yanjiu* [Manchu Minority Research], 2 (1999), pp. 58–62, 60–61, point out that after the original Jurchen hunting parties the prey was evenly divided among the participants. Elliott has referred to the imperial hunting parties of the Qing emperors as "invented tradition". See Elliott, *The Manchu Way*, p. 187.

The number of these assignments was quite out of proportion to the actual proportion of the population whom the banner people represented.[42] Yet, with the banner population increasing over time, and despite the trend to create jobs for them by all means, a rising number of banner people were registered as "idle" (*sula*) and could receive only temporary work assignments. In the palace in Peking alone, between fifty and a hundred temporary assignments for the *sula* were envisaged per day.[43]

In the context of the impact of state policies, it is important to note that estimates for 1730 based on both the historiography and archival records suggest that perhaps as much as between twenty-one and twenty-five per cent of the annual state budget was allocated to support the banner system, the constituents of which formed a strategically very important elite comprising just two per cent of the entire population of the Qing empire.[44] Moreover, according to Elliott's calculation, most of the expenses for the banners were used to feed not the officers and soldiers but family dependants and horses.[45] Military tributary labour in the banners was thus unfree, but advantageous and privileged if the soldiers could obtain their wages. This was not always the case. Crossley mentions that most of the garrison populations "did not receive stipends, but lived as the dependents of those men between the ages of 15 and 60 who were eligible for, *and lucky enough to actually secure*, the payments".[46]

It was a political choice to maintain this elite group of fighters, who, until the restrictions on their occupations were lifted in 1863, were not supposed to work for subsistence or for the market.[47] The reasons for this were evidently the trust that the Qing rulers and the Imperial Household Department as the core court institution placed in persons of the same region of descent, often defined as enlarged family. In the case of the Han Chinese members of the banners, what counted was the proven loyalty at a certain critical period in the transition from the Ming to the Qing. Evidently, this was an uneconomic way of keeping an army, the dependants of which were continuously increasing due to demographic reasons, which led to poverty among many of its members. Like other contemporaneous states in the world where standing armies were maintained,[48] the Qing state

---

42. *Ibid.*, pp. 176–196.

43. Rawski, *The Last Emperors*, p. 169.

44. Elliott, *The Manchu Way*, p. 311, referring to Chen Feng's figures in *Qingdai junfei yanjiu* [A Study of Military Expenses in the Qing Dynasty] (Wuhan, 1992).

45. *Ibid.*, p. 310.

46. Crossley, *The Manchus*, p. 82. Italics added.

47. Elliott, *The Manchu Way*, p. 311.

48. Michael Sikora, "Change and Continuity in Mercenary Armies: Central Europe, 1650–1750", in Erik Jan Zürcher (ed.), *Fighting for a Living: A Comparative Study of Military Labour 1500–2000* (Amsterdam, 2013), available at http://www.oapen.org/search?identifier=468734 last accessed 31 August 2016, pp. 201–241, 202; John Brewer, *The Sinews of Power: War, Money, and the English State,*

had to shoulder a huge financial burden in order to maintain its privileged Eight Banner fighters. The intention of Qing rulers was to protect the distinction of the ruling elite, even if this did not seem to be economically rational. This was all the more the case since the banners were not the only Qing army.

LABOUR RELATIONS IN THE OTHER QING ARMY: THE GREEN STANDARDS

Apart from the political decision to support the Eight Banner Army, the Qing sustained an army of paid Han Chinese soldiers. This was, as Ulrich Theobald and I have shown, the second large shift in labour relations in the service of the state.[49] The Green Standard Army, which was recruited mainly from Ming divisions who had deserted, consisted of professional soldiers working in commodified labour relations. This employment was intended for a lifetime. Soldiers' sons turning sixteen had the right, not the obligation, to serve in the army.[50] As to the size of the Green Standards compared with the Eight Banners, the rule-of-thumb figure is 600,000 and 200,000 men respectively.[51] The Green Standards commanded not only land, but also marine forces. As to combat power, the numerical ratio between banner and Green Standard soldiers serving on the battlefield was typically 1:10,[52] but in some wars, especially against the Dzunghars, banner troops were deployed in a larger proportion.

Previously, the Ming army had a corvée military service, and the transition to the professional Green Standard Army can be qualified as one from tributary to commodified labour.[53] Yet, already during the Ming era (1368–1644), powerful and resourceful private households, and even military and civilian officials, privately hired soldiers, so that this transition should be seen as gradual.[54] It hinged upon the weakening of state power in the latter

1688–1783 (London [etc.], 1989), p. 40; Jari Eloranta, "Military Spending Patterns in History", available at http://eh.net/encyclopedia/military-spending-patterns-in-history/, last accessed 29 February 2016.

49. Christine Moll-Murata and Ulrich Theobald, "Military Employment in Qing Dynasty China", in Zürcher, *Fighting for a Living*, pp. 353–391, 371, 382.

50. Luo Ergang, *Luying bingzhi* [Treatise on the Green Standards] (Beijing, 1984), p. 231.

51. For a discussion of competing figures on the army sizes, see Moll-Murata and Theobald, "Military Employment in Qing Dynasty China", p. 357, fn. 18.

52. Ulrich Theobald, *War Finance and Logistics in Late Imperial China: A Study of the Second Jinchuan Campaign (1771–1776)* (Leiden, 2013), p. 46f., quotes figures of seventy per cent for Green Standard troops, eight per cent for banner troops, and twenty-two per cent for locally recruited supplementary troops.

53. Moll-Murata and Theobald, "Military Employment in Qing Dynasty China", p. 357, and David M. Robinson, "Military Labour in China, circa 1500", in Zürcher, *Fighting for a Living*, pp. 43–80.

54. Robinson, "Military Labour in China", pp. 67, 79–80.

half of the Ming dynasty and the increasing financial liquidity due to the silver influx during this period. In the expansionary phase of the Qing, military conscription was not inflicted upon the Han Chinese population, and apart from the Green Standard Army free wage labour was used also for transport workers and experts, especially for arms producers, who were not continuously employed in the army.[55] Thus, in contrast to the Ming, whose standing army consisted of military households entitled to land and which were supposed to feed themselves, in the case of the Han Chinese army the Qing resorted from their inception to commodified military labour.

In Tilly's sense, the above setting points to a tendency towards the capital-intensive rather than coercion-intensive path for recruitment in the military sector in the course of the seventeenth and eighteenth centuries. In the Jurchen/Manchu case, in the pre-conquest era the government profited both from tributary military and agricultural labour in the new territories of Liaodong. Yet, after the rule of the Qing had been consolidated south of the Great Wall, although the labour of the banner soldiers was of a tributary nature, that of the Green Standard Army was not. Moreover, both constituted a small proportion of the population that was overwhelmingly engaged in agriculture in reciprocal and commodified labour relations.

WARFARE WITH THE DZUNGHARS: DESTRUCTION AND EXPULSION OF A LABOUR FORCE

During the period of Qing expansion between the 1690s and the 1780s, frequent wars were waged against adversaries north, west, and south of the empire. All of these battles involved high death tolls. The longest conflict was against the contenders for primacy in the huge steppe empire of the Dzunghars. These semi-nomadic groups of Oirat Mongols, whose power base lay in present-day Xinjiang (see Figure 2), had not accepted Qing supremacy. Like the Jurchen, and at about the same period, their leaders acquired weapons technology, and resettled in their own territory captives from ethnic groups well versed in agriculture (mostly those later referred to as Uighurs; that is, Muslim Turkic-speaking non-nomadic people), who were coerced to work in tributary labour relations. The Dzunghars exploited the mineral resources of the region, controlled trade revenues, and tried to combine various groups of the Oirat Mongols to consolidate their power.[56] The Dzungharian population worked mostly as animal herders,

---

55. See Moll-Murata and Theobald, "Military Employment in Qing Dynasty China", pp. 365–366, for the example of the second military campaign to the Gold River Valley on the Sichuan/Tibet border (1771–1776): blacksmiths who produced sabres, swords, daggers, and halberds were "official craftsmen" within the banners, but the Green Standard Army used hired labour for arms production. For more details, see Theobald, *War Finance and Logistics in Late Imperial China*.

56. Millward, *Eurasian Crossroads*, pp. 90, 92.

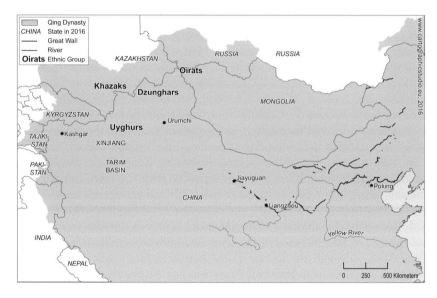

Figure 2. Qing expansion into the Dzungharian territory.

practising nomadic pastoralism. As such, their labour relations correspond to those of the Jurchen before the conquest, working in reciprocal labour relations 4a, 4b, and 5. Like the Jurchen, the Dzunghars employed war captives both for animal herding,[57] but also for agriculture.[58] This was unfree labour, and since the slaves had no right to leave, the corresponding labour relation is 11. The sources hardly warrant a quantification of the people engaged in commodified labour relations. Figures given in the literature quoting total sales from eight Dzungharian trade missions in 1752 suggest the possibility of a partly commodified economy.[59]

The wars with the Qing empire were first fought between 1689 and 1696, when the Dzunghar leader Galdan (1644–1697) was defeated. The final conflict, between 1752 and 1758, was a retaliatory campaign for the insubordination of a potentially dangerous Dzungharian rival. As a result, a region corresponding to present-day Northern Xinjiang was depopulated. In an account published in 1842, the historian Wei Yuan quotes a figure of

57. Cai Jiayi, "Zhunga'er de muxuye. Zhunga'er shehui jingji chutan zhiyi" [Animal Husbandry of the Dzunghars: First Explorations of the Dzunghar Social Economy, 1], *Minzu yanjiu* [Ethno-National Studies], 1 (1985), pp. 54–63, 61.
58. Wang Xilong, "Zhunga'er tongzhi shiqi de Tianshan beilu nongye laodongzhe de laiyuan he zushu" [The Ethnic Affiliation and Origin of the Agricultural Workers in the Northern Tianshan District during the Period of Dzungharian Rule], *Minzu yanjiu*, 5 (1993), pp. 97–101, 97–100.
59. Accordingly, 386,012 sheep, 13,343 horses, 7,199 cows and oxen, and 9,424 camels were sold in one year. Cai Jiayi, "Zhunga'er de muxuye", p. 56.

several hundred thousand households (600,000 people, according to Peter Perdue), of which forty per cent died of smallpox, twenty per cent fled to Russia and Kazakhstan, thirty per cent were killed by the Qing army in battle,[60] and the remaining women, children, and the elderly were enslaved and given over to serve in Manchu and Mongol banners.[61]

The area was resettled with military farms, a pattern in use in Chinese empires since the Han dynasty (206 BCE to AD 220). Here, at first, Chinese soldiers and exiled convicts, but also resettled Uyghurs from the Tarim Basin, worked mainly in tributary labour relations to secure the upkeep of the garrison forces, initially about 40,000 men (c.1760). Half of them were Mongols and Manchu banner people, and half were Chinese soldiers.

As a result of the escalating conflict between the Qing and the Dzungharian empires, a harsh cut in terms of the size of the labour force ensued. Decimation was an intentional policy, and the practice of subjugation of the remaining population had direct consequences on labour relations, causing an extreme shift from predominantly reciprocal to tributary relations. This could hardly have happened had it not been for the war and subjugation.

Interestingly, shortly after this culmination of Qing expansion into central Asia, ethnically related groups also resettled in what had previously been Dzunghar territory. As Dmitry Khitrov explains in his contribution to the present Special Issue, the Kalmyks had fled from Dzungharia in the first half of the seventeenth century. Like the Dzunghars, they belonged to the Oirat group, but formed a distinct subgroup, the Torghuts. These people searched for more open pastures in the north-west, their migrations in the 1620s and 1630s taking them as far as the Lower Volga. Yet, after the experience of being subjected to coerced military service in Russia, about 150,000 of them remigrated to Dzungharia in 1771, and between 50,000 and 70,000 were settled in Northern Xinjiang (Figure 3).[62]

UNFREE LABOUR SOUTH OF THE GREAT WALL IN THE LATE MING AND EARLY QING

While between the early 1600s and the mid-seventeenth century, the far north thus experienced a reconfiguration of labour relations depending upon status and ethnicity, and empire-wide the armed forces were converted from a corvée army in the Ming to the commodified Green Standard Army during the Qing, simultaneously in central China and in the south a change in labour relations emerged that can be characterized as an

---

60. Wei Yuan, *Shengwu ji* [An Account of the Holy Warfare (of the Qing Dynasty)], ch. 3, fol. 11a/b (Peking, 1844). See Perdue, *China Marches West*, p. 285.
61. Millward, *Eurasian Crossroads*, p. 95.
62. *Ibid.*, pp. 89, 100.

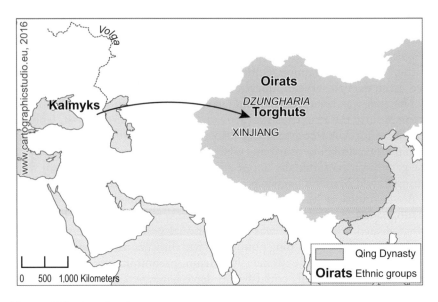

Figure 3. Kalmyk remigration.

increase in unfree labour.[63] This trend started from about the 1550s in many regions in China, but it is especially well documented for the central and southern provinces. Among the reasons that led to the immiseration that brought about this particular turn, an increase in state expenditure on warfare and consequently higher taxation, bad harvests, and little state support for the destitute were most important.[64]

In a recent article, Claude Chevaleyre cites the classic study by Ho Ping-ti,[65] who assumed that about one per cent of the Ming population were of a lower

63. This has been studied by Chinese scholars, first in an article by Xie Guozhen in 1932, followed by many articles and several book-length contributions by Japanese and Chinese historians, including Oyama Masaaki, Niida Noboru, and especially Fu Yiling, and in sinological social history research by Andreas W. Mixius, *"Nu-pien" und die "Nu-p'u" von Kiangnan. Aufstände Abhängiger und Unfreier in Südchina 1644/45* (Hamburg, 1980), Joseph P. McDermott, "Bondservants in the T'ai-hu Basin during the Late Ming: A Case of Mistaken Identities", *The Journal of Asian Studies*, 40:4 (1981), pp. 675–701, and Harriet Zurndorfer, *Change and Continuity in Chinese Local History: The Development of Hui-chou Prefecture from 800 to 1800* (Leiden, 1989).

64. Claude Chevaleyre, "Acting as Master and Bondservant: Considerations on Status Identities and the Nature of 'Bond-Servitude' in Late Ming China", in Alessandro Stanziani (ed.), *Labour, Coercion, and Economic Growth in Eurasia, 17th–20th Centuries* (Leiden, 2013), p. 242, gives a few other reasons for entering into servitude: avoidance of punishment, the hope of protection by a powerful individual, or extraordinary expenses due to family events.

65. Ping-ti Ho, *The Ladder of Success in Imperial China: Aspects of Social Mobility, 1368–1911* (New York, NY, 1962), p. 19.

legal status than the commoner population. Chevaleyre concludes that this may have meant 700,000 to two million people around 1600, most of whom were probably bondservants, but more exact figures cannot be ascertained.[66]

There was a variety of forms of this type of unfree labour: hereditary and non-hereditary; some of these servile labourers were more bound to the household of the masters, both in the countryside and in cities, others worked the fields. The service obligation tied them not to the land, but to the master, in whose household register the servants were usually included as dependants. Ownership of bondservants was not reserved for the nobility; as a rule, the masters were commoners. Harriet Zurndorfer has described the wide variety of possible arrangements, pointing out that although the bondservants belonged to the lowest legal category, they could own and dispose of land and exploit other bondservants.[67] Variegated as the category was, there were several ways in which people could become bondservants: through purchase, adoption, marriage (if a free man married a bonded woman, his status and that of their children would be commuted to that of bondservants), debt bondage, coercion, and self-commendation.[68] In spite of the negative consequences for personal freedom, in some cases people entered into bond service in order to escape criminal indictment or to garner the protection of an influential family for their own advancement. Not all types of bond service implied permanent servitude and completely forsaking one's previous property.[69]

Although the search for protection, and perhaps even the hope of working as a manager or overseer of agricultural estates or in wealthy households as a "luxury slave" or "brazen servant" (*haonu*), might have prompted some to commend themselves, in most cases bonded labour simply meant toil and exploitation. The recorded bondservant rebellions in Middle and South China confirm this assumption. Mixius has analysed these movements, which contributed to the upheaval at the end of the Ming dynasty. He assumes that the unrest was caused by the immediate great

66. Chevaleyre, "Acting as Master and Bondservant", p. 270.
67. Zurndorfer, *Change and Continuity in Chinese Local History*, p. 198; Christine Moll-Murata, "Work Ethics and Work Valuations in a Period of Commercialization: Ming China, 1500–1644", *International Review of Social History*, 56 (2011), Special Issue *The Joy and Pain of Work*, pp. 165–195, 175–176. See also Chevaleyre, "Acting as Master and Bondservant", pp. 241–242, for the wide scope of bondservant identities and occupations, which were not restricted to agricultural labour.
68. McDermott, "Bondservants", pp. 680–685. According to McDermott, p. 683, commendation (*touchong, toukao*) refers to the process of selling or presenting oneself, one's family, and one's property to a wealthy household for protection, a route into bond servitude that might have been the most common in the area around Lake Tai, close to Suzhou and Shanghai, and, for the wealthy gentry, a common manner to enlarge their landholdings.
69. *Ibid.*, pp. 284–285.

economic and social pressure on the bonded people.[70] There are records of about one hundred such incidents involving between several dozen and up to 5,000 participants between the 1620s and the 1660s.[71] It needs to be stressed that the Qing armies, when they met with rebellious bondservants on their conquest in 1644 and 1645, crushed these insurrections and for the time being opted to restore law, order, and the previous property and work relations rather than to propose and realize immediate change.[72]

The loss of life due to the violence seen during the southern expansion did reduce the entire labour force. However, this was not a deliberate policy, in the sense of extermination, even if the consequences were accepted by the conquerors. In general, if appeasement and accommodation were actively sought after (and this was certainly not always the case), it was targeted at elites rather than at the population. In 1660, the banner people were forbidden by government order from accepting any further self-commendations of the Han Chinese population. The reason was most certainly not an emancipatory concern for those who were willing to serve in unfree labour conditions, but that the stipends of the banner people were not high enough to pay for an increasing number of servants.[73]

During the eighteenth century, the broad tendency towards emancipation, and the rise of tenancy and wage labour in agriculture rather than unfree labour, has been discussed in the historiography.[74] Bond service gradually disappeared in most regions during the eighteenth century.[75] Demography and market forces may have played a more important role in this respect than state policies, since there was an available labour force in many Chinese regions due to the increase in population, and a labour market existed.[76]

---

70. Mixius, *"Nu-pien"*, p. 135. He argues that immediate indignation rather than pronounced egalitarian thought might have caused their uprisings.

71. *Ibid.*, p. 27.

72. *Ibid.*, p. 52.

73. *Ibid.*, p. 50, records this order; Crossley, *The Manchus*, p. 83, records the concern of the government about the rising indebtedness of the banner people, due also to the increasing number of servants they paid and/or accommodated. See also Elliott, *The Manchu Way*, pp. 228–230, for the situation of servitude in several garrisons.

74. The impulses given by the most activist of the Qing emperors, Yongzheng (reigned 1723–1735), to the emancipation of further groups of outcast classes are summarized by Madeleine Zelin, "The Yung-cheng Reign", in Peterson, *The Cambridge History of China*, pp. 183–229, 220ff. Zelin interprets Yongzheng's emancipation edicts as related to the emperor's vision that all subjects should be uniformly subjected to the law, p. 221.

75. Zurndorfer, *Change and Continuity*, p. 120, for a view from the perspective of the Huizhou prefecture in Anhui province. Chevaleyre, "Acting as Master and Bondservant", p. 271, points to the much later complete and formal abolition of slavery and human trafficking enacted in 1910, one year before the end of the Qing dynasty.

76. *Shenshi nongshu / Bu nongshu* [Mr Shen's Book on Agriculture, alternative title: The Farmer's Help], compiled by Zhang Lüxiang (Beijing, 1956), which I have introduced elsewhere (Moll-Murata, "Work Ethics and Work Valuations", p. 176), is a solitary example that discusses

This becomes evident if legislation and legal cases are considered. Concerning the arbitration of the Qing state in labour issues, major turning points were the gradual acknowledgement that cases involving crimes committed by short-term hired labourers should be treated similarly to those of ordinary, free people.[77] Previously, the status of hired workers resembled that of a bondservant, because economic dependence implied legal inferiority. After 1735, the discrimination linked to the quasi-bonded status of long-term hired workers who were engaged for a year or longer was also gradually eased.[78] This means that status inequality expressed in legal codification as to the value of the life of a master versus a bonded servant no longer applied in its harshest form. In judicial practice, the proceedings for cases including homicide (when masters killed servants) had to be reported to the central government and appeared in the routine memorials presented by the provincial authorities to the Ministry of Justice.[79] This is not an example of active intervention in labour relations by the government. Rather, it can be interpreted as an acknowledgement of a change in the social valuation of labour; the government followed, and did not take the lead. Yet, the mere fact that the government did take it onto itself, even if formally (backlogs were great), to arbitrate cases between workers and employers, and later also dealt with issues of wage labour, shows a perspective of the functions that governments can and did take in mediating in labour disputes and labour relations.

At the same time, it is important to bear in mind that wage labour both in agriculture and in the production of commodities did not account for a large percentage of the population.[80] By far the largest economic sector, which covered the greatest part of the Chinese population, was self-sufficient agriculture, with slowly increasing commodification. Here, the impact of the state and tributary labour relations was slightest. As Tilly observed,

---

hiring and remunerating agricultural and proto-industrial workers by middling landowners in the Jiangnan region. Yet, seen together with the large number of court cases involving hired labourers from throughout China, the existence of a labour market is evident. See Wu Liangkai, "Qingdai qianqi nongye gugong de gongjia" [Wages of Hired Agricultural Labourers in the Early Qing], *Zhongguo shehui jingjishi yanjiu* [Journal of Chinese Social and Economic History], 2 (1983), pp. 17–30.

77. Mixius, *"Nu-pien"*, pp. 126, 192; Moll-Murata, "Work Ethics and Work Valuations", p. 177.

78. Kang Chao, *Man and Land in Chinese History: An Economic Analysis* (Stanford, CA, 1986), p. 144.

79. I have discussed this in more detail in Christine Moll-Murata, "Legal Conflicts Concerning Wage Payments in Eighteenth- and Nineteenth-Century China: The Baxian Cases", in Jane Kate Leonard and Ulrich Theobald (eds), *Money in Asia (1200–1900): Small Currencies in Social and Political Contexts* (Leiden, 2015), pp. 265–308, 275–276.

80. Christine Moll-Murata, "Methodological Paper China 1800", p. 9, available at https://github.com/rlzijdeman/labrel/blob/master/data/China/China_1800_Methodological_Paper.pdf, last accessed 17 July 2016.

below the level of the district governments "even the mighty Chinese Empire ruled indirectly via its gentry".[81]

CONCLUSION

How can the government actions outlined above be interpreted in the framework of Charles Tilly's paradigm of capital and coercion? Looking at the larger picture, the implications of the capital-coercion nexus for labour relations consist of a clearly conceivable coercive element in the form of military recruitment by banner formation north of the Great Wall during the expansionist phase of Jurchen/Manchu rule. From the perspective of the Qing government, this also had a more paternalistic side of concern for the well-being of the ethnic core group and its dependants. Both the rebellious Dzunghars and the Kalmyks who had returned from the Volga region experienced more or less extreme forms of coercion by decimation or by resettlement and forced change of occupation and lifestyle. The factor of "capital", if applied to labour relations, pertains to the commodified types. The trend to commercialization during the Qing proved to be irreversible, even if gradual: at least the rights of tenants and wage labourers were raised to the same level as those of commoners in the legal codes.

Returning to the question of which types of labour relations were actively shaped by the expanding Qing empire and which were subjected more to other influences, as defined by the Global Collaboratory on the History of Labour Relations (economic, demographic, social and geographic mobility, urbanization, technological), the formation of the banners stands out clearly. This type of state intervention related to a (post-conquest of China) small percentage of the population, but it changed the configuration of military labour relations in a distinct manner. The unfree labour relations of the bondservants in conquered China, and the status of hired workers (and tenants), were arbitrated and acknowledged ex post facto, rather than directly impacted. In this field, economic institutions and evolutionary change played a more important role.

Tilly's ideas about the specific Chinese combination of capital and coercion derived from a relatively stable setting with a landowning gentry and merchants representing capital and state power embodying coercion. Looking at the period of the enormous upheavals in the course of the dynastic transition and consolidation renders a more dynamic view of a part of the world where the compounded capital-and-coercion mode had been in existence in different combinations but as least as long as in Europe.

---

81. Tilly, *Coercion, Capital, and European States*, p. 127.

IRSH 61 (2016), Special Issue, pp. 49–70 doi:10.1017/S0020859016000420
© 2016 Internationaal Instituut voor Sociale Geschiedenis

Tributary Labour in the Russian Empire in the Eighteenth Century: Factors in Development*

DMITRY KHITROV

Faculty of History, Lomonosov Moscow State University
Lomonosovsky Prospekt, 27–4, 119991, Moscow, GSP-1,
Russian Federation

E-mail: dkh@bk.ru

ABSTRACT: This article addresses the system of state-organized and state-controlled tributary labour in the Russian Empire in the eighteenth century. On the basis of the taxpayers' registry of 1795, it focuses on the social groups obliged to perform military service or labour directly for the polity. They included the numerous "service class" of the southern and eastern frontier regions, including Russian, Ukrainian (mainly Cossack), and indigenous (Bashkir and Kalmyk) communities, and the group of *pripisnye*, peasants "bound" to industries and shipyards to work for their taxes. The rationale behind the use of this type of labour relation was, on the one hand, the need of the state to secure the support of labour in distant and poorly populated regions, and, on the other, that the communes of labourers saw performing work for the state as a strong guarantee of their landowning privileges.

INTRODUCTION

In the eighteenth century, the Russian Empire experienced rapid economic growth and a significant transformation of its social structure. With the country's industrialization and the modernization of the military sphere, it became one of the world's leading powers. This geopolitical success was backed by a significant demographic expansion (with the population increasing from 10.5 million in 1678 to 38 million in 1795, owing both to natural growth and the acquisition of new territories),[1] followed by massive migration and the rapid agricultural development of the frontier regions, especially in the southern and eastern steppe borders of the empire.

---

* This article is based on research that was partially supported by the Russian Foundation for Humanities (RFH), project No. 16-01-0068.
1. Ja.E. Vodarskij, *Naselenie Rossii za 400 Let (XVI – nachalo XX veka)* [The Population of Russia over a Period of 400 Years: Sixteenth to the Early Twentieth Centuries] (Moscow, 1973), p. 27.

It is fairly clear, however, that the mechanisms used to achieve these results were significantly different from those of West European countries, where the development of markets, growth of industry, and rapid urbanization led to the decline of mediaeval estates and fostered a specialization of labour. An abundant historiography, both Soviet/Russian and Western, focused on the economic issues of that period, generally agrees that market institutions, especially the labour market, developed significantly less than in Western Europe,[2] and the role of estates in the ordering of society remained important and actually grew.[3] The question arises, then, as to what instruments were used by the state to substitute the market mechanisms.

In terms of the history of labour, this outlines the need for the advanced study of the relations identified in the Collaboratory taxonomy as tributary.[4] As a rule, such direct obligations were described as *sluzhba* (service) or *povinnosti* (duties). They were widespread in Muscovy, being directly linked to landowning: "all men should bear service from their land, and no one should own land gratuitously", the decree of 1701 stated.[5] In the eighteenth century, the direct link between landowning and obligatory service was broken for the nobility, as in 1714 Peter I proclaimed service to be obligatory for all nobles, regardless of their land possessions, and in 1762 Peter III abolished obligatory service but left landowning untouched. For the large non-noble groups within the population, however, the system of obligatory works and services imposed by the state continued to be very important from both an economic and a social point of view. We will address this later in this article, when we discuss the factors behind the emergence and enduring nature of these relations.

We focus on the eighteenth century, which was critical for the history of the territorial expansion of Russia as it was a period when the broad belt of southern and eastern border regions became safe and started to

2. See the modern overview of these discussions in A. Stanziani, *After Oriental Despotism: Eurasian Growth in a Global Perspective* (London, 2014), pp. 15–26.

3. L.V. Milov, *Velikorusskij Pakhar i Osobennosti Rossijskogo Istoricheskogo Prozessa* [The Ploughmen of Great Russia and the Specifics of the Russian Historical Process] (Moscow, 2001), pp. 162–197; B.N. Mironov, *A Social History of Imperial Russia*, 2 vols (Boulder, 2000). For a general overview and references see "Krestyanstvo perioda pozdnego feodalizma (seredina XVI veka—1861 g.)", in *Istorija Krestyanstva SSSR, 3* [The History of Russian Peasantry] (Moscow, 1993); D. Moon, "Peasants and Agriculture", *The Cambridge History of Russia: Volume 2, Imperial Russia, 1689–1917* (Cambridge, 2006), pp. 449–467.

4. Karin Hofmeester *et al.*, "The Global Collaboratory on the History of Labour Relations, 1500–2000: Background, Set-Up, Taxonomy, and Applications", available at: https://datasets. socialhistory.org/dataset.xhtml?persistentId=hdl:10622/4OGRAD, last accessed 20 September 2016.

5. L.E. Shepelev, *Tituly, mundiry, ordena v Rossijskoj imperii* [Titles, Uniforms, Medals in the Russian Empire] (Leningrad, 1991), p. 28.

attract large migration flows; it was also when the paradigm of the interaction of the state with its subjects significantly changed, and the newly established imperial administration began to actively shape social structures and labour relations. To a large extent, the framework of relations between the imperial administration and the estates, elaborated in the course of the eighteenth century, continued to exist until the end of the imperial period.

SOURCES AND DATABASE

Fortunately, the Russian Empire in the eighteenth century had an advanced system of population statistics. The poll tax was the key element in the country's financial system and, to this end, periodic taxpayers' registries, so-called *revizias*, were compiled approximately every twenty years, in 1719–1724, 1744, 1763, 1781, and 1795.

This article primarily addresses the large database (over 400,000 records) that is one outcome of the Collaboratory. It covers the project benchmark for 1800, based on the fifth *revizia* (1795).[6] Being one of the world's most accurate censuses at the time,[7] it covers nearly the entire population of the empire, organized by provinces and social groups, and provides a solid ground for comparison and retroactive estimates.[8] The system of social stratification in the late eighteenth century was quite multi-layered, and each social group was identified according to its position in society and its obligations to the state. Some of them can be found in all regions (like state peasants), others existed only in several provinces, or just one. Drawing on the historiography and legislation, this gives us an opportunity to determine ethnicity, urban/rural residence, and sector of the economy (agriculture, trade, industry, or civil service) for each of these social groups, showing also the major corresponding labour relations. We should remember, however, that the *revizia* focused on the formal obligations of social groups, and can therefore sometimes obscure actual labour relations. For instance, if a certain commune hired workers to perform those duties for them (such cases,

6. The aggregated results of the registry are published in L.G. Beskrovnyj, Ja.E. Vodarskij, and V.M. Kabuzan, *Perepisi naselenia Rossii. Itogovye materialy podvornykh perepisej I revizij 1646–1858* [The Population Registers of Russia, 1646-1858], 14 vols (Moscow, 1972), VI. See also V.M. Kabuzan, *Narodonaselenie Rossii v XVIII –pervoj polovine XIX v. (Po Materialam Revizij)* [The Population of Russia in the Eighteenth and the First Half of the Nineteenth Centuries, According to *Revizia* Materials] (Moscow, 1963).
7. Ja.E Vodarskij, "Perepisi naseleinja v XVII v. v Rossii I drugikh stranakh Evropy", in *Feodalnaya Rossija vo vsemirno-istoricheskom processe* [Population Censuses of the Seventeenth Century in Russia and Other European Countries] (Moscow, 1972).
8. Dmitry Khitrov and Gijs Kessler, "Global Collaboratory on the History of Labour Relations, 1500–2000. Dataset: Russia", July 2012, available at: https://github.com/rlzijdeman/labrel/blob/master/data/Russia/Russia_1500_1650_1800_1900_2000_Methodological_Paper.pdf, last accessed 20 September 2016.

although not very common, can be found in the historiography),[9] this will
not be visible from this type of source. Moreover, these materials have a
tendency to underestimate the size of migration and the level of urbanization,
generally tending to record the migrants (both seasonal and permanent) in the
places they originally lived. The other problem is the project framework
required to consider the different gender and age groups. Women were
recorded and the age of each person was indicated in the *revizskie skazki*, the
primary documents of the *revizia*; unfortunately, these data were never
aggregated as they were of no interest to the tax authorities. So, we had to use
a range of samples to estimate the size of the female population and of the
different age groups.[10]

To study the dynamics of the process, we also consider material from
earlier *revizias* – those of 1719–1724, 1744, and 1763.[11] Unfortunately,
direct comparisons between them are hindered because of the reforms of
1775, which significantly changed the territorial-administrative divisions,
making the new districts and provinces incomparable with earlier ones. As a
result, changes can be tracked only for social groups as a whole.

LABOUR RELATIONS IN RUSSIA IN 1795: A GENERAL OVERVIEW AND THE ROLE OF TRIBUTARY LABOUR[12]

First, it is necessary to outline the general structure of labour relations in
imperial Russia. It was a predominantly agrarian society; for over ninety-six
per cent of the total population primary labour relations were connected
to their households (as heads of families, working family members,
seniors, and children, LabRel 1, 4a, 4b, and 5). All other relations, including
tributary, were secondary. Only small groups of the urban population,
mainly merchants and skilled artisans, but also the nobility providing
military service and civil administrators, can be identified as self-employed
or wage earning; this category did not exceed two per cent of the
total population, and, together with the other two per cent (regular
army soldiers), they make up the remaining four per cent of the population.
The actual proportion of free wage labour was generally higher than our

9. A.S. Orlov, *Volnenija na Urale v Seredine XVIII v.* (Moscow, 1979), pp. 44–48.

10. See Khitrov and Kessler, "Global Collaboratory on the History of Labour Relations".

11. Beskrovnyj *et al.*, *Perepisi*, vols 2–4.

12. See the presentations: Gijs Kessler and Dmitry Khitrov, "Transitions in Labour Relations
in Eastern Europe: Russia, 1500–2000", paper presented to the Third European Congress on
World and Global History, Session Transitions in Labour Relations World Wide 1500–2000,
London School of Economics, London, 14–17 April 2011; Gijs Kessler and Dmitry Khitrov,
"Labour Relations in Eastern Europe: Russia, 1500–2000", paper presented to the Final
Workshop, Global Collaboratory on the History of Labour Relations 1500–2000, Amsterdam,
11–12 May 2012.

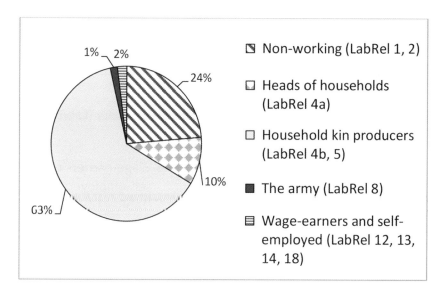

1% — 2%
24%
10%
63%

- Non-working (LabRel 1, 2)
- Heads of households (LabRel 4a)
- Household kin producers (LabRel 4b, 5)
- The army (LabRel 8)
- Wage-earners and self-employed (LabRel 12, 13, 14, 18)

Figure 1. Primary labour relations, 1795.

sources suggest, but it certainly did not involve large masses of the population.[13]

The picture of secondary labour relations of the two main economically active groups (heads of households and household kin producers) presented in Figure 2 is significantly more diverse, however, as large numbers of peasant households were involved in labour migration (*otkhodnichestvo*), waged work, or self-employed work in rural industry (*promysly*), or performed certain labour obligations that can be classified as tributary.

As can be seen, forty-four per cent of the economically active population were involved in various forms of tributary labour (LabRel 10). The absolute majority (eighty-eight per cent) of them were serfs, working in the corvée fields of their landlords.

The long discussion in both Russian and Western historiography of the factors in the development of this institution and its similarity with serfdom in Central and Eastern Europe led specialists to suggest that the creation of the manorial jurisdiction of landlords in 1592–1593 was the government's response to an economic crisis, an attempt to stop the

---

13. N.L. Rubinshtejn, "Nekotorye Voprosy Formirovaniya Rynka Rabochej Sily v Rossii v XVIII v." [Some Questions on the Development of Labour Markets in Eighteenth-Century Russia], *Voprosy istorii*, 2 (1952), p. 95. See also *Ocherki Istorii SSSR. Period Feodalozma. Rossiya vo vtoroj polovine XVIII v.* (Moscow, 1956), p. 112.

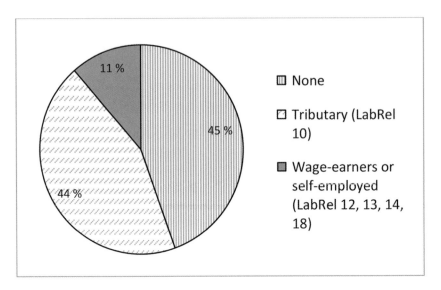

Figure 2. Secondary labour relations of heads of households and household kin producers.

massive relocation of peasants and to provide the lesser nobility with working hands.[14] Russian historiography, generally, concentrated on the issue of whether the prohibition on peasants leaving the estates of their masters, about 1592, was enforced by a government decree, which has never been found however, or whether it was the result of purely economic factors. Although the majority of specialists now agree that the 1592 decree did in fact exist,[15] modern works nevertheless tend to see the development of the manorial economy of the nobility (with the nobility settling in their newly acquired villages between the late fifteenth and early seventeenth centuries) as a major driver in the development, if not the emergence, of serfdom; much later, from the second half of the eighteenth century, we can also track the significant impact of the market economy and growing agricultural exports, which encouraged landlords to develop the corvée and increase the labour obligations of dependent peasants, generally in the sense

14. See the economic explanation for this process in E. Domar, "The Causes of Slavery or Serfdom: A Hypothesis", *The Journal of Economic History*, 30:1 (1970), pp. 18–32. It would be too simple to regard it as the response of the nobility to massive migration to the steppes. Serfdom was fully established by the Code of Laws of 1649, when the absolute majority of the population were still located in the country's historic centre, and the frontier regions remained unsafe and scarcely populated. J. Burbank and F. Cooper, *Empires in World History: Power and the Politics of Difference* (Princeton, 2010).
15. B.N. Florya, "Ob Ustanovlenii 'Zapovednykh Let' v Rossii" [The Establishment of "zapovednye gody" in Russia], *Otechestvennaya Istoriya*, 5 (1999), pp. 121–124.

suggested by Engels and Kula.[16] Initially, however, in the country's central regions market institutions had no significant impact on those relations.

In recent years, several studies have appeared examining the various labour duties performed by the groups of population considered "tax paying" (*tyaglye*). Merchants and craftsmen in the cities were obliged to serve in the customs service and to organize the production and sale of goods over which the state had a monopoly;[17] peasants were responsible for keeping the roads in their neighbourhoods in an acceptable condition,[18] helped in the reconstruction of fortifications, and provided housing for troops (*postoi*)[19] and carts for government transport (*podvody*). The latter obligation was divided between the peasants and a large group of professional coachmen, *yamshiks*, who dated back to the early Muscovy period and whose status and services would require a quite separate study. The problem for scholars is that those services were imposed by local authorities, which makes them extremely hard to study owing to the lack of extant archival material and the absence of aggregated data. For now, the picture we have is too fragmented to allow any generalizations to be made.

In this article, we will not consider these issues further and instead focus on those groups who, according to data from the fifth *revizia*, performed labour duties for the polity as their major obligation.

"Services" (*sluzhba*) and "duties" (*povinnosti*) of different estates, performed in kind, were very widespread in Muscovy[20] and probably had their origins in the earliest stages of the development of mediaeval Russian society.[21] In Russia, with its open borders, severe climate, and long

---

16. W. Kula, *Problemy i Metody Historii Gospodarczej* (Warsaw, 1963). See also I.D. Kovalchenko, *Ruskoe Krepostnoe Krestyanstvo v Pervoj Polovine XIX veka* [Russian Peasantry of the First Half of the Nineteenth Century] (Moscow, 1967).

17. M.B. Bulgakov, *Gosudarstvennye sluzhby posadskikh ljudej v XVII veke* [State Services of City Dwellers in the Seventeenth Century] (Moscow, 2004); E.N. Nasedkin, *Kazennye sluzhby moskovskogo kupechestva v 20e – 30e gody XVIII veka* [State Services of Moscow Merchants in 1720s–1730s] (Moscow, 2011).

18. John Randolph, "Russian Route: The Politics of the Petersburg-Moscow Road, 1700-1800", in Mark Bassin, Christopher Ely, and Melissa K. Stockdale (eds), *Space, Place, and Power in Modern Russia: Essays in the New Spatial History* (DeKalb, 2010); M.V. Kalinin, "Stroitelstvo i Remont Dorogi Moskva-Peterburg v 1726–1733 gg". [The Construction and Maintenance of the Moscow-Petersburg Road, 1726–1733], *Rus', Rossija. Srednevekovje I Novoe vremia*, 4 (Moscow, 2015), pp. 544–548.

19. L.E. Subboitna, "Naturalnyj Postoj v XVIII-XIX vv.: Cherez Lgoty k Civilizovannym Formam Otnoshenij Armii i Obshestva" [Billeting for the Army in the Eighteenth and Nineteenth Centuries], *Vestnik Tambovskogo universiteta. Seriya Gumanitarnye nauki*, 2 (46) (Tambov, 2007), pp. 136–140.

20. See V.O. Kluchevsky, *A History of Russia*, 5 vols (New York, 1960), I, pp. 272–285.

21. B.N. Florya, "Sluzhebnaya Organizatsia i Eyo Rol' v Razvitii Feodalnogo Obshestva u Vostochnykh I Zapadnykh Slavyan" [Service Organization and its Role in the Development of Feudal Societies in Eastern and Western Slavonic Countries], *Otechestvennaya istoria*, 2 (1992), pp. 56–65.

distances, the demand for large amounts of labour, especially for military and transport purposes, emerged much earlier than the state's ability to pay to meet that demand.[22] Normally, this work was remunerated in the form of land rather than money; even more generally, landowning, for all the estates, was linked directly not only to paying taxes (*tyaglo*) but also to performing certain work (although the ratio of monetary to labour obligations varied).[23] Theoretically, these services were imposed "on land", not on people, and those who abandoned the land were no longer obliged to perform "service".[24] A century-long discussion in Russian historiography has revealed the overall similarity of those relations to the land-based commendation in mediaeval Europe, but also revealed significant differences, especially the direct and overall nature of service to the state and the more active role of communes, both peasant and urban, in its performance.[25] As the empire treated its subjects in accordance with their major obligations, the imposition of such obligations led to the formation of specific social groups, with the specifics of their status more or less documented.

The burden of direct labour obligations was significantly relieved by the role of the communes, which were especially strong and influential in Russian society. The communes had their own institutions, were collectively responsible for obligations to the state, and had the right to redistribute this burden among its members. New studies have revealed that the communes were not always silent and content with the administration.[26] Tax increases especially could result in a reluctance to pay, which, given the

---

22. The lack of financial resources in the time of Peter I is specifically discussed in P.N. Milukov, *Gosudarstvennoe Khoziaistvo Rossii i Reforma Petra Velikogo* [The State Economy and the Reforms of Peter the Great] (Moscow, 1905). See also E.V. Anisimov, *Podatnaya Reforma Petra I* [The Taxation Reforms of Peter I] (Leningrad, 1982).

23. The most obvious example of *sluzhba* was the obligatory state service (either civil or military) of the nobility. In this case, the two types of obligation were distinctly separate – the landlord performed "service", while the peasants remained responsible for paying taxes. In the eighteenth century, however, the direct link between landowning and mandatory service was broken, with the latter being determined by the Decree on Single Inheritance (1714) as an attribute of a noble, not a landowner (which meant that landless nobles were not exempt). State service remained the dominant occupation of noblemen until they obtained the right to retire in 1762 (or later, as research by I.V. Faizova has revealed: see I.V. Faizova, *Manifest o Volnosti i Sluzhba Dvoryanstva v XVIII veke* [The Manifest of the Freedom of Nobility and the State Service of Nobles in the Eighteenth Century] (Moscow, 1999)), but these labour relations are significantly different. The nobles earned salaries, and, more importantly, had the right to choose the place and type (military or civil, as well as the branch of the military, etc.) of service (in reality, of course, the options were usually limited).

24. Kluchevsky, *A History of Russia*, I, pp. 286–312.

25. See, for instance, N.P. Pavlov-Silvanskij, *Gosudarevy sluzhilye lyudi* [The Tsar's Service Class] (Moscow, 1898).

26. V.A. Aleksandrov and N.N. Pokrovskii, "Mir Organizations and Administrative Authority in Siberia in the Seventeenth Century", *Soviet Studies in History*, 26:3 (1987), issue on Coercion and Community Interest Representation in Muscovite Local Government, pp. 51–93.

lack of means of coercion available to the administration, often resulted in the accumulation of debt. Surprisingly, the peasants were often less reluctant to accept demands to perform certain duties in kind and even serve in the imperial army, which took the men away from their homes for twenty-five years. These issues require more detailed studies, but it is fairly clear that the commune members performed such tasks on a rotation basis, and also used the recruitment system to relieve communities of undesired members.[27] Generally, the direct claim on tributary labour forced the commune to collaborate with the administration, while the attempt to use market mechanisms (i.e. raising payments due in order to force peasant households to release labour) led to discontent, which usually took the form of collective petitions in which the commune members insisted that they were unable to pay the increased sum. The other reason is that, because of the high volatility of both labour and grain markets, the direct labour obligations were more predictable for a commune and a household (in terms of the amount of work to be done) than the efforts needed to collect money for monetary payments. This was especially true in years of natural disaster, when the massive supply of labour outstripped the need for workers, and, surprisingly, in years of bumper harvests, when the supply of grain exceeded demand.[28]

For the groups we are discussing, their tributary labour obligations lay either in the military sphere or in industry. These workers numbered about 1,700,000. Based on previous studies, we have estimated the size of the free wage market to have been 3,200,000, and the size of social groups not involved directly in agriculture at around 779,000, according to the database, so we can conclude that about twenty-six per cent of workers in the non-agricultural sphere were mobilized using tributary labour relations. The numerous social groups present in the sources can be combined into two larger clusters according to the nature of their labour obligations.

First, we have the "service class" groups, who performed military service for the state and whose status was determined by that fact. They included the Cossacks of Don, Yaik, the North Caucasus, Volga region, and Siberia, whose communities were formed in the steppes belt in the course of the sixteenth and seventeenth centuries, largely from fugitives from the central serfdom area, and later integrated by the tsar; and the Bashkirs and the Kalmyks, large indigenous nomadic and semi-nomadic groups. Two other groups considered here are the *odnodvortsy* of Central Black Earth Region, the descendants of the lesser nobility of the former frontier, with no (or very few) serfs and a transitional status between that of the nobility and the peasantry, and the Ukrainian

---

27. See E.N. Shvejkovskaya, *Russikij krestyanin v dome I mire* [The Russian Peasant at Home and in the Commune] (Moscow, 2012), pp. 44–55.
28. N.N. Petrukhntsev, *Vnutrennyaya Politika Anny Ioannovny (1730–1740)* [The Internal Policy of Anna Ioannovna, 1730–1740] (Moscow, 2014).

Cossacks of Hetmanate (Left-Bank) and Slobodskaya Ukraine. By 1795, their service had been replaced by monetary payments, but it was still performed in the course of eighteenth century.

Secondly, we have groups of peasants bound to different industries (*pripisnye*) and shipbuilders (*lashmans*). Although the binding of certain peasant communes to industries was a sporadic phenomenon in the seventeenth century, this group was generally constituted during and after the reforms of Peter I, in particular with the rapid growth of the Urals metals industry.

The territorial distribution of these two groups is illustrated in Figure 3. Small groups of service class and *pripisnye* were scattered throughout the country, including its central provinces, but it was only in the wide belt of the southern and eastern frontier regions that they formed a group exceeding three per cent of the total population. The service class was localized mainly in the steppes and forest steppes of Left-Bank Ukraine, the Black Sea, and Lower Volga regions, as well as in the Southern Urals, where the Bashkirs formed another large group in this stratum. The *pripisnye* were generally located to the north-east of them, in the forest areas of Middle Volga and the Central Urals.

This wide "belt of tributary labour" flanked the country's central regions from the south and the east. The ratio of the groups bound to obligatory work and services significantly varied however (Figure 4).

As can be seen, those groups formed the majority of the population in the forest areas of Middle Volga and the Southern Urals, as well as in the frontier, poorly populated semi-desert province of Astrakhan. In the developed agricultural regions of Left-Bank Ukraine and the Black Sea, as well as in the central provinces of the Volga region, they varied from one-quarter to one-half of the total population, decreasing to just a few per cent in the densely populated Nizhny Novgorod, Simbirsk, Saratov, and Voronezh regions, where the area of significant tributary labour coincided with the main area of serfdom, linked to the country's inner regions.

"SERVICE CLASS"

We now review the history of those groups, starting with those whose work for the state was considered to be "service" – a mark of semi-privileged status. We should note, however, that the legislation and the state in general never treated those groups as a single estate, preferring to deal with each of them separately, although sometimes the documents generalize them as "the military citizens", or "service class".[29] Running their own households

---

29. The identification of this strata as "performing service" resembles the concept of "*sluzhilye liudi*" in Muscovy. However, the meaning of the term is significantly different here. In the

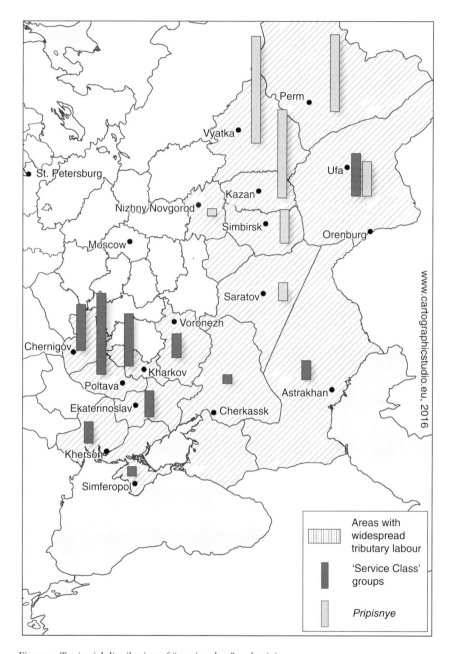

Figure 3. Territorial distribution of "service class" and *pripisnye*, 1795.

seventeenth century it meant both nobles and non-nobles performing military service directly for the tsar; "the military citizens" were non-nobles and possessed non-privileged lands.

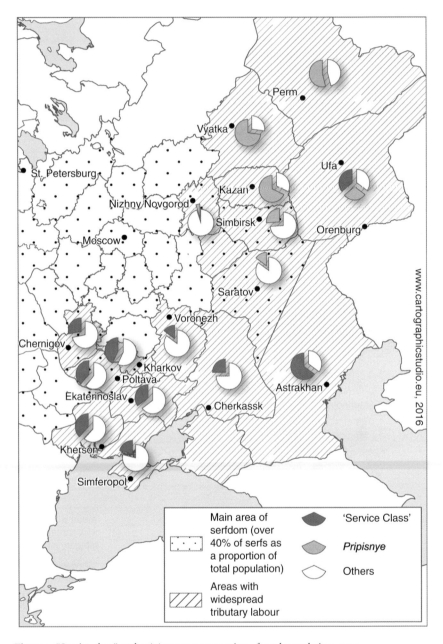

Figure 4. "Service class" and *pripisnye* as a proportion of total population, 1795.

(or, in the case of nomads, sustaining their traditional way of life), they were not taxed but instead obliged to perform military service or work for military institutions. The Russian empire had an open southern border of more than 2,500 kilometres in the European part of the country, and this significant military force, although ineffective against the regular armies of the European powers, remained essential there.[30]

The composition of these strata is very mosaic. The *revizia* outlines about forty different groups, each with a specific legal and social status. Four major circles can be distinguished among them however – Ukrainian Cossacks (*cherkasy*, according to the *revizia* terminology), the Cossacks of Don, Bashkirs, and Kalmyks. Close to them are the *odnodvortsy*, descendants of poor nobles in the former frontier provinces of Central Black Earth Region, who had lost their noble privileges and whose landowning and service obligations had become communal (unlike nobles, who owned land and served personally) by the late seventeenth century, alongside a large number of small groups that originally served along the fortified lines ("ploughing soldiers", "fortification guards", etc.).

With the significant trend towards regional studies in Russian historiography, a large number of monographs have appeared in recent decades discussing these groups from the point of view of changes in their status and obligations. Several attempts were also made to generalize those results, focusing on the issues of the status of ethnic minorities[31] or on migration and the economic development of new regions.[32] We will try, here, to focus on the long-term shifts in labour obligations that took place.

The origin of those groups was different: the Don Cossacks owe their origins to the migration of the Russian population to the area of the Lower Don, which at that time was not controlled by the government; the Ukrainian Cossacks emerged as an organization of armed people on the south-east frontiers of the Polish state, which was seized by Russia in the second half of the seventeenth century; the Bashkirs were the autochthonous population of the southern Urals region, with a semi-nomadic way of life; and the Kalmyks, classic nomads, migrated to the Lower Volga from Dzungaria in the first half of the seventeenth century. The fortified lines in the Central Black Earth Region, *zaseki*, constructed in a major flurry of activity in the mid-seventeenth century, were a place of service for diverse and numerous groups of military, and some of them retained their specific status even after being abandoned when the military moved south in the final decades of that century.

---

30. L.G. Beskrovnyj, *Russkaya Armiya i Flot v XVIII veke* [The Russian Army and Fleet in the Eighteenth Century] (Moscow, 1958).

31. See, for instance, A. Kappeler, *The Russian Empire: A Multi-Ethnic History* (London, 2001).

32. N.I. Nikitin, *Russkaya Kolonizatsiya s Drevneyshich Vremen do nachala XX veka* [Russian Colonization from the Beginning to the Early Twentieth Century] (Moscow, 2010). M. Khodarkovsky, *Russia's Steppe Frontier: The Making of a Colonial Empire, 1500–1800* (Bloomington–Indianapolis, 2002).

The majority of those groups, excluding the Black Earth Region service class, had certain elements of political autonomy in the seventeenth century, but, in general, that autonomy was ended or severely curtailed during the reign of Peter I. The autonomy of Hetmanate in Left-Bank Ukraine, granted to the Cossacks in 1654, was largely abandoned after the first hetman, Ivan Mazepa, defected to the Swedes in 1708. The elective institutions of the Don Cossacks were put under direct control after Bulavin's rebellion in 1708. Ayuka Khan's death in 1723 triggered a long-drawn-out power struggle between the different groups of Kalmyks, which resulted in the Russian administration assuming greater control.[33]

At the same time, the nature of their service had to change. In the seventeenth century, the armed communities pledged to protect the borders of the state, as well as to perform various tasks for the government, such as escorting ambassadors to neighbouring states, and preventing attacks from within their territory on the inner regions of the country. In response, they were recognized as "service class", which guaranteed their self-rule and landowning, gave them a number of economic privileges (such as the exemption from duties on distillation awarded to the Ukrainian Cossacks and the exemption from the payment of duties on salt production granted to the Bashkirs), and the right to receive a regular *zhalovanie*, the wage for service. An important part of the agreement was the right to directly appeal to the monarch; the history of the steady stream of embassies sent by the Cossacks and Bashkirs to the tsars continued throughout the seventeenth century,[34] and during the same period the Hetmans and Kalmyk Khans ran a largely independent policy. These were guaranteed by a series of charters, the initial terms of which were revised from time to time in light of changed circumstances however.

Russia's foreign policy successes and changes in the military sphere led to these areas gradually becoming the inner regions of the country. The Turkish fortress at Azov, at the mouth of the Don, was seized by Peter the Great in 1696, marking the start of a permanent Russian garrison there (though Azov was returned to Turkish rule in 1711–1739). With the construction of Orenburg and the line of forts on the Yaik, in 1739 the Bashkirs also found themselves within the empire's expanding borders. Due to tensions in relations with Poland and Turkey, the number of Russian troops in Ukraine also gradually increased during the eighteenth century.

33. For an overview of those issues see Yu.V. Krivosheev (ed.), *Rossija i stepnoj mir Evrazii* [Russia and the Steppes World of Eurasia] (St Petersburg, 2006).
34. N.A. Mininkov, *Donskoe Kazachestvo v Epochu Pozdnego Srednevekov'ya (do 1671 g.)* [The Don Cossacks in the Late Medieval Period (to 1671)] (Rostov-on-Don, 1998); N.F. Demidova, "Bashkirskie Posol'stva v Moskvu v XVII veke", *Ot Drevney Rusi k Rossii Novogo vremyani* [The Embassies of the Bashkirs to the Russian Court in the Seventeenth Century] (Moscow, 2003).

The Kalmyks, who occupied the steppes on both sides of the Lower Volga, were less affected, but in 1771 most of them migrated back to Dzungaria, and the rest chose to stay on the right bank of the Volga and were surrounded by territories under direct Russian control.[35] This led to significant changes in the character of military service.

Firstly, the state began to require participation in long-distance military expeditions and large campaigns. In 1695–1696, the Don Cossacks played a significant role in Peter I's campaign against Turkey, acting largely separately.[36] By the time of the 1735–1739 campaign they had become an irregular part of the army, acting under the command of regular officers. The Bashkirs and the Kalmyks took part in the Seven Years' War (1756–1763), also as part of the Russian army. In the second half of the century, this practice became common, and the presence of Cossacks and irregular steppes cavalry became one of the most characteristic features of the Russian army.

Systematic service on the borders was even more important. The Don Cossacks had regularly been sent to endangered parts of the steppe borders since the 1720s. Moreover, the government periodically moved certain groups of Cossacks to form new regiments where they were needed. In 1730, 600 Cossack families were sent to settle at the Tsaritsyn line, and in 1792–1793 three Don regiments were relocated to the North Caucasus. The Bashkirs had largely been responsible for servicing the system of fortified lines in Yaik since the late 1730s. In the same decade, the irregular services of Ukrainian Cossacks and the Black-Earth Region service class were significantly reshaped with the formation of a corps of border guards, the so-called Land Militia, which was also commanded by regular officers.

Because it involved removing men from their families for long periods and required expensive equipment and supplies, such service became a heavy burden for the ordinary members of the commune. At the same time, there began a period of rapid migration to these regions, as they were no longer frontier regions and dangerous. The formation of large non-serving (mainly peasant) groups in those lands led to the growing involvement of the imperial administration in local affairs, as large numbers of "regular citizens" appeared in the region and, behind them, the centralized state.[37]

35. E.V. Dordjieva, *Ischod Kalmykov v Kitay v 1771 g.* [The Exodus of the Kalmyks to China, 1771] (Rostov-on-Don, 2002), pp. 254–260. V.I. Kolesnik, *Poslednee Velikoe Kochevie: Perechod kalmykov iz Zentral'noy Azii v Vostochnuyu Evropu I Obratno v XVII i XVIII vv.* [The Last Great Nomad Migration: The Move of the Kalmyks from Central Asia to Europe and Back] (Moscow, 1993).
36. M.M. Bogoslovskiy, *Petr I. Materialy dlya biographii* [Peter I: Material for a Biography] (Moscow, 2005), 1, pp. 435–451.
37. See the detailed quantitative study of the issue in V.M. Kabuzan, "Chislennost' I Razmeshenie Kazakov Rossijskoj Imperii v XVIII – nachale XX veka" [The Number and Location of the

Attempting to distinguish between the privileged and non-privileged population, the government tried to compile registers of service class, and encountered much difficulty in doing so. Attempts to hold a census among the Bashkirs had little success until the 1750s,[38] when the first reliable Don census was conducted in 1756,[39] and estimates of the nomadic Kalmyk population remained quite approximate until 1771, when the majority of them migrated to China.[40]

At the same time, the local elite were extremely keen to be ennobled.[41] The landowning of the "service class" communities was corporative, and they benefited most from the communal redistribution of land; the problem was that even the large landholders continued to depend on the commune. Achieving the status of a noble (either by being promoted to the rank of an officer in military service or by proving the noble origins of one's family) opened the way to privatizing those plots of land, although this was always met with resistance on the part of the commune. The result of this internal conflict depended on the strength of communal traditions of land owner-ship and on the position of the government, as turning these lands into noble estates inevitably led to the decline of military service. In eighteenth-century Ukraine, much of the land was privatized by the Cossack elite, which very early on had marked its claim to noble status and finally obtained it in the 1780s, in response to its consent to the abolition of the autonomy of the Cossack administration. As a large amount of land was taken out of the hands of Cossack communities, they went into decline and it became difficult for them to bear service. By 1795, the position of Ukraine's remaining service class was rapidly changing towards that of state peasants, as their military service was becoming more and more incidental, being replaced by tax payments. Contrarily, similar tendencies among the Don elite were suppressed by the government, interested in the vast military power that the Voisko supplied for the wars against Turkey and Iran.[42]

The growth of the non-service population implied the increasing pre-sence of the imperial administration, searching for fugitive serfs, regulating conflicts between the service community and newcomers, and attempting to

Cossacks in the Russian Empire in the Eighteenth to the Early Twentieth Centuries], *Trudy instituta rossijskoj istorii*, 7 (Moscow, 2008), pp. 302–325.

38. M.M. Zulkarnaev, "Analiz istochnikov o chislennosti Bashkir v kontse XVII – nachale XVIII v." [Study of the Sources on the Number of Bashkirs in the Late Seventeenth to the Early Eighteenth Centuries], *Rus', Rossija. Srednevekovje I Novoe vremia*, 4 (Moscow, 2015), pp. 351–358.

39. A.P. Pronshtejn, *Zemlya Donskaya v XVIII Stoletii* [The Land of Don in the Eighteenth Century] (Moscow, 1961), p. 26.

40. V.I. Kolesnik, *Demograficheskaya Istoriya Kalmykov v XVII-XIX vv.* [The Demographic History of the Kalmyks in the Seventeenth to the Eighteenth Centuries] (Elista, 1997).

41. Pronshtejn, *Zemlya Donskaya v XVIII Stoletii*, pp. 131–135.

42. *Ibid.*, pp. 230–234.

influence traditional authorities. It led to numerous conflicts throughout
the eighteenth century: in Ukraine, Hetman Mazepa defected to the Swedes
in 1709; the Don Cossacks rebelled in 1708 and again in 1793–1794,
the Bashkirs in 1737–1739, 1755, and 1772–1774. After such events, the
government usually significantly curtailed the autonomy of the local
elective institutions responsible for local affairs and the organization of
military service, but economic privileges remained untouched and were
reconfirmed.

Summarizing the above, during the eighteenth century the evolution of
those groups, although very different in terms of origin, ethnicity, and in
how they were integrated into Russian society, generally followed the same
path. Their military service shifted from the defence of their own territory,
with minimum intervention from the civil or military administration in
their affairs, to a kind of universal (for those groups) conscription, under the
direct control of the military administration. There is no reason to think
that this institution gradually declined in the eighteenth century; on the
contrary, the number of "military citizens" grew, and new groups (like the
Cossacks along the newly constructed fortified lines) emerged. Moreover,
none of those groups actually disappeared in the eighteenth century. Even
those that, due to the shifting of the frontier, had found themselves in the
inner regions of the country and stopped performing actual military service
by the mid-eighteenth century (like the *odnodvortsy*, who had to make
payments instead of service) continued to exist, continuing their semi-
militarized way of life and not dissolving within the larger social strata.

What factors contributed to their stability? On the one hand, all those
groups had a privileged status, officially confirmed, and owned land; they
were organized into communes and had means, both legal and armed, to
defend their rights. Although the understanding of some privileges, the size
of their land, and the role of their elective institutions in local affairs could
be disputed and periodically even caused conflicts, the government generally honoured its agreements with them. On the other hand, the government itself was interested in their service. Numerous, having experience
of service at the frontier and cultivating their military traditions, they
provided the Russian army with a significant supply of well-trained and
dedicated irregular cavalry, which had played a significant role in military
campaigns not only in the steppes but also in the European theatre of
warfare.

The real threat to the specific status of these communes came from inside,
not outside. The tendency of local elites to privatize the land and to obtain
noble status can be traced in all of them. The existence of communal institutions, as well as the government's demand for military service, were
obstacles to this privatization, and where the process of the nobilitation of
local elites developed rapidly the decline of local communes was inevitable.
Even the groups that had completely terminated their military service

(*lashmans*, Hetmanate, and Slobodskaya Ukraine Cossacks, *odnodvortsy*) did not completely lose their status before the end of the eighteenth century. One characteristic of enlightened absolutism was its reluctance to accept forced changes in the status of different social groups.[43]

PRIPISNYE

The next group to be addressed are the numerous workers in industry and transport. As is well known, at that time, even a comparatively small manufacturer required a large number of workers to produce and deliver the raw materials. In metallurgy, ironstone had to be mined and charcoal produced; in the potash industry, oak logs and ash had to be prepared; in shipbuilding, trees had to be felled and timber dried.

Unlike those groups associated with military service, the emergence of most of the groups associated with industry and infrastructure dated to the imperial period, especially the time of Peter I. The creation of Peter's new army and navy, and the onset of military and economic rivalries with European powers, demanded the creation of a fairly extensive military industry (especially metallurgy and the production of potash, a necessary component of gunpowder and shipbuilding). It required a very large amount of unskilled labour. The situation was complicated by the fact that both the theatres of war and the most valuable resources were located on the periphery of the state, in the thinly populated regions. At the time, the best ore mines were located in the Urals; the large hardwood forests were also mainly located outside the interior of the country, especially in the Middle Volga region. The government solved this problem by imposing tributary obligations on the local population. The two largest groups in the database are "those assigned to the Admiralty" and "those bonded to the steel and potash plants".

Despite the similarity of their status and obligations, the origin of these groups was very different. The group of *lashmans* was formed based on the indigenous service class groups of the Volga region, mostly Tatars. By the early eighteenth century this region had become part of the country's interior, and there was less need for them to contribute military service; in a 1718 decree,[44] Peter I ordered military service to be replaced by work in the Admiralty in Kazan, and called the newly organized group "the *lashmans*" (from the Low German *laschen*, to cut logs).[45] Having lost

---

43. O.A. Omel'chenko, *"Zakonnaya monarkhia" Ekateriny II* [The "Lawful Monarchy" of Catherine II] (Moscow, 1994).

44. *Polnoe Sobranie Zakonov Rossijskoj Imperii* [The Complete Code of Laws of the Russian Empire], vol. 5, no. 3149, p. 533.

45. A.I. Nogmanov, *Tatary Srednego Povolz'ya I Priural'ya v Rossijskom Zakonodatel'stve vtoroj poloviny XVI–XVIII vv.* [The Tatars of the Middle Volga and Urals Regions in the Russian

their service status, the *lashmans* preserved some of their traditional privileges, including their militarized social organization, with elected *decani* and *centurions*, and the right to bear arms.[46] They were not recruited, and their communes enjoyed an autonomy generally more extensive than that of the region's tax-paying population. The size of this group changed over time, but the main core, located in the Middle Volga region, remained stable over time. The size of the Tatar "service class", which soon became a group of *lashmans*, was 63,000 in 1719, growing to 69,000 in 1744 and 76,000 in 1763.

The need for labour for the newly established Urals metallurgy and Volga region potash industry was even greater. Peter I found the solution in his manifest of 1/24, the so-called *Plakat*.[47] Under this law, certain peasant communes (state peasants, as a rule) could be "bound" to a nearby factory for the purpose of paying taxes, without the right to be paid in monetary form. This arrangement went by the name of *pripisnye*. The daily wage for this work was set by law at a rate much lower than the free wage in those regions, where the supply of wage labour was quite low.[48] This practice, invented in the Urals metallurgy industry, was expanded later to other regions and branches of industry, such as potash production in the Middle Volga.[49]

The size and territorial presence of this group expanded in the course of the first half of the eighteenth century, following the expansion of metallurgy in the region,[50] with the new peasant communes being bound to the numerous newly constructed factories. In 1719, only 97,000 men were recorded in this group, increasing to 161,000 in 1744 and 184,000 in 1763; soon after, following a series of revolts, the government officially stopped the practice of binding peasants to the factories, but those already bound remained so.

Legislation of the Second Half of the Sixteenth to the Eighteenth Centuries] (Kazan, 2002), pp. 35, 38–41.

46. See D. Mustafina, "Bunt tatar-musul'man v 1748 g. — nesostoyavshijsya fakt ili vymysel?" [The Rebellion of the Muslim Tatars in 1748: An Insinuation or an Unsuccessful Attempt?], *Gasyrlar avyzy – Echo vekov*, 2 (2008), pp. 159–175.

47. *Polnoe Sobranie Zakonov Rossijskoj Imperii*, vol. 7, no. 4533, pp. 310 *et passim*.

48. So if, for some reason, the commune chose to hire a worker instead of sending a member, it had to pay him several times more than the sum they had to work off. See A. Kahan, *The Plow, The Hammer, and the Knout: An Economic History of Eighteenth-Century Russia* (Chicago, 1985), pp. 84–86.

49. E.D. Bogatyrev, *"Dlya Umnozheniya Kazny Gosudarevoj": kazannaya potashnaya promyshlennost' v kontze XVII – tret'ej polovine XVIII veka* [For the Increase of the Tsar's Income: The State-Owned Industry of Potash in the Late Seventeenth to the Mid-Eighteenth Centuries] (Saransk, 2006).

50. S.G. Strumilin, *Istoriya Chernoy Metallurgii v SSSR* [The History of Iron Metallurgy in the USSR] (Moscow, 1954), N.I. Pavlenko, *Istoriya Metallurgii v Rossii XVIII veka* [The History of Russian Metallurgy in the Eighteenth Century] (Moscow 1962).

If a factory were privatized, which often happened, especially in the 1740s, when the influential aristocracy discovered that factories could be highly profitable, this did not end the peasants' obligations. Instead, the new owner assumed the obligation to pay to the treasury the poll tax, which was then worked off by the *pripisnye*. This practice increased over time – whereas in 1719 only a few per cent had been bound to privately owned factories, this had increased to over one-third by 1763.[51] Even the large landowners used it, because it was much harder to relocate their serfs from the interior of the country than to use local peasants as *pripisnye*; and it was especially important for the non-noble manufacturers, who could not own serfs (Peter I's decree of 1721 allowed it, but the serfs, *posessionnye*, were considered the property of the factory, not of the owner). The *posessionnye* were much less widespread than the *pripisnye* however. For the mid-eighteenth century, we know even of cases in which state peasants (those who lived in the tsar's lands and were statutorily defined as "free rural citizens") were bound to private factories.

Still, from a legal point of view, *pripisnye* were not turned into serfs. The state administration periodically tried to establish its control over the use of their labour, and in 1762–1763, after a series of rebellions, a major government commission led by Prince A.A. Vyazemsky, one of Catherine II's most trusted advisers, established a system of norms concerning relations between the factory owners and the communes of the *pripisnye*. Due to Orlov's extensive study,[52] we know that the major complaints of the *pripisnye* were linked to "misattitudes" on the part of the administration, including wrongly calculating the number of days worked, reluctance to include days spent on the road to the factory as days worked, and, especially, the attempts of the administration to intervene in the communal redistribution of duties. The peasants insisted that the use of communal institutions permitted them to perform their duties with the minimum of damage to their own households (the administration said, probably not without reason, that they tended not to send the best workers and the best horses to the factory, especially during the agricultural season).

A small but very important group of industrial workers were skilled masters and apprentices. Initially, this group was formed as free wage, but in 1735, after a series of petitions from factory owners, they were bound to the factories as *vechnootdannye*. The owners insisted that there was an urgent need to keep these people at the factories and to avoid situations in which their original communes exercised their right to have them returned or to send them to the army as recruits. They asked that those workers not be

51. V.I. Semevskij, *Krestjane v tzarstvovanie Ekateriny II* [The Peasants in the Reign of Catherine II], 2 vols (Moscow, 1902), II, p. 305 See also R. Portal, *L'Oural au XVIIIe siècle: Étude d'histoire économique et sociale* (Paris, 1950).
52. Orlov, *"Volnenija na Urale"*.

allowed to be freed, but to have them bound to the factories, however, following the general idea that the social status of a social group must be determined according to its major obligations.[53]

So, the newly established industry required large amounts of labour, and the administration solved the problem by both changing the nature of the service to be performed by the "service class" groups and by "uncommodifying" the obligations of groups of taxpayers. It is interesting that, in itself, this solution did not become a source of discontent.[54] While the government's attempts to commodify the obligations of "military citizens" often became the reason for their rebellion, the reverse was not regarded as unacceptable.

CONCLUSIONS

The system of state-organized and state-controlled tributary labour, which existed in Russia in the eighteenth century, appeared in response to the needs of the state, which was developing large industries and building systems of border protection in desolate and under-populated regions. The population there made a livelihood through agriculture, trade, and other traditional activities, and it was unlikely that the state would be able to make them significantly change their traditional way of life through economic measures (whether by offering sufficiently attractive wages or by imposing a sufficiently heavy tax burden).

At the same time, in a society where the majority of the population was, in different ways, bound to the soil, and therefore had very limited mobility, it was very unlikely to attract enough labour migrants to these territories; also, the supply of large groups of highly specialized workers or military personnel would inevitably become a problem, given the weak development of markets and transport. In these circumstances, the polity had no option other than to impose direct military and labour obligations on the local peasant communes. The direct nature of these obligations made them more predictable than monetary ones, and performing them on a rotational basis allowed the communes to also preserve their traditional way of life; this act on the part of the government usually did not therefore lead to open discontent.

The development of a system of obligatory work was facilitated by the fact that the idea of the necessity of performing different types of work in addition to, or instead of, paying taxes was very natural for Russian society.

53. M.A. Kiselev, "Sozdanie vechnootdannych v 1730–e gg. v kontekste istorii soslovnoj politiki Rossii" [The Formation of the Vechnootdannye Estate in the Context of Russian Social Policy], *Rus', Rossija. Srednevekovje I Novoe vremia*, 4 (Moscow, 2015), pp. 478–483.
54. See, for instance, Ja.A. Balagurov, *Kizhskoe vosstanie 1769–1771* [The Kizhi Rebellion, 1769–1771] (Petrozavodsk, 1969).

Direct "service" for the polity (especially military service) was considered honourable and linked to a range of privileges.

Such privileges could include different specific social and economic rights (such as the exemption from duties on the production of salt granted to the Bashkirs), but the basic and most important of them was a strong guarantee of the semi-privileged status of landowning. Unlike state peasants, the "service-class" groups could not be turned into serfs by an act of "donation" on the part of the emperor; even the *pripisnye*, bound to the private factories, could appeal to the royal administration if their obligations were unlawfully increased by the factory owner. For the local elites, administering these works and services strengthened their position within the communes, and performing military service allowed them to achieve the rank of officer and, in certain circumstances, become a member of the nobility.

The system of tributary labour obligations in place in eighteenth-century Russia emerges as an arrangement better suited than monetary and market mechanisms of mobilizing and allocating labour and other resources to meeting the interests of both the state (which needed a large amount of labour to protect its borders and develop new industries) and of those groups on which these obligations were imposed. This was partly a matter of geography, with tributary labour relations being most widespread in thinly populated border regions, and of a certain, historically determined, predilection for such types of arrangements.

IRSH 61 (2016), Special Issue, pp. 71–92 doi:10.1017/S0020859016000456
© 2016 Internationaal Instituut voor Sociale Geschiedenis

Colonial Organization of Mine Labour in Charcas (Present-Day Bolivia) and Its Consequences (Sixteenth to the Seventeenth Centuries)

Raquel Gil Montero

National Council of Science and Technology,
Institute of Geography, History and Social Sciences,
National University of the Centre of Buenos Aires Province
Pinto 399, Tandil (Buenos Aires), Argentina

E-mail: raquelgilmontero@conicet.gov.ar

Paula C. Zagalsky

National Council of Science and Technology,
Regional History Research Institute, National University of Jujuy
Otero 262, Jujuy, Argentina
and
University of Buenos Aires, Argentina

E-mail: pzagalsky@gmail.com

ABSTRACT: This article analyses the changes in the organization of labour during the sixteenth and seventeenth centuries in colonial Charcas, present-day Bolivia, focusing on the role that different colonial authorities played in this process and its consequences. The Spanish took advantage of the pre-Hispanic organization of labour from the beginning of their conquest. However, in a colonial context, labour relations changed significantly, and the architect of those alterations was Viceroy Francisco de Toledo. We examine the transformations in mine labour carried out by the Spanish colonial polity; these had a significant effect not only on mining, but also on all labour relations in the southern colonial Andes.

INTRODUCTION

This article analyses changes in the organization of labour during the first two colonial centuries, focusing on the role played by the different colonial authorities in this process and its consequences. Our starting point is the reforms carried out by Viceroy Francisco de Toledo during the 1570s, while we also consider past labour organization. This allows us to cast light on the role the colonial authorities played in labour relations and how that role changed during Toledo's rule. Engaging with the broader framework of this special issue, we suggest that those colonial authorities were mobilizers and allocators of labour; only occasionally were they direct employers.

In this article, we understand Charcas – a term with multiple meanings – in an operative way *sensu* Barnadas:[1] a historically cohesive territory, the central force of which was Potosí. Between 1542 and 1776, Charcas was included in the Peruvian Viceroyalty and, after 1561, it was the centre of the jurisdiction of the Royal Audience of Charcas (supreme court of justice). The geographical scope of our study extends from Lake Titicaca in the north to the southern border of present-day Bolivia, excluding those indigenous territories on the eastern lowlands that were not under external control at that time (Figure 1). This complex territory, inhabited by a range of ethnic groups, was conquered by the Incas during the fifteenth century and during the 1530s by the Spanish. The relationship those groups had with the Incas, and later on with the Spanish, varied from war to alliance, and the first colonial decades were especially conflictive.

Although mining activities began with the Spanish conquest, the exploitation of the most important centre, Potosí, did not get underway until 1545, in the context of the civil war among the conquerors. In 1548, the Crown managed to put an end to the rebellion, but the power of the local Spanish lords did not diminish until the arrival of the fifth Viceroy of Peru, Francisco de Toledo (1569–1581). Before Toledo, the Crown had granted privileges to particular Spaniards who had actually carried out the conquest. They were given rights (*encomienda*) to obtain tributes from the indigenous peoples, paid in the form of goods, silver, gold, labour, or personal services.

In this article, we focus especially on the changes made to the indigenous tributary system and on the forced mine labour, known as *mita*, which Toledo introduced for the Potosí silver mines and mills. Here, we want to stress one of the changes introduced by Toledo, namely dividing indigenous obligations into two: all indigenous tributaries (men between eighteen and fifty years' old) had to pay a monetary tribute to the Crown, and a proportion of those men had to work for Spaniards, mainly in mining activities, for a specific period of time (*mita*). The *mita* was a state-coordinated form of draft labour that influenced the lives of the majority of the indigenous population in Charcas, as we will see. These changes were central to the evolution of labour relations in the following century.

The seventeenth century saw a massive process of migration of indigenous peoples, caused by the changes mentioned above, since they were forced to obtain money to pay the tributes or to pay for a replacement

---

1. Josep M. Barnadas, *Charcas, orígenes históricos de una sociedad colonial* (La Paz, 1973).

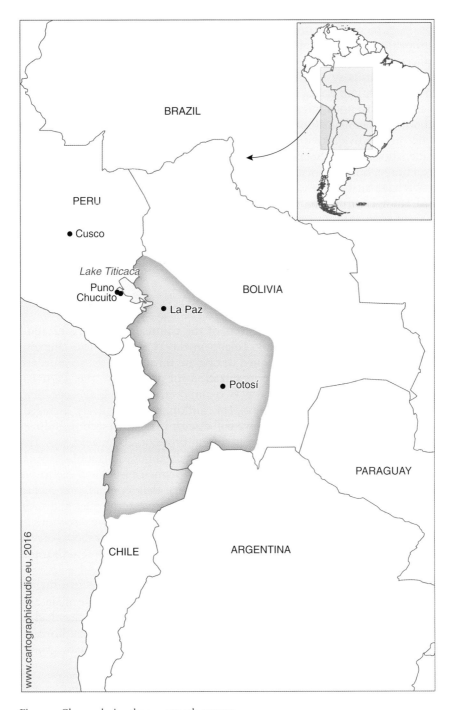

Figure 1. Charcas during the seventeenth century.

for the *mita*, or alternatively responded by running away from their ethnic authorities or colonial obligations. Despite migration posing complications concerning the payment of tributes, as well as concerning the observance of the mining *mita* system, the colonial authorities did not respond. We argue that an important causal factor in this official reticence was the fact that this massive indigenous migration process favoured the private acquisition of labour by the Spanish owners of other mines and haciendas, as well as of other productive activities. Hence, we examine the changes carried out to mine labour by the Spanish colonial polity and its consequences not only for mining, but also for all labour relations in the southern colonial Andes.

We have analysed a range of concepts, including tribute, payment, and free labour, within the framework of the taxonomy of labour relations developed by the Global Collaboratory on the History of Labour Relations (Collaboratory). In our final section, we will reflect upon the changes in labour relations in the light of this taxonomy.

INITIAL ORGANIZATION OF COLONIAL LABOUR

This section focuses on those aspects of the colonial labour organization that were reformed by Viceroy Toledo in the 1570s, and that, later on, constituted a model that continued to operate throughout the seventeenth century. The early colonial organization of labour in the Peruvian Viceroyalty was based partly on two important defining aspects: first, indirect rule, and second pre-existent, although substantively changed, forms of labour organization. As we will discuss in the final section, indirect rule implied a combination of two different types of labour relations. The first was between the beneficiary of the indigenous obligations (which could be an individual Spaniard, the Crown, or the church) and the native authorities responsible for those obligations that their communities had to fulfil. The second type was between the local native authorities and their people. This was the organizational key: indigenous people went to work in the mines or on the coca lands, paid their tributes in silver, or did whatever they had to, because of the relationship they had with the native authorities (Spanish: *caciques*)[2] based on different types of reciprocity.

The Spanish took advantage of the Inca tributary system. According to Murra,[3] before the conquest, all communities had to provide male and female labour to periodically perform a range of different tasks; they had to produce goods for the Inca authorities or for their own local authorities, and goods – offerings – for the gods. However, men from a specific group,

---

2. There were different levels of native authorities, and their regional names varied (*curacas, hilacatas, mallku*), but here we use the term *cacique*, meaning all those authorities collectively.
3. John V. Murra, *La organización económica del Estado inca* (Mexico, 1989 [1978]).

the *yana*, were in a different position, since they were separated from their communities and native authorities and were placed in the service of the Incas themselves, or in the service of other authorities.[4] Their children inherited their status, and they were not obliged to perform the same periodic tasks that other natives were required to. This pre-Hispanic distinction between natives belonging to a community and the *yanas* persisted after the conquest, although in a colonial system.

What specific mechanisms were used by the Spanish to recruit native labour for their enterprises during the first few decades of the conquest? In general terms, indigenous slavery was forbidden soon after the demographic collapse in the Caribbean islands. The most widespread form of labour recruitment, especially in the Peruvian Viceroyalty, was the *encomienda*, legitimized by the Crown. This royally sanctioned institution entailed some of those Spaniards taking part in the conquest acquiring rights to receive tributes from a native authority and from any people subjected to it. In return, the beneficiary had to promote their welfare and guarantee that the indigenous people would embrace Christianity. The beneficiary was also obliged to contribute to the military defence of his jurisdiction of residence.[5] Indigenous people were obliged to pay tributes in the form of goods, silver, gold, labour, or personal services. Right from the beginning, then, the Spanish could access the labour, and sometimes the capital, needed to develop agricultural, mining, and ranching enterprises.[6] Most *encomiendas* benefited individuals, though a few were under the direct control of the Crown.

The second form of labour recruitment, which was present only in the Peruvian Viceroyalty, was the *yanaconazgo*. Although the *yana* population has its origins in the pre-Hispanic period, its significance changed completely during colonial times. Since the earliest decades of the conquest, they were a kind of servant and were not present in other regions – such as Mexico – at least not in the same number.[7] There were different types of *yanaconas*, working for individuals, for the Crown, or for the church, although the largest group were those attached to the land, working on Spanish haciendas. From 1566, they were obliged to pay tribute in cash to the Crown, but usually they did not pay at all.

4. John H. Rowe, "Inca Policies and Institutions Relating to the Cultural Unification of the Empire", in George A. Collier, Renato I. Rosaldo, and John D. Wirth (eds), *The Inca and Aztec States, 1400–1800: Anthropology and History* (New York, 1982), pp. 93–118.
5. Barnadas, *Charcas*; Ana M. Presta, *Encomienda, familia y negocios en Charcas colonial (Bolivia). Los encomenderos de La Plata 1550-1600* (Lima, 2000).
6. Teodoro Hampe Martínez, "La Encomienda en el Perú en el siglo XVI", *Histórica*, 6:2 (1982), pp. 173–216; Presta, *Encomienda, familia y negocios*.
7. Juan and Judith Villamarin, *Indian Labor in Mainland Colonial Spanish America* (Newark, DE, 1975).

We want to stress two aspects of the organization of labour in this period that are important for our analysis. First, the *encomienda* implied a community and its native authority, which mediated the community's relationship with the *encomendero*, being a Spanish individual or the Crown.[8] They preserved their land and their internal socio-political organization. The native authorities collected and paid their tributes to the *encomendero* in the form of silver and goods. Indigenous people included in the *encomienda* were also obliged to perform some public and private tasks, coordinated by their own native authority (such as carrying post, taking care of the upkeep of roads, building churches, and providing food for priests). After the extinction of their *encomiendas,* these indigenous people became royal tributaries and some of them were conscripted for the *mita*. Second, the *yanaconas* were separated from their communities; they had no land, nor did they recognize a native authority.[9] They had to work for Spanish individuals, in mines, houses, on haciendas, or for the church. In most cases, they served the Spanish, without any mediation, but there were also *yanaconas* working for themselves, especially in urban contexts. They were not obliged to take part in the *mita*, nor bound by other collective obligations. Until 1566, the *yanaconas* did not have to pay tribute to the Crown.

These two forms of labour organization were the most important in terms of numbers involved, and because they were official. Moreover, many of those who belonged to an *encomienda* were forced to fulfil colonial obligations only part of their time, depending on the community, the tasks they had to undertake, and their status. Not all indigenous individuals were necessarily included in those forms, and in a way they were "free"; there were some who could work for themselves, the most important of them being traders and artisans, who were inside the colonial economy but relatively independent.

MINING AND LABOUR IN THE ANDES: VICEROY TOLEDO

From the mid-sixteenth century, and almost until the present, the Americas produced most of the world's silver and gold. Between 1550 and 1800, Mexico and South America accounted for over eighty per cent of the world's silver production, and over seventy per cent of all gold production.[10] During the

8. In this article, we understand "community" to be a colonial construction. Some *encomiendas*, therefore, did not have the same organization or composition as the pre-Hispanic groups.
9. There were some *yanacona* authorities in the sixteenth century that emerged in the colonial context.
10. Harry E. Cross, "South American Bullion Production and Export, 1550–1750", in J.F. Richards (ed.), *Precious Metals in the Later Medieval and Early Modern Worlds* (Durham, NC, 1983), pp. 397–424.

sixteenth and seventeenth centuries, the Viceroyalty of Peru was notable for its mining production, while the Viceroyalty of New Spain was the most important mining region during the eighteenth century. One feature that distinguished these two places was the centrality of a unique mine in Peru: Potosí. During its heyday, it accounted for over ninety per cent of the Viceroyalty's production. Its silver production was so important that, even when in decline, it continued to dominate global Spanish-American production.[11] In this section, we focus on the main aspects of the mine labour system at Potosí, including both free and coercive labour.[12] We suggest that, directly or indirectly, mining was the activity that organized the colonial labour world, not only in Charcas, but throughout the Viceroyalty of Peru.

In the context of a Crown besieged by debt, the extraction of precious metals was a royal priority. Within this context, towards the end of the sixteenth century Viceroy Toledo introduced a range of reform measures. Firstly, these reforms aimed to increase Peruvian silver production, which had started to decline in the 1560s because of the extinction of the high-grade ores. To achieve this, silver was amalgamated with mercury and a system of lakes built in order to supply the silver refineries (*ingenios*).[13] Further, a compulsory labour system, the *mita*, was introduced for Potosí silver production.[14]

Secondly, the reforms tried to increase control over the indigenous population, with varying degrees of success. This was effected through the so-called process of *reducción*, an attempt to concentrate in colonial towns the indigenous population living in dispersed settlements. This process affected more than one million people, and it aimed to make more effective the organization and fulfilment of colonial obligations, being both tribute and *mita*, as well as to improve evangelization and to impose a cultural model through European urban life patterns.

---

11. Richard L. Garner, "Long-Term Silver Mining Trends in Spanish America: A Comparative Analysis of Peru and Mexico", *American Historical Review*, 93:4 (1988), pp. 898–935.

12. Various aspects of Potosí's history have been studied by many authors, whose findings offer a collective knowledge that has been essential to our article. Otherwise, it would have been neither possible to cover so many of the subjects necessary to help us understand the early colonial process, nor to examine all the disparate documentary sources. A recent review can be found in Paula Zagalsky, "La mita de Potosí: una imposición colonial invariable en un contexto de múltiples trasformaciones (siglos XVI–XVII; Charcas, Virreinato del Perú)", *Chungara*, 46:3 (2014), pp. 375–395. Some of the subjects mentioned in this section have been widely analysed in Raquel Gil Montero, "Free and Unfree Labour in the Colonial Andes in the Sixteenth and Seventeenth Centuries", *International Review of Social History*, 56 Special Issue 19, *The Joy and Pain of Work: Global Attitudes and Valuations, 1500–1650* (2011), pp. 297–318.

13. The new phase made possible by amalgam technology implied that the social means of production were almost completely concentrated in Spanish hands.

14. Peter Bakewell, *Miners of the Red Mountain: Indian Labour in Potosi, 1545–1650* (Albuquerque, NM, 1984). Jeffrey A. Cole, *The Potosí Mita, 1573–1700: Compulsory Indian Labor in the Andes* (Stanford, CA, 1985).

Thirdly, Viceroy Toledo massively monetized the tributary system. This system calculated the tribute per capita for the male indigenous tributary population in each *repartimiento de indios* (fiscal and administrative unit), but responsibility for payment lay with the *caciques*.[15] This monetized tribute obliged indigenous people, one way or another, to participate in commodified relationships, offering their products in the market or their labour in exchange for money. The labour relationships, even those mediated by money, could be both voluntary and coercive.[16] In order to achieve these three main goals, Viceroy Toledo developed a fourth measure: a general *visita*, or inspection of the Viceroyalty, which recorded the number of individuals and their resources. The inspection played a key role in the reconfiguration process and in the imposition of a new order that involved the *mita* system, the payment of tributes, and the relocation of the indigenous population to new rural towns.

The characteristics of Potosí's mine labour system have been widely studied, so we will merely summarize its central elements here. The Potosí *mita* was a state-coordinated form of draft labour, systematically organized since 1573. Its major objective was to reorganize mine labour according to royal needs and the increasing political power of the state. Toledo's mining *mita* had pre-Hispanic precedents: the system was inspired by how the Incas had organized labour. Toledo's mining *mita* also had colonial antecedents taken from the first period of Potosí silver production, then dominated by native technology known as the *huayra* stage.[17]

The *mita* system established the forced migration to Potosí of a percentage of the male indigenous tributaries, *mitayos*, and their families for one year from the sixteen highland *corregimientos* (provinces) in the region between Cuzco and the southern border of present-day Bolivia (Figure 1). In 1575, Toledo determined the percentages of *mitayos* each region should send annually: between thirteen per cent and seventeen per cent of their tributaries. Different viceroys established the annual total, *"mita gruesa"*, which varied only during the initial years of the system: between 1573 and 1575, the number of *mitayos* varied from about 9,500 to around 11,000; but from 1578 to the 1680s, it was fixed at around 14,000. The *mita* labour system divided the annual contingent into thirds: one-third were

15. In the early colonial period, *repartimientos de indios* were groups of native people assigned to a certain *encomendero*, so they were fiscal and administrative units. In addition, since the seventeenth century they were considered territorial units being parts of a province's district.
16. Carlos S. Assadourian, "La despoblación indígena en Perú y Nueva España durante el siglo XVI y la formación de la economía colonial", *Historia Mexicana*, 38:3 (1989), pp. 419–453.
17. *Idem*, "La producción de la mercancía dinero en la formación del mercado interno colonial. El caso del espacio peruano, siglo XVI", in Enrique Florescano (ed.), *Ensayos sobre el desarrollo económico en México y América latina (1500–1975)* (Mexico, 1979), pp. 223–292. Bakewell, *Miners of the Red Mountain*. Gil Montero, "Free and Unfree Labour".

obliged to work weekly, while the other two-thirds rested, although only theoretically.[18] *Mitayos* were obliged to work weekly for a limited number of Spanish owners of mines and mills.[19] In 1575, Viceroy Toledo established the *mita* "*capitanías*" to organize and ensure *mitayo* labour in Potosí. This institution appointed native leaders, who were responsible for the mobility and presence of forced mine labourers. In the beginning, this was a position of great power and prestige, but by the seventeenth century it had become a heavy and difficult burden to bear.

The polity fixed the wages of forced labourers at a rate below those paid to "free" labourers. In theory, wages were paid in money and were insufficient to ensure the reproduction of labour power. In addition to wages, *mitayos* also had resources from their communities of origin, which thereby subsidized colonial mining production.[20] *Mitayos* women also contributed to their household economy by working in the urban markets.[21] Apart from paying their tributes (almost ninety per cent of their income), *mitayos* were also obliged to contribute part of their wages to pay the salaries of royal officials, *mita* captains, and hospitals.[22] Finally, they needed money to pay for their individual and family livelihood, such as food, clothes, housing, and candles for the mines. Clearly, they had no choice but to look for other job opportunities as "free" labourers during their period of "rest".[23] This guaranteed mine owners a permanent supply of "free" labour.[24] Assadourian has estimated that at the beginning of the seventeenth century – during the mining boom in Potosí – seventy per cent of the labour force was hired and thirty per cent was forced.[25] Hired labour was important in terms of numbers, particularly in specialized and better-paid tasks.[26] The *mita* could be fulfilled in person, but substitution (*conmutación*) was also permitted. This meant that it was possible to pay a fixed sum of money for each absent *mitayo*. With that money, termed "silver Indian", it was possible to hire and pay a labourer. However, the

---

18. This system of "thirds" was not effective and, presumably during the seventeenth century, it was replaced by one in which the contingent was divided into two (Cole, *The Potosí Mita*).

19. This system excluded many Spaniards who arrived too "late" to benefit from this source of labour. Many of those excluded submitted complaints centred on the *mita*, even questioning it strongly in the second half of the seventeenth century.

20. Assadourian, "La producción de la mercancía".

21. Jane Mangan, *Trading Roles: Gender, Ethnicity, and the Urban Economy in Colonial Potosí* (Durham, NC [etc.], 2005).

22. Assadourian, "La producción de la mercancía".

23. Bakewell, *Miners of the Red Mountain*.

24. Assadourian, "La producción de la mercancía".

25. *Ibid*.

26. *Ibid*., pp. 252–257; Enrique Tandeter, *Coacción y mercado. La minería de la plata en el Potosí colonial, 1692–1826* (Buenos Aires, 1992); Paula Zagalsky, "Trabajadores indígenas mineros en el Cerro Rico de Potosí. Tras los rastros de sus prácticas laborales (siglos XVI y XVII)", *Revista Mundos do Trabalho*, 6:12 (2014), pp. 55–82.

money paid in compensation was not always used to hire a replacement; often it remained in the pockets of the Spanish beneficiaries of the *mita* (mine owners and mill owners).

There are two different ways of evaluating the numbers covered by the *mita*. On the one hand, we have the official list of annual *mitayos*, that is the estimated number of *mitayos* forced to work in the mines and mills of Potosí; on the other hand, we can also consider the effective number of *mitayos* who really went there and worked. At around 14,000 per annum the estimated number was very stable until the end of the seventeenth century, but the effective numbers – information not easily found and not systematic[27] – corresponded closely to silver production: they fell throughout the century. It was not until the government of Viceroy La Palata in the late 1680s that the theoretical and effective numbers tended to coincide (Figure 2).

Only Potosí and a few other mining centres benefited from the *mita*, which means that, in almost all other mining camps, hired labour prevailed. These kinds of labourers quickly increased in number from the last quarter of the sixteenth century onwards, partly because of growing demand for specialists in mercury amalgam technology and partly because of the end of the *encomienda* system.[28] Hired and paid labour, however, did not mean a modern labour market. The owners of mines and mills organized their labour force in such a way as to combine mechanisms of attraction, more-or-less forced recruitment methods, and forced retention of labourers. The two principal ways of attracting people were the combination of better wages, something possible in the new rich mines, and the opportunity labourers had to work for themselves during the weekends.[29]

Many testimonies and ordinances indicate that the notion of "hired" was interpreted liberally in relation to mine labour: coercion was very common, and it was permitted under various circumstances because mining contributed to the royal "fifth" (*quinto*) – a tax imposed on silver production. The Spanish, for example, had the right to take indigenous people living in the vicinity of their mines and oblige them to work.

---

27. Tandeter, *Coacción y Mercado*. Cole, *The Potosí Mita*.
28. Bakewell, *Miners of the Red Mountain*.
29. Zulawski suggested that the wages were necessary, but not sufficient, to tempt labourers, and that they were probably only half of what workers were capable of earning had they been allowed to prospect for minerals themselves. Ann Zulawski, "Forasteros y *yanaconas*. La mano de obra de un centro minero en el siglo XVII", in Olivia Harris, Brooke Larson, and Enrique Tandeter (eds), *La participación indígena en los mercados surandinos. Estrategias y reproducción social. Siglos XVI a XX* (La Paz, 1987), pp. 159–192. María C. Gavira Márquez, "Reclutamiento y remuneración de la mano de obra minera en Oruro, 1750–1810", *Anuario de Estudios Americanos*, 57:1 (2000), pp. 223–250. Gil Montero, "Free and Unfree Labour". Raquel Gil Montero, "Mecanismos de reclutamiento indígena en la minería de plata. Lípez (sur de la actual Bolivia), siglo XVII", *Revista América Latina en la Historia Económica*, 21:1 (2014), pp. 5–30.

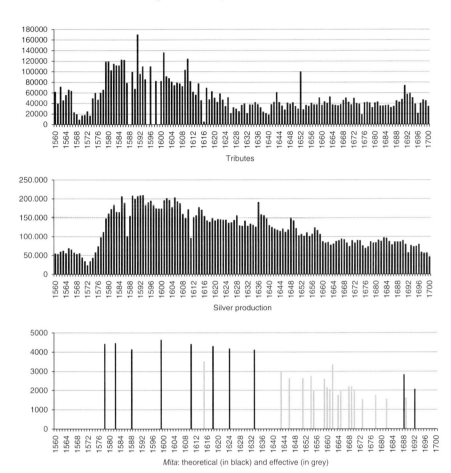

Figure 2. Tributes, silver production, and the *mita*, Potosí, 1560–1700.
Sources: Tributes (in pesos) and silver production (in kilos), TePaske (http://www.insidemydesk. com/hdd.html); *mita* (number of *mitayos*), Cole, *The Potosí Mita*, pp. 41, 72; Tandeter, *Coacción y mercado*, pp. 39–48.

This activity was sometimes known as "hunting".[30] This right was already enshrined in Toledo's ordinances.[31] There were other practices in relation to labourers, including the abduction or retention of their wives, and the pursuit and capture of runaways. There are documents that record the "sale" by native authorities of labourers; we have treated then as hired

---

30. Gil Montero, "Mecanismos de reclutamiento".
31. Mining Ordinances, Ordinance III, Francisco de Toledo, *Relaciones de los Vireyes y Audiencias que han gobernado el Perú: Memorial y Ordenanzas de D. Francisco de Toledo*, 4 vols (Lima, 1867), I, p. 274.

labour. Working in a mine, however, meant the possibility of earning more money, principally for those who were specialists and could earn better wages. Many indigenous people acquired technical knowledge relating to the amalgam process in Potosí, and, with it, they could command higher wages in new mines such as Oruro and San Antonio de Lípez.[32]

MITA, TRIBUTE, AND LABOUR: A DISCUSSION

Toledo's enduring reforms profoundly changed the colonial reality. In our article, we stress the relevance of the *mita* in the organization of labour relations. This hypothesis is based on the number of people directly forced to work in the mines and mills, on *mita*'s role in the mining boom at Potosí, and, principally, on the related migrations that modified the demography of the Viceroyalty and influenced almost all other forms of labour. The *mita* also occupied a central place in official concerns: it was present in debates, correspondence, and viceroys' reports, while the tribute lost importance. In our analysis, we reconsider some classic interpretations, focusing on the tribute, of the mechanisms that forced native peoples to work in colonial enterprises. These mechanism, we believe, were very important at the beginning of the colonial period, but over time they lost their centrality because of the transformation of the economy and society in the Peruvian Viceroyalty.

How did the Spanish oblige native populations to participate in the colonial economy as labour? Assadourian proposed a number of interpretations for the colonial period that have profoundly influenced the historiography,[33] and we now re-evaluate them, focusing on labour and tribute. Assadourian wrote that the tributes indigenous people had to pay increased significantly, first with the inclusion of the *yanaconas* in 1566 and then with the reforms introduced by Viceroy Toledo, who augmented the value of the tributes each community had to pay and monetized them.[34] These reforms pushed native people to sell their labour or goods, thus stimulating the internal economy and augmenting royal incomes. Demography and the economy – Assadourian argues – developed in reverse, at least until 1630. Demography was the limiting factor in the growth of tributes: the size of the native population fell. This drove the government to put mining at the centre of its utilitarian politics.[35] Assadourian analysed the shipments of silver to Spain and the increase in royal incomes as indicators of economic growth and of the increase in the tax burden. In particular, he emphasized the differential pressure on native

---

32. Gil Montero, "Mecanismos de reclutamiento".
33. Assadourian, "La despoblación indígena".
34. *Ibid.*, p. 427.
35. Assadourian, "La despoblación indígena", p. 427.

peoples, both in tributes and in labour, between Mexico and Peru, where the burden was much worse.

We base our discussion of Assadourian's hypothesis on TePaske's impressive work in collecting data on and interpreting royal income and expenditure in Spanish America.[36] Drawing on his work, we used two sets of data taken from the records of Potosí's *Caja Real*:[37] on tribute income and silver production. Tributes were an explicit component of royal income, unlike the other obligations that the native people had to fulfil, so we prioritized the colonial obligation, which can be analysed as serial data and quantified. We know that other demands were made that are difficult to quantify. For example, the forced acquisition of goods, where native people were compelled to buy unnecessary goods sold to them by local authorities at high prices; services that natives owed to their authorities, such as transport using their own animals; and food and services they owed to the priests. These are not included here. The data on silver production were processed by TePaske, based on the Potosí royal incomes (Figure 2). We also looked for data on the *mita*, both theoretical and effective. The data available are not all of the same quality, but we can observe a general tendency. Finally, we added information on population (Table 2).

In Potosí, tributes and mining taxes accounted for ninety per cent of royal income during the sixteenth and seventeenth centuries.[38] Serial data on both show how they developed differently over time. To explain this variation, Klein suggested that, in general, the royal fifth tax was linked to silver production, while tributes followed indigenous demography.[39]

However, the tribute data show a closer relationship to colonial politics. We observed four cycles in the tribute series, although a small variation at the end of the period could be interpreted as a fifth cycle (Table 1). Before Toledo, tribute income accounts for just thirteen per cent of total income reaching the royal treasury, and it was not especially important, measured in pesos.

---

36. The data assembled by TePaske and an important group of researchers are available at: http://www.insidemydesk.com/hdd.html, last accessed 2 December 2015. Part of the published analysis starts in 1680. See, for example, Herbert Klein, *The American Finances of the Spanish Empire: Royal Income and Expenditures in Colonial Mexico, Peru, and Bolivia, 1680–1809* (Albuquerque, NM, 1998). For a more extended analysis, see Bernard Slicher van Bath, *Real Hacienda y economía en Hispanoamérica, 1541–1820* (Amsterdam, 1989). For a critical study, see Raquel Gil Montero, "El tributo andino reinterpretado. El caso del corregimiento de Lípez", *European Review of Latin American and Caribbean Studies*, 99 (2015), pp. 69–88.

37. The *Caja Real* was the royal treasury, which recorded all royal income and expenditure. Some provinces, and other minor jurisdictions, had one. Potosí's *Caja Real* included records not only for the city, but also for the province (Porco) in which Potosí was located and for other neighbouring provinces (including Lípez and Chichas).

38. Here, we also included income from quicksilver, which was a monopoly of the Crown. Klein, *The American Finances*.

39. *Ibid.*

At that point, few *repartimientos de indios* were paying in Potosí, and those that did paid infrequently. With Toledo, three important changes occurred: it was made compulsory for the *yanaconas* to pay; most of the *encomiendas* lapsed and the tributes associated with these rights reverted to the Crown; and there was an important and successful official effort to oblige all tributaries to comply with their obligations. Royal incomes increased in a clear context of population decline, as Assadourian noted. However, from the beginning of the seventeenth century tributes started to lose their relevance compared with the *mita*, not only for the royal treasury, but also for the authorities. One sees a clear and rapid decrease in tribute income. The fourth cycle shows relative stability in those incomes, which were at their lowest level during colonial times, even though the number of *repartimientos* obliged to pay the tribute was greater. The last cycle was brief, and showed a sharp decrease in expected *repartimientos* and a slight, but significant, increase in tributes: those were the years of La Palata's general inspection.[40]

Toledo's government marked a period of unprecedented involvement by the colonial state and its agents, organizing and controlling tributaries. Their presence led to a temporary increase in tribute income. However, at that time, the principal concern was to organize the collection of the royal fifth,[41] and so the state stopped pressing indigenous labourers in relation to tribute and instead continued to press them in relation to the *mita*. Table 1 shows that, over time, although more *repartimientos* were obliged to pay tributes to the Crown, not all of them did so every year. In Potosí, tributes lost their importance in terms of value, since taxes on mining production became the chief source of income.

Regarding the demographics of the seventeenth century (the second factor in Assadourian's argument), massive migrations in the Andes seemed to be related to mining activity since a large proportion of the labour force was directly or indirectly involved in silver production. When it comes to assessing this relationship, the worst problem we face is that most of the regional silver boom took place between the two general inspections (Toledo's in the 1570s, and La Palata's in the 1680s) in which the Andes population was enumerated. A second problem is that those inspections excluded an important part of the indigenous population living in the cities that had emerged around centres of silver production. To compensate for this, we used other evidence that shows the direction of migration during the seventeenth century (Table 2), and this implies we need more than Potosí to understand that migration: we also need the *mita*. The evidence comprises two observations: first, that it was the

---

40. The cause of the decrease in the number of *repartimientos* expected to pay was a reorganization of the royal treasury: some of the *repartimientos* started to pay in 1609 in another *Caja Real*; some of them disappeared from the official records.
41. The royal fifth accounted for two-thirds of total royal income in Potosí.

Table 1. *Tributes: royal treasury of Potosí, 1560–1700.*

	No. of *repartimientos* expected to pay*	No. of *repartimientos* that paid each year (average)	Tributes as % of total income (average)	Tributes: average total annual payment (in pesos ensayados)
1560–1573	20	9	13	37,796
1574–1601	31	19	9	96,349
1602–1626	31	12	5	64,061
1627–1687	38	11	4	38,080
1688–1700	16	11	5	46,509

Source: TePaske (http://www.insidemydesk.com/hdd.html)
* *Yanaconas* were not included

Table 2. *Distribution of indigenous people recorded in the general inspections of Toledo and La Palata (%)*

Regions	Toledo (1570s)	La Palata (1680s)
Cuzco + Puno + Chucuito	64	32
La Paz	17	27
Charcas	19	41

Sources: Toledo (Noble David Cook, *Tasa de la Visita General de Francisco de Toledo* (Lima, 1975)); La Palata (Ignacio González Casasnovas, *Las dudas de la corona. La política de repartimientos para la minería de Potosi (1680–1732)* (Madrid, 2000)).

region around Potosí that grew most; and, second, that the provinces that lost most in terms of population were those obliged to send *mitayos*.

Mining, *mita*, and migrations were strongly connected, as many migrants from the northern *mita* provinces did not return to their homes, and stayed in Potosí, as we can see in Table 2, which summarizes the demographic changes that occurred in the Peruvian Viceroyalty.

To explain the mechanisms developed by the colonial state and that permitted this kind of migration – probably as an undesired effect – we propose to separate tributes from other forms of labour, and to examine what happened between the 1570s and 1680s.[42] In some cases, trends coincided, but in many others they did not. We found three different situations: one in which some tributaries had to pay their tributes in money, and they worked to earn this money; another in which they had to work as forced labourers (*mitayos*) and to pay their tributes as well;

42. Andean historiography generally analysed *mita* and tributes together with the other obligations that indigenous people had to pay (in the form of labour for example), regarding them all as part of the "tribute" they had to pay as Crown subjects. Zagalsky, "La mita de Potosí".

and a third in which they sometimes had to work and were not obliged to pay tributes in money, as was the case with the *yanaconas* mentioned earlier.

Regarding tributes, Toledo reinforced a tendency that had already begun and that might explain the timing of migration: most of the tributes were paid to the Crown at the royal treasury and not to the private sector *encomenderos*. This was a consequence of Crown policy, started in the 1560s, to eliminate the social, political, and material power of the *encomenderos*. As a result, indigenous people were no longer subject to a particular beneficiary, a situation that allowed labour to migrate and to be recruited for the most important activity benefiting the Crown: mining. In this context, Philip II said about the mine labourers: "The profit that one of these natives [mine labourer] generates is greater than that given by twenty tributaries".[43] Mobility disfavoured the control that native authorities had on their people and thus affected the payment of tributes. However, although the officials knew from the beginning about the decrease in these incomes and about the massive migration, they took no action until the arrival of La Palata in the 1680s.

Geographical mobility was, and still is, important in the mine labour world. We believe that two factors permitted and promoted mobility during the seventeenth century: the fact that the tributes were paid to the Crown, and not to private individuals; and the organization of the *mita*. Becoming royal tributaries, without personal links to a particular Spaniard, allowed indigenous *caciques*, groups, and people to "choose" where to sell their labour or goods, and to earn money to fulfil their obligations. Further, the power that Potosí mine owners and the authorities had at that time allowed them to prioritize the *mita*, arguing that it helped them to increase the royal fifth. This had a practical result: tributes decreased dramatically during this period, but the authorities took no action.

There were two types of labour: one mobile and one attached to the land. The first group, people affected by the *mita*, who fled – either to avoid the obligation or to find money for a substitute – provided labour for various activities that did not rely on forced labour: these activities included work on estates, in other mining centres, and in the transportation of goods to supply the important urban market that was developing during the seventeenth century. The second group was established by the agricultural estates, which promoted greater geographical stability for labourers, using a range of mechanisms to bind them to the land. One such mechanism involved Spanish landowners paying the tributes to the Crown and the indigenous labourers being indebted to them in return. Another involved

---

43. Nicolás Sánchez Albornoz, *Indios y tributos en el Alto Perú* (Lima, 1978), p. 46. Our translation.

landowners attracting or accepting fugitive tributary natives, who became *yanaconas*, thus establishing a personal relationship with the Spanish and becoming less free to move.

There has been a conflicting debate about the demographic crisis at the end of our period, in the 1680s and 1690s. On the one hand, the royal authorities claimed that the principal cause of the decrease in tribute income and in the number of *mitayos* was the indigenous people running away and avoiding their colonial obligations. On the other hand, indigenous organizers of the *mita* in Potosí maintained that people were obliged to flee from their rural towns because of abuse by the *caciques*, the local Spanish authorities, and because their lands had been sold. Moreover, during the seventeenth century, further burdens were added to the existing ones – tributes and *mita* – already imposed on the natives. One of these became the most important: the forced acquisition of goods, sold by local Spanish authorities to the natives, from the first half of the seventeenth century. Indigenous people were forced to buy non-useful and very expensive goods sold by the local authorities, a practice legalized by the Crown in the 1750s. This practice had its origins in the seventeenth century, when the Crown began to sell official positions, especially that of local governor. The appointee then attempted to recover the money paid to the Crown by selling goods to the tributaries.

Although beyond our period, a description of what happened during the eighteenth century helps to put the previous two centuries into a broader context. According to various sources, during the first half of the eighteenth century *mita* substitution and the compulsory purchase of goods by indigenous people were the most oppressive obligations for the royal tributaries. In this context, royal officials also made various attempts to oblige indigenous people to pay their tributes regularly.[44] In the context of the new reforms introduced by the Crown, the native response to all these pressures was the increase in violence that began in the 1740s, culminating in massive rebellion during the 1780s. The compulsory purchase of goods was subsequently forbidden, and the way tributes were paid was radically reformed: people had to pay per capita, and the tribute payable was related to their place of residence and not their place of origin. The indirect forms of labour control discussed earlier lost much of their significance. As a result, in the late 1780s, for the first time in the colonial history of Charcas, the value of the tribute collected by the royal officials exceeded that of silver production. The importance of the

---

44. The context was actually more complex than this. See Sergio Serulnikov, *Subverting Colonial Authority: Challenges to Spanish Rule in Eighteenth-Century Southern Andes* (Durham, 2003). The Bourbon monarchs made important reforms during the second half of the eighteenth century which modified the so-called colonial pact and significantly affected the local population (not only the indigenous people).

tribute grew significantly and became the main source of Crown income in the Andes.

COLONIAL POLICIES AND SHIFTS IN LABOUR RELATIONS

In presenting our case study of the definitions of labour relations proposed by the Collab, we want to stress, first, that all the labour relations we have noted existed in a colonial context. This context influenced all labour relations, especially those of indigenous peoples. Second, we use the term "state" in a broader sense, as proposed by the editors, and, of course, as distinct from the "nation state". During colonial times in Spanish America, political power was devolved to various decentralized poles, often with conflicting interests. However, there was a significant difference between what we have called private individuals and the authorities, although in many cases they were one and the same. Third, one of the characteristics of the relationship between conquerors and natives was the role of indirect rule. This characteristic partly explains the survival of Andean communities, because they maintained their right to organize themselves – at least at some levels – and retained part of their original lands and resources – in theory – as long as they fulfilled their colonial obligations, namely tribute and *mita*. Platt proposed the notion of "pact" to understand this relationship.[45]

In what follows, we analyse each tributary category using the Collaboratory's taxonomy (Figure 3). Broadly speaking, almost all the population living on communal land were household producers, leading and kin, at least part of the year. In addition, and because of their reciprocal relationships, they also had to fulfil communal obligations, such as tribute and *mita*. Then, part of the year and sometimes during a whole year, a percentage of the tributaries and their families migrated to Potosí to work in the mines or mills, or they went elsewhere to earn the money they needed to meet their communal obligations. People belonging to a community (i.e. everybody except the *yanaconas* and those we have termed "free" indigenous people) had to fulfil jointly all the many obligations, as we have seen above, and not just the tributes. The *cacique* was responsible for fulfilling these obligations to the colonial authorities. Some wealthier groups or people were able to avoid selling their labour: instead, they sold their goods in urban markets, went as merchants to various parts of the Viceroyalty, or had enough llamas to transport their goods or those of others.

All the relationships we have noted in the previous paragraph were within the ethnic group; however, indigenous peoples also had labour relations with the Spanish. In the *mita* system, for example, we find a combination of inter- and intra-ethnic relations. On the one hand, there

45. Tristan Platt, *Estado boliviano y ayllu andino* (Lima, 1982).

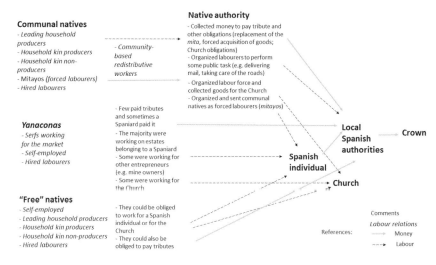

Figure 3. Overview of labour relations during the seventeenth century, Charcas.

were the colonial obligations all indigenous peoples had as Crown subjects that legitimized the state-coordinated form of draft labour organized by Viceroy Toledo for the benefit of individual Spaniards; on the other, there was the asymmetrical reciprocal relationship indigenous people had with their native authority, which forced them to fulfil their obligations. All indigenous individuals were Crown subjects, but this relationship was mediated by their native authorities.

Although *mita* was not tributary labour in the sense proposed by the Collaboratory – because the polities did not benefit directly, as the mines were exploited not by the state but by individual Spaniards – initially only royal authorities had the power to force indigenous people to migrate and to work in mining, coordinated through their *caciques*. The benefit to the Crown was indirect: indigenous labour produced silver, and, owing to the royal fifth tax paid by private silver producers, this was the main source of the increase in royal income.

The state regulated the amount of money that *mitayos* received for their labour from individual Spaniards. This amount was less than the wages paid to hired labourers, and when the *mita* was first organized it was calculated per day. However, during the seventeenth century the miners regulated the *mitayo*'s weekly work, imposing a production quota, and the money they actually received was therefore less than the level theoretically set by the state. As *mitayos* they had to pay their tribute, for their food, all the equipment needed for their work, for the hospital, and the salaries of their priests and of the colonial authorities.

There were various types of indigenous people involved in Potosí's mining activities: forced labourers (*mitayos*) as well as "hired" labourers and *yanaconas* belonging to the Crown. All of them were Crown subjects, although not all were obliged to work in the mines. Why did indigenous people who were not *mitayos* go to Potosí or to other mines? Colonial relationships explain this. For example, Spanish miners had the right to oblige a small number of indigenous people living close to their mines to work there, just because they were Crown subjects. In other mining centres in south Charcas we found people who had been forced to stay, by being locked inside a room for the night, or because their wives and children were prevented from leaving.[46]

What we have here called "hired" labourers were people who went to the mines, attracted by the incomes they could earn there. They were usually "well-paid" skilled labourers, though it would be more accurate to say "better paid"; they were sometimes the same *mitayos*, working in their free time. Although they were free to move to other places and mines, they were not really free to decide to stay in their communities if they wanted. They could also be obliged to stay in a mining camp against their will. As we have already seen, they, too, had to find money to pay their obligations and not only for their survival: their reciprocal relationships with their communities "forced" them to go.

Among the *yanaconas*, we found no indirect rule, as they had no reciprocal obligations to their communities. However, they were also Crown subjects. In almost all mining centres, there were three different types of *yanaconas*: some worked for particular individuals (as a kind of servant), others for themselves (forced only to pay the tribute to the Crown), while others worked for the church (and paid tribute to the Crown).

There were also indigenous peoples living in places other than the communal lands, mines, and estates we have described. Many of them lived in the cities, sometimes with strong relationships to their communities, through paying their tributes, sending money for the *mita* substitute, or for other reasons; there was sometimes no such relationship. The latter were "free" indigenous people, who did not recognize a native authority, who did not work for a Spaniard, fixed to the land as *yanaconas*, and who did not pay tribute. They lived, avoiding obligations, on the margins, but they played a role in the colonial economy as traders or muleteers; sometimes, they worked in peripheral lands or mines, or as highland pastoralists. In the seventeenth century they were few in number, but by no means insignificant.

In summarizing the role of the state in labour relations, we would stress some of the factors that defined those relations. The first is that all

---

46. Gil Montero, "Mecanismos de reclutamiento".

indigenous people were subjects of the Spanish Crown, and that allowed private individuals and various authorities to force them to work. The state defined many of the tasks that almost all tributaries living in communal lands had to perform. They were also obliged, by the state, to send some of their men to work in specific mines and mills, and to pay their tributes to the Crown. The state set the wages that *mitayos* received and, in general, all obligations relating to this particular form of labour. Other non-official obligations, such as paying for their substitutes in the *mita*, or buying the obligatory goods sold to them by the local governor, could be considered indirect methods to force them to acquire money, through the sale of their labour or goods. Finally, the passive role of the authorities was also important: for example, like the *encomenderos* before them, royal officials did not control the tribute indigenous people had to pay to the Crown, or their spatial movements.

CONCLUSIONS

Right from the beginning of the conquest, the Spanish took advantage of the Inca's organization of labour. However, in a colonial context labour relations changed significantly. The architect of the changes that affected those relations until the end of the eighteenth century, and, in some respects, until independence, was Viceroy Francisco de Toledo. In this article, we have stressed four aspects of his reforms that were important for the new configuration of labour relations: the organization of the *mita*, the extinction of the *encomiendas*, the increase in the amount each community had to pay, and the obligation to pay in money. The reforms freed the tributaries from their *encomenderos* and permitted the massive migrations that took place from the seventeenth century onwards.

Why would a native leave his land and work for the conquerors? The historiography traditionally argues that the increase in the tribute, and the obligation to pay it in money, forced them to migrate and to look for ways to earn money in order to pay it. This is, of course, part of the answer. However, we have seen that there were also indigenous people who were not obliged to pay, but instead required to work for the Spaniards (*yanaconas*); further, the obligations involved more than paying tributes, and the other obligations were sometimes more important. It was the colonial relationship indigenous people had with the Crown that legitimized the different forms of direct and indirect coercion.

Direct coercion was exerted, for example, through the *mita* system, and through some royal labour regulations. Indirect coercion is more difficult to identify. Indigenous peoples, and, more specifically, those peoples of more limited means, were forced to leave their land and to look for ways to earn money to fulfil their colonial obligations. There were at least three reasons for this: the need to pay for substitutes for the *mita*, the obligation to buy goods sold by the local governors, and the tributes themselves. The latter lost their importance during the seventeenth century, while the first two became more important. Regarding the Collaboratory's taxonomy, we want to stress that, although the state regulated the tasks and identity of labourers, the major beneficiaries were private individuals.

Why did indigenous peoples fulfil their obligations? The key factor was indirect rule: those natives belonging to a community wanted to retain their rights by collaborating with their communities, paying their tributes, and meeting all other obligations. In exchange, they could organize their own government and keep their lands.

Natives who did not belong to a community, typically the *yanaconas*, did not have reciprocal labour relations and communal obligations. Some of them had inherited their *yanacona* status and worked for a Spaniard right from the start of the conquest. Some had tried to escape their obligations, principally the *mita*, by running away and ended up as *yanaconas* on estates or working in other enterprises. Royal officials did not force them to return to their communities, partly because there were an increasing number of Spanish landowners and mining entrepreneurs who did not have the advantage of forced labour – such as the *mitayos* – and who therefore needed such labour.

IRSH 61 (2016), Special Issue, pp. 93–114 doi:10.1017/S0020859016000511
© 2016 Internationaal Instituut voor Sociale Geschiedenis

Dynamics of Continuity and Change: Shifts in Labour Relations in the Potosí Mines (1680–1812)*

ROSSANA BARRAGÁN ROMANO

International Institute of Social History
PO Box 2169, 1000 CD Amsterdam, The Netherlands

E-mail: rba@iisg.nl

ABSTRACT: Labour relations in the silver mines of Potosí are almost synonymous with the *mita*, a system of unfree work that lasted from the end of the sixteenth century until the beginning of the nineteenth century. However, behind this continuity there were important changes, but also other forms of work, both free and self-employed. The analysis here is focused on how the "polity" contributed to shape labour relations, especially from the end of the seventeenth century and throughout the eighteenth century. This article scrutinizes the labour policies of the Spanish monarchy on the one hand, which favoured certain economic sectors and regions to ensure revenue, and on the other the initiatives both of mine entrepreneurs and workers – unfree, free, and self-employed – who all contributed to changing the system of labour.

The Potosí silver mines are said to have been present at the birth of global trade, which began to grow in the sixteenth century. The mines continued to be exploited until the first few decades of the nineteenth century.[1] Throughout that long period, the mines were worked by the indigenous population, most particularly under the system of *mita* or

---

* This article is based on the Potosí archives in Sucre, and on archives in Buenos Aires and Seville. It also draws on a rich historiography. See R. Barragán, "'Indios Esclavos'. En torno a la mita minera y los servicios personales, 1790–1812", in Clément Thibaud *et al.* (eds), *Les révolutions des empires Atlantiques. Une perspective transnationale* (Paris, 2013); R. Barragán, "Extractive Economy and Institutions? Technology, Labour and Land in Potosí (16th to 18th Century)", in Karin Hofmeester and Pim de Zwart (eds), *Colonialism, Institutional Change and Shifts in Global Labour Relations* (Amsterdam, forthcoming); R. Barragán, "Working Silver for the World: Mining Labor and Popular Economy in Potosí", in *Hispanic American Historical Review*, (forthcoming). For further historiography, see footnote 2.

1. After the decline of silver, at the end of the nineteenth century, Potosí's mountain produced tin, and since the last few decades of the twentieth century it has produced zinc, lead, tin, and silver (again).

unfree work, which was established in the final decades of the sixteenth century and remained in place until it was abolished in 1812.[2] Behind the continuity of the *mita* lay important changes that will be examined in this article. It will look, too, at other forms of work, both free and self-employed. The analysis is focused on how the "polity" could shape labour relations, especially from the end of the seventeenth century (1680) and throughout the eighteenth century. The role of the state as conqueror in early times, as employer more recently, and as redistributor over the past few centuries has been pointed out by the editors of this Special Issue. This article scrutinizes both the labour policies of the Spanish monarchy, which favoured certain economic sectors and regions to ensure revenue and the initiatives of mine entrepreneurs and workers, who contributed to changing the system of labour.

My point of departure was to think about the complexities of what the "state" is.[3] In contrast to the concept of a well-defined and identified institution, over the past decade academics have criticized the notion of a geographical and political centre of power conceived as one entity with a single coherent policy, and any clear distinction between the state and civil society. The approach taken here is to consider the state as an ensemble of political and administrative levels interconnected through policies and practices. Those policies and practices are conceived of as the result of conflicts and struggles between different actors, groups, and regions, generating a dynamic with often unpredictable consequences.

---

2. The classic studies of Potosí and Indian labour remain Alberto Crespo Rodas, "La 'mita' de Potosi", *Revista Histórica*, 22 (1955–1956), pp. 169–182; Peter Bakewell, *Miners of the Red Mountain: Indian Labor in Potosí, 1545–1650* (Albuquerque, NM, 1984); Jeffrey Cole, *The Potosí Mita, 1573–1700: Compulsory Indian Labor in the Andes* (Stanford, CA, 1985) for the early periods; and Rose Marie Buechler, *Gobierno, Minería y Sociedad. Potosí y el "Renacimiento" Borbónico, 1776–1810* (La Paz, 1989); Enrique Tandeter, "Forced and Free Labour in Late Colonial Potosí", *Past and Present*, 93 (1981), pp. 98–136; and *idem*, *Coacción y Mercado. La minería de la plata en el Potosí colonial, 1692–1826* (Buenos Aires, 1992) for the later periods.
3. Scholars have differentiated between a political-legal organization, a collection of instruments and institutions, and a state system, on the one hand, and the construction of consensus and hegemony, the functions of cohesion and unification, the ideological project, and the "idea of the state" or imaginary unity, on the other. See Philip Abrams, "Notes on the Difficulty of Studying the State (1977)"; *Journal of Historical Sociology*, 1:1 (1988); Philip Corrigan, "State Formation", in Gilbert M. Joseph and Daniel Nugent (eds), *Everyday Forms of State Formation: Revolution and the Negotiation of Rule in Modern Mexico* (Durham, NC, and London, 1994), pp. xvii–xxi; Martin Smith, *Power and the State* (Basingstoke, 2009); Bob Jessop, "From Micro-Powers to Governmentality: Foucault's Work on Statehood, State Formation, Statecraft and State Power", *Political Geography*, 26:1 (2007), pp. 34–40. Sharma and Gupta wrote that instead of viewing states as preconstituted institutions that perform given functions, they are produced through everyday practices: Aradhana Sharma and Akhil Gupta (eds), *The Anthropology of the State* (Oxford, 2006), p. 27.

The first part of this article summarizes my view of the main labour relations and their shifts over four periods from 1545 to 1812. After an initial period of exploitation, based mainly on a system of sharecropping, *mita* or unfree labour was established in 1574–1575 during the second period and coexisted with free *minga* labour. Through the years, *mita* changed along with the whole labour system, and I shall describe its main characteristics and shifts. With this panorama, which complements the contribution by Raquel Gil Montero and Paula Zagalsky in the present Special Issue, this article focuses on the struggles to widen or abolish *mita* unleashed almost a hundred years after its implementation (1680–1732). Here, my analysis centres on the interaction between the authorities at different levels within the Spanish monarchy.

The second part of the article draws on the debates that took place within the different levels of the state, while the third examines workers' initiatives in response to developments in state policy that influenced the entirety of labour relations. In the eighteenth century, self-employed workers or *kajchas* emerged and consolidated their position in close association with rudimentary ore-grinding mills, called *trapiches*, where silver was refined. The peculiarity of the eighteenth century lies in the fact that the main sources reveal that both unfree *mitayos* and free *mingas* could have been the same self-employed workers. That means that workers' control over production and processing was growing, and explains why coerced labour could not be transformed either into completely free labour, or into completely unfree labour. The result was a combination of different settings in which labour fell into distinct categories, but this did not mean that there were necessarily always distinct groups of workers.

Finally, in the fourth part, I shall analyse a new wave of discussion dealing with the right of the Crown to favour the Potosí mines and their tenants as if they formed part of the state public sector. That was a significant debate and should be placed in the general context of the projects and reforms of the monarchy in the eighteenth century and changes in the political process from 1808–1812 that led to the disintegration of the Spanish Empire.[4] The debate involved functionaries in different administrative and political layers of the economic and political establishment. As we shall see in more detail in

---

4. The political crisis started with the conflicts linked to Napoleon Bonaparte, who invaded Portugal (1807) and Spain (1808). Charles IV, King of Spain, abdicated in favour of his son Ferdinand VII, who was overthrown by Napoleon. Spain was subsequently entrusted to Joseph Bonaparte. In May 1809, a rebellion broke out in Madrid against the French occupation. Local and regional assemblies were organized (*juntas*) in favour of the Spanish king. The same happened in the Americas. A *central junta* then convened an Extraordinary and General Assembly, or Cortes de Cádiz, which promulgated the first Spanish Constitution in 1812. In the Spanish Americas, the crisis led to a series of struggles, particularly after 1814, which ended with the political independence of most of South America.

the last part of this article, this included the mine owners and mercury millers (*azogueros*) of Potosí, the authorities in the cities, and the judicial and religious authorities of the Audiencia de Charcas (see Figures 2 and 3). One of the highest authorities of the *audiencia* questioned the general assumption that silver was the "blood of the political body".[5] The discussion undermined the legitimacy not only of the authorities, but also of the *mita*, because it was a burning issue over a large geographical area and had consequences for the next twenty years until its formal abolition in 1812 in the Cortes de Cádiz that gave Spain its first constitution. In the process, the *mita* became a symbol of inequality, oppression, and of a system of labour associated with the *ancien régime* and the conquest of America.

SILVER PRODUCTION AND THE MAIN SHIFTS IN LABOUR RELATIONSHIPS IN POTOSÍ, 1545–1812

The Potosí mines were "discovered" in 1545 and very quickly began to be exploited for the benefit of the Spanish Crown. Legislation maintained the legal doctrine of royal ownership of the subsoil, allowing it to be exploited by individuals in exchange for a tax on what they produced. In principle, the king granted rights to his vassals and subjects, whatever their status. However, with some exceptions, the indigenous people did not own the seams of Potosí's mines and became workers.[6]

Production figures for Potosí (Figure 1), as reconstructed by Garner and TePaske[7] and based on the royal tax levied on the production of silver pesos,[8] shows a spectacular boom between 1549 and 1605, a decline during the seventeenth century, and then recovery between 1724 and 1790.[9]

5. "Discurso", in Ricardo Levene, *Vida y Escritos de Victorian de Villaba* (Buenos Aires, 1946), p. xxxi.
6. For an analysis of property in mines and on land, see Barragán, "Extractive Economy and Institutions?".
7. The main evaluations come from the work of John TePaske and Herbert Klein, *The Royal Treasuries of the Spanish Empire in America*, 3 vols (Durham, NC, 1982). Those accounts are published on the website of Richard Garner, available at www.insidemydesk.com, (last accessed 26 August 2016. See also Richard Garner, "Long-Term Silver Mining Trends in Spanish America: A Comparative Analysis of Peru and Mexico", *The American Historical Review*, 93:4 (1988), pp. 898–935; John TePaske, *A New World of Gold and Silver* (Leiden, 2010); and *idem*, "New World Silver, Castile and the Philippines, 1590–1800", in J. Richards (ed.), *Precious Metals in the Later Medieval and Early Modern Worlds* (Durham, NC, 1983).
8. The high-quality eight-real coin, also known as the Spanish dollar due to its wide circulation in the period.
9. The royal taxes (twenty per cent of production in Potosí) are converted into pesos (value in pesos). On the peso, see Carlos Marichal, "The Spanish-American Silver Peso: Export Commodity and Global Money of the Ancien Regime, 1550–1800", in Steven Topik, Carlos Marichal, and Zephyr Frank (eds), *From Silver to Cocaine: Latin American Commodity Chains and the Building of the World Economy, 1500–2000* (Durham, NC, 2000), pp. 25–52. For the general

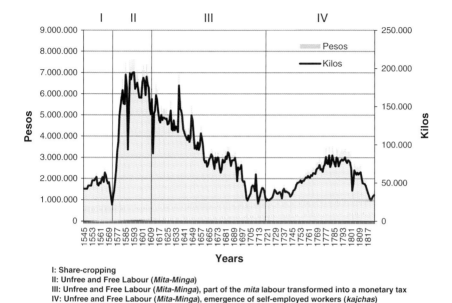

Figure 1. Silver production in Potosí (1545–1817) and the main forms of labour relations
Source: Garner Peru sheets, based on TePaske, available at www.insidemydesk.com. The labour relations have been added by me. The vertical axis to the left gives the value of silver in pesos. See footnotes 7, 8, and 9.

As we shall see, those trends are related mainly to the richness of the ores and to labour policies.

In terms of labour relationships, I distinguish four periods. The first runs from the Spanish discovery of the mines until 1573–1575. Then, Viceroy Francisco de Toledo instituted the *mita* system, which began the second period, when Potosí reached its apogee. The third of these periods runs from 1610 to 1720, when production decreased for many reasons, chief

---

trends emanating from America and the circulation of silver around the world, see Dennis Flynn and Arturo Giráldez, "Cycles of Silver: Global Economic Unity through the Mid-Eighteenth Century", *Journal of World History*, 13:2 (2002), pp. 391–427; Arturo Giráldez, "Born with a Silver Spoon: China, American Silver and Global Markets during the Early Modern Period" (Ph.D. dissertation, University of Amsterdam, 2002); Richard Garner, "Where Did all the Silver Go? Bullion Outflows 1570–1650: A Review of the Numbers and the Absence of Numbers", October 2006, available at www.insidemydesk.com/lapubs/NetDraft-SilverGoRev.pdf, (last accessed 26 August 2016). About the revival in the eighteenth century, Garner wrote: "Without Potosi's eighteenth-century revival, both the mining economy and the general economy might have remained stalled down to the end of the colonial period" (Garner, "Long-Term Silver Mining Trends", pp. 910–911). For Tandeter, the revival was between 1731 and 1800. Even with a diminished role towards the 1770s, Potosí accounted for forty per cent of the silver originating from the Viceroyalty of Peru. Tandeter, "Forced and Free Labour", p. 100.

among which were the impoverishment of the ores and a shortage of labour. Over those one hundred years the *mita* system "metamorphosed", with corvée labour changing to cash payments as production declined. Finally, the fourth period was marked by a renaissance in the production of silver in Potosí after 1720. Although that rise in production appears small in comparison with the first, it was, nevertheless, important. Output of silver rose, partly because in 1736 the tax on silver was reduced from a fifth to a tenth of its value, but also because of the additional mercury supplied from Almaden[10] and as a result of a consolidation of the activities of self-employed workers, or *kajchas*.

Let us analyse this overview in more detail. In the first period, the extraction process, smelting, and casting in wind-blown furnaces (a traditional pre-Hispanic technique called *huayras*), and the sale of the silver in local markets were all controlled by the indigenous population. They carried out the extraction using their own means of production, exploiting part of the mines at their own cost and largely for their own benefit. It was a system of sharecropping, or a kind of leasing of property.[11]

Figure 1 shows an astonishing increase in production after 1575. The period was marked by the rule of Viceroy Francisco de Toledo, who, in the 1570s, organized the "colonial system",[12] which involved re-launching mining from Potosí (due to the scarcity of high-grade metals), introducing technological changes and the *mita* as a method of continuous provision of labour. The amalgamation process, in which pulverized ore was blended with mercury, required the provision of mercury from the Huancavelica mine in Peru, water for the refining mills, and an important contingent of manpower – through the *mita* system.

The institution consisted of a constant supply of labour based on the pre-Hispanic system of work, the *mita*, meaning "turn". Toledo organized the system, which involved an Indian labour force of 14,000 men between eighteen and fifty years of age being recruited from seventeen provinces to work in Potosí, taking their families with them. They worked in Potosí's mines and mills for a year under the leadership of local Indian authorities (*caciques*, or *curacas*).

The *mita* workers (draft labour) were therefore one part of Potosí's labour system, while the *minga* workers made up the rest. Insofar as the *mita* were considered *unfree* labour, the *mingas* can be considered *free* labour. However, my recent research has led me to conclude that instead of two separate and opposed categories, we should think in terms of a single system of work, the *mita-minga* system, which I found applies particularly

---

10. TePaske, *A New World of Gold And Silver*, p. 146.
11. Carlos Sempat Assadourian, *El Sistema de la Economía Colonial. Mercado Interno, Regiones y Espacio Económico* (Lima, 1982), pp. 22 and 295; Bakewell, *Miners of the Red Mountain*, p. 51.
12. Sempat Assadourian, *El Sistema de la Economía Colonial*.

to the eighteenth century. To understand that, we must remember that every year the total number of *mitayo* or unfree workers was divided into three contingents of labourers. The contingent not working were considered to be in "*huelga*", or "on strike", indicating that they were effectively on leave. Turns of work alternated each week so that, in principle, everyone worked for one week and "rested" (in "*huelga*") for two weeks. The *mitayos* then had to work seventeen weeks or four non-consecutive months, which they did throughout the year. Some sources indicate that the free workers, or *mingas*, were recruited precisely from among men who were "*de huelga*", in other words the *mitayos*.[13] If that was so, then the *mingas* were, on the whole, the same people as the *mitayos*.

Mitayos (corvée, or unfree workers) and *minga* workers (paid by the day, or free workers) were present from the sixteenth to the eighteenth centuries, but the continuity of terms for workers can obscure changes that began in the first few decades of the seventeenth century, when some workers avoided unfree *mita* work by transforming their obligation to work into a payment in cash, a process generally channelled through their authorities (*caciques*). During that third period, what Cole has called a metamorphosis of the *mita* took place.[14] The money paid by the workers through their own native authorities could be used by the mine and mill owners to employ free labour or *minga* workers, but in some cases they simply kept it for themselves.

During the seventeenth century, an enormous amount of regional migration occurred as people from communities obliged to send *mita* workers decamped to other provinces[15] where they were not registered or where they would not be liable to *mita* service. The result of all these changes explains why the number of *mitayo* workers declined from the 14,000 established by Toledo in 1573–1575 to no more than 4,000 by the end of the seventeenth century. That was a fall in excess of seventy per cent, and in the eighteenth century the number declined even further to approximately 3,000.[16]

In the fourth period, from about 1730, an upturn in mining activity meant cash payments from workers became less important. Now, the most important feature was the emergence of *kajchas*, who, as far as mine owners were concerned, were simply thieves who stole ore during the weekends. The self-employed *kajchas* undoubtedly challenged and questioned the

13. Cole, *The Potosí Mita*, pp. 9, 12, 14.
14. *Ibid.*, pp. 23–45.
15. See Nicolás Sánchez-Albornoz, *Indios y Tributos en el Alto Perú* (Lima, 1978); Sempat Assadourian, *El Sistema de la Economía Colonial*; Thierry Saignes, *Caciques, Tribute and Migration in the Southern Andes: Indian Society and the 17th Century Colonial Order* (London, 1985). There followed a far-reaching redistribution of the Andean population, which took place largely in the seventeenth century.
16. There were, nevertheless, only 3,199 *mitayos* workers each year, instead of 17,000 (Decree of Viceroy Castelfuerte, 1736; Tandeter, "Forced and Free Labour", pp. 102–103).

ownership and the exploitation of the ores, as the *kajchas* exploited them by processing them in their own rudimentary mills or *trapiches* (Figure 4). The combination of *mitayo* and *minga* workers, as well as that of *kajchas* and *trapiches*, was characteristic of the eighteenth century.

In 1812, the first national legislative assembly took place in Cadiz, which, as a result of the French occupation of Spain by Napoleon, claimed to represent the whole of the peninsula and Spanish territory in America. Cadiz therefore represents a climactic point in the political crisis that began in 1808, and scholars have highlighted the political revolution that put an end to the *ancien régime*. The Assembly of the Cortes de Cádiz formally ended the *mita* system.

This overview shows that among the most important changes was the switch from corvée labour to payment in cash and a constant reduction of the number of workers going to Potosí, which led to endless complaints and requests by the mine and mill owners. There was also significant discussion of the situation among the authorities.

THE DEBATES ON WHETHER TO EXTEND OR ABOLISH THE *MITA* (1680–1735): BETWEEN POTOSÍ, LIMA, SEVILLE, AND MADRID

The continuous drop in the number of workers going to Potosí and the changes introduced led to intense debates about reforming Potosí's mining industry. The owners pushed for a new allocation of labour for the *mita*, while various members of the bureaucracy opposed their request, considering them a group operating in a region privileged by state policies. I propose to distinguish two phases in the struggle, the first occurring between 1689 and 1700 and the second between 1710 and 1735. In both of them it is fascinating to analyse the requests of Potosí's guild of mine and mill owners (*azogueros*).[17]

A first request was made in the form of a petition submitted by representatives of Potosí's mine and mill owners to the Consejo de Indias, Madrid, 1633.[18] It is important to note that the mine and mill owners claim to be speaking on behalf of the whole city (Villa Imperial de Potosí). The first paragraph of the petition recalls the importance of the discovery of Peru for the monarchy, for the Empire, and for Spain, and refers to the imperial city of Potosí. The three main measures were for taxes to be reduced (from twenty per cent to ten per cent); a new census to be held, and labour reallocated; and a better distribution of mercury or *azogue*.

---

17. The name comes from *azogue*, mercury, used to produce silver by amalgamation.
18. *Pretensiones de la Villa Imperial de Potosi propuestas en el Real Consejo de las Indias* (Madrid, 1633).

Most interesting is the interaction between the different levels of the public administration: the intervention by members of the *audiencias* of Lima and Charcas, by the Viceroy of Peru,[19] and by the Consejo de Indias in Spain (Figures 2 and 3). It is clear that opinions on the matter were expressed at all levels, and the abolition of the *mita* system was one option discussed. The highest Spanish authorities tried to sustain a policy of equilibrium, which explains the continuation of the *mita*, for though they did not permit its expansion, they did not support its abolition either.

Scrutinizing the procedures and decisions in both phases allows some conclusions. First, it is evident that consecutive viceroys from Peru (Melchor de Navarra, Duke of Palata, 1681–1689; and Melchor Porto-carrero, Count of Monclova, 1689–1705) sometimes had different or even opposing labour policies in relation to Potosí. This is not to say that the authorities in Spain did not take a consistent position regarding support for or the abolition of the *mita*. The reality "on the ground", though, was that the implementation of state policy was mediated through conflicts and struggles of different groups and sectors, leading to unpredictable consequences. Second, the debates were referred to Spain, where members of the Consejo de Indias intervened to take a decision. Third, Potosí's mine and mill owners' guild sent its own representatives to Spain, and their arguments, too, were crucial. Fourth, it is true that, at first glance, the decisions taken do not seem to have changed the labour system radically, although they were the result of negotiations between antagonistic points of view. None of the positions stated predominated, although, while unable to impose its own preference, the mining industry led by the mine and mill owners' guild did succeed in blocking proposals to abolish the *mita*, which continued albeit on a smaller scale and with some changes.

The first phase in the debate developed after failure of the great reforms that the Viceroy the Duke of Palata had tried to implement in 1689. He organized a new census to cover a vast region in order to revise the number of *mitayos* that every village and province was obliged to provide to Potosí. The census was to include the migrant population (*forasteros*), who had appeared after the previous census of 1575. The idea was to rein-vigorate the *mita* by raising its number from 3,000–4,000 workers to the 12,000–14,000 workers of 1575. The reform also sought to impose tighter fiscal control.

19. The Viceroyalty of Peru, created in 1542, had jurisdiction over most of Spanish South America. Its capital was Lima. The viceroy represented the King of Spain and his immense territory was divided into a number of *audiencias*. The *audiencias* were the supreme tribunal courts, but they also had some legislative and government responsibilities. Two of the most important were the Audiencia de Lima, created in 1543, and the Audiencia Cancillería Real de La Plata de los Charcas, established in 1559 in La Plata (modern-day Sucre), containing an important part of what is now Bolivia. Potosí was in the Audiencia of Charcas.

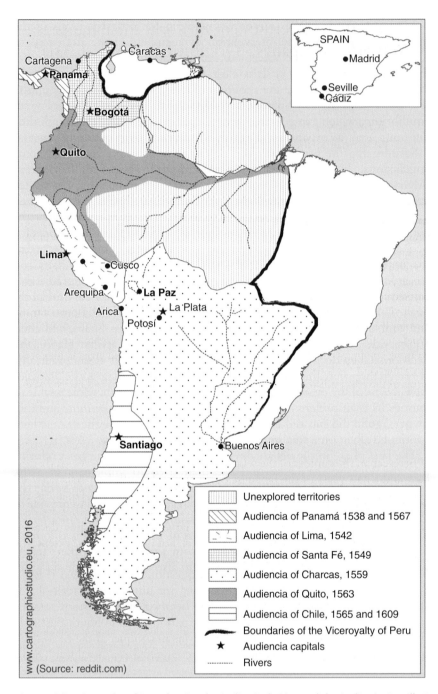

Figure 2. The Viceroyalty of Peru showing the Audiencia de Lima and the Audiencia Cancillería Real de La Plata de los Charcas, c.1650.
Source: http://homepages.udayton.edu/~santamjc/Caribbean1.html.

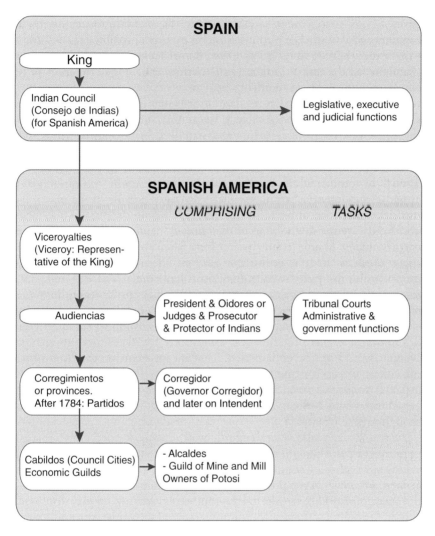

Figure 3. The political levels of authority in Colonial Spanish America
Source: Diagram prepared by the author.

His successor as viceroy, Monclova, adopted a completely different policy. He organized a council in 1691, attended by various authorities of the Viceroyalty of Peru, for the purpose of analysing the situation. This they did for almost fifteenth months, until finally two positions emerged. There were those who pleaded for the *mita* system to be abolished and those who wished it to be continued.

Initially, the first group, in favour of abolishing the *mita*, predominated. The *mita* was considered a form of extortion because it had changed from corvée labour to payment in cash – which favoured owners – with the complicity of a number of authorities. This position explained the reduction in tax revenues from silver going to the Royal Treasury (Real Hacienda) as systematic fiscal fraud, a result not only of the weakening of the monarchy's economic and political control, but also of the over-exploitation of indigenous labour.[20] It was at that time that Matías Lagunez, the Prosecutor, or *Fiscal*, of the Audiencia de Lima, wrote his *Discurso sobre la mita*. For him, there were two *mitas*, the one that had been legally sanctioned and the other that was actually practised.[21] Constant violation of the existing law made the operative *mita* illegal, and Lagunez also held that there was a network of actors, including indigenous authorities, who were involved in the abuse of indigenous labour for their own purposes. It was Lagunez, too, who developed the important idea that the mining industry was being subsidized[22] by the low salaries of the *mitayos*[23] and that the Potosí mining centre would be unable to survive if it were forced to pay everyone wages as high as those of the free workers or *mingas*. There was, then, a conviction that the era of unlimited wealth for Potosí had come to an end, but that it was not true that without the *mita* (Indians) and Potosí's wealth Peru itself would not exist.[24]

The competing position took the form of decisive support for mining that basically meant ensuring the best conditions for the sector so that tax revenues would not be endangered. That meant ensuring the flow of and convenient prices for the *azogue*, or mercury, but also necessitated a sustained supply of *mita* workers. From that viewpoint, if Potosí failed, everything would be lost: "the Indies would end" and this "would be felt throughout the world".[25]

The result was a *juste milieu* (middle way). It was decided not to increase the number of workers for the *mita* and not to extend it to new regions or to include new peoples (migrants or *forasteros*) as the Duke of Palata had planned. However, a royal decree issued in Lima in 1692 established a new allocation of workers to just thirty-four mills (leaving twenty-four mills without workers), although their numbers were set at just 4,108 in total or 1,367 per week.[26] However, the guild of the *azogueros* was able to reduce workers' wages.[27]

20. See Ignacio González Casasnovas, *Las dudas de la Corona. La política de repartimientos para la minería de Potosí* (Madrid, 2000), p. 270.

21. *Ibid.*, pp. 260, 271, 282–283 and 292.

22. The term used was "saving" money.

23. González Casasnovas, *Las dudas de la Corona*.

24. *Ibid.*, pp. 337, 400.

25. *Ibid.*, pp. 336–337.

26. *Ibid.*, pp. 318–319 and 367.

27. *Ibid.*, pp. 325 and 327.

The documents were duly analysed in Madrid in 1694.[28] The Consejo de Indias and other administrative bodies decided that the *mita* should continue but with certain restrictions. A Royal Decree of 1697 (18–II) confirmed the measures introduced in 1692 but ordered the addition of four new points: (i) the wages of unfree workers (*mitayos*) and free workers (*mingas*) were to be equalized, (ii) commutation of work for payment in cash was to be forbidden; (iii) the fixed amount in ores required from workers was to be reduced; and (iv) the costs incurred by workers in travelling to Potosí should be paid in advance. Some authorities in the *audiencias* of Lima and La Plata, along with the Archbishop of La Plata, and the mine and mill owners (*azogueros*) rejected the measure.[29] Equalizing wages was one of the more controversial points. Some people believed it was intended to conceal the desired end of the *mita*.

In the second phase of the debate, the contraction in silver production at Potosí was drastic. It was no accident that four requests (memorials) were presented by the mine and mill owners between 1708 and 1714. In 1719 they opened a debate, once again, about the *mita*. There were more reports in the 1730s, which culminated in measures taken in 1735–1736 that lasted until the end of the eighteenth century.

Particularly in 1709–1710, the mine and mill owners reiterated old requests, namely that the price of mercury be lowered, that royal taxes be reduced, and that there be a new allocation of workers. The owners demanded more effective intervention by the *audiencia* to guarantee the number of workers allocated, and complained about the *corregidores*, the regional authorities of the provinces, whom the owners saw as mainly responsible for the diversion of Indian labour for use in other enterprises and businesses. In 1714, the owners demanded a ban on the conversion of corvée labour into cash payment, a practice that the owners said was against their own interests. They also wished to reduce the two weeks of rest enjoyed by the *mitayos* to just one week because they could then engage the same *mitayos* as free labourers for just one week instead of having to do so for two. [30] Finally, they claimed that a fifty-quintal box of ore cost one hundred pesos, but they obtained just fourteen quintal of silver from it, for which they were paid only ninety-one pesos.[31]

In 1719, the Consejo de Indias in Spain examined a file entitled "Considerations concerning the abolition of the forced labour of the *mita*". The arguments in favour of abolition included the deterioration in Potosí's mines, decreased tax revenues, and the negative consequences of forced

---

28. *Ibid.*, pp. 334 and 337.
29. *Ibid.*, pp. 341, 344–345.
30. *Ibid.*, pp. 389.
31. Silvio Zavala, *El servicio personal de los indios en el Perú, extractos del siglo XVIII*, 3 vols (Mexico, 1980), III, p. 34.

labour for the indigenous population. Three main measures were proposed, namely the abolition of the *mita*, a reduction in the price of mercury (*azogue*), and tax cuts.[32] In the event, the region was hit by a major epidemic, which somehow paralysed the decision-making process.

Later, in 1727, the *azogueros* again requested the abrogation of the 1697 measure, particularly the requirement to equalize wages between unfree and free workers. There followed a lockout in Potosí.[33] Subsequently, a total of nine reports were written in the 1730s by the magistrates of the Audiencia de Lima and the Audiencia de Charcas. Two ideas coalesced: the "common utility" or the public good for the political body of the kingdom, and the recruitment of free workers during the weeks of rest enjoyed by the unfree *mitayos*,[34] the general view being that the allocation of *mitayos* or unfree labour was inevitable. The main argument of one such report was that such political subordination was not contrary to Christian liberty, that it was one thing to serve, but a completely different thing to be a serf. The Viceroy of Lima sent the votes of the assembly of the magistrates to Spain; most of those magistrates agreed with the *mita*,[35] whereupon a new royal decree was issued in Seville in 1732 ordering the continuation of the *mita*, though calls to equalize the wages for unfree labour and free labour were set aside. The one week of work and two weeks of rest of the *mitayos* was reconfirmed and Indian migrants (*forasteros*) were included among the *mita* workers.[36]

Clearly, the preferred option of the mine and mill owners that their allocation should revert to approximately 14,000 workers instead of 4,000 – a demand they had also submitted to the Viceroy the Duke of Palata – was no longer feasible. However, at least the threat of abolishing the *mita* never materialized either. The long-awaited demand that taxes be reduced from twenty per cent to ten per cent promulgated by royal decree on 28 January 1735[37] seems to have been introduced to compensate the persistence of the mine and mill owners, and in response to the reduced purity of the ore in Potosí.

THE WORKERS INITIATIVES: THE SELF-EMPLOYED
KAJCHAS AND *TRAPICHES*

It is certain that one of the most relevant changes in the eighteenth century was the emergence of *kajchas*, who were associated with the rudimentary

32. González Casasnovas, *Las dudas de la Corona*, p. 406.
33. Zavala, *El servicio personal de los indios en el Perú*, III, pp. 35–36.
34. González Casasnovas, *Las dudas de la Corona*, p. 430 and 434.
35. Zavala, *El servicio personal de los indios en el Perú*, III, pp. 19 and 23, 31.
36. *Ibid.*, pp. 32–33, and González Casasnovas, *Las dudas de la Corona*, pp. 441–442.
37. Zavala, *El servicio personal de los indios en el Perú*, III, p. 36.

ore-grinding mills called *trapiches*. They were self-employed workers, according to the taxonomy of the Global Collaboratory on the History of Labour Relations of the International Institute of Social History (IISH).

The owners of the mines called the *kajchas* the "weekend thieves", but the tradition of fairly free access to the ores had existed since the first few decades of Potosí's mine exploitation. Viceroy Toledo, who established the *mita* and the amalgamation process, himself stated in the legal regulations he drew up that the owners of the mines were obliged to give the workers a quarter of the mines as "had been done until then", on condition that they sell the metals they obtained back to the owners of the mines and refineries.[38] It is possible that such indulgence shown to the indigenous population working on the Cerro de Potosí was considered some sort of compensation and actually originated as the natives began to be denied free access to the ore. What might have looked like a concession had therefore become established as a right, whose origins had been largely lost in the mists of time. The existence of the *kajchas* meant therefore that neither ownership of the mines, nor the exclusive property rights of the Spanish mine owners were entirely accepted by the workers, who, for their part, insisted on their own rights of access to the silver mines, such as they had had since early times. Similarly, although deprived of actual ownership of the mines, as *kajchas* the *mita* and *minga* workers nevertheless maintained control over a substantial portion of the ore.

The *kajchas* exploited the ore, and the role of the *trapicheros* was to refine it. In 1759, a *trapiche* (Figure 4) was described as the place where the ore was ground, which was done using large rocks[39] rather than the sophisticated machinery of a trituration mill or the water mill of the *ingenio* used for refining. In the *trapiches*, after ore had been crushed, the powder was mixed with mercury, salt, and sometimes tin. The ore was then washed to create a silver/mercury amalgam, which settled in the water. The amalgam could be sold as it was, directly to the dealers, or it could be "burned" to obtain pure silver that could then be sold to the bank established by the Spanish Crown.[40]

The sources reveal the growing strength of the *kajchas* and *trapiches* from 1750 onwards. One of the most interesting aspects of a 1761–1762 report is

---

38. "Ordenanza X", in *Relaciones de los Vireyes y audiencias que han gobernado el Perú*, Vol. I: Memorial y Ordenanzas de D. Francisco de Toledo (Lima, 1867), p. 357.

39. The *trapiche* consisted of stones to grind the ore and one or two *cochas* or small ponds to wash it.

40. See "Testimonio de la visita de cerro yngenios y *trapiche*s del cerro rico y ribera de la imperial Villa de Potosi con expresion de los nombres de las minas, sus varas, rumbos y frontis [...] 1789–1790", Charcas 700, fol. 123v.–24, Archivo General de Indias de Sevilla [hereafter, AGI].

Figure 4. *Trapiche* according to Frézier, 1732. B = *Trapiche* mill to crush minerals. D = Ponds to wash the amalgam. H = Furnaces to extract the mercury.
Source: Relation du voyage de la mer du Sud aux côtes du Chili, du Perou, et du Bresil, fait pendant les années 1712, 1713 & 1714 *par M. Frezier, Paris, 1732, plate XXII, p. 138.*

that more than 200 *trapiches* were listed. Spaniards owned 58 of them, some were the property of *mestizos* (those of European and American descent) and *mulatos* (those of mixed white and black origin), while 160 of the *trapiches* were in the hands of indigenous people, both men and women.[41]

These self-employed workers and the *trapicheros* provoked frequent debates about what should be done with them. While the interests of the mine and mill owners were supported by some local authorities who sought to eliminate the *kajchas* and the *trapiches*, the higher colonial authorities sometimes opted for a degree of acceptance because of the tax the *kajchas* paid to the Crown. Official "tolerance" was therefore essentially a tax-driven policy, imposed against the will of the mines' entrepreneurs, the *azogueros*.

On the other hand, the detailed daily logbooks of the San Carlos Bank for 1762 recording sales of silver to the bank reveal that the *trapicheros* numbered almost 500 people and that in relation to 1,500 transactions they accounted for sixteen per cent of total sales (in pesos), while the *azogueros* accounted for eighty-three per cent. Although the great majority of *trapicheros* were men, a significant number were women – 39 of more than 200.[42]

It is important to emphasize that some documents noted that the "*yndios trapicheros*" were also employed not only as *kajchas*, but also as unfree *mitayos* and free workers. They included the pick-men in the mines. Such sources might exaggerate the intermingling, but the important thing to note is that the people working in the *trapiches* were associated with workers in the mines and, certainly in a number of cases, they were the same people.[43]

The independent economy of the *kajchas* and *trapicheros* in the eighteenth century is a clear example of a practice that had begun in the sixteenth century and which, by the eighteenth century, had helped improved the situation for mineworkers.

THE *MITA* AS SLAVERY? FROM DEBATE TO ABOLITION IN 1812

In the final decade of the eighteenth century the *mita* system had again come close to being abolished. In 1793, Victorián de Villaba,[44] Attorney General of the Audience de Charcas, wrote his *Discurso sobre la mita de Potosí*,[45]

41. See AGI Charcas 481, no. 19, 1763–1769.
42. Archivo Histórico de Potosí, AHP BSC 313, for the *trapicheros*, and AHP BSC 360 for the *azogueros*. This topic is dealt with in depth in my article in the Hispanic American Historical Review.
43. See AGI Charcas 481, no. 19.
44. Born in Aragon, Villaba died in Charcas in 1802. He was Professor of Law at the University of Huesca. He translated fragments of the great work of the famous Gaetano Filangieri (*La Scienza della legislazione* (1780–1785), 5 vols) and of *Lezioni di commercio* (1769) by Antonio Genovesi. He was also the author of *Apuntes para una Reforma de España, sin trastorno del gobierno monárquico ni la religión* (1797). He was appointed Attorney General of the Audiencia de Charcas, where he arrived in 1791.
45. The *Discurso sobre la mita de Potosí* comprises some twelve folios in four parts, developing the four arguments of the author: (1) the mines of Potosí were not a public work; (2) that even if the work done was public, there was no right to oblige Indians to work; (3) that Indians were not

using the same title as the abolitionist document written a century earlier by Lagunez. Starting with a religiously inspired motto from St Ambrose ("It is a better thing to save souls for the Lord than to save treasures"), Villaba attacked the *mita*'s existence, arguing that the mines of Potosí could not be regarded as being controlled by the sovereign, and that even if the work done there was for the public good or for the *res publica*[46] (the government and the state) no one had any right to oblige Indians to work there. The response was immediate. Potosí's highest authority, the Governor Francisco de Paula Sanz and his adviser Pedro Vicente Cañete,[47] both asserted that, all over the world, since ancient times, mines had been considered to be under the direct dominion of kings, who had duly exploited them;[48] the Spanish king might therefore exploit the mines directly or indirectly. In the latter case, the king gave his vassals "possession" but not ownership, and for that "concession" received the right of regalia in the form of a proportion of production.

In this great debate between Villaba and Sanz/Cañete, one of the issues discussed was, again, the interpretation of what was public and whether it was rational to continue with a policy that favoured channelling labour to Potosí. Villaba clearly opposed Sanz and Cañete, who, in 1787, wrote a guide to the government of Potosí and a legal code for the mines.[49]

so indolent as it was thought; and (4) that even if they were indolent there was no right to coerce them to work. See the important and pioneering work of Levene, *Vida y Escritos de Victorian de Villaba*. Villaba's *Discurso sobre la mita*, the response, and the *Contra réplica* published by Levene in 1946 are just three pieces of this debate, of which there are thousands of pages in the Archivo General de la Nación and at least thirty-two documents related directly to Villaba (in the Archivo Nacional de Bolivia), many of which are from 1795 and 1796. This is a wide topic that we will be discussing in another article. For a broad view on Villaba, see José Portillo Valdés, "Victorián de Villava, fiscal de Charcas: Reforma de España y nueva moral imperial", *ANUARIO de Estudios Bolivianos, Archivísticos y Bibliográficos*, 13 (Sucre, 2007). Sanz took over one hundred pages to reply to Villaba's twelve pages.

46. In the early seventeenth century, a number of writers distinguished between coerced and unpaid work on the one hand and obligatory paid work in favour of the *res publica* on the other (see Zavala, *El servicio personal de los indios en el Perú*, II, pp. 18 and 21–22).

47. Francisco de Paula Sanz was administrator of the royal tobacco monopoly in Río de la Plata from 1777 to 1783 and Governor Intendant of Potosí from 1788 to 1810. He was born in Málaga in around 1745 and died in December 1810. Pedro Vicente Cañete was born in Asunción (Paraguay) in 1749–1750 and died in 1816. He studied in Santiago, Chile. In 1781, he was designated Adviser to the Governor of Paraguay; later, he became General Adviser and War Auditor to the Viceroy in Buenos Aires and, in 1783, he was appointed Adviser to the Intendancy in Potosí.

48. The jurist Solórzano suggested, in 1647, that kings had coercive powers over their vassals whenever they believed that this was for the public good. He argued that the members of the republic had to help each other, as if they were members of the same human body. Juan de Solórzano y Pereyra, *Política Indiana* (Buenos Aires, 1972), I, pp. 267–268.

49. Pedro Vicente Cañete, *Guía histórica, geográfica, física, política, civil y legal del Gobierno e Intendencia de la Provincia de Potosí* (1787), idem, *Código Carolino de Ordenanzas Reales de las Minas de Potosí y demás provincias del Río de la Plata* (1794) and *Catecismo Real Patriótico* (1811).

Both men, Sanz and Cañete, thought the *mita* constituted "the principal centre and support of the welfare of the state" and that without "forced Indians" it would not be possible to make progress.[50]

Villaba asserted instead that mining was not a "public" affair controlled by either the nation, or the sovereign because it benefited private actors, namely the mine and mill owners – the *azogueros*[51] – and so effectively represented a policy that today we would call "subvention" for a privileged sector and economic group. As a result of this royal concession, the mine and mill owners benefited from the *mita*, which was designed to "extract the immense wealth of the ramifications of the earth" for the treasury, for the kingdom, and for the splendour and glory of the monarchy.[52]

Villaba's point of view contained another crucial idea. The abundance of money was not the "nerve of the state and the blood of the body politic", because it was a universal commodity[53] that did not create national happiness. Potosí, said Villaba, remained an example of the fact that "in mining regions, we see only the opulence of the few and the misery of infinite numbers".

A reply to Villaba was published in 1793[54] and some years later, in 1796, the different corporations of Potosí (mainly the mine and mill owners, and the civic authorities) drafted an "Apologetic Representation" expressing their unity in opposition to Villaba, who had published a paper openly calling the *mita* a tyranny. They attacked Villaba for receiving the support of the Church and accused the priests of a "scandalous" use of indigenous labour, which was why the Church opposed the *mita*. The corporations also accused the *audiencia* of meddling in the "exclusive dominion" of the government of Potosí by acting as a "theocratic government". They asserted that Villaba wanted to abolish the *mita* "to make his name famous in America" and that the real offence was "dismantling the use of the earth's immense riches and impeding the glory and splendour of the Monarchy". Finally, they asserted that "those powerful men that the natives hear, listen to, and faithfully obey [Villaba and the Indian authorities] sought to win them at the cost of the ruin of sovereignty and the royal jurisdiction, which constitutes a state offence and a crime of *lèse-patria* and *lèse-majesté*."[55]

What was the outcome of this process? The impossibility, once again, of abolishing the *mita*, the unfeasibility of broadening it, and the paralysis stemming from the Mining Code. However, above all it was a fierce attack

---

50. Sanz and Cañete in Portillo, "Victorián de Villava", p. 451.
51. "Discurso", in Levene, *Vida y Escritos de Victorian de Villaba*, pp. xxxi–xxxiii.
52. ABNB Minas 1796, 129/13 f.2/10v and f.135–17.
53. "Discurso", in Levene, *Vida y Escritos de Victorian de Villaba*, p. xxxi.
54. Contextación al Discurso sobre la mita de Potosí escrito en La Plata a 9 de Marzo de 1793. Archivo General de Indias. MP Buenos_Aires, *v273*, MP Libros_Manuscritos, 76 Charcas 676.
55. All this information is taken from the document ABNB Minas 1796, 129/13 f.2/10v.

on the institution of the *mita*. Villaba, in the first paragraph of his *Discurso sobre la mita*, insisted that it was "temporary slavery", even if the Indians were not legally slaves.[56] Nevertheless, Villaba's was clearly a strategy intended to portray the mine owners as slave owners and to delegitimize the *mita*, and it seems that his approach did indeed affect the number of *mitayo* workers going to Potosí.

The *mita* became an important issue over the following decades. The arguments used against it reappeared for example in 1802 in the writings of Mariano Moreno, later a political leader of the Buenos Aires movement for independence. Other radical writers of the period put forward the same arguments.[57]

In 1810, Napoleon Bonaparte's invasion of the Iberian Peninsula prompted a political crisis in Spain, with, as a result, the first sessions of the Cortes de Cádiz – the first Assembly of Spain and the Americas. Representatives repeatedly discussed the situation of the indigenous people.[58] Those who argued against the *mita* in Cadiz were well-known individuals who would eventually go on to have long political careers in the independent states of Latin America, men of the same generation as Simón Bolívar, such as José Joaquín de Olmedo, the delegate for Guayaquil, or Florencio del Castillo of Nicaragua and Costa Rica. Although Castillo and Olmedo might not have been familiar with Villaba's writings, they made use of all the arguments generally deployed about the *mita*, and added some new

56. He made indistinct use of the terms "slave" and "serf" present in Roman law and in the Castilian *Partidas*. In the classic manual of Roman law, slavery "or" servitude was explained as "an institution [...] by which a man was found subjected against his nature to the domination of another". See Eugene Lagrange, *Manual del Derecho romano o explicación de las Instituciones de Justiniano* (Madrid, 1870), pp. 100–101. The parallel between Villaba and Las Casas is noteworthy. Las Casas wrote an important tract (*Sobre la materia de los Indios que se han hecho esclavos*) (1552) to prove the unlawfulness of all slavery in the Indies. See David Thomas Orique, "The Unheard Voice of Law in Bartolomé de Las Casas's *Brevísima relación de la destruición de las Indias*" (Ph.D. dissertation, University of Oregon, 2011), p. 202.

57. Villaba's influence was present in the radical "Diálogo entre [the Inca] Atahualpa y [the King] Fernando VII en los Campos Elíseos" (1809), an imaginary work questioning the legitimacy of the Spanish king, in the proposal "in favour of the Indians in general" in the context of the insurgent project of Jiménez de León y Mancocápac, Manuel Victoriano Aguilario de Titichoca, and Juan Manuel Cáceres of 1810–1811, and in the declarations of Juan José Castelli, one of the leaders of the May Revolution in Buenos Aires in 1810. See María Luisa Soux, "Los discursos de Castelli y la sublevación indígena de 1810–1811", in Carmen McEvoy and Ana María Stuven (eds), *La República Peregrina. Hombres de armas y letras en América del Sur 1800–1884* (Lima, 2007); and María Luisa Soux, "Castelli y la propuesta indígena de 1810–1812. Oralidad, discursos y modernidad", in *Memoria del Coloquio. El Pensamiento Universitario de Charcas y el 25 de mayo 1809 y 1810* (Sucre, 2010).

58. Scarlett O'Phelan, "Ciudadanía y Etnicidad en las Cortes de Cádiz", in Cristóbal Aljovín de Losada and Nils Jacobsen (eds), *Cultura política en los andes (1750–1950)* (Lima, 2007); Marie Laure Rieu-Millan, *Los Diputados americanos en las Cortes de Cádiz (Igualdad o independencia)* (Madrid, 1990).

liberalist-inspired ones of their own. In their view, the *mita* system was a symbol of the conquest itself and of barbarously feudal legislation.[59] So abolition of the *mita*, already a moribund institution in any case, was duly decreed on 21 October 1812.

CONCLUSIONS

We can arrive at a better understanding of the labour system in Potosí, with its continuities as much as its shifts, by closely examining the official policies relating to it, and the discussions concerning those policies. Official policy was, of course, promoted from above, first by the different levels of the Spanish monarchy – whether in Madrid, Seville, Lima, or Potosí – and then modified by the requests at a local level of the mine and mill owners. We can also consider the strategies of workers, who, of course, had to respond to their situation from below.

From the very beginning, in Colonial Spanish America the *mita* raised the problem of "personal service"; that is to say, the tension between the freedom of the Indians considered as vassals of the Crown and the obligations imposed on them to work in the mines. However, it was equally clear that coercion was based on two commonly articulated reasons for the silver mining industry's economic importance: first, its role in contributing to the public good, and more specifically its contribution through tax to the financial well-being of the monarchy.

The decrease in production, tax yield, and in the number of workers going to Potosí during the seventeenth century gave rise to competing requests and proposals, particularly from the mine and mill owners who championed a new allocation of labour for their enterprises. Their failure to secure their desired reform prompted decades of reports, proposals, and debates between the authorities at the different political levels of the Spanish monarchy between 1692 and 1732. A hundred years after its implementation, the *mita* could not be revitalized from its now diminished role, as the mine and mill owners from Potosí had hopefully proposed, although its abolition as advocated by other economic and political groups did not come about either. Potosí's mining sector had certainly lost ground, but the Spanish Crown dared not put an end to the industry's privilege because of the resources it still generated. That situation explains why the *mita* continued despite the changes. For example, in the eighteenth century there were no more than 3,000 workers, compared with 14,000 at the end of the sixteenth century.

59. José Joaquín de Olmedo, *Discurso sobre las mitas de América pronunciado en las Cortes, en la sesión de 12 de Agosto, de 1812* (London, 1812); Alberto Calderón Vega, *Florencio del Castillo Villagra y las Cortes de Cádiz. Mociones y proposiciones* (Costa Rica, 2010).

The labour system in the Potosí mines in the eighteenth century emerges as much more complex, the result of intertwined factors. State policies did not revitalize it by increasing the number of *mita* labourers, but they did decrease taxes and facilitated access to mercury to boost production. For the mine and ore-mill owners the *mita* was important even after the number of *mitayos* had decreased considerably, because it was the main mechanism for attracting a significant workforce to Potosí from a population that already had its own land and resources. The workers themselves showed their agency and sought additional gains by exploiting the mines during weekends. The *mitayos* and *mingas* could simultaneously be *kajchas* or have agreements with them. The *kajchas* were also closely associated with the *trapiches*, and both of them revealed their empowerment in the mid-eighteenth century, when the Potosí mountain would be divided between the owners of the mines and the *kajchas*.[60]

In the *mita* debate at the end of the colonial period, Villaba's discourse in favour of the Indians had much more to do with enlightened concepts of wealth, and humane Christian values. This humanistic perspective was present among the intellectual generation of the late eighteenth and early nineteenth century, who saw the Indians as victims of oppression. By about 1809, the *mita* became the symbol of the conquest, with its brutal and feudal legislation, and the obligations of the system represented the absence of freedom for the Indians. The *mita* became a powerful symbol of America itself in the minds of some, including a number of American assembly members of the Cortes de Cádiz in 1812. However, the paradox is that the vision of Villaba, who was the most vigorous to defend the Indians, also did most to paint a pitiful picture of their agency, which historians are now trying to overcome.

60. They continued exploiting the ores during the nineteenth century and right up to the 1930s, when cooperatives, still extant, were organized.

IRSH 61 (2016), Special Issue, pp. 115–135 doi:10.1017/S0020859016000468
© 2016 Internationaal Instituut voor Sociale Geschiedenis

Political Changes and Shifts in Labour Relations in Mozambique, 1820s–1920s*

FILIPA RIBEIRO DA SILVA

International Institute of Social History
PO Box 2169, 1000 CD Amsterdam, The Netherlands

E-mail: filipa.ribeirodasilva@iisg.nl

ABSTRACT: This article examines the main changes in the policies of the Portuguese state in relation to Mozambique and its labour force during the nineteenth and early twentieth centuries, stemming from political changes within the Portuguese Empire (i.e. the independence of Brazil in 1821), the European political scene (i.e. the Berlin Conference, 1884–1885), and the Southern African context (i.e. the growing British, French, and German presence). By becoming a principle mobilizer and employer of labour power in the territory, an allocator of labour to neighbouring colonial states, and by granting private companies authority to play identical roles, the Portuguese state brought about important shifts in labour relations in Mozambique. Slave and tributary labour were replaced by new forms of indentured labour (initially termed *serviçais* and latter *contratados*) and forced labour (*compelidos*). The period also saw an increase in commodified labour in the form of wage labour (*voluntários*), self-employment among peasant and settler farmers, and migrant labour to neighbouring colonies.

INTRODUCTION

With the independence of Brazil in 1821, Portugal lost its most important source of overseas revenue. This led to a "colonial crisis", which fuelled an intense debate about the future of the empire. The debate made clear that the prospects for overseas economic revival lay in Africa and led to the establishment of institutions such as the Portuguese Geographical Society, the Portuguese National Commission for the Exploration and Civilization of

---

* The research that forms the basis of this study was carried out within the framework of three research projects: the Global Collaboratory on the History of Labour Relations, 1500–2000, hosted by the International Institute of Social History and sponsored by the Gerda Henkel Foundation and the Netherlands Organization for Scientific Research (NWO); the Labour Relations in Portugal and the Lusophone World, 1800–2000: Continuities and Changes project; and the Counting Colonial Populations: Demography and the Use of Statistics in the Portuguese Empire, 1776–1890 project, both sponsored by the Portuguese Foundation for Science and Technology.

Africa, in 1875, and the organization of a series of scientific expeditions to the continent.[1]

These expeditions, together with Portugal's historical presence in Africa, laid the foundations for the territorial claims made at the Berlin Conference (1884–1885), covering the heartlands of Central Africa between Angola and Mozambique. Portuguese claims were repudiated by Britain and Germany because of their major interests in the region. In the General Act of the Conference, the principle of effective occupation prevailed. Colonial powers could obtain rights only over those territories that they effectively occupied, either by way of agreements with local leaders or by establishing an administrative and military apparatus to govern and guarantee the rule of law. Effective occupation also became the criterion to solve colonial border disputes.[2]

Together, these political and economic changes forced Portugal to take action. To promote occupation, the state put in place a series of measures that fostered settlement, expansion of administrative and military structures, as well as economic development, either through its own initiative or by sponsoring private entities. These changes in Portuguese colonial policies led to important transformations in the politics, economies, and world of labour in Lusophone Africa, including Mozambique, marking the beginning of a new imperial economic cycle – which William Clarence-Smith has termed the "Third Portuguese Empire" – based on the extraction of raw materials and production of export crops through coercive and semi-coercive systems of labour exploitation.[3]

This study examines the main changes in the policies of the Portuguese state in relation to Mozambique and its labour force during the nineteenth and early twentieth centuries, stemming from political changes within the Portuguese Empire, the European political scene, and the Southern African context, and their impact on forms of labour and labour relations, by applying the taxonomy of labour relations and associated methodological approach developed by the Global Collaboratory on the History of Labour Relations, 1500–2000 to this specific case study. To meet the challenges involved, while at the same time facing a difficult economic and financial situation at home, the Portuguese colonial state

---

1. Valentim Alexandre, *Origens do colonialismo português moderno (1822–1891)* (Lisbon, 1979). *Idem* and Maria Cândida Proença, *A questão colonial no Parlamento (1821–1910)* (Lisbon, 2008). Valentim Alexandre, *Os sentidos do Império: questão nacional e questão colonial na crise do Antigo Regime português* (Porto, 1993). *Idem, Velho Brasil, novas Áfricas: Portugal e o Império (1808–1975)* (Porto, 2000). See, for example, Hermenegildo Carlos de Brito Capello and Roberto Ivens, *De Angola à Contra-Costa*, 2 vols (Lisbon, 1886). *Idem, De Benguella às terras de Iácca* (Lisbon, 1881).
2. Final Act of the Berlin Conference, Article 35.
3. William Clarence-Smith, *The Third Portuguese Empire: 1825–1975* (Manchester, 1985).

made use of the most abundant and valuable resource available – labour, and put in practice an old tool used in empire building and management – outsourcing. By becoming a main employer in the territory, but also by granting private companies and neighbouring colonial states power to mobilize and allocate labour, the Portuguese state brought about important changes in labour relations in Mozambique. Slave and tributary labour was replaced by new forms of indentured and contract labour (*serviçais/contratados*) and forced labour (*compelidos*), while commodified labour in the form of wage labour (*voluntários*), the self-employment of peasant and settler farmers, and migrant labour to neighbouring colonies increased.

Our study discusses the impact of political change as an explanatory factor in shifting labour relations in Mozambique. The analysis is based on a dataset built using demographic and statistical information gathered from several Portuguese archives and libraries, including population counts, census data, reports from state and concessionary companies' officials, and secondary literature, in particular the seminal studies by Frederick Cooper and the award-winning book *Slavery by Any Other Name* by Eric Allina, which gave voice to the labour experiences of Africans and their agency in labour struggles against colonial exploitation in Mozambique.[4] The classification of labour relations is based on the taxonomy developed by the Global Collaboratory on the History of Labour Relations, and the analysis focuses on the comparative study of two chronological cross sections: 1800 and 1900.[5]

PORTUGUESE RULE, ECONOMY, AND LABOUR RELATIONS, C.1800

By the early nineteenth century, Portuguese influence in East Africa was still limited to a strip of land along the Zambezi Valley, starting on the coast between Sofala and Quelimane and stretching towards the heartlands, reaching as far as Sena, Tete, and Zumbo.[6] In the course of the century,

---

4. Frederick Cooper, *Decolonization and African Society: The Labor Question in French and British Africa* (Cambridge, 1996). Eric Allina, *Slavery by Any Other Name: African Life under Company Rule in Colonial Mozambique* (Charlottesville, 2012).
5. Preliminary results for the dataset under construction can be found in Filipa Ribeiro da Silva, "Relações Laborais em Moçambique, 1800", *Diálogos*, 17 (2013), pp. 835–868.
6. On the earlier Portuguese presence in the region, see, among others, Allen Isaacman, *Mozambique: The Africanization of a European Institution, the Zambezi Prazos, 1750–1902* (Madison, WI, 1972), Malyn Newitt, *Portuguese Settlement on the Zambesi: Exploration, Land Tenure and Colonial Rule in East Africa* (New York, 1973), and Michael N. Pearson, *Port Cities and Intruders: The Swahili Coast, India, and Portugal in the Early Modern Era* (Baltimore, 1998), Introduction and ch. 1. Eugénia Rodrigues, "Portugueses e Africanos nos Rios de Sena, Os Prazos da Coroa nos Séculos XVII e XVIII" (Ph.D., Universidade Nova de Lisboa, 2002).

Portugal also came to control several coastal areas, including the Quirimbas islands, Ibo, Angoche, Inhambane, and present-day Maputo. During this period, Portuguese influence also reached south-east Zambia and southern Malawi (Figure 1).

Free Africans (*colonos*) constituted the majority of the economically active population (c.eighty-seven to ninety per cent) both in and outside the areas controlled by and under the influence of the Portuguese state and *Prazos da Coroa*, located along the Zambezi Valley and held by families of Portuguese descent. The *Prazos da Coroa* was a system of land tenure, regulated by the same principles as the Roman law contracts of emphyteusis, and put in place by the Portuguese Crown from the seventeenth century onwards to attract settlers to the region of the Zambezi Valley.[7] From an economic viewpoint, they were similar to medieval manors in how they were run and the types of relationship established between land tenants and peasants. However, as Allen Isaacman and Malyn Newitt explain, "from the African point of view they were essentially chieftaincies and as such part of a complex system of social and economic relations bounding together all the people in the region".[8] The *Prazo* system was a form of outsourcing used by the Portuguese state also to promote the development of activities such as mining, agriculture, and trade, without having to invest much in human and financial resources. The management of trade routes between Mozambique and Goa (the headquarters of the Portuguese Estado da Índia) had also been under private management. This was a common and old practice used by the Portuguese state also in the Atlantic, where settlement and economic development were initially carried out by private entrepreneurs and consortia.[9]

---

7. Under Roman Law, emphyteusis was a contract by which a landed estate was leased to a tenant, either in perpetuity or for many years, upon payment of an annual rent or canon, and on condition that the lessee improved the property, by building, cultivating, or otherwise, with the lessee having the right to alienate the estate at his pleasure or pass it to his heirs by descent, and with the property being free from any right of revocation, re-entry, or claim of forfeiture on the part of the grantor, except for non-payment of the rent. The right granted by such a contract was designated *jus emphytcuticum*, or *emphytcuticarium*.

8. Newitt, *A History of Mozambique* (Bloomington, 1995), p. 217. Each *Prazo* varied in size, but usually included an area under the direct administration of the land tenant and several attached villages of free and enslaved Africans. Isaacman, *Mozambique: The Africanization of a European Institution*. Newitt, *Portuguese Settlement on the Zambesi*. Allen Isaacman and Barbara Isaacman, "The Prazeros as Transfrontiersmen: A Study in Social and Cultural Change", *International Journal of African Historical Studies*, 8:1 (1975), pp. 1–39.

9. A great deal of the early Portuguese maritime exploration, settlement and economic development, tax collection, and management of royal trade monopolies had been outsourced to private entrepreneurs, businessmen, and consortia. See, among many others, António Vasconcelos de Saldanha, *As Capitanias e o Regime Senhorial na Expansão Ultramarina Portuguesa* (Funchal, 1992), Leonor Freire Costa, *O transporte no Atlântico e a Companhia Geral do Comércio do Brasil (1580–1663)*, 2 vols (Lisbon, 2002), and António Carreira, *As Companhias Pombalinas de*

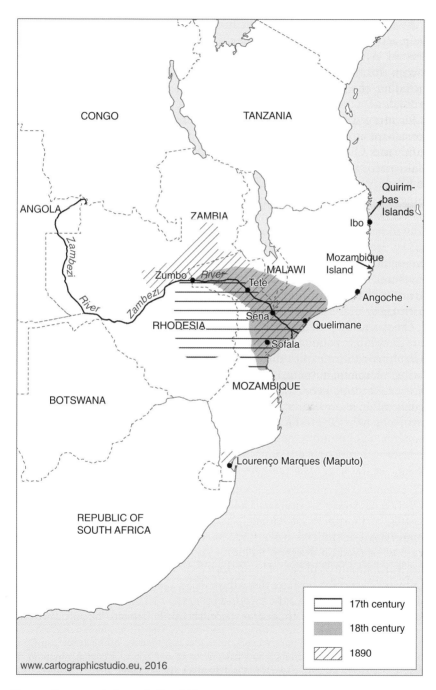

Figure 1. Portuguese influence in East Africa, 1500s–1970s.
Source: Malyn Newitt, *Portuguese Settlement on the Zambesi: Exploration, Land Tenure and Colonial Rule in East Africa* (New York, 1973), p. 15.

Alongside work in the *Prazos*, Free Africans were also engaged in five main activities: gold extraction in surface-mining workings located in the Central African heartlands; elephant hunting (as a source of meat and ivory); foraging for honey, wax, and wood; subsistence agriculture, including the production of maize, millet, wheat, sugar, tobacco, and groundnuts (and oil); as well as the transport of agricultural surplus, ivory, gold, foraged goods, and enslaved Africans to important inland-[10] and coastal-trading centres, such as Tete, the Island of Mozambique, Inhambane, and Quelimane.[11] The slave trade was controlled mainly by the Makua people, whereas elephant hunting was dominated by Maravi, Lunda, and Bisa peoples. Caravan trade between the interior and the coast, on the other hand, was dominated by the Yao people.[12] In all communities, agriculture was mainly the women's concern, with male seasonal participation only to help clear the fields and during harvesting.[13] Part of the gold, ivory, honey, wax, and agricultural production ended up in the hands of local authorities, either of African or Portuguese descent, in the form of tribute payment.[14] Tribute in the form of labour was often also demanded by African village and community chiefs as well as by the *Prazo* tenants of Portuguese descent, in exchange for the protection they offered.

The work and products paid as tribute to the *Prazo* tenants were not only for domestic consumption, but also to supply small urban centres, provision ships, and for export through the coastal ports. The products obtained through farming, hunting, fishing, and foraging also fed villages and families of Free Africans. Free Africans were, therefore, involved in various labour relations. In their capacity as village leaders and heads of families, their involvement in the production of goods to guarantee the livelihoods of their family and community members should be seen as work for the household, as leading kin producers, and community redistributive workers (LabRel 4a + 7, see Table 1). The remaining members of these villages and families,

---

Navegação, Comércio e Tráfico de Escravos entre a Costa Africana e o Nordeste Brasileiro (Porto, 1969).

10. Newitt, *A History of Mozambique*, p. 194.

11. Inland trading centres were called *feiras* in Portuguese sources.

12. Newitt, *A History of Mozambique*, p. 183. On the Mozambican slave trade and its inland and overseas dimensions, see, among others, Edward A. Alpers, *Ivory and Slaves: Changing Patterns of International Trade in East Central Africa to the Later Nineteenth Century* (Berkeley, 1975), Pedro Machado, "A Forgotten Corner of the Indian Ocean: Gujarati Merchants, Portuguese India and the Mozambique Slave-Trade, c.1730–1830", *Slavery & Abolition*, 24:2 (2003), pp. 17–32, José Capela, "Slave Trade Networks in Eighteenth-Century Mozambique", in David Richardson and Filipa Ribeiro da Silva (eds), *Networks and Trans-Cultural Exchange: Slave Trading in the South Atlantic, 1590–1867* (Leiden, 2014), pp. 165–194.

13. Kathleen E. Sheldon, *Pounders of Grain: A History of Women, Work, and Politics in Mozambique* (Portsmouth, NH, 2002), ch. 1.

14. Newitt, *A History of Mozambique*, pp. 237–242.

Table 1. *Labour relations in Mozambique, c.1800 (guestimates).*

Types of labour				Labour relations codes	Guestimate (%)
Non-working				1 + 2 + 3	26
Working	Reciprocal labour			4a + 4b + 5 + 6 + 7	45
	Tributary labour			8 + 9 + 10 + 11	9.5
	Commodified labour	For market	Free	12a + 12b + 13 + 14	2
			Unfree	15 + 16 + 17	17
		For non-market Institutions		18	0.5
	Subtotal				74
Total					100

including women and other dependants able to work, were often involved in the production of goods for domestic consumption within the family and village as dependent family members, i.e. kin producers (LabRel 4b, see Table 1, and Table 2 for combinations of labour relations). In addition, the labour relations established between the *colonos* and *Prazo* tenants fall into another type of employment, i.e. tributary work and commodified labour for the market (LabRel 10 + 16, see Table 1). In this category the tribute assumed two forms: work and products. Thus, the *colono* had simultaneously a relationship of dependence towards the *Prazo* tenant, being obliged to work his land, as well as being obliged to pay a tribute in kind to the aforementioned *Prazo* tenant, which was mainly directed to supply the market economy. It is likely that identical labour relations existed between Free Africans and African local chiefs.

Enslaved Africans formed the second largest group among the economically active population – about nine to twelve per cent. This group comprised three main categories: rural and urban slaves, and slaves for export. Rural slaves formed the largest group. Most of them lived and worked in the Zambezi *Prazos* or nearby villages under the jurisdiction of *Prazo* tenants. Many of these slaves had been attached to the land and its tenant through a "system of reciprocal obligations". In this sense, the relationship between master and slave approached more that of feudal patronage and dependence than the forms of slavery that emerged in the Americas. In most cases, these slaves had their families and lived in their own villages, which fell under the jurisdiction of the *Prazos* and the local chiefs in territories outside the Portuguese sphere of influence. They often performed several tasks for *Prazo* tenants and local chiefs, while carrying out other activities, such as hunting, fishing, and foraging to guarantee their own subsistence. Over time, these slaves became known as *Chicunda* and were employed by their masters in the collection of taxes from the *colonos*, as well as on diplomatic missions, in the defence of the *Prazo* and dependent areas, and in trade, on

Table 2. *Combinations of labour relations in Mozambique, c.1800 (guestimates).*

Types of labour		Labour relations codes	Guestimate (%)
Non-working Non-combined LabRels		1	26
		2	
		3	
Working	Combination Type 1	4a + 10 + 16	15
	Combination Type 2	4b + 10 + 16	45
	Combination Type 3	5 + 10 + 16	5
	Combination Type 4	4a + 11 + 17	1.5
	Combination Type 5	4b + 11 + 17	4
	Combination Type 6	5 + 11 + 17	0.5
	Combination Type 7	4a + 13 + 18	0.5
	Combination Type 8	4b + 13 + 18	1
	Combination Type 9	5 + 13 + 18	0.5
	Non-combined LabRels	6	0.5
		14	0.5
Total			100

Sources: Based on late eighteenth- and early nineteenth-century population charts, and inventories of the *Prazos* of the Mozambican territory controlled by the Portuguese, including information on professions, available in the Portuguese Overseas Historical Archive (AHU).
Observations: Calculations made by the author, based on the taxonomy of labour relations. For further details, see Filipa Ribeiro da Silva, "Relações Laborais em Moçambique, 1800", *Diálogos*, 17 (2013), pp. 835–868, 860–861.

behalf of *Prazo* tenants. The *Chicunda*, or Achicunda, in fact, comprised most slaves at the time. The remaining slaves also lived dependent on or in the *Prazo* itself and had a wide variety of roles. For example, the "Jesuit *prazos* employed cooks, bakers, barbers, tailors, washerwomen, masons, fishermen, seamstresses, carpenters, tillers, ironsmiths, boat-builders and gold miners as well as household and garden slaves".[15] There were, however, some distinctions in the type of activities performed by male and female slaves. Most female slaves were occupied in agriculture and mining.

Urban slaves and slaves for export, on the other hand, were a constant presence in the Portuguese cities and fortresses along the coast, as well as in the Portuguese fleets sailing in the Indian Ocean and *Carreira da Índia* (i.e. the Portuguese Indiamen). They were either in transit as "slaves for sale", or as workers – often as "slaves for hire". In the latter case, they performed a variety of tasks associated with daily life in these spaces, including domestic service, street sale of products, and craftwork (LabRel 17, see Table 1, and Table 2 for combinations of labour relations).

15. *Ibid.*, p. 241.

Like the *colonos*, African slaves were involved in various labour relations. As village chiefs and heads of families (in the case of the *Chicunda*), they were engaged in the production of items at the village and family level to guarantee their survival and the livelihoods of their families and communities. In this capacity, they were household leading producers (LabRel 4a, see Table 1). The remaining slaves in these villages and families, including women, and other dependants able to work also contributed to the production of goods for domestic consumption, and should be seen as household kin producers (4b, see Table 1). The labour relations established between the slaves and the *Prazo* tenants were of another type, the so-called tributary work (LabRel 11, see Table 1, and Table 2 for combinations of labour relations). However, a significant part of the activities developed by slaves in rural areas was directed towards the production of foodstuff for local consumption, and goods for the market economy (LabRel 17, see Table 1, and Table 2 for combinations of labour relations). Revenue from the foodstuffs and goods produced for their master were kept by the latter.

In contrast, the population of Portuguese, mulatto, and Indian origin represented a small fraction of the economically active population – just 0.4 to one per cent. Many of these individuals combined different activities, including the leasing and management of *Prazos* in the Zambezi Valley, and military and/or administrative service to the Portuguese Crown, alongside trade in various products and enslaved Africans. On the one hand, as *Prazo* tenants they were employers of free Africans (*colonos*) and of enslaved Africans. They were, therefore, engaged in various types of working relationships (LabRel 12a + 13 + 14 + 18, see Table 1). On the other hand, many of these individuals, both men and women (particularly widows), were usually heads of households, which at the time functioned as production units, for both domestic and market consumption. They were, therefore, household leading producers (LabRel 4a + 13, see Table 1) and their spouses and descendants were household kin producers. In the territory that fell outside Portuguese control, labour relations were likely similar to those outlined above, as *Prazo* tenants often adopted the practices of local African leaders to extract labour and wealth from the population living under their jurisdiction.

Evidence suggests that by 1800 labour relations in Mozambique were dominated by reciprocal labour, often in combination with tributary and commodified labour. Subsistence agriculture appeared to be combined with the sale of surplus to the market. Harvest activities were carried out in combination with other tasks, such as hunting, working as porters, etc. Work for subsistence of the household (reciprocal labour) was combined with production of surplus for the market (work for the market), as well as with tributary labour for heads of villages, chiefs, and Portuguese *Prazo* tenants. In terms of the gender division of labour, men hunted and cleared fields for harvest, worked as porters, and as an armed defence guard; women took care of household chores, agricultural production, the sale of surplus in the market, and mining. Children also participated in the economy of the household and the rural community by helping in light household chores and in agricultural activities.

There is no evidence of a real free wage labour market. In the main port towns engaged in coastal, regional, and intercontinental trade, Portuguese, Swahili, and Banyan merchants resorted to slave labour for domestic work, for offering all kinds of services ("slaves for hire"), for equipping the ships operating through these ports, and for work in the production of foodstuff in the surrounding fields to supply the towns. The number of people working exclusively for the market appears to have been rather small, especially the number of those working for wages paid in currency and who could freely dispose of their labour as a commodity.

This system of combinations of labour relations was broken with the advent of the modern colonial era in Mozambique and the development of a colonial economy that obeyed the capitalist logic of catering to international markets and maximizing profits, at the lowest possible financial cost and with the minimum of risk.

PORTUGUESE RULE, ECONOMY, AND LABOUR RELATIONS IN MOZAMBIQUE AFTER THE 1890S

With the triumph of the principle of "effective occupation" at the Berlin Conference (1884–1885) and given the interests of the British and German governments in Mozambique, land occupation and population control became urgent matters. To face these challenges, the Portuguese state resorted to outsourcing – outsourcing the responsibilities of occupation, but also the financial and human costs associated with such type of enterprise.

The outsourcing of sizeable sections of Mozambique in the late nineteenth century is often portrayed in the literature as something new. However, outsourcing had a long history within the Portuguese empire, even as regards labour recruitment. Since the mid-sixteenth century (at least) there had been a long tradition of outsourcing the supply of labour within overseas territories, in particular within the Atlantic World, where Portuguese, and later Brazilian, private merchants and state-sponsored chartered companies catered to the demands of planters and miners in the New World. In this context, the state outsourced the acquisition along the African coast, the transport across the Atlantic, and the sale in the Americas.[16] However, the "recruitment" of Africans in the continent itself,

---

16. Fréderic Mauro, *Portugal, o Brasil e o Atlântico (1570–1670)*, 2 vols (Lisbon, 1997). Enriqueta Vila Vilar, *Hispanoamerica y el comercio de esclavos* (Seville, 1977).

either by purchase or enslavement through kidnapping or war, was never controlled by the Europeans (neither by the Portuguese, nor by others), and was never really outsourced to private consortia or entrepreneurs.[17]

In Mozambique itself, there was a tradition of outsourcing dating from the sixteenth and seventeenth centuries, as referred to before.[18] Thus, by the end of the nineteenth century, when faced with financial constraints, international political pressure, and economic rivalries, outsourcing the empire appeared to be the solution – an old solution. As in previous cases of colonial outsourcing, in Mozambique the state outsourced sections of territory where there was little or no Portuguese settlement, no defensive structures, no significant economic development, no bureaucratic apparatus, and no control over local African states/polities and their populations. So, the area of central Mozambique and the northern part of the territory were outsourced to two main companies chartered by the state: the Mozambique Company (1892–1942) and the Niassa Company (1891–1929) (see Figure 2).[19]

In contrast, the areas along the Zambezi Valley, where Portuguese presence dated from the late sixteenth and seventeenth centuries, including the districts of Tete and Quelimane, and the Island of Mozambique, were kept under the direct administration of the state. The same strategy was used in relation to the southern region of Mozambique – the so-called districts of Lourenço Marques (present-day Maputo), Gaza, and Inhambane, where settlement dated mainly from the nineteenth century in response to the growing interests of the British in the region – as control over these areas provided the British access to a port (Lourenço Marques), essential for the export of the raw materials and minerals being extracted in the Witwatersrand region and the Copperbelt, as well as to labour (migrants labourers) (see Figure 2).[20]

---

17. In the Portuguese Empire, the single exception to this was in Angola, where officials of the Crown were authorized to enslave Africans and/or to purchase them from Africans at fairs or demand payment of tribute from African leaders in slaves – the so-called *Tributo dos sobas*. Beatrix Heintze, "Angola nas garras do tráfico de escravos: as guerra do Ndongo (1611–1630)", *Revista Internacional de Estudos Africanos*, 1 (1984), pp. 11–60.

18. Isaacman, *Mozambique: The Africanization of a European Institution.* Newitt, *Portuguese Settlement on the Zambezi.* Eugénia Rodrigues, *Portugueses e Africanos nos Rios de Sena: os prazos da Coroa em Moçambique nos séculos XVII e XVIII* (Lisbon, 2013).

19. Barry Neil-Tomlinson, "The Mozambique Chartered Company, 1892–1910" (Ph.D., University of London, 1987). *Idem*, "The Nyassa Chartered Company: 1891–1929", *Journal of African History*, 18:1 (1977), pp. 109–128. Leroy Vail, "Mozambique's Chartered Companies: The Rule of the Feeble", *Journal of African History*, 17:3 (1976), pp. 389–416. Allina, *Slavery by Any Other Name.*

20. Alan K. Smith, "The Idea of Mozambique and Its Enemies, c.1890–1930", *Journal of Southern African Studies*, 17:3 (1991), pp. 496–524. *Idem*, "The Struggle for the Control of Southern Mozambique, 1720–1835" (Ph.D., University of California, Los Angeles, 1971).

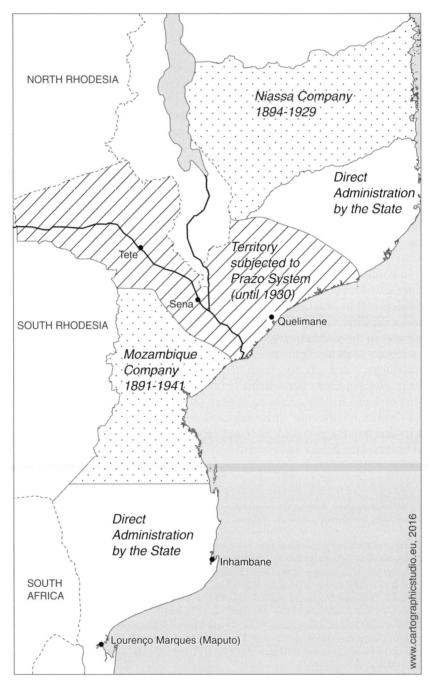

Figure 2. Mozambique, c.1900. Areas administered by the state and concessionary companies. *Source*: *Malyn Newitt*, A History of Mozambique *(Bloomington, IN, 1995), p. 366.*

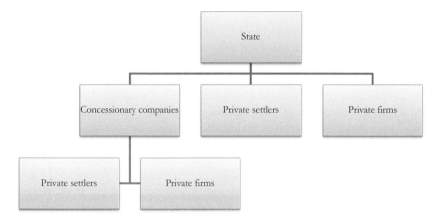

Figure 3. Outsourcing management of land and labour, Mozambique, 1890s–1940s: A chain.

Although these sections of the territory remained under the direct administration of the Portuguese state, the state also granted concessions to private firms and entrepreneurs within its territories. Similar prerogatives were granted to the concessionary companies. We can, therefore, regard this whole outsourcing scheme as a chain (see Figure 3).

In keeping with the Portuguese tradition of colonial outsourcing, companies were made responsible for land occupation, settlement, the rule of law, economic development, construction of infrastructure, and the recruitment and management of labour within their territories. For this, they were granted permission to organize and retain an active police and military force, to establish an administrative apparatus, to issue their own legislation, to collect taxes, to take population censuses, as well as to act as recruiters, allocators, and employers, and as mediators in labour conflicts.[21]

However, in late nineteenth-century Mozambique outsourcing was done on a larger scale and reached a whole new level. For the first time, vast areas of the African continent were being granted to companies authorized to issue their own regulations and have their own currency and police force.[22] Also, for the first time, private enterprises were explicitly allowed and encouraged to subjugate African leaders, enrol the African population, and

---

21. For a general overview of the Portuguese-speaking African territories, see Philip J. Havik, Alexander Keese, and Maciel Santos, *Administration and Taxation in Former Portuguese Africa: 1900–1945* (Cambridge, 2015), ch. 4.

22. In the Portuguese Empire, the single exception to this was in Angola, where, in the sixteenth century, the Portuguese Crown granted to Paulo Dias de Novais a captaincy to promote settlement and economic development. Ilídio do Amaral, *O Consulado de Paulo Dias de Novais: Angola no último quartel do século XVI e primeiro do século XVII* (Lisbon, 2000).

in this way recruit, allocate, and control labour in the African continent itself. In fact, the establishment of the Mozambican concessionary companies brought the outsourcing of labour supply and transport that had dominated Portuguese participation in the transatlantic slave trade into the African continent. In the areas controlled by the companies, company officials engaged directly in the enrolment of people declared "fit to work", the forceful "recruitment" of workers, and their allocation to various employers and different tasks. In those areas directly administered by the state, officials were involved in similar activities. However, to perform their roles as recruiters, allocators, employers, and mediators, companies and the state were to a great extent dependent on the voluntary or coerced cooperation of African chiefs of villages and of vaster territories, as previously with the supply of slaves for the early modern transatlantic slave trade and as is explained in greater detail in the following paragraphs. More importantly, for the first time concessionaries had at their disposal the means of the modern state: advanced military technology, a police force, modern statistics, etc. These allowed companies to exercise an unprecedented level of control over land and population in Africa – even though their control was limited geographically and the local population developed strategies to circumvent control by the state and the concessionary companies.

In order to become recruiters and allocators of labour, the Portuguese state and the concessionary companies needed a legal basis and a moral justification. For this, the Portuguese state issued a new labour code in 1899.[23] This new code determined that all men "fit to work" had the moral obligation to do so – *contratados*. Work was, in fact, the means through which Africans could "civilize themselves". As a consequence, men "fit to work" found without work or not having a clear professional occupation were deemed outlaws and, therefore, forcefully compelled to work – *compelidos*.

The new labour code gave the state and the concessionary companies the power to determine who was not "fit to work", and to put in place the necessary means to "recruit" either voluntarily or forcefully those "fit to work". Under the labour code, all men and youngsters older than fourteen years were, in principle, "fit to work". Children under fourteen, women, and the elderly were exempt from the obligation to work. The same applied, too, to those with any physical and mental illness that incapacitated them from performing any work. However, in practice, children, women, and the

---

23. Joaquim Moreira da Silva Cunha, *O Trabalho Indígena: Estudo de Direito Colonial* (Lisbon, 1955), p. 147, 149. This labour code was deeply influenced by the political and colonial thought of António Enes, former Governor of Mozambique and Minister of Naval and Overseas Affairs. See António Enes, "A colonização europeia de Moçambique", in Ministério das Colónias (ed.), *Antologia Colonial Portuguesa* (Lisbon, 1946), I, pp. 7-21; António Enes, *Moçambique: Relatório Apresentado ao Governo* (Lisbon, 1971) [1st ed. 1893].

elderly were often obliged to work, especially when men and youngsters over fourteen deemed "fit to work" were scarce. In 1907, the new Portuguese labour code required each African to work for four months per year.

The Portuguese labour codes were to be applied in the territories under the direct administration of the state and served as a guideline for the specific labour regulations issued by concessionary companies in their territories. However, in the territory of the Mozambique Company the period of work referred to in the regulations often exceeded the number of months defined in the labour code. In 1911, the Company set the obligation to work at six months and in 1920 extended it to one year.[24]

However, labour codes and regulations alone were not sufficient to compel Africans to work for wages, because they had at their disposal a variety of means to guarantee their survival and to amalgamate wealth without being dependent on selling their labour to the Portuguese. In order to force Africans to sell their labour for wages, the Portuguese state introduced the hut tax. Initially, it could be paid with labour, but over time payment in currency was made mandatory. So, the goals of the labour codes and regulations and the tax system introduced by the state and companies were threefold: obtain manpower, extract revenue, and force Africans to enter the emerging colonial wage labour market. The obligations towards the colonial state and its concessionary companies were, in fact, strongly bound together, as failure to pay the hut tax resulted in coercion to work.

To organize the hut tax collection and recruit workers, the state and the concessionary companies used their administrative apparatus, setting up what looked like a labour recruitment chain. In the case of the Mozambique Company, the headquarters in Lisbon delegated these responsibilities to the Native Labour Department (in existence between 1911–1925). These responsibilities were then transferred down the chain to the secretary general in the territory, and subsequently to the district administrators, their assistants, and police officers. The district administrators, either in person or through their assistants, were responsible for population censuses, tax collection, and workers' recruitment. To do so, they relied on local chiefs

---

24. On regulations on native labour recruitment and management within the territory administered by the Mozambique Company, see "Regulamento do Trabalho Indígena", *Boletim da Companhia de Moçambique*, 174 (16 November 1900); *Boletim da Companhia de Moçambique*, 10 (16 May 1907); "Regulamento geral do trabalho dos Indígenas no Território da Companhia de Moçambique", *Boletim da Companhia de Moçambique*, 18 (16 September 1907); "Regulamento provisório para o recrutamento e fornecimento de mão d'obra indígena pela Companhia de Moçambique", *Boletim da Companhia de Moçambique*, 14 (17 July 1911); "Regulamento provisório para o recrutamento e fornecimento de mão d'obra indígena pela Companhia de Moçambique", *Boletim da Companhia de Moçambique*, 4 (16 February 1915); "Código do trabalho dos indígenas nas colónias portuguesas", *Boletim da Companhia de Moçambique*, 6 (19 March 1929); "Código do trabalho dos indígenas nas colónias portuguesas", *Boletim da Companhia de Moçambique*, 20 (23 October 1930).

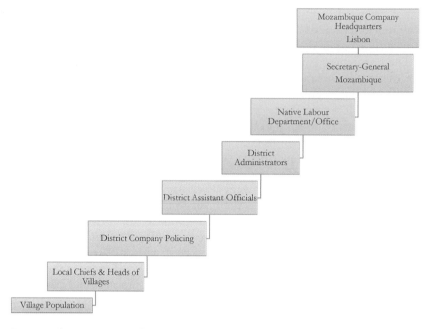

Figure 4. Labour recruitment chain – Mozambique Company, 1911–1925.

and heads of villages. These were expected to collaborate with the officials of the Mozambique Company (as well as the officials of the state in the territories under direct administration) in selecting and providing men "fit to work", collecting the hut tax, capturing workers who had left their assigned jobs before the end of their contract, and/or providing replacements for missing workers (see Figure 4).

Chiefs often resisted these demands. The colonial state and its concessionary companies had, therefore, to resort to various strategies to gain their cooperation.[25] Violence, threats, hut tax exemption, gifts in cash and/or goods, payment of fixed amounts in cash, or payment of a fixed sum per worker supplied were among the most common practices used to entice and/or compel chiefs to cooperate.[26] It is, however, worth noticing that, despite agreeing to collaborate with the colonial authorities, chiefs tried to safeguard their own interests and the interests of their communities. This was often achieved through negotiations, which could include offers of free

---

25. Resistance assumed different forms, from daring refusals to supply workers and pay taxes, to relocation of their population to another location, by crossing the borders between different colonies or between territories administered by state and concessionary companies. Allina, *Slavery by Any Other Name*, p. 92.
26. *Ibid.*, pp. 107–118.

work in the region in exchange for exemption from the obligation to work four or more months in other regions.[27] This way chiefs could keep manpower within their territory and guarantee that men worked for the companies and colonial state when they were not needed for agricultural work and other tasks. Chiefs thereby tried to keep the local economy and labour force in balance. This allowed communities to produce enough for their subsistence, as well as some surplus to sell in the closest markets. Men still had time throughout the year to find short-term wage labour. The payment received for their work as well as the money made by selling any surplus were used to pay the hut tax.

After 1926, in reaction to the growing criticism of the League of Nations and the International Labour Organization (ILO) concerning forms of labour and labour conditions in the Portuguese-African colonies, the directors of the Mozambique Company abolished the Native Labour Department and authorized a privately run Native Labour Association to operate in the territory. However, its recruitment activities were not very successful, resulting in a labour crisis in the territory in subsequent years. This was made worse by several natural disasters, forcing the Company to reassume its role as labour recruiter.

The "labour crisis" was widespread because the Company used to recruit and redistribute workers to other employers. White settler farmers, firms in the financial, shipping, and agricultural sectors, like the Bank of Beira and the Buzi Company, involved in sugar production, were among the main beneficiaries.[28] The labourers recruited were often allocated to work on maize farms, in clearing operations in the bush to reclaim agricultural land, and in mines, as carriers (*machileiros*) (see Figure 5), on plantations, and in construction, etc. For private employers, this labour supply came at a price. Employers had to pay for each worker supplied and were expected to pay a wage, provide clothing, accommodation and food, and grant workers a two-hour break daily for rest and Sunday as a holiday.

In those areas directly administered by the state, the recruitment process is likely to have run along similar lines.[29] The state catered to its own labour needs, and also acted as indirect allocator of labour for private entities by authorizing concessionary companies, including the Mozambique

---

27. *Ibid.*, pp. 162–170.
28. *Ibid.*, pp. 51–52, 63, 151–152.
29. On the labour migration of Mozambican workers to South Africa and Southern Rhodesia, see, among others, Patrick Harries, *Work, Culture, and Identity: Migrant Laborers in Mozambique and South Africa, c.1860–1910* (Portsmouth, NH, 1994). Alan H. Jeeves, *Migrant Labour in South Africa's Mining Economy: The Struggle for the Gold Mines' Labour Supply 1890-1920* (Montreal, 1985), Simon E. Katzenellenbogen, *South Africa and Southern Mozambique: Labour, Railways, and Trade in the Making of a Relationship* (Manchester, 1982), and Charles van Onselen, *Chibaro: African Mine Labour in Southern Rhodesia, 1900–1933* (London, 1977).

Figure 5. Machileiros in Mozambique. This photograph shows a Norwegian colonist in Mozambique being carried by the traditional Machila, c.1900. The use of Machilas to transport Europeans and wealthy people was common practice in the Portuguese empire in the eighteenth and nineteenth centuries, including in Angola and Brazil.
Private collection of Elsa Reiersen. Used with permission.

Company, and foreign labour recruitment associations to operate in those areas under its control. In the southern districts (Lourenço Marques, Gaza, and Inhambane), under the agreements between South Africa and Portugal – the first dating from 1897 – a South African recruitment agency by the name of the Witwatersrand Native Labour Association (WENELA) was authorized to operate a recruitment station there. The Rhodesian Native Labour Bureau, established in 1903 to cater to the labour demands of the Rhodesian Copperbelt and its mining sector, was also authorized to recruit in the same areas.

How did all these changes affect workers, their forms of employment, their working conditions and their labour relations with their employers? By 1900, the state and concessionary companies had forced the development of a wage labour market, mainly for males, promoting the development of labour as a commodity for the capitalist-oriented market. Although labelled "contract" labour, the recruitment and employment systems were put in place using coercion, because, even though employees were paid, many workers were unwilling to sell their labour freely to the market. Working conditions were identical to what nowadays is defined as modern forms of slavery. Non-payment, delayed payment, deduction of workdays from salaries, insufficient clothing, food rations, and poor accommodation facilities were common complaints among workers against their private employers. The use of violence, threats, extension of contracts beyond the fixed duration, and refusal to grant daily hours for rest and Sundays as a day off were also usual. Some workers performed labour equivalent to indentured work for the market (immediately after the abolition of slavery indentured workers were often called *serviçais*, over time they also became known as *contratados*); others were in situations of effective forced labour for the market (*compelidos*). This represented an increase in unfree commodified labour for the market (see Table 3). In fact, only skilled workers retained some freedom of choice – the *voluntários*. They were able to voluntarily offer their work to the wage labour market and were often better paid and had better working conditions.

African men declared "fit to work" lost a lot of their freedom in relation to labour choices: when to work, whom to work for, how long to work, what work to do, and for how much they were willing to work, etc. This loss of freedom of choice changed their labour relations and had several consequences. On the one hand, they were forced to enter the wage labour market that was expanding under the sponsorship of the colonial authorities and concessionary companies. On the other, they were often assigned work for long periods of time and in places distant from their home villages and communities.

The emergence of these new labour regimes also brought about transformations in the economies of households and rural communities in the region. Men involved in labour for the benefit of the household and community – reciprocal labour – decreased in number, while women were increasingly engaged in reciprocal labour, as, in principle, colonial authorities did not seek their work for the development of the commercial agricultural, industrial, and mining sectors. So, women were to a great extent excluded from the wage market that was forcefully emerging in the region under the "sponsorship" of the state and its concessionaries. It seems likely, too, that the number of children and elderly working, especially in reciprocal labour, increased to replace those men who were recruited to work elsewhere.

However, the development of colonial capitalism in Southern Africa and the subsequent expansion of the mining and commercial agricultural sectors also offered business opportunities to African farmers. The construction of compounds to house labourers near mining fields and plantations created new consumption markets for foodstuffs traditionally produced by local farmers, such as maize and brewed beer. These products, often produced by women and which had in the past been a by-product of subsistence agriculture, would now be commercialized in Mozambique and exported to

Filipa Ribeiro da Silva

Table 3. *Labour relations in Lourenço Marques and its outskirts, 1912.*

Main population groups	Main types of labour	Description of labour relations	Total population (no.)	Total population (%)
Non-working		1. Incapable of working or not expected to work	3,414	13.1
		2. Affluent	73	0.3
		3. Unemployed	0	0.0
		Non-working subtotal	*3,487*	*13.4*
Working	Reciprocal labour	4. Household leading producers (only part of their time)	140	0.5
		5. Household kin producers	1,200	4.6
		6. Household servants	1,605	6.2
		7. Community redistribution agents		
		Reciprocal work subtotal	*2,945*	*11.3*
	Tributary labour	8. Forced labourers	800	3.1
		9. Indentured labourers		
		10. Serfs		
		11. Slaves		
		Tributary work subtotal	*800*	*3.1*
	Commodified labour	12. Self-employed	1,288	4.9
		13. Employers	624	2.4
		14. Wage earners	3,965	15.2
		15. Indentured workers (only part of their time)	11,153	42.8
		16. Serfs		
		17. Slaves		
		18. Wage earners for non-market institutions	1,817	7.0
		Commodified labour subtotal	*18,847*	*72.3*
		Working subtotal	*22,592*	*86.6*
Total			26,079	100.0

Sources and observations: Calculations by the author based on data from the Census of the Population of Lourenço Marques – 1912 (present-day Maputo) and the Census of the Population living in the outskirts of Lourenço Marques – 1912, and on the taxonomy of labour relations developed by the Global Collaboratory on the History of Labour Relations, 1500–2000.

Southern Rhodesia and South Africa, in particular to the Copperbelt. Thus, apparently, the rise of the colonial state and colonial capitalism also stimulated the formation/expansion of a group of prosperous African independent farmers and cattle breeders, with profits from catering to the new consumption needs of male wage workers in the mining, agricultural, and industrial areas. Catering to the needs of the growing white colonial elites was also a profitable business. Others acquired the status of independent farmers with the help of remittances sent by their relatives who were migrant workers in Southern Rhodesia and South Africa, with these remittances being invested in the acquisition of livestock, land, seeds, and in the payment of hut taxes.

Although we lack comprehensive census data and information on the occupational structure of the entire Mozambican population for 1900, the data available for the city of Lourenço Marques and its outskirts, dating from 1912, illustrate the aforementioned changes in labour relations in the territories under the direct administration of the Portuguese state (see Table 3). Similar patterns are likely to be found in the territory of the Mozambique Company.

CONCLUSION

The evidence analysed here suggests that on the eve of the twentieth century the Portuguese colonial state became the main employer and redistributor of labour, both in relation to its own subjects and to subjects of other countries. On the one hand, the state developed into an important recruiter and allocator of labour within two specific regions of the territory of Mozambique, while simultaneously authorizing private entrepreneurs and firms to operate also as recruiters and employers within these same regions. These prerogatives were granted not only to its own subjects, but also to subjects of other states and their colonies, in particular South Africa and Southern Rhodesia. By using an old solution to promote settlement, development, and empire management – outsourcing – the state transferred state-like powers, though for the first time including recruitment and redistribution of labour, to two main concessionary companies, which carried out operations in central and northern Mozambique.

Together, the state and the concessionary companies brought the outsourcing of labour recruitment to the African continent and introduced to Mozambique important changes in the world of labour, including the development of a wage labour market, mainly for men, often working either in conditions identical to indentured work or forced labour, and the expansion of labour migration to neighbouring regions. The removal of men from the households and rural communities affected subsistence and local economies, leading to an increasing number of women, children, and the elderly engaged in reciprocal labour. However, the expansion of the colonial economy also contributed to the formation of a group of independent African farmers producing for the market and of skilled African workers also able to more freely offer their labour in the market – contributing to an increase in commodified labour.

IRSH 61 (2016), Special Issue, pp. 137–164 doi:10.1017/S0020859016000481
© 2016 Internationaal Instituut voor Sociale Geschiedenis

Grammar of Difference? The Dutch Colonial State, Labour Policies, and Social Norms on Work and Gender, c.1800–1940*

ELISE VAN NEDERVEEN MEERKERK

*Department of Rural and Environmental History,
Wageningen University
PO Box 8130, 6700 EW Wageningen, The Netherlands*

E-mail: elise.vannederveenmeerkerk@wur.nl

ABSTRACT: This article investigates developments in labour policies and social norms on gender and work from a colonial perspective. It aims to analyse the extent to which state policies and societal norms influenced gendered labour relations in the Netherlands and its colony, the Netherlands Indies (present-day Indonesia). In order to investigate the influence of the state on gender and household labour relations in the Dutch empire, this paper compares as well as connects social interventions related to work and welfare in the Netherlands and the Netherlands Indies from the early nineteenth century up until World War II. At the beginning of the nineteenth century, work was seen as a means to morally discipline the poor, both in the Netherlands and the Netherlands Indies. Parallel initiatives were taken by Johannes van den Bosch, who, in 1815, established "peat colonies" in the Netherlands, aiming to transform the urban poor into industrious agrarian workers, and in 1830 introduced the Cultivation System in the Netherlands Indies, likewise to increase the industriousness of Javanese peasants. While norms were similar, the scope of changing labour relations was much vaster in the colony than in the metropole.

During the nineteenth century, ideals and practices of the male breadwinner started to pervade Dutch households, and children's and women's labour laws were enacted. Although in practice many Dutch working-class women and children continued to work, their official numbers dropped significantly. In contrast to the metropole, the official number of working (married) women in the colony was very high, and rising over the period. Protection for women and children was introduced very late in the Netherlands Indies and only under intense pressure from the

* This article is a result of the NWO-funded Vidi research project "Industriousness in an Imperial Economy: Interactions of Households' Work Patterns, Time Allocation and Consumption in the Netherlands and the Netherlands-Indies, 1815-1940". I would like to thank the editors of this Special Issue for their useful comments on earlier drafts. An earlier version is available online as CEGH working paper: http://www.cgeh.nl/sites/default/files/WorkingPapers/CGEHWP58_vannederveenmeerkerk.pdf.

international community. Not only did Dutch politicians consider it "natural" for Indonesian women and children to work, their assumptions regarding inherent differences between Indonesian and Dutch women served to justify the protection of the latter: a fine example of what Ann Stoler and Frederick Cooper have called a "grammar of difference".

INTRODUCTION

This article aims to study the role of the Dutch colonial state with respect to changing household and gender labour relations in the nineteenth and early twentieth centuries. It explicitly takes the *colonial state*, rather than the *nation state*, as its point of departure. Over the past two decades, post-colonial and post-nationalist studies have criticized the widespread idea of nations as self-contained units of analysis. Rather, they claim, colonialism ought to be considered as a *consequence* as well as a *constituting element* of European state and nation building since the seventeenth century.[1] From the late eighteenth century onwards, colonialism intensified, and the imperial project became a more explicit constituent of state formation. Moreover, this was the period when increasing colonial encounters highlighted the contrasts between the "advanced" colonial administrators and settlers on the one hand, and the "backward" indigenous population on the other. Such contemporary paradigms of modernity and backwardness, as well as notions of the "civilizing" mission of Europeans *vis-à-vis* non-European populations, have often been adopted by historians, who have taken developments in Western Europe and North America as blueprints for the "road to modernity" of other societies and cultures.[2] Instead, both postcolonial and "new imperial" historians have argued that, because of their interwoven histories, we need to study historical developments in "the East" *as well as* in "the West" in relation to each other, in order to better understand them.[3]

In their inspirational work, Ann Stoler and Frederick Cooper have emphasized the many ambivalences of colonial rule, and pointed to the importance of recognizing how colonialism shaped the histories not only of

---

1. David Held *et al.*, *Global Transformations: Politics, Economics and Culture* (Cambridge, 2011), p. 41.

2. For an already classic account see Dipesh Chakrabarty, *Provincializing Europe: Postcolonial Thought and Historical Difference* (Princeton, 2008).

3. Sebastian Conrad and Shalini Randeria (eds), *Jenseits des Eurozentrismus. Postkoloniale Perspektiven in den Geschichts- und Kulturwissenschaften* (Frankfurt am Main, 2002), pp. 10, 12; Frederick Cooper, *Colonialism in Question: Theory, Knowledge, History* (Berkeley and Los Angeles, 2005); Chris Bayly, *The Birth of the Modern World 1780–1914: Global Connections and Comparisons* (Oxford, 2004). Although Bayly explicitly distances himself from postcolonial history, he aims to show interconnectedness and interdependencies in world history.

the colonies, but also those of the metropoles. While the effects of such mutual influences on the metropole have often been indirect or even obscured, such "tensions of empire" are relevant for both the history of former colonies and former colonizers. Therefore, we need to "examine thoughtfully the complex ways in which Europe was made from its colonies".[4] When we read or reread the historical archival material from this perspective – placing colonial history not solely in the context of domination and subordination – a more dynamic historical narrative emerges, characterized by tensions, anxieties and paradoxes, collaboration and resistance.[5] Examining these tensions and *mutual* influences will not only lead to a better understanding of the metropolitan as well as the colonial past, it can also help more fully explain the postcolonial remains of these complex relationships.[6]

In order to investigate the influence of the state on gender and household labour relations in the Dutch empire, this paper compares as well as connects social interventions related to work and welfare in the Netherlands and the Netherlands Indies[7] from the early nineteenth century up until World War II. This was the period in which the Dutch increasingly attempted to gain political control over the Indonesian archipelago, leading to an intensification of colonial contacts and significant social and economic consequences on both sides of the empire. I aim to show how state intervention, in this case by the Dutch nation state *and* colonial state, although differing in content and extent, was strikingly similar in terms of *ideology* and *timing* in both parts of the empire until the end of the nineteenth century. However, around the turn of the twentieth century, when in Europe – including the Netherlands – welfare states rapidly started to develop, social policies between metropole and colony diverged both in timing and effects. These differences were reinforced by changes in ideology, entailing strong gender as well as racial components, impacting drastically on diverging trajectories of labouring households in both parts

---

4. Cooper, *Colonialism in Question*, p. 3.
5. Ann L. Stoler, *Along the Archival Grain: Epistemic Anxieties and Colonial Common Sense* (Princeton, 2009).
6. Ann L. Stoler and Frederick Cooper, "Between Metropole and Colony: Rethinking a Research Agenda", in Frederick Cooper and Ann L. Stoler (eds), *Tensions of Empire: Colonial Cultures in a Bourgeois World* (Berkeley, 1997), pp. 1–56, 33.
7. This article focuses on the region that in the nineteenth and early twentieth centuries was called the Netherlands Indies, or the Netherlands East Indies, which more or less comprises the territory of present-day Indonesia. Until the end of the nineteenth century, the Dutch predominantly colonized the island of Java, and most literature and archival sources in the period under investigation relate to this, most densely populated, island of the archipelago. Despite its shifting boundaries, it is almost standard practice among historians to call this area "Netherlands Indies" throughout the colonial period, and I have therefore opted to adopt this convention too.

of the world. While early nineteenth-century initiatives have been studied in the same analytical framework,[8] to my knowledge no similar exercise has yet been undertaken for the remainder of the colonial period.[9]

This is highly relevant because important changes took place in the late nineteenth century, in which the welfare state slowly but surely emerged, at least in the metropolitan parts of the Dutch empire, whereas social legislation in the Netherlands Indies lagged seriously behind. Moreover, important ideological changes occurred in this period, which I believe contributed first to the simultaneity and later to the divergence of social policy in the different parts of the empire. In the beginning of the century, the political elites considered work by all members of the labouring classes – men, women, and children – to be the key to an industrious and blossoming society and economy, both in the Netherlands and in the Netherlands Indies. Towards the end of the century, however, the well-being of the poor and working classes became increasingly defined as a "Social Question" in the Netherlands, in which child labour and women's work formed an important concern. Similar concerns led to the "Ethical Policy" in the Netherlands Indies in 1901, although attitudes towards the work of women and children here were far more ambivalent, as I will show. In the 1920s and 1930s, the ideal of the male breadwinner society had gained solid ground in the metropole, culminating in draft legislation to prohibit any paid work by married women in 1937, whereas work by women and children in the colony was conceived as rather unproblematic and even "natural" in the same period.

WORK AND SOCIAL DISCIPLINE: THE NETHERLANDS AND THE NETHERLANDS INDIES COMPARED (C.1800–1870)[10]

Already in the early modern period, both in the Dutch Republic and the Netherlands Indies the rhetoric and policies of the authorities increasingly started to associate poverty with idleness. In the context of

---

8. Albert Schrauwers, "The 'Benevolent' Colonies of Johannes van den Bosch: Continuities in the Administration of Poverty in the Netherlands and Indonesia", *Comparative Studies in Society and History*, 43:2 (2001), pp. 298–328; Ulbe Bosma, "Dutch Imperial Anxieties about Free Labour, Penal Sanctions and the Right to Strike", in Alessandro Stanziani (ed.), *Labour, Coercion, and Economic Growth in Eurasia, 17th–20th Centuries* (Leiden, 2013), pp. 67–74.
9. With the notable exception of a study on child labour by Ben White, "Childhood, Work and Education, 1900–2000: The Netherlands and the Netherlands Indies/Indonesia Compared", *Brood en Rozen*, 4 (2001), pp. 105–120.
10. Parts of the following section have appeared, in a slightly modified version, in Elise van Nederveen Meerkerk, "Industriousness in an Imperial Economy: Delineating New Research on Colonial Connections and Household Labour Relations in the Netherlands and the Netherlands Indies", *Workers of the World*, 1:3 (2013), pp. 107–112.

eighteenth-century economic decline, the answer to the growing problem of poverty was work: the idle poor should be transformed into hard-working and productive citizens. This rhetoric applied to lower-class men, women, and children alike. For example, Dutch welfare institutions increasingly restricted provisions for unemployed immigrants, begging was forbidden, and beneficial entitlements became increasingly dependent on people's work efforts.[11] On Java, Dutch colonizers likewise condemned migration and "vagrancy" by the indigenous population as being economically counterproductive.[12] The number of local initiatives, such as workhouses and spinning contests to stimulate the production of fine yarns – typically the work of women and children – mushroomed in the Netherlands in the latter half of the eighteenth century. However, most of these initiatives failed. Often, the poor refused to work, or soon left the workhouse because of its bad reputation or because women and children could earn more and be more flexible elsewhere in the labour market.[13]

Many early nineteenth-century policymakers as well as intellectuals believed that poor relief formed a disincentive for creating industrious, law-abiding citizens.[14] After the Dutch Kingdom was established in 1815, initiatives to combat poverty were taken at the national as well as the imperial level. Remarkably, King William I entrusted one particular person to implement his plans to counter pauperism by stimulating the industriousness of poor families, first in the Netherlands and later on Java. The man in question was Johannes van den Bosch (1780–1844), who had served as a military officer in the Netherlands Indies since 1799. He owned a plantation on Java, where he experimented with the cultivation of cash crops between 1808 and 1810. However, Governor General Daendels expelled Van den Bosch to the Netherlands in 1810, probably because of his criticism of colonial policy. Here, Van den Bosch successfully fought against the French in 1814–1815, a fact that did not go unnoticed by the later king.[15]

After the Vienna peace treaties of 1815, Van den Bosch spent most of his days designing plans to combat poverty in the Netherlands. He wrote an elaborate book on the problems of poverty, unemployment, and the desired role of the state. Although poverty was particularly dire in Dutch towns, Van den Bosch was convinced that – unlike in Britain – *agriculture* instead

11. Marco van Leeuwen, "Amsterdam en de armenzorg tijdens de Republiek", *NEHA-Jaarboek*, 59 (1996), pp. 132–161.

12. Jan Breman, *Koloniaal profijt van onvrije arbeid. Het Preanger stelsel van gedwongen koffieteelt op Java* (Amsterdam, 2010), p. 41.

13. Elise van Nederveen Meerkerk, *De draad in eigen handen. Vrouwen en loonarbeid in de Nederlandse textielnijverheid, 1581–1810* (Amsterdam, 2007), pp. 177–179.

14. Frances Gouda, *Poverty and Political Culture: The Rhetoric of Social Welfare in the Netherlands and France, 1815–1854* (Amsterdam, 1995), p. 20.

15. J. Boerma, *Johannes van den Bosch als sociaal hervormer: De maatschappij van weldadigheid* (Groningen, 1927), pp. 2–4.

Figure 1. Count Johannes van den Bosch (1780–1844). Governor General in the Netherlands Indies (1830–1833).
Cornelis Kruseman. Donated by jkvr. J.C.C. van den Bosch, Den Haag. Rijksmuseum Amsterdam. Public domain.

of industry would be the answer to the problem in the Netherlands. His earlier experiments with cash-crop cultivation on Java probably formed the foundation for Van den Bosch's ideas.[16] He argued that the urban poor

16. Schrauwers, "The 'Benevolent' Colonies", p. 301.

should gain the "right to work", by having them relocated to rural regions where they could learn how to cultivate agricultural crops for their own subsistence, selling their surpluses in the market. With private funds Van den Bosch established the Maatschappij van Weldadigheid (Benevolent Society) in 1818 to set up agricultural colonies in Drenthe, an under-populated province in the east of the Netherlands consisting mostly of peatland. Tens of thousands of – mostly urban – pauper families migrated (and later were even deported) to these "peat colonies". The idea was that several years in the countryside would turn them into industrious agrarian workers. Eventually, they were supposed to leave the colonies with some savings and an improved mentality.[17]

Suitable colonists nevertheless proved hard to find, and "industrious-ness" soon needed to be enforced to a great extent. Some of the dwellings were transformed into penal institutions for convicted paupers. Even in the "free" peat colonies, regulations were strict and detailed. Throughout the 1820s, Van den Bosch regularly corresponded with the overseers, ensuring that they saw to it that "no household would be bereft of the necessary, but that it itself would earn these necessities".[18] The meticulous detail of Van den Bosch's calculations for the bare subsistence needs of households strikes the historian's eye when reading the archival material. While undoubtedly benevolent in intent, the experiment with the peat colonies clearly shows that, to the elite, the poor were really a "foreign country", as Frances Gouda has argued.[19] The initiative was an example of social engineering, and its overseers eschewed neither intensive control nor, at times, even force over the daily lives of ordinary people. A strict regime of meals, work, and rest was established, including only limited leisure time. Wages for field work were set at two-thirds of regular Dutch adult male wages, from which the costs of daily subsistence were subtracted.[20] Part of whatever a colonist family earned in excess of this had to be put into a health fund, part had to be saved, and part was paid out as pocket money. Their savings would enable the family to leave the institution within a couple of years.[21] In terms of the taxonomy of labour relations as defined by the Global Collaboratory,[22] this would thus entail a shift from labour relation 3 (unemployed) to labour relations 4a and 4b (leading producers and

---

17. *Ibid.*, pp. 303–313.
18. National Archive (NA), Van den Bosch Collection (vd Bosch), inv. no. 58, Benevolent Society, fol. 79v.
19. Gouda, *Poverty and Political Culture*, p. 2.
20. NA, vd Bosch, inv. no. 58, fol. 14v.
21. R. Berends *et al.*, *Arbeid ter disciplinering en bestraffing. Veenhuizen als onvrije kolonie van de Maatschappij van Weldadigheid 1823-1859* (Zutphen, 1984), pp. 60–61.
22. In full: The Global Collaboratory on the History of Labour Relations, 1500-2000. For the most recent taxonomy of labour relations, see https://collab.iisg.nl/c/document_library/get_file?p_l_id=273223&folderId=277142&name=DLFE-202901.pdf, last accessed 2 October 2015.

kin producers), 18 (wage earners working for non-market institutions), and 12a and b (possible surpluses sold in the market by heads of households and kin respectively).

In practice, though, the peat colonies increasingly came to resemble forced labour relations for a non-market institution (labour relation 8). Although Van den Bosch opposed slavery in principle, he could scarcely see the distinction between "forced" and "free" labour.[23] After all, every wage labourer was to some extent enslaved, as he (and less commonly she) was always economically dependent on a boss or employer, and therefore Van den Bosch was not against the coerced adoption of the poor.[24] Indeed, colonists coming to Drenthe voluntarily formed an exception: every year between 1830 and 1860 an average of just twenty-two families arrived of their own volition.[25] As far back as the early 1820s, the peat colonies relied extensively on state financing,[26] and in 1859 the colonies were taken over by the state, thus officially becoming a public institution. From then on, most of the thousands of families and individuals in the peat colonies were sent to or detained in the "beggars institutions" by local urban authorities. In 1875, 2,809 people were still living there, only ten of whom had volunteered.[27] Instead of transforming poor men, women, and children into hard-working citizens, the colonies had turned into a fully fledged penal institution, to which undesired elements from urban society were sent. Judged by their original intention, the peat colonies can thus be considered a failure. Nevertheless, an important effect of these social experiments was that they set an example for similar initiatives, both within and outside Europe.[28] More strikingly, the peat colonies formed a blueprint for the Cultivation System on Java, designed and implemented by their inventor Johannes van den Bosch when he was Governor General in the Netherlands Indies (1830–1833).

Much has been written about the Cultivation System, but for the purposes of this paper the relatively underexplored links with Van den Bosch's benevolent colonies in the Netherlands are particularly interesting. Both can be seen as "development projects" with state support, focusing on the agricultural production of cash crops by the poor, who would not only work for their subsistence, but also receive a cash bonus for surplus crops.

23. Bosma, "Dutch Imperial Anxieties", p. 68.

24. J.J. Westendorp Boerma, *Een geestdriftig Nederlander. Johannes van den Bosch* (Amsterdam, 1950), pp. 39–40.

25. C.A. Kloosterhuis, *De bevolking van de vrije koloniën der Maatschappij van Weldadigheid* (Zutphen, 1981), p. 243.

26. Westendorp Boerma, *Een geestdriftig Nederlander*, p. 38.

27. "Bevolking der Rijksbedelaars Gestichten", *De Economist*, 24:2 (1875), pp. 732–736.

28. In the southern Netherlands for example. Westendorp Boerma, *Een geestdriftig Nederlander*, p. 37; and in France: Gouda, *Poverty and Political Culture*, p. 114.

Moreover, in both cases the objective was to transform "lazy" paupers into industrious workers, and to this end a certain degree of coercion was tolerated.[29] Indonesian *men* especially were seen as idle, as opposed to their wives, whom the Dutch as well as the English portrayed as particularly industrious and entrepreneurial. For instance, Thomas Stamford Raffles, Governor General during the British interregnum in the East Indies (1811–1816), noted in 1817 that "[t]he labour of the women on Java is estimated almost as highly as that of the men".[30] Indeed, early colonial officials in Java estimated that women spent about twice as much time on rice cultivation as men did.[31] Apart from subsistence agriculture (labour relation 4), which was presumably the most important labour relation on Java around 1800, both men and women performed communal agricultural tasks, as a sort of risk-spreading for the *desa*, the village community (labour relation 7), and they had to give part of their produce to the village head as a form of tribute (labour relation 8).

Van den Bosch stated that Javanese peasants needed to work only a few hours per day to survive. In order to make them produce also for the market, their industriousness needed to be enhanced, for their own benefit as well as that of the imperial economy.[32] To achieve this, Javanese peasants were expected to set aside a proportion of their land to produce export crops, such as coffee, sugar, and indigo, for the Dutch authorities. While peasants obtained monetary compensation for their production, this predominantly served to pay land rents to indigenous elites and Dutch civil servants. The system remained in place until around 1870, and although its effects varied greatly from one part of Java to another[33] it had tremendous effects on both the Javanese and the Dutch economies.

29. Schrauwers, "Benevolent Colonies", pp. 313–314.
30. Cited in Elsbeth Locher-Scholten, "Female Labour in Twentieth Century Java: European Notions – Indonesian Practice", pp. 40–42, in *idem* and A. Niehof (eds), *Indonesian Women in Focus: Past and Present Notions* (Dordrecht [etc.], 1987), pp. 77–103; White, "Childhood, Work and Education", pp. 110–111. See also H.W. Daendels, *Staat der Nederlandsche Oostindische bezittingen. Bijlagen, Organique Stukken, Preparatoire Mesures 31* (The Hague, 1814), p. 104; Peter Boomgaard, "Female Labour and Population Growth on Nineteenth-Century Java", *Review of Indonesian and Malayan Affairs*, 15:2 (1981), p. 7.
31. Barbara Watson Andaya, *The Flaming Womb: Repositioning Women in Early Modern Southeast Asia* (Honolulu, 2006), p. 106. This is exactly why I have problems with the division between "leading producers" and "kin producers" in the taxonomy – it is not at all clear to what extent men were more important than women, or women more important than men, in sub-sistence agriculture in Java (and presumably this also goes for other parts of the world, including Africa). See also Ester Boserup, *Woman's Role in Economic Development* (New York, 1970).
32. J. van den Bosch, "De consideratiën en het advies van den 6 Maart 1829, uitgebragt door den benoemden Gouverneur-Generaal van N. Indië J. van den Bosch, op het rapport van den heer Du Bus over de kolonisatie" [1829], in D.C. Steyn Parvé, *Het koloniaal monopoliestelsel getoetst aan geschiedenis en staatshuishoudkunde* (The Hague, 1850), pp. 294–328, 304.
33. Robert Elson, *Village Java under the Cultivation System, 1830–1870* (Sydney, 1994), pp. 43–44.

The effects of the Cultivation System on household labour in the Netherlands Indies, in particular on the work of women and children, are very much underexplored territory. Angus Maddison has concluded that the introduction of the system did not mean that Indonesian workers were impoverished, but that they had to work harder to meet their daily needs.[34] While Maddison did not explore the economic activities of Javanese women and children, my argument here is that their work did indeed increase. Ben White has recently stated that the Cultivation System "required fundamental reorganization of the household's division of labour".[35]

Firstly, the labour input of women and children in subsistence agriculture increased, because men had to devote more of their time to cultivating cash crops. Although quantitative evidence is scarce, Peter Boomgaard has contended that in areas suitable for export crops the extra annual labour that was needed to fulfil the criteria of the Cultivation System was between 120–130 days per household.[36] This would have required women to devote more time to rice production, in which they had traditionally already been involved.[37] Thus, their activities in the form of subsistence labour (labour relation 4b) increased further.

Secondly, although this was explicitly *not* the intention of the authorities, women and children assisted or worked full time in the cultivation of cash crops as well.[38] Simultaneously, the labour-intensive production of second crops, for instance on garden plots, did not decline but increased during the Cultivation System, and Boomgaard has argued that this was an activity women tended to combine with their activities in the home.[39] Garden crops were sold mostly in the market, so the involvement of women in self-employed agriculture rose as well (labour relation 12b).

Thirdly, there is empirical evidence that women and children living in villages that were exempt from the cultivation duties performed free wage labour in neighbouring villages that were obliged to contribute, for instance by picking tea leaves[40] and on coffee plantations.[41] This means that the

---

34. Angus Maddison, "Dutch Income in and from Indonesia 1700–1938", *Modern Asian Studies*, 23:4 (1989), pp. 645–670.

35. Ben White, "Labour in Childhood's Global Past: Child Work and Colonial Policies in Indonesia, 1800–1949", in K. Lieten and E. van Nederveen Meerkerk (eds), *Child Labour's Global Past, 1650–2000* (Berne, 2011), p. 485.

36. Peter Boomgaard, *Children of the Colonial State: Population Growth and Economic Development in Java, 1795–1880* (Amsterdam, 1989), p. 82.

37. Barbara Watson Andaya, "Women and Economic Change: The Pepper Trade in Pre-Modern Southeast Asia", *Journal of the Economic and Social History of the Orient*, 38:2 (1995), p. 172.

38. NA, Koloniën, 1850–1900, inv. no. 5830, Geheime verbalen, no. 47, 12 February 1852. See also Boomgaard, "Female Labour", p. 9.

39. Boomgaard, *Children of the Colonial State*, p. 107.

40. Arsip Nasional Jakarta (ANRI), inv. no. 1621, Cultuurverslag Preanger Regentschappen 1862.

41. J.H. van den Bosch, *Een viertal verhandelingen over de belangrijksten quaestien, thans omtrent Java aan de orde van de dag* (The Hague, 1850), p. 42. Van den Bosch explicitly says that these female coffee pickers "can only be hired out of their own free will".

system also brought about a greater involvement of women and children in wage labour (labour relation 14). After 1850, wage labour opportunities, for instance on sugar plantations, increased even more – for men as well as for women.[42]

This enhanced work effort by women and children, caused by a state-supported system of resource extraction, might have originated mostly out of increasing poverty, as Boomgaard argues.[43] However, other historians suggest that the colonial interactions also entailed new consumptive possibilities for Indonesian households. More generally, the rise of waged labour severely affected labour relations in the Javanese economy and households, as well as their consumption patterns.[44] In this sense, Van den Bosch's initial aims – enhancing market production by the agrarian population – appear to have been more successful in the Netherlands Indies than in the Netherlands. Interestingly, in the Netherlands, Van den Bosch's initiatives led to a (minor, because of the more modest scale of the "peat colonies") shift in labour relations from non-working to mainly *non-market* economic activities, predominantly reciprocal labour in the form of penal work, whereas in the Netherlands Indies commodified labour relations were on the rise.

Without doubt, this difference in outcome related to the fairly effective grip the colonial state had on the Javanese economy. Ironically, this tight grip led to millions of guilders from the Cultivation System and other tax benefits flowing to the Dutch treasury during much of the nineteenth century (see Table 1).

Especially after the 1850s and 1860s, when the surplus from the Netherlands Indies had been at its largest relative to the Dutch state's tax revenues, male real wages started to rise spectacularly, and faster than in other Western European countries.[45] Moreover, compared to other European countries the registered labour force participation of women declined earlier and faster in the Netherlands, and this has often been related

---

42. Ulbe Bosma, "The Discourse on Free Labor and the Forced Cultivation System: The Contradictory Consequences of the Abolition of the Slave Trade in Colonial Java, 1811–1870", in Marcel van der Linden (ed.), *Humanitarian Intervention and Changing Labor Relations: The Long-term Consequences of the Abolition of the Slave Trade* (Leiden and Boston, 2011), pp. 387–418, 411.

43. Boomgaard, "Female Labour".

44. Jan Luiten van Zanden and Arthur van Riel, *The Strictures of Inheritance: The Dutch Economy in the Nineteenth Century* (Princeton, 2004), p. 116.

45. Ewout Frankema and Frans Buelens, "Conclusion", in *idem* (eds), *Colonial Exploitation and Economic Development: The Belgian Congo and the Netherlands Indies Compared* (London, 2013), p. 275. For a comparison of the development of real wages in Europe between 1860 and 1913, see Elise van Nederveen Meerkerk, "Vergelijkingen en verbindingen. De arbeidsdeelname van vrouwen in Nederland en Nederlands-Indië, 1813–1940", *Low Countries Historical Review*, 130:2 (2015), pp. 13–43, 32.

Table 1. *The "Batig Slot" (colonial surplus) from the Netherlands Indies, 1831–1877*

Period	Colonial surplus (in guilders)	% of Dutch GDP	% of total tax income
1831–1840	150,600,000	2.8	31.9
1841–1850	215,600,000	3.6	38.6
1851–1860	289,400,000	3.8	52.6
1861–1870	276,700,000	2.9	44.5
1871–1877	127,200,000	1.7	26.5

Sources: 1831–1870: estimates by Van Zanden and Van Riel, *Strictures of Inheritance*, p. 180, including hidden subsidies. 1870–1877: J. de Jong, *Van Batig Slot naar ereschuld. De discussie over de financiële verhouding tussen Nederland en Indie en de hervorming van de Nederlandse koloniale politiek, 1860–1900* (The Hague, 1989), pp. 133, 262; Jan-Pieter Smits, Edwin Horlings, and Jan Luiten van Zanden, *Dutch GNP and its Components, 1800–1913* (Groningen, 2000), pp. 173, 177.

to the rising real wages of male labourers.[46] This rise in real wages was due not so much to higher *nominal* wages but to the reduction in excises, made possible in part because the Dutch treasury received a major share of its income from the colonies (see Table 1, last column). Of course, reducing indirect taxes on consumables was relatively favourable for the working classes, who had to spend a comparatively large share of their income on foodstuffs and fuels. As one historian has put it: "The surplus from the Indies enabled the government to lower the tax burden for the 'common man' without simultaneously raising it for the bourgeoisie."[47] Although the male breadwinner ideology was still far from being attainable for all working-class households, the development in real wages, which were closely linked to colonial remittances, most probably did create the conditions for a relatively widespread adoption of at least the *ideal* of the married woman at home. As I will argue below, this did not mean that married women stopped working. It did, however, entail a shift from work in formal wage labour and self-employment to more hidden and informal types of labour relations, such as performing wage labour activities in the home, which has often escaped the attention of officials and historians, and eventually, in the first few decades of the twentieth century, to a retreat into unpaid domestic tasks (labour relation 5).

Another effect of colonial economic policies on the Dutch economy in this period was rapid industrialization, which, in turn, affected the work

46. Janneke Plantenga, *Een afwijkend patroon. Honderd jaar vrouwenarbeid in Nederland en (West-) Duitsland* (Amsterdam, 1993), p. 193; Ariadne Schmidt and Elise van Nederveen Meerkerk, "Reconsidering the 'First Male-Breadwinner Economy': Women's Labor Force Participation in the Netherlands, 1600–1900", *Feminist Economics*, 18:4 (2012), pp. 69–96.
47. De Jong, *Van Batig Slot naar ereschuld*, p. 42.

patterns of households in the Netherlands. The semi-governmental Nederlandsche Handel-Maatschappij (Dutch Trading Company), established in 1824 by the Dutch king to monopolize trade with the Netherlands Indies, not only transported the cash crops gained from the Cultivation System on Java back to the Netherlands, it was also responsible for shipping cotton cloth produced in the Netherlands to the Indonesian market. To this end, new cotton factories were set up in the proto-industrial eastern provinces of the Netherlands.[48] Because of the increased monetization of the Javanese economy, Indonesian households shifted from home production of cotton to buying textiles imported from the Netherlands. On the one hand, mechanization caused the rapid decline of hand-spinning, seriously decreasing demand for homespun yarn among both Dutch and Indonesian women and children. On the other, it temporarily drew children and young women to the factories in the Netherlands, affecting wage labour relations in Dutch households.[49] In the late nineteenth century, especially in rural areas, Dutch wives and children accounted for twenty per cent of total household income on average. On top of this, their work in subsistence agriculture also contributed significantly to the family budget.[50]

WORK, THE SOCIAL QUESTION, AND ETHICAL POLICY (1870–1901)

Towards the end of the nineteenth century, the intensification of industrialization in the Netherlands and the social problems it brought about increasingly gained the attention of contemporary publicists and politicians. The labour of Dutch children and women formed an important aspect of the Social Question. Progressive liberals, in particular, started to debate the social consequences of industrialization, and they established their own societies and journals. Their attention was directed primarily towards the labouring classes, to prevent them from falling prey to the emerging labour unrest and socialism.[51] Nevertheless, some social liberals were also genuinely concerned about the miserable plight of many working poor, and they believed that the state should act to alleviate some of the

---

48. Ton de Graaf, *Voor Handel en Maatschappij, Geschiedenis van de Nederlandsche Handel-Maatschappij, 1824–1964* (Amsterdam, 2012), pp. 59–63.
49. Corinne Boter, "Before She Said 'I Do': The Impact of Industrialization on Unmarried Women's Labour Participation 1812–1932", CGEH Working Paper No. 56, http://www.cgeh.nl/sites/default/files/WorkingPapers/cgehwp56_boter.pdf; Cor Smit, *De Leidse Fabriekskinderen. Kinderarbeid, industrialisatie en samenleving in een Hollandse stad, 1800–1914* (Leiden, 2014).
50. Corinne Boter and Elise van Nederveen Meerkerk, "Colonial Extraction and Living Standards: Household Budgets, Women's Work and Consumption in the Netherlands and the Dutch East Indies, ca. 1860–1940", unpublished paper presented at the XVIIth World Economic History Conference, Kyoto, 3–7 August 2015, available from the authors on request.
51. Van Zanden and Van Riel, *Strictures of Inheritance*, p. 245.

worst injustices of industrialization. Although demanding social legislation was a bridge too far for these liberals, they agreed on legislation on one particular issue: child labour.[52] After fierce parliamentary debate, in 1874 Samuel van Houten, one of the progressive liberals active in these circles, succeeded in getting his Child Labour Act (*Kinderwetje*) passed, which prohibited *industrial* work for children younger than twelve. Though far from comprehensive, it constituted the very first piece of Dutch labour legislation.

Apart from child labour, women's work – and especially *married* women's work – was on the agenda of bourgeois efforts to civilize society. One of the goals was to transform married women from the labouring classes into devoted, neat, and frugal housewives, who would lay the foundations of a stable family life, preventing disorderly behaviour such as alcoholism by their husbands or vandalism by their children. Being a proper housewife was thus incompatible with full-time work outdoors.[53] In the 1880s, such private initiatives also gained political weight. Both the women's movement and the emerging liberal, confessional, and social democrat political parties started to get involved in the debate on labour. Their discussions concerned not only the need to protect women and children against exploitation, but, more fundamentally, the suitability of married women for work, both on physical and moral grounds.[54] These concerns led to the 1889 Employment Act, containing regulations against "excessive and hazardous labour by juvenile persons and women". Among other things, this law restricted the working day for women and children under sixteen to a maximum of eleven hours, and prohibited Sunday and night labour for these groups.[55]

During this period, a particular socio-political context had developed in the Netherlands that historians have termed "pillarization". From the 1870s onwards, interest groups emerged organized according to ideology (Catholic, orthodox Protestant, or socialist), establishing associations and organizations in many societal domains. The "pillars" had to collaborate with each other and with the less organized "rest" (liberals and non-orthodox Protestants) because no single group could obtain a political majority. This led to a transformation in the direction of society, from a

---

52. Marco H.D. van Leeuwen, "Armenzorg 1800–1912: Erfenis van de Republiek", in J. van Gerwen and M.H.D. van Leeuwen (eds), *Studies over zekerheidsarrangementen. Risico's, risico-bestrijding en verzekeringen in Nederland vanaf de Middeleeuwen* (Amsterdam, 1998), p. 289.
53. Smit, *Fabriekskinderen*, p. 385.
54. See, for example, Jacques Giele, *Een kwaad leven. De arbeidsenquête van 1887* (Nijmegen, 1981), p. 87; Ulla Jansz, *Denken over sekse in de eerste feministische golf* (Amsterdam, 1990), p. 36; Stefan Dudink, *Deugdzaam liberalisme. Sociaal liberalisme in Nederland 1870–1901* (Amsterdam, 1997), p. 105.
55. Selma Leydesdorff, *Verborgen arbeid – vergeten arbeid: een verkennend onderzoek naar de gevolgen van de arbeidswetgeving voor vrouwen en hun verdringing naar de huisindustrie in Nederland* (Amsterdam, 1975), p. 33.

more liberal to a more "neo-corporatist" tendency, in which all the pillars were to resolve as many of their problems as possible within their own group, with minimal public support. In this new order, the Social Question had a distinctive place. The elites among the newly organized confessional groups – orthodox Protestants and Catholics – in particular, but also the socialists, adopted the strategies of civilizing the working classes that had already been adopted by the liberal bourgeoisie.[56]

Indeed, confessional politics became increasingly important in constituting some form of social security towards the end of the century. With increasing industrialization, the labourer had gained a more important role in the economy and society, and this was also reflected in contemporary theological ideas about labour. Instead of being a curse for sin, originating in Adam and Eve's expulsion from the Garden of Eden, manual labour was increasingly seen as virtuous (at least for the lower social strata). Modern theologians depicted labour as the driving force behind the societal and economic progress that was God's will. On these grounds, ministers and confessional politicians would have to convince the labouring classes that they should not contest their position through strikes or work stoppages,[57] that their superiors ought to promote their best interests, and that the state should set some minimum conditions for monitoring labour protection. To this end, the orthodox Protestant politician Abraham Kuyper had already made quite revolutionary propositions in parliament in 1874, but the time was not yet ripe.[58] Only fifteen years later, the 1889 Employment Act, with its restrictions on women's and children's work, was introduced by the very first Christian administration in the Netherlands, a coalition of Catholics and orthodox Protestants.

Some historians have defined this particular socio-political culture, in which the elites of the diverse pillars aimed to promote the best interests of their less fortunate followers, as "patronizing citizenship".[59] As the historian Elsbeth Locher-Scholten showed in 1981, this specific Dutch political culture may likewise help explain the development of a changing attitude towards the Netherlands East Indies in this period.[60] Politicians

---

56. Van Zanden and Van Riel, *Strictures of Inheritance*, pp. 242–249.

57. Mirjam Fokeline Buitenwerf-van der Molen, *God van vooruitgang: de popularisering van het modern-theologische gedachtegoed in Nederland (1857–1880)* (Hilversum, 2007), pp. 173–177.

58. Jeroen Koch, *Abraham Kuyper, een biografie* (Amsterdam, 2006), p. 154. Kuyper had been a fierce critic of Van Houten's first law against child labour because, in his view, this law was intended merely to regulate labour and not to serve "to protect the child". *Ibid.*, p. 151.

59. Berteke Waaldijk and Susan Legêne, "Ethische politiek in Nederland. Cultureel burgerschap tussen overheersing, opvoeding en afscheid", in Marieke Bloembergen and Remco Raben (eds), *Het koloniale beschavingsoffensief. Wegen naar het nieuwe Indië 1890–1950* (Amsterdam, 2009), p. 187.

60. Elsbeth Locher-Scholten, *Ethiek in fragmenten. Vijf studies over koloniaal denken en doen van Nederlanders in de Indonesische archipel 1877–1942* (Utrecht, 1981).

and social commentators became increasingly aware that the excessive financial revenues derived under the Cultivation System and, after its abolition, the huge tax revenues derived from the Netherlands Indies, had negatively affected the financial state of the Netherlands Indies. The devastating consequences for the welfare of the archipelago and its native inhabitants increasingly raised the indignation of several contemporaries. In a famous article, publicist and lawyer Conrad Theodor van Deventer pleaded for this "debt of honour" (*eereschuld*), which ran into millions of guilders, to be repaid and invested in the well-being of the population, for instance by providing basic education and improving infrastructure.[61]

In the spirit of the age, the second confessional administration of the Netherlands, led by the Protestant Kuyper, implemented the Ethical Policy in the Netherlands Indies at its inauguration in 1901. In her annual speech to parliament, the young Queen Wilhelmina stated that "the Netherlands was to fulfil a moral calling towards the population of these provinces".[62] As Kuyper had already declared in "Our Programme" in 1879, his Anti-Revolutionary Party aspired to a form of "custody" over Dutch overseas possessions, rather than exploitation or colonialism. This custody was to be achieved by the moral uplifting of indigenous populations, in the first place by Christianizing them.[63] The Ethical Policy had two main objectives: improving the welfare of the indigenous population and, at the same time, increasingly subjecting them to the colonial state. This policy followed from the fact that, as a Christian nation, the Netherlands had a duty towards the indigenous inhabitants of the East Indies. This entailed missionary work, the protection of contract labourers, and a general investigation into the "lesser welfare" of the Indonesian population.[64] This attitude towards the common indigenous people had striking similarities with the attempts made in previous decades at civilizing the working classes in the metropole. According to the Anti-Revolutionaries, the labouring classes in the Netherlands also had to be morally uplifted, and protected in ways that resembled practices of custody.[65] Another parallel was that responsibility for their living standard was no longer placed solely on the working poor, and that society and – to a limited degree – the state ought to create vital minimum conditions for its population's welfare, both in the metropole and the colony.

One element of the Ethical Policy was a focus on Javanese households, and particularly the place of women. In some sense, concerns about the

61. C.T. van Deventer, "Een Eereschuld", *De Gids*, 63:3 (1899), pp. 205–252.
62. As cited in S.C. van Randwijck, "Enkele opmerkingen over de houding der zending tegenover de expansie van het Nederlands gezag", *Low Countries Historical Review*, 86:1 (1971), p. 55.
63. Abraham Kuyper, "Ons Program" (5th edn, Hilversum, 1907) [1st edn 1879], pp. 331–332.
64. Koch, *Abraham Kuyper*, p. 462.
65. Kuyper, "Ons Program", pp. 369–370.

position of married women in the Netherlands Indies and their working activities mirrored those about Dutch housewives, but apart from class, ethnicity invigorated paternalism. As noted above, the traditional image of the Javanese woman was that she was very active, both within the household and in the labour market, in contrast to her husband, "the average coolie, who does not work unduly hard".[66] Around 1900, the general image of the Javanese woman was still that "[s]he toils and drudges as long as her powers allow her to".[67] Nevertheless, European notions of the role of Indonesian women had become more differentiated in the course of the nineteenth century. This was due partly to the more intensive encounters between Javanese and Dutch people, the latter having increasingly settled (with their families) in the colony. Partly, however, these new ideas were related to increasing concerns in the Netherlands about the standard of living of the indigenous population. Indonesian women were regarded as important actors in the civilization offensive this new attitude entailed.[68]

Like almost a century earlier, the industriousness of the Javanese population was considered important, but the newest insight on this issue was that the loose family ties on Java supposedly led to a lack of diligence and entrepreneurship, thus hampering the region's economic development. To strengthen these ties and guarantee a more stable family life, the wife needed to function as the centre of the household, and it was recommended that she withdraw from the public domain.[69] Furthermore, Christian missionaries tried to impose "Western" family norms on the households they converted. Their attention was initially directed towards combatting polygamy and convincing Indonesian women that their most important role was to be a housewife and mother, whose primary obligation lay in their household duties.[70]

However, ideal and practice were far apart. For one thing, large differences continued to exist between various social groups. The two lowest – and largest – groups in society were the poor and "common" *desa-vrouwen* (village women). From an early age, they helped their parents in the fields,

66. As ventilated, for example, by P. Levert, *Inheemsche arbeid in de Java-suikerindustrie* (Wageningen, 1934), p. 247.
67. *Onderzoek naar de mindere welvaart der Inlandsche bevolking op Java en Madoera, IXb3, Verheffing van de Inlandsche vrouw* (Batavia, 1914), p. 1.
68. One volume of the extensive research report (comprising twelve volumes, but with its sub-volumes totalling thirty-six volumes) was entitled *Verheffing van de Inlandsche vrouw* [The Elevation of the Indigenous Woman].
69. Elsbeth Locher-Scholten, "Door een gekleurde bril… Koloniale bronnen over vrouwenarbeid op Java in de negentiende en twintigste eeuw", *Jaarboek voor Vrouwengeschiedenis*, 7 (1986), pp. 41–44.
70. Sita van Bemmelen, "Een adatrechtstudie in historisch perspectief. J.C. Vergouwen over Toba-Batakse vrouwen", *Jaarboek voor Vrouwengeschiedenis*, 7 (1986), pp. 71–72.

or watched over their younger siblings. After marriage, they usually continued to work hard on the land or in their own small business, "since only few women are being sufficiently sustained by their husbands".[71] Moreover, they were traditionally active in all kinds of industries, including handweaving, which continued to be of importance until the 1920s, food processing, and woodworking, such as the plaiting of bamboo and rattan.[72] There were also the *santri* women, Muslim women generally from the middle classes who received some form of religious instruction and who usually became obedient and thrifty housewives. Finally, there were the *priyayi* (elite) women, often highly educated and wealthy, who usually outsourced their domestic tasks and were considered lazy and extravagant by Dutch observers.[73]

These are, of course, all stereotypes, but my point is that the rhetoric with regard to Indonesian women continued to revolve around their industriousness (or lack of it). The promotion of Western family values in the Netherlands Indies most prominently affected the role of *priyayi* and Christian women, who were of course minorities in a society largely consisting of Muslim small farmers. However, both economic interests and racist prejudices were too entrenched to allow the cult of "domesticity" to extend to include the majority of women, non-Christian *desa* women, whose labour would actually become more important, as we will see in the next section. As opposed to the *communis opinio* on Dutch women, the idea that Indonesian women should not be performing work outdoors at all was uncommon. Unlike in the metropole, satisfactory protective labour legislation and education for indigenous women and children were not yet considered necessary in the colony.

FURTHER LEGISLATION AND THE "MALE BREADWINNER SOCIETY" (1901–1940)

Not only in the Netherlands Indies, but also in the Netherlands, ideology and practice sometimes diverged. The 1874 Child Labour Act, for instance, covered only industrial labour by children up to the age of eleven, and the agricultural and service sectors were long exempt from regulation. The 1889 Employment Act, too, made exceptions, for instance for Sunday work for women in dairy processing. Also, even after the Kuyper administration had enacted the first law on compulsory schooling for children aged up to twelve, many children stayed at home, for instance to help on the family farm, especially in seasons when their labour was dearly needed.[74] In the

71. *Verheffing van de Inlandsche vrouw*, p. 3.
72. J.E. Jasper and Mas Pirngadie, *De inlandsche kunstnijverheid in Nederlandsch Indië. Vol. I, Het vlechtwerk* (The Hague, 1912).
73. *Verheffing van de Inlandsche vrouw*, pp. 3–5.
74. Nevertheless, there were large regional differences, resulting from the different agricultural systems (for example, capital vs labour intensive). See Willemien Schenkeveld, "Het werk van

early 1920s, just after the minimum age for child labour had been raised to fourteen years, many parents complained to the Labour Inspectorate that this law obliged their children to remain at home idle for two years: they no longer had to go to school, but they were not yet allowed to work.[75] The archives of the Labour Inspectorate show that, despite society's changing norms, child labour was still very much a feature.[76] As late as 1928, for example, the Director General of Labour, C. Zaalberg, complained: "in industrial centres one sees the questionable phenomenon of housefathers being unable to find work and living off the earnings of their daughters".[77]

Likewise, work by married women had not completely disappeared by the beginning of the twentieth century. Although the official censuses show a clear decline in the participation of women in the Dutch labour market, particularly in the category of registered gainful employment by married women, part of this decline must be ascribed to under-registration of wives who worked in the family business or in domestic industry.[78] In the 1910s, a study and exhibition focused attention on the situation in Dutch domestic industry, in which many women and children worked part-time. It is hard to estimate their numbers, in part owing to shortcomings in the study, shortcomings that the Director General of Labour at the time, H.A. van Ysselsteyn, acknowledged.[79] We do know for certain, however, that many women performed paid work at home, rolling cigarettes, wrapping sweets, and canning vegetables for example. Interestingly, these women also produced for the colonies. They made trimmings for sale in the Netherlands Indies, but sometimes also fabricated military accessories, such as badges and "embroidered grenades".[80]

Still, the male breadwinner model had already taken root in the Netherlands by the turn of the twentieth century. For instance, the official participation rate of women older than sixteen had declined from twenty-four per cent in 1849 to seventeen per cent in 1899, which was very low compared with other Western European countries at the time.[81] Because under-registration was a reality in other countries as well, we can safely conclude that women's participation was comparatively low in the

kinderen in de Nederlandse landbouw 1800–1913", *Tijdschrift voor Sociale en Economische Geschiedenis*, 5:2 (2008), pp. 28–54.

75. NA, Arbeidsinspectie, inv. no. 1746, various petitions.

76. As is also claimed by Smit, *Fabriekskinderen*, p. 484.

77. NA, Arbeidsinspectie, inv. no. 267, letter from C. Zaalberg to Jac. van Ginneken, 1 August 1928.

78. Schmidt and Van Nederveen Meerkerk, "Reconsidering", pp. 80, 82.

79. NA, Arbeidsinspectie, inv. no. 331, letter from H.A. van Ysselsteyn to Prof. N.W. Posthumus, 28 December 1912.

80. NA, Arbeidsinspectie, inv. no. 334, documents concerning labour circumstances in domestic industry in general.

81. Schmidt and Van Nederveen Meerkerk, "Reconsidering", p. 81.

Figure 2. Postcard promoting that mother's place is in the home, not in the factory. *Katholiek Documentatie Centrum Nijmegen. Used with permission.*

Table 2. *Legislation on child labour and schooling, 1901–1921*

Year	Type of law	Most important coverage
1901	Compulsory schooling	six years' compulsory primary education for children under 13
1911	Employment	Minimum age raised to 13; protective measures for children under 17
1919	Employment	Minimum age raised to 14; protective measures for children under 18
1921	Compulsory schooling	seven years' compulsory primary education

Source: Based on Smit, *Fabriekskinderen*, p. 11.

Netherlands around 1900.[82] Moreover, the percentage of *married* women with an occupation recorded in the census was only slightly over four per cent, which is low however you look at it.[83] An increasing proportion of the female population had thus either switched to performing economic activities in the home, either as wage earners or self-employed (labour relations 14 and 12b respectively), or were able to become full-time housewives (labour relation 5).

Also, the first few decades of the twentieth century witnessed further legislation in an effort to reduce the participation of children in the labour market and, perhaps more importantly, keep them in school longer (see Table 2).

Further labour legislation in the Netherlands in this period again targeted women's work. In 1937, the conservative Catholic Secretary of State Carl Romme even proposed legislation to prohibit all work by married women. Eventually, his bill was watered down to apply only to female state employees. The documents drawn up by the committee preparing the bill provide interesting information on the discussions between conservative, confessional, liberal, and socialist members, most of whom did not disagree so much on the "true calling" of the married woman, but on the question of whether the state ought to prescribe this ideal or leave it up to households themselves.[84]

In the Netherlands Indies, developments were very different. As we know, the work of married women outside the household and family farm, for instance as wage labourers on tobacco or rubber plantations, was perhaps frowned upon, but it was never intended to be eradicated. The lobby of important businessmen and plantation owners, making widespread use

---

82. Hettie Pott-Buter, *Facts and Fairy Tales about Female Labor, Family and Fertility: A Seven-Country Comparison 1850–1990* (Amsterdam, 1993), p. 31.
83. Centraal Bureau voor de Statistiek [hereafter, CBS], *Uitkomsten der achtste algemeene tienjaarlijksche Volkstelling van een en dertig december 1899* (The Hague, 1902), p. 186.
84. NA, Arbeidsinspectie, inv. no. 271.

Figure 3. Women picking tea leaves for the Tjimoelang tea company at Buitenzorg. *Collections KITLV. Used with permission.*

of "cheap and compliant" labourers, was simply too powerful. Many sugar and coffee plantations employed not only indigenous men, but also their wives and children. A sample of 400 plantation workers shows that, on average, seventy per cent of their wives also worked independently of their husbands for wages in all kinds of manual agricultural labour, accounting for an average of almost thirty per cent of household income.[85] Thus, although ever since the introduction of the Ethical Policy the advantages of the role of women as a stable factor within the household had been stressed, economic incentives to employ them outside the house were too strong. Moreover, as many plantation owners allowed whole households to live on the plantation, they perhaps thought they could hit two birds with one stone.

A similarly ambivalent attitude towards the work of Indonesian children prevailed. As we have seen, work by children, especially under the age of twelve, had been a matter of growing concern and intense debate in the Netherlands in the second half of the nineteenth century, with legislation being introduced in 1874. In contrast, a total disregard for the issue prevailed in the Netherlands Indies. Interestingly, while the minimum age for child labour in the Netherlands had been raised to fourteen in 1919

85. Boter and Van Nederveen Meerkerk, "Colonial Extraction and Living Standards".

(see Table 2), in 1926 it was set at twelve for Indonesian children. This becomes clear moreover if we look at school enrolment rates. By 1900, ninety-five per cent of all Dutch children younger than twelve attended school, whereas only 0.5 per cent of all Indonesian children received schooling.[86] As part of the Ethical Policy, from around 1900 the colonial government increasingly invested in a schooling system for indigenous children. However, this was a highly hierarchical system, with "European" schools being accessible only to children from the elites, "standard" schools aiming at middle-class children, and *desa* (village) schools being visited mainly by children from lower social groups. Although the indigenous schooling system was in principle open to both boys and girls, it was meant primarily to provide boys with the necessary education to enable them to maintain a family, or – for the higher classes – to prepare them for a career within the colonial administration. Moreover, most indigenous parents objected to their daughters being in the same classroom as boys.[87] These obstructions are reflected in reported school enrolments rates for the period 1909–1922, which indicate that girls constituted only about eight per cent of the total number of pupils.[88] Likewise, the scarce data available on literacy rates also reveal low family investment in the education of girls: according to the 1930 census only 2.2 per cent of indigenous women could read and write, while 10.8 per cent of indigenous men were registered as literate.[89] Among Dutch officials and citizens, this was not perceived as a problem, and it was believed that educating a small number of *priyayi* women would suffice to disseminate knowledge and values further to ordinary women (*desa* women or *volksvrouwen*).[90]

From the 1920s onwards, the issue of restricting female and child labour in the colony was increasingly debated in the Dutch parliament following severe criticism by the international community of Dutch reluctance to implement legislation restricting female night work and child labour in the Netherlands Indies. In 1926, the International Labour Office (ILO) called on the Netherlands to introduce labour legislation in the colonies. The 1930 census of Java and Madura lists almost thirty per cent of all married women with a *registered* occupation, predominantly in agriculture and industry. Compared with the low official figures for the Netherlands (where only

86. White, "Childhood, Work and Education", pp. 105–109.
87. Frances Gouda, "Teaching Indonesian Girls in Java and Bali, 1900–1942: Dutch Progressives, the Infatuation with 'Oriental' Refinement, and 'Western' Ideas about Proper Womanhood", *Women's History Review*, 4:1 (1995), p. 27.
88. J.E.A.M. Lelyveld, "…Waarlijk geen overdaad, doch een dringende eisch…" Koloniaal onderwijs en onderwijsbeleid in Nederlands-Indië 1893–1942 (Ph.D. dissertation, Utrecht University, 1992), pp. 83, 152.
89. CBS, *Volkstelling 1930 Vol. VIII* (The Hague, 1932–1934), p. 29.
90. Gouda, "Teaching Indonesian Girls", p. 28.

six per cent of all married women were recorded as having an occupation in 1930), this percentage was very high.[91]

To give an impression of the type of work Indonesian women and girls performed, I have listed the five occupations most frequently reported in the 1930 Census, both for married and unmarried women. Not surprisingly, given the agrarian nature of Javanese society at that time, most women worked in small-scale agriculture. However, compared with Indonesian men, a much larger proportion of women with an occupational record worked in the industrial and service sectors, most notably in food and textile production and retailing. For unmarried women, domestic service was quite common (see Table 3). It should be noted, however, that, like the Dutch census, the Netherlands Indies census registered only what the authorities considered to be "gainful employment": those types of labour that generated "compensation (be it in money, or in kind), [excluding] mere refreshments".[92] Thus women working in subsistence agriculture (labour relation 4b) or performing communal agricultural services (labour relation 7) were not included in the statistics.

Proponents of work by Indonesian women and children stated that indigenous culture and traditions made women's hard physical labour customary, and that children were better off working than being idle.[93] These opinions were voiced primarily by Western entrepreneurs and liberal politicians, who viewed Indonesian women and children as a source of cheap labour and opposed state intervention. But it was not only the business community that stressed the inherent differences between Dutch and Indonesian women. In 1925, publicist Henri van der Mandere wrote:

> It is self-evident that women in Western society are excluded from hazardous and tough labour [...]. Women's position in Indonesian society is incomparable to that of the Dutch woman. Whereas manual labour is an exception in the Netherlands, it is the rule here; there are even regions where it follows from *adat*[94] that almost all work is done by women.[95]

This quote indicates that it was not only considered "natural" for Indonesian women to work, the inherent differences between Indonesian and Dutch women also made it self-evident that the latter were to be protected from hazardous work. This is a fine example of what Ann Stoler and Frederick Cooper have called "the grammar of difference".[96]

91. Own calculations based on CBS, *Volkstelling 1930, Vol. III* (1934), pp. 94–95.
92. *Ibid., Vol. I*, p. 82; *Vol. II*, p. 84.
93. Locher-Scholten, "Female Labour in Twentieth Century Java"; White, "Childhood, Work and Education", pp. 110–111.
94. Indigenous customs and traditions – EvNM.
95. H.C.G.J. van der Mandere, "Internationale wetgeving en Indië", *De Indische Gids*, 1 (1925), p. 25. I am grateful to Nynke Dorhout for providing me with this quote.
96. Stoler and Cooper, "Between Metropole and Colony", p. 3.

Table 3. *Five most frequently recorded occupations for married and unmarried women, Java and Madura, 1930*

Rank	Branch	No. of married women	Share of total (%)	Rank	Branch	No. of unmarried women	Share of total (%)
1	Small-scale farming	934,297	35.4	1	Small-scale farming	886,538	42.0
2	Textile production	325,549	12.3	2	Trade in foodstuffs	139,053	6.6
3	Trade in foodstuffs	315,859	12.0	3	Domestic service	132,081	6.3
4	Foodstuff production	199,349	7.6	4	Textile production	130,326	6.2
5	Woodwork production	159,889	6.1	5	Foodstuff production	94,631	4.5

Source: CBS, *Volkstelling 1930, Vol. III*, pp. 94–95.

CONCLUSION

This article has analysed the role of the state as a regulator and arbiter in changing labour relations, focusing on the work of women and children from the perspective of the colonial connections between the Netherlands and the Netherlands Indies. During the nineteenth century, the Dutch state increasingly intervened in social affairs, both in the metropole and the colonies. I have shown that the *principles* underlying changes towards further interventionism were quite similar in both parts of the empire at least until the end of the nineteenth century. However, the *scope* and *effects* of intervention differed tremendously in the Netherlands and the Netherlands Indies. The explanatory framework I have used for this "simultaneousness of the non-simultaneous" is the different ideological attitudes towards the working classes in the Netherlands and the Netherlands Indies, which seem to have further diverged in the course of the nineteenth century. In the early nineteenth century, combatting idleness and encouraging the poor to work was still on the agenda in the metropole as well as in the colony. In fact, it may be stated that Dutch elites tended to view the working poor in the Netherlands as "a foreign country" almost as much as they did the Javanese commoners. Thus, similar initiatives were taken in 1818 and 1830, respectively, to reform the population's labour ethic, not coincidentally by one and the same man, Johannes van den Bosch, and supported by King William I.

Apart from their initiator, there were several other striking parallels between the peat colonies of the Maatschappij van Weldadigheid and the Cultivation System. Both were state-supported, focusing on raising market production in the agricultural sector. In both projects, the objective was to educate "lazy" paupers in order to transform them into thrifty workers, and a high degree of social engineering, and even force, was occasionally used. Also, in both cases it was expected that women and children would contribute to the family economy, although most commonly on the family farm. A major difference between the two initiatives was their scope: although several thousand Dutch families went to the peat colonies, it remained a peripheral phenomenon, and from the beginning many workers considered it to be a penal colony, which it would eventually turn into. Conversely, the Cultivation System would have tremendous effects on Javanese society and labour relations there. Moreover, at the same time, as I have argued here, the gains from the Cultivation System and other extractive colonial policies influenced economic development and labour relations in the Netherlands.

Important effects on the Javanese economy included rapid monetization, and an increased workload by women and children, in subsistence agriculture but also in self-employed and waged labour. The role of women in subsistence agriculture had traditionally been large, but the forced shift by men towards cash-crop cultivation made this role increasingly important. More importantly, the monetization and commodification of the entire economy, in which the Cultivation System played a decisive role, increased opportunities for women to sell their products in the market or to perform wage labour on plantations or for neighbours. Simultaneously, the state-subsidized imports of Dutch textiles into Java stimulated the take-off of industrialization in the Netherlands, especially in traditional proto-industrial areas, where the factories were looking primarily for cheap wage labourers, such as young children and women. While in a totally different – urbanized and industrializing – context than in the Netherlands Indies, this did initially (up to about the 1880s) raise the proportion of young as well as married women in the labour force. However, simultaneously, a counter effect was achieved by the enormous flows of capital from the trade in Javanese cash crops, and other taxes, into the Dutch treasury. These cash flows allowed for excise reforms in the metropole, contributing directly to a rise in male wages, implying the foundation of the financial realization of the breadwinner–homemaker ideal for an increasing number of households in the Netherlands. Even though for most working-class households this goal became attainable only in the first few decades of the twentieth century, from the last decade of the nineteenth century it motivated married women to switch from labour outside the home to economic activities in the private sphere.

In the same period, industrialization and the growing importance of wage labour, as well as the "pillarization" in which class distinctions in the Netherlands were partly overruled by ideological differences, led to a different take on the position of work and labourers in the metropole. Although the Social Question was born primarily out of concerns about labour unrest, a growing number of contemporaries were genuinely worried about the well-being of the lower classes. This apprehension was further induced by the rise of confessional parties from the 1870 onwards; they were not opposed to a mild form of state regulation, and even legislation. Though the 1874 Child Labour Act had been drawn up by a liberal, even at the time some Protestants, such as Kuyper, believed it did not go far enough.

While civilizing the working classes was not a confessional prerogative – it was an objective shared by liberal and socialist elites alike – the Christian parties gave it their own twist. Gender played an increasingly important role in the debate after the issue of work by very young children had been resolved by the 1874 legislation. The moral concerns regarding men and women working together in factories, and particularly the central role of the clean and thrifty housewife within the labouring household, were central issues in the debate. Throughout the entire period, we can observe a shift among married women from wage and self-employed labour to more informal paid work and subsistence agriculture around 1900, and subsequently to the status of housewives (labour relation 5) by the late 1930s.

Christian values also played a role in the development of the Ethical Policy in the Netherlands Indies, symbolizing the moral responsibility towards the underdeveloped population of the archipelago. The Ethical Policy followed from a broader discontent that had been growing under the Dutch elites, due to the increasing realization that the Dutch state and economy profited immensely from the gains made from the colony, and that the indigenous population suffered from this extraction. However, after its implementation, the Ethical Policy was concerned primarily with the Christian mission and with definitively making the Javanese subjects of the Dutch state. Although according to the ethical rhetoric Indonesian women were crucial in modelling indigenous family life according to "modern" Western values, in practice the labour of women and children – especially for the lower classes and farmers – was not explicitly opposed, or even protected against. Moreover, the ideals of domesticity would not have been as financially attainable as they were in the metropole, simply because the taxes and profits drained from the colony were too high to allow higher living standards for the majority of the indigenous population. Only a small minority, comprising elite and higher middle-class Indonesian women, could afford to adjust to live up to "Western" ideals of domesticity.[97]

Unlike the Dutch working classes, Javanese households thus remained "a foreign country" to the elites in the Netherlands. While labour protection as well as education became increasingly available to Dutch women and children in the beginning of the twentieth century, these provisions were scarcely extended to their Indonesian counterparts. Conveniently, within the context of the decline of coerced labour on Java, women and children formed a source of cheap labour that entrepreneurs in the Netherlands Indies wished to employ. Until well into the 1920s, politicians and contemporary observers utilized a rhetoric of innate culture and traditions, not only to legitimize the absence of social legislation in the colony but also to stress that these inherent differences justified the fact that Dutch women and children were indeed protected by law. Moreover, whereas in the Netherlands there was a state body to counteract possible excesses (the Labour Inspectorate), no such institution had been set up in the Netherlands Indies, and ultimately the ILO had to monitor the implementation of social policies in the Dutch colony. A "grammar of difference" moulded the state's intervention, in the colony as well as the metropole.

---

97. Bela Kashyap, "Who's in Charge, the Government, the Mistress, or the Maid? Tracing the History of Domestic Workers in Southeast Asia", in Dirk Hoerder, Elise van Nederveen Meerkerk, and Silke Neunsinger (eds), *Towards a Global History of Domestic and Caregiving Workers* (Leiden and Boston, 2015), p. 351.

IRSH 61 (2016), Special Issue, pp. 165–185 doi:10.1017/S0020859016000390
© 2016 Internationaal Instituut voor Sociale Geschiedenis

The Labour Recruitment of Local Inhabitants as *Rōmusha* in Japanese-Occupied South East Asia*

Takuma Melber

Karl Jaspers Centre for Advanced Transcultural Studies
Voßstraße 2, Building 4400, 69115 Heidelberg, Germany

E-mail: takuma_@gmx.de

Abstract: During World War II, Japan, as occupying power, mobilized thousands of labourers in South East Asia. While the history of Allied prisoners of war (POWs) deployed as forced labourers on the Burma-Siam "Death Railway" is well known, the coercive labour recruitment of local inhabitants as so-called *rōmusha* has, until today, remained an almost completely untold story. This article introduces *rōmusha*, with a particular focus on the Burma-Siam Railway, and presents the methods used by the occupying powers to recruit local inhabitants in Java, Malaya, and Singapore, initially as volunteers, and increasingly using force. We look, too, at the tactics and strategies of avoidance the locals were able to deploy. The article offers insights into the poor working conditions on the railway, discusses the body count, and gives an idea of the huge impact of the forced labour recruitment not only in economic terms, but also in terms of the effect it had on the social structure at both the micro and macro levels.

INTRODUCTION

When seen in the context of the whole of human history, it is obvious that the four and a half years of the Japanese occupation of South East Asia between 1942 and summer 1945 were a short period. Prior to this, Japan, as the new imperialist player in Asia, had annexed an area of North East Asia (Korea, Taiwan, and Chinese territories) larger than itself. For decades, historians have been debating whether or not and to what extent the Japanese empire through its imperialism caused postwar changes in South East Asian societies, although it is beyond question that World War II was a decisive turning point in the region's history, for until the outbreak of war almost all South East Asian countries had been ruled by Western colonial empires. However, before the independent nation states in South East Asia emerged after World War II, the empire of Japan conquered the region and controlled it during the war years. The war, conducted as a "total war", had a

---

* Personal names of Japanese individuals are given according to the Japanese style of family name followed by given name.

huge social impact and deeply affected labour relations not only in Japan itself, but also in the occupied South East Asian countries, as especially during the second part of the occupation Japan felt compelled to mobilize labour on a large scale. The first months of the Pacific War, which began with the surprise attack on Pearl Harbor, proved to be very successful for Japan's army and navy, and the fall of Singapore on 15 February 1942 and the attendant surrender of British forces there was the climax of the Japanese invasion of the Malay Peninsula. As part of their Burma Campaign, Japanese troops captured Rangoon on 8 March 1942 and very quickly occupied all the islands of the Dutch East Indies. However, the naval Battle of Midway at the beginning of June 1942 proved to be the turning point of the war, as it marked the moment that Japan gradually began to lose control of the Pacific.

Japan's war leaders saw that the military situation in the Asia-Pacific theatre was steadily deteriorating, along with the food supply, which was now going from bad to worse. The Japanese empire and its South East Asian possessions were economically isolated from international trade, and Japan's economic situation worsened from the middle of 1942. The military administration adopted drastic measures in their attempts to solve the problem of shortages of food and essential goods, as well as to guarantee the production of war materials to strengthen the domestic economy of the so-called Greater East Asia Co-Prosperity Sphere (*Daitōakyōeiken*). Further, the aim of Japan's leadership was to continue to wage war and, of course, to maintain wartime logistics, such as the movement of raw materials essential for the war effort. In addition, because of Japan's steadily worsening military situation fortifications were constructed in the occupied zone in preparation for an Allied invasion.[1] With the aim of improving productivity as well as to exploit available manpower for military and economic needs, Japan increasingly conducted "total mobilization" of its society, right up to the end of the war. For example, Japanese women were set to work in factories, replacing men who were then conscripted to the battlefronts in the Asia-Pacific region.[2] In contrast to Western countries at war – especially Great Britain, where, from an early stage, the mobilization of women had been conducted highly systemically and on a large scale – Japan began to

1. Paul H. Kratoska, *Nihon senryōka ni okeru tōnanajia no keizai jōkyō* [The Economic Conditions in Japanese-Occupied South East Asia], in Kyeungdal Chō *et al.* (eds), *Higashiajia kingendai tsūshi* [East Asian Contemporary History], vol. 6: *Ajia taiheiyō sensō to "daitōakyōeiken", 1935–1945* [The Asia-Pacific War and the "Greater East Asia Co-Prosperity Sphere", 1935–1945] (Tokyo, 2011), pp. 260–280, 269f.; Shigeru Satō, *"Rōmusha"*, in Peter Post (ed.), *The Encyclopedia of Indonesia in the Pacific War* (Leiden, 2010), pp. 197–201, 197.
2. For the role of women in Japan's war economy, see Thomas R. Havens, "Women and War in Japan, 1937–45", *American Historical Review*, 80:4 (1975), pp. 913–934, 913ff.; Regine Mathias, "Women and the War Economy in Japan", in Erich Pauer (ed.), *Japan's War Economy* (London, 1999), pp. 65–81, 66ff.

enlist women as labourers for the war economy comparatively late. The conscription of female labourers in Japan did not begin before 1943 and was intensified only from 1944 onwards, when deteriorating war conditions and the shortage of labour had made it unavoidable, rather a last resort. But diverse objections prevailed against female labourers in wartime Japan generally. From the state's point of view, the Japanese woman should not play a role as a productive human resource, for her role was motherhood, its value being in the production literally of *man*power.

But the consequences of the war were not limited to the Japanese homeland. The impact of the war as well as the influence of Japan as the occupying power was huge on labour relations in the occupied territories too. Generally speaking, from 1942 to 1945 the whole economy of South East Asia was subordinated to the principal aim of the imperialist state, which was to win the war at all costs. Initially, the Japanese empire had planned to build an Asian economic bloc, under Japanese leadership, of course. The occupied North East Asian territories were to be developed as a centre of industrial production, while South East Asia was to function as a base for the supply of raw materials and as a market for industrial goods.[3] Japan's short-term plan intended to cut off its enemies from South East Asia's natural resources – vital for strategic purposes – as well as to secure and exploit them for itself.

However, Japan's industry had to align itself to the war effort and US submarines kept up a solid campaign against Japanese cargo ships. For that reason, the Japanese empire was unable to establish a real exchange of South East Asian raw materials for the production of goods in Japan, on the one hand, and of consumer goods from Japan for sale in South East Asia, on the other. So what had originally been planned as a relationship – however naturally unequal – of exchange became in the main one-way traffic along a road of exploitation.[4] The occupying power looked on South East Asia purely as a source of war resources – meaning not only raw materials such as petroleum, rubber, tin, bauxite, or lumber, but also the "human resource" of the local inhabitants.

Accordingly, following its aim to exploit South East Asia's resources to the greatest degree, Japan's armed forces tried to systematize one quite specific kind of labour by mobilizing forced labour. Forced labour existed alongside other types of labour, such as contract work or normal wage labour, but was considered indispensable by Japan's authorities owing to economic necessity and for strategic military reasons. The outcome of the

3. Shigeru Satō, "Relocation of Labor and the *Rōmusha* Issue", in Post, *The Encyclopedia of Indonesia in the Pacific War*, pp. 245–260, 253.
4. Norman G. Owen, "Economic and Social Change", in Nicholas Tarling (ed.), *The Cambridge History of Southeast Asia, Volume Two: The Nineteenth and Twentieth Centuries* (Cambridge [etc.], 1992), pp. 467–527, 469.

Battle of Midway led Tokyo to decide to transform conditions in South East Asia, especially in the last two years of Japanese occupation, and one of the changes was the forced recruitment of *rōmusha*,[5] in other words, the local inhabitants of the South East Asian territories. The prime function of the *rōmusha* would be to do manual labour.

This article, then, will focus first on the recruitment by the Japanese of the local inhabitants of South East Asia, particularly Malaya and Singapore, for forced labour, but will also explain how some locals were able to avoid recruitment. The continued general lack of data makes research on *rōmusha* rather difficult: "the exact scale of mobilization [of labour] for military and civilian purposes cannot be ascertained, as the official statistics are incomplete and also because there was much unofficial mobilization by both the military and the Military Administration".[6] However, by looking at the forced deployment of indigenous workers from Malaya, Singapore, and Java for manual labour, this article presents a very important part of the mobilization of forced labour during the Japanese occupation of South East Asia in general, and forms an addendum to the much better researched fate of Allied POWs as forced labourers. And we shall see how the case of the *rōmusha* is a simultaneous example of how Japan shaped labour during the war for its own imperialist ends.

---

5. Satō defined the term "*rōmusha*" as follows: "*rōmusha* is a Japanese word meaning an unskilled laborer who carries out temporary construction work. Such a laborer typically is a single male, lives in laborers' quarters as long as his employment lasts, and moves on when it ends, looking for another job". Satō, "*Rōmusha*", p. 197. In her classic work on the history of *rōmusha*, Kurasawa underlined the fact that in Indonesia the term "*rōmusha*" does not mean just "labourer". *Rōmusha* were "persons who were recruited by force during the Japanese occupation period to do hard physical work". Aiko Kurasawa, *Nihon senryōka no Jawa nōson no henyō* [Transformation in the Rural Areas of Japanese-Occupied Java] (Tokyo, 1992), p. 180. In the pre-occupation period, the term "coolie" (Dutch *koelie*) was commonly used for day labourers or contract workers. The Chinese transcription of "coolie" (苦力) included the characters 苦 (*kū*), which can be translated as "suffering", "pain", or "sorrow", and 力 (*li*), for (physical) strength or labour. Because of this quite negative connotation, the Japanese occupying force introduced the term "*rōmusha* (労務者)", using the characters 労 (*rō*) to mean "work", "labour", 務 (*mu*) meaning "duty", "service", and 者 (*sha*) meaning "person". Shigeru Satō, *War, Nationalism and Peasants: Java under the Japanese Occupation, 1942–1945* (Armonk, NY, 1994), p. 154, fn. 1. According to Lieutenant Colonel Sugiyama, it was forbidden for Japanese soldiers on the Burma-Siam Railway to use the term "coolie". One alternative to "*rōmusha*" was the neutral term "*kōin*" (工員), meaning a factory worker. But the use of the term "*kōin*" caused problems on the Burmese side: "But, since the [Japanese] soldiers who come from the north of the Kanto district pronounce 'i' as 'e', 'Koin' became 'Koen'. This word 'Koen' is somewhat similar to Burmese 'KOE', 'dog', which at times gave rise to their [Burmese forced labourers'] feelings of animosity towards us." In Paul H. Kratoska (ed.), *The Thailand-Burma Railway, 1942–1946: Documents and Selected Writings*, vol. 4 (London, 2006), p. 71.
6. Satō, "Relocation of Labor", p. 251.

FORCED LABOUR DURING THE JAPANESE OCCUPATION

By February 1942, the Japanese investigation committee for the inspection of all southern territories had already created the expectation in Singapore that Java should become the key source of "human labour", presumably because of its relatively large population and its convenient central location in South East Asia. On 10 July 1942, the Japanese army and navy together arranged the transport of *rōmusha* from Java, which was under the administration of the Japanese army, to territories controlled by the Japanese navy. At a later conference, the directors responsible for *rōmusha* affairs within the Southern Army declared Java a key source for the supply of *rōmusha*. Finally, in September 1944, the provisional House of Councillors in Tokyo ordered an increase in their supply.[7]

Forced labour on the Burma-Siam Railway (*Taimentetsudō*) has remained the most famous example of its use in Japanese-occupied South East Asia. Construction of the 415-kilometre-long railway connection between Ban Pong in Siam and Thanbyuzayat in the south-east of Burma began in July 1942. The Japanese occupying power hoped to utilize the Burma-Siam Railway both to avoid having to transport supplies by dangerous sea routes from its South East Asian territories to the front in Burma, and ultimately to link Bangkok in Siam and Rangoon in Burma.[8]

In spring 1943, the Japanese 29th Army was required to supply contingents of labourers for the Burma-Siam Railway.[9] Apart from 92,000 Burmese *rōmusha*, 78,204 forced labourers from Malaya, mainly indigenous Malays and Tamils, made up the second largest group on the "Death Railway". Seventy thousand of those 78,204 Malayan *rōmusha* were recruited and sent to the railway between April and September 1943, and approximately 41 per cent of those 70,000 died as a consequence.[10]

It must be mentioned that systematic large-scale recruitment of *rōmusha* on Java began only after completion of the Burma-Siam Railway, which was built between July 1942 and October 1943.[11] As is still the case today,

---

7. For the decisions concerning the labour mobilization see Kenichi Gotō, *Nihon senryōki indoneshia kenkyū* [Research on the Japanese Occupation Period in Indonesia] (Tokyo, 1989), p. 99, and Satō, *War, Nationalism and Peasants*, p. 156.

8. Toshiharu Yoshikawa, "Taimentetsudō" [The Burma-Siam Railway], in Chō *et al.*, *Higashiajia kingendai tsūshi*, p. 42f.

9. Michiko Nakahara, "Nihon senryōki eiryōmaraya ni okeru *rōmusha*dōin – taimentetsudō no bāi" [The Mobilization of *Rōmusha* in Japanese-Occupied British Malaya: The Case of the Burma-Siam Railway], in Aiko Kurasawa (ed.), *Tōnanajiashi no naka no nihon senryō* [The Japanese Occupation in South East Asian History] (Tokyo, 2001), pp. 171–198, 178.

10. The National Archives of the UK, Public Record Office, London [hereafter, PRO], WO 203–5823, SEATIC Bulletin No. 246: Burma-Siam Railway, 8 October 1946.

11. Satō, *War, Nationalism and Peasants*, p. 155.

seventy per cent of the population of Indonesia (seventy million people) lived on Java,[12] hence Java becoming the primary source of forced labourers during the Japanese occupation. It is, therefore, no surprise that the research community tends to use the generic term *rōmusha* more or less as a synonym for forced labourers from Java.

In total, between 200,000 and 300,000 forced labourers were sent from Java to other territories in Japanese-occupied South East Asia – 31,000 of them to Malaya alone.[13] The majority, more than forty per cent, of those Javanese *rōmusha* sent overseas arrived on the island of Sumatra, which lies between the Malay Peninsula and Java. During the first year of the Japanese occupation from 28 March 1942 to April 1943, Sumatra was a single administrative and political unit with Malaya.[14] According to a Dutch intelligence report, a total of about 120,000 Javanese and Chinese *rōmusha* were transported from Java to Sumatra during the Japanese occupation.[15]

Japanese primary sources reveal that the Japanese 29th Army in Malaya requested 55,477 forced labourers from Java between April 1944 and March 1945. Their request was granted by Southern Army Headquarters in Singapore, which sent 22,100 *rōmusha* from Java to the Malay Peninsula.[16] It seems that, faced with dwindling powers, the occupying force could manage only a limited exploitation of that source of *rōmusha*.

METHODS OF RECRUITMENT

The Southern Army and the Japanese military administration in Malaya (*Marē Gunseikanbu*) demanded the recruitment of 100,000 labourers to be

---

12. *Idem*, "Relocation of Labor", p. 245.

13. Kurasawa, *Nihon senryōka no Jawa nōson no henyō*, p. 180ff.; Remco Raben, "Indonesian *Rōmusha* and Coolies under Naval Administration: The Eastern Archipelago, 1942–45", in Paul H. Kratoska (ed.), *Asian Labor in the Wartime Japanese Empire: Unknown Histories* (Armonk, NY, 2005), pp. 197–212, 197; Satō, *War, Nationalism and Peasants*, p. 158f. Besides the 300,000 Javanese forced labourers who were sent abroad, many Javanese, too, were impressed for forced labour on Java. Kratoska, *Nihon senryōka ni okeru tōnanajia no keizai jōkyō*, p. 269. Examples for railway construction work, shipbuilding, and mining can be found in Satō, *War, Nationalism and Peasants*, p. 179ff.

14. Satō, "*Rōmusha*", p. 201.

15. NIOD Instituut voor oorlogs-, holocaust- en genocidestudies, Indische Collectie, Amsterdam [hereafter, NIOD], Netherlands Forces Intelligence Service (NEFIS), Dept. I – Section II (Economic Technical Department): Report concerning data in the hands of the above-mentioned Section of NEFIS concerning the number of romusha's outside Java, March 1946.

16. The notes of Mori Fumio (Mori Fumio, Gunsei Shubo = 森文雄、軍政手簿) are available in the *Bōeikenkyūjo* (防衛研究所), The National Institute for Defence Studies, Tokyo. The statistic can be found in Kurasawa, *Nihon senryōka no Jawa nōson no henyō*, p. 232, as well as in Satō, *War, Nationalism and Peasants*, p. 159. Miyamoto Shizuo, staff officer of the 16th Army on Java, mentioned the same number: 22,100 *rōmusha* were sent from Java to Malaya in 1944. Shizuo Miyamoto, *Jawa shūsen shoriki* [Records at the End of the War in Java] (Tokyo, 1973), p. 41.

Table 1. *Transport of* rōmusha *from Java to other Japanese-occupied territories (1944).*

Destination	Number
Malaya	22,100
Sumatra	92,700
Northern Borneo	17,000
(Lesser) Sunda Islands[17]	6,000
Sulawesi (formerly known as Celebes)	20,000
Reserve	7,200
Subtotal	*165,000*
Territories occupied and administered by the Japanese navy[18]	63,000
Total	228,000

Source: Miyamoto, *Jawa shūsen shoriki*, p. 41.[19]

used for construction work on the Burma-Siam Railway. All organizations, from local labour bureaus and village headmen (called *penghulu* in Malay) to commercial companies, were called upon to provide fixed quotas of labourers.[20] To meet the first labour force requirements, the Singapore Rubber Association (*Shōnan Gomu Kumiai*), which controlled the rubber industry on the whole Malay Peninsula, sent 8,000 of their labourers from Perak province alone. The Indian Independence League and the Overseas Chinese Association, likewise coerced into cooperating with the Japanese authorities, sent numbers of *rōmusha* in July and August 1943 and again in spring 1944.[21]

At the beginning of recruitment for construction of the Burma-Siam Railway some people even volunteered to work. The Japanese promise of comparatively good pay for a work period limited to between

17. In the original text, Miyamoto wrote "Sunda Islands", which means the Lesser Sunda Islands (from Bali to Timor), east of Java, which the Japanese called Sunda.

18. Sulawesi, Southern Borneo (formerly Dutch Borneo), the Moluccas, the Lesser Sunda Islands, New Guinea, and Guam were administered by the Japanese navy. Burma, and the Philippines (until becoming independent in 1943) as well as Hong Kong, Northern Borneo, Sumatra, Malaya, and Java were administered by the Japanese army. But there were also some naval bases located in army territory. Harry J. Benda, James K. Irikura, and Koichi Kishi (eds), *Japanese Military Administration in Indonesia: Selected Documents* (New Haven, CT, 1965), pp. 5, 53f.

19. The 7th Japanese Army (Southern Army) sent *rōmusha* from Java to the occupied territories. The Southern Army was installed in Singapore in mid-March 1944, meaning that the numbers of recruits mentioned above do not cover the whole of 1944.

20. Nakahara, "Nihon senryōki eiryōmaraya ni okeru *rōmusha*dōin", p. 181; Michiko Nakahara, "Malayan Labor on the Thailand-Burma Railway", in Kratoska, *Asian Labor in the Wartime Japanese Empire*, pp. 249–264, 256.

21. Paul H. Kratoska, *The Japanese Occupation of Malaya: A Social and Economic History* (London, 1998), p. 182f. According to an article published in a Perak newspaper and dated 10 August 1943, the Overseas Chinese Association of Perak sent more than 700 forced labourers as a "first batch" to Siam. In Kratoska, *The Thailand-Burma Railway*, p. 3.

three and six months appeared attractive in the face of continuing unemployment and miserable living conditions in the villages.[22] The majority of Malaya's lower classes were illiterate, so in rural areas recruitment for the Japanese was done mainly by word of mouth. Village headmen, foremen on plantations, civil servants at labour bureaus, and Japanese soldiers advertised for construction workers to work on the Burma-Siam Railway in Malaya. Consequently, many people applied for *rōmusha* after hearing about the Japanese recruitment programme either directly or from friends, neighbours, or relatives.[23]

A certain Shinozaki Mamoru, who as chief of the Ministry for Social Affairs (*Kōseika*) in Singapore gained deep insights into the labour mobilization, reported on the recruitment of labour in Singapore City. After the war, he placed on record that the offer had appeared to be very good at the beginning of the recruitment drive: "When the Siam-Burma railway started, the Railway Regiment also came to ask for Labour. The document requesting recruits, came to me and I studied it carefully. The terms were very good. [...] The salaries offered were very high compared to other labour wages."[24] Finally, a department of the Ministry of Social Affairs, which had been established specially for the recruitment of *rōmusha* (*Rōdōjimukyoku*),[25] was able to send three contingents of 200 men each from Singapore to Siam. These first recruits were mainly unemployed men, who, according to Shinozaki, set out completely unsuspectingly for the north.[26]

When the first deserters from among the labourers returned to their villages and told of the real working conditions on the Burma-Siam Railway, the Japanese military administration in Malaya began to use deception or coercion in the mobilization of new labourers, an approach tolerated or even supported by the Malayan village headmen, the *penghulu*. Many documents report on local individuals who were suddenly snatched from their everyday life, press-ganged on the street by

22. Abu Talib Ahmad, "The Malay Community and Memory of the Japanese Occupation", in Patricia Lim Pui Huen and Diana Wong (eds), *War and Memory in Malaysia and Singapore* (Singapore, 2001), pp. 45–89, 68; PRO, WO 203–5823, SEATIC Bulletin No. 246.

23. Nakahara, "Nihon senryōki eiryōmaraya ni okeru *rōmusha*dōin", p. 178f.

24. Mamoru Shinozaki, *My Wartime Experiences in Singapore. Interviewed by Lim Yoon Lin* (Singapore 1973), p. 61. Shinozaki, who was interrogated by the Allies after the war, mentioned that wages were thrice as high in comparison with wages generally in Singapore. For that reason, many people volunteered. Compare Kratoska, *The Thailand-Burma Railway*, p. 73.

25. Mamoru Shinozaki, *Shingapōru senryō hiroku. Sensō to sono ningenzō* [Secret Documents about the Occupation of Singapore: The War and the Corresponding Ideal Image of Human Beings] (Tokyo, 1976), p. 92. According to Nakahara, the *rōmujimukyoku* (労務事務局) had been installed in every province of Japanese-occupied Malaya after October 1943. Nakahara, "Nihon senryōki eiryōmaraya ni okeru *rōmusha*dōin", p. 180.

26. Shinozaki, *My Wartime Experiences in Singapore*, p. 61f.

Japanese soldiers, loaded onto trucks and effectively kidnapped. Coercive recruitments of that kind happened frequently in public places such as street cafes, cinemas, or after Muslim Friday prayers. There are reports of raids on rubber plantations too.[27] Coercive recruitment of that kind led to social disorder in village communities and within families, as well as disrupting cultivation and causing supply problems in production not only in Malayan rural areas, but also in every Japanese-occupied South East Asian territory.[28]

A report by Kuji Manabu, governor of the West Coast province in Northern Borneo (*Kita Boruneo*), which was separately administrated by the Japanese, serves as an example of the kind of problems that occurred. Kuji reported that locals were urged to perform forced labour to improve the infrastructure, working on the expansion of the road network and the construction of airfields, both vital for the supply of food and raw materials. However, the recruitment of forced labour caused problems within village communities, and those problems had to be solved by the Japanese civil administration in Northern Borneo's West Coast province. Taking local circumstances into account, a rotation scheme was established: "[...] Kuji instituted a time-shift system, whereby small detachments were taken from each village in rotation, to work for one week and then allowed to return to the village, until their turn came again. Regard was paid in the allocation of these units to the conditions prevailing in their *kampongs* [villages], conditions, for example, differing in a farming community from these in a fishing area".[29]

Furthermore, on the Japanese side, conflicts of interest had arisen between the Southern Army and the civilian administration of the occupied territory. During the first recruitment campaign Singapore's labour department, *Rōdōjimukyoku*, had been unwilling to send young men to the Burma-Siam Railway. Indeed, the *Rōdōjimukyoku* kept them back as labour for the construction of fortifications in Singapore itself. Consequently, the Japanese military protested – and the regiment responsible for the railway construction loudest of all – complaining "Why is Syonan not

27. Ahmad, "The Malay Community", p. 66; Kratoska, *The Thailand-Burma Railway*, p. 13; Nakahara, "Nihon senryōki eiryōmaraya ni okeru *rōmusha*dōin", p. 184ff.; Nakahara, "Malayan Labor on the Thailand-Burma Railway", p. 256.

28. Raben, "Indonesian *Rōmusha* and Coolies under Naval Administration", p. 212; Satō, *War, Nationalism and Peasants*, pp. 165, 178.

29. PRO, WO 203–6317, SEATIC Intelligence Bulletin No. 237, 15 June 1946. Kuji Manabu was the governor of Northern Borneo's West Coast province, one of five provinces in this territory, from 20 November 1943 to 1 June 1945. Its seat of government was in Jesselton (today: Kota Kinabalu). According to Kuji, 3,000 Javanese *rōmusha* were used in this province for the construction of roads and airfields. In Malaya, a similar system of part-time work was used in the agricultural sector (especially for (forced) plantation workers). Kratoska, *Nihon senryōka ni okeru tōnanajia no keizai jōkyō*, p. 269.

cooperating?"[30] The administrative units of all the other Malayan provinces, including Sumatra, which had sent forced labourers to the Burma-
Siam Railway, wondered, too, and asked "Why is Syonan not sending?
Why only us? This is unfair."[31] For that reason, the administration of the
occupied territory asked Shinozaki in his role as chief of the social ministry
in Singapore and the corresponding labour department, *Rōdōjimukyoku*, to
meet the labour quota for restoring economic peace: "Send some labour
recruits there, even if it is only a small number, never mind. We are in a
difficult position."[32] According to Shinozaki, in the end the homeless and
beggars were collected from the streets, piled onto lorries and transported
to where forced labour was needed.

> At that time there were many vagabonds in the streets, beggars and homeless
> people, some from Sumatra. There had been requests from the citizens to clean up
> the streets; these people were very dirty, some with skin diseases. We were
> thinking how to do this. Some had been picked up and sent to the reformatory
> home. The police and the district committee decided to pick up these people and
> put them into the homes where they were cleaned, fed and treated for a few days.
> After they had recovered, the Labour Office asked them: "Mau pergi Siam kerja?"
> ("Want to go and work in Siam?"). Some didn't want. Some accepted. So we sent
> those who agreed to go.[33]

From the contemporary Japanese point of view, that was a clever move at
the time. On the one hand, the *Rōdōjimukyoku* was able to meet the
designated thirteen contingents as the quota for the labour force, and some
3,000 persons were sent from Singapore to the Burma-Siam Railway.[34] On
the other hand, Singapore's streets were "cleaned". The operation may be
understood as the Japanese parallel to the Nazi regime's *Zigeunerpolitik*
(gypsy policy), even if the subjects of it were deported not to extermination
camps but to forced labour.[35] However, the forced labour in Japanese-
occupied South East Asia definitely had an eliminatory characteristic,
at least on the Burma-Siam Railway. Incidentally, the "cleaned" streets in
the South East Asian metropolis did not remain so for very long, for in
spring 1945 there were something like 500 beggars living on the streets of
Singapore. They were *rōmusha* from Java and their lot was the result of

---

30. Shinozaki, *My Wartime Experiences in Singapore*, p. 62. Japanese-occupied Singapore was
named *Shōnan* or *Syonan*, which means "light of the south".
31. *Ibid.*, p. 63.
32. *Ibid.*
33. *Ibid.*
34. Shinozaki reported that he had been requested to send 3,000 forced labourers (recorded as
"coolies") from Singapore. Kratoska, *The Thailand-Burma Railway*, p. 72f.
35. Concerning the *NS-Zigeunerpolitik*, see Michael Zimmermann (ed.), *Zwischen Erziehung
und Vernichtung. Zigeunerpolitik und Zigeunerforschung im Europa des 20. Jahrhunderts*
(Stuttgart, 2007).

Japan's war economy and policy: "On account of maltreatment, illness or undernourished they had been unable to work and had been dismissed. Some had run away because of the beatings that were administered. […] the Japanese do not care whether the coolies run away or not. They get enough replacements from Java."[36]

"COLLABORATION" AS AN AVOIDANCE STRATEGY

A forced labour organization on Sumatra, which has previously received little attention in research, is the subject of an Allied intelligence report. "Palembang Si" (*Parenban-shi*), the city administration of the city Palembang in south-eastern Sumatra, organized the Badan-Pembantoe Pemerintah (BPP),[37] "a corporation of unskilled labourers for local administrative purposes". This organization was something like a recruitment office, based on orders from Palembang's Japanese governor, who asked the village headmen to meet a certain quota per village as a labour force. Of course, there were local differences in the implementation of the recruitment, which was handled arbitrarily on the whole. In particular, the ranks of the BPP were filled with imports of labourers from neighbouring Java. Reading the Allied documents, we clearly see the coercive nature of the labour recruitment. In the area around Palembang, local people could hardly elude recruitment: "If by chance a man who is selected refuses to join, all his possessions are confiscated and he has to leave his home-town, but wherever else he goes to he is caught by the Japanese and compelled to join the BPP. This only counts for small towns, but in the big towns they are told to join the BPP whether they like it or not."[38] Following the forced recruitment, the BPP labourers received working clothes: a red-striped shirt, a pair of black work trousers, plus two pairs of underpants, and a straw hat. Moreover, the labourers were identified by a badge that showed a green six-pointed star on a white background and the initials BPP. For a three-month period, the BPP labourers had to work for the Japanese in Palembang, the seat of the local government, away from their home towns. The work consisted of manual labour on so-called government projects, such as construction work on public and government buildings, the construction of roads and bridges, and the repair of bunker installations; but they were also forced to work on rubber plantations. While it is true that the forced BPP labourers were paid for their work, they suffered from poor medical treatment and wholly inadequate

---

36. NIOD, Labour Requirements Migration: Forced Javanese Labour, 25 June 1945.
37. The abbreviation BPP was also translated as "Badan Pendukung Pemerintah (Government Supporting Organization)". The Indonesian term *Pendukung* is a synonym for *Pembantoe* or *Pembantu* (literally "assistant"). Shigeru Satō, "Occupation: Administration and Policies", in Post, *The Encyclopedia of Indonesia in the Pacific War*, pp. 61–147, 69.
38. NIOD, Romusha: BPP (Badan-Pembantoe-Pemerintah), 30 April 1945.

nutrition. In cases of illness, individuals were forced to continue to work, which naturally resulted in a correspondingly high death rate. At the end of the three-month work period, BPP labourers received a certificate exempting them from further recruitment by the occupier for forced labour.[39]

Among the mainly Chinese immigrant local population of the Malayan provinces of Perak and Kedah – where the Japanese occupying forces had been encouraging iron production – an early strategy to avoid similar forced recruitment as *rōmusha* instead of BPP was to specialize in the production of iron nails and other building materials. All such products were then sold to the Japanese, who also accepted the braiding of strong ropes as similarly suitable alternative work, which saved the locals from forced recruitment. In addition, anyone who collaborated economically with the occupying power received diverse grants from the Japanese army.[40]

A number of documents show that collaboration with the occupying force was a promising avoidance strategy for escaping *rōmusha* recruitment. After the war, the Dias brothers, Charles and Anthony, born to a Eurasian father and a Chinese mother, testified that they had agreed to spy for the headquarters of the military police (*Kenpeitai*) for one reason only, that they wished to avoid forced-labour recruitment and deployment to Siam to work on the construction of the Burma-Siam Railway.[41]

Seventy-five per cent of the Indian National Army (INA), which in summer 1945 numbered 16,000 to 20,000 men, were Tamil civilians. A British intelligence report had this to say about the INA: "[...] However it must not be overlooked that many of them [the Tamils] were forced into the INA to avoid being press-ganged into Japanese labour gangs [...]".[42]

During the war, the unemployed in South East Asia were in particular danger of being recruited as *rōmusha*, which explains why service in the paramilitary *heiho* became an attractive alternative. As auxiliary troops, *heiho* were guaranteed basic needs such as clothes, food, and accommodation, while wages for *heiho* were twice those of the *rōmusha*, leading many young men on Java to volunteer for the *heiho*.[43] According to the Japanese historian

---

39. *Ibid.*; Satō, "Occupation", p. 69.
40. Shinozaki, *Shingapōru senryō hiroku*, p. 92.
41. PRO, WO 203–5808, SEATIC Intelligence Bulletin No. 211, 6 October 1945.
42. PRO, WO 203–2298, Supplementary Guide to JIFC (Indian) Activities (Malaya), 16 August 1945.
43. Kurasawa, "Nihon senryōka no Jawa nōson no henyō", p. 205; Kaori Maekawa, "Taheiyō-sensō ni okeru nihongun no horyoseisaku to ajiakei horyo no gunjidōin – Indoneshia ni okeru heiho seido o chūshin ni" [The Japanese Army's Policy Concerning Prisoners of War during the Pacific War and the Mobilization of Asian Prisoners of War for War Purposes – with special focus on the *heiho* system in Indonesia] (Ph.D. dissertation, Sophia University Tokyo, 2009), p. 97.

Maekawa Kaori, in the context of the worsening war situation local administrators, such as village headmen, confronted many such young men with the choice of either becoming *rōmusha* or volunteering for the *heiho*. The occupying power spared no one from the general mobilization, and each family was required to provide at least one individual,[44] meaning that in many places the young men were forced to choose "the lesser of two evils".[45]

In this context, the destinies of forcibly recruited *rōmusha* and members of collaborating paramilitary troops were closely linked. One example is a *heiho* platoon from Malaya's north-western province Kedah. The *heiho* was installed on guard duty at the Tamarkan Camp on the Burma-Siam Railway and received orders to shoot disobedient *rōmusha*.[46]

In reality, most voluntary recruits of the *heiho*, who received military training similar to that of Japanese soldiers,[47] did work resembling that done by the coercively recruited *rōmusha*, being set to dig ditches, mend roads, or to do agricultural work.[48] So the institution of the *heiho*, which started on the Malay Peninsula in May 1943, must be understood as another part of the general mobilization of labour in South East Asia.[49]

COERCED LABOUR IN THE INFRASTRUCTURE: INTERPRETATIONS IN TERMS OF LABOUR RELATIONS

Our knowledge of coerced labour during the Japanese occupation of South East Asia is still severely limited because of the general shortage of primary sources and limited access to documents from Japanese commercial companies active in occupied South East Asian territories from 1942 to 1945. It is therefore very difficult to formulate any comprehensive definition of

44. Maekawa, "Taheiyōsensō ni okeru nihongun no horyoseisaku to ajiakei horyo no gunjidōin", p. 99.
45. Joyce C. Lebra, *Japanese-Trained Armies in Southeast Asia: Independence and Volunteer Forces in World War II* (Hong Kong, 1977), p. 117f.
46. Ahmad, "The Malay Community", p. 71. According to documents of the 16th Japanese Army (Java), the majority of the *heiho* did service as guards. Waseda daigaku ajia taiheiyō kenkyū sentā [The Asia-Pacific Research Institute of the Waseda University in Tokyo], Nishijima Collection, JV 45, The Headquarters of the 16th Army. Explanations Regarding All Kinds of Armed Bodies, 1945.
47. Waseda daigaku ajia taiheiyō kenkyū sentā.
48. Ban Kah Choon and Yap Hong Kuan, *Rehearsal for War: Resistance and the Underground War against the Japanese and the Kempeitai, 1942–1945* (Singapore, 2002), p. 68; Joyce C. Lebra, "The Significance of the Japanese Military Model for Southeast Asia", *Pacific Affairs*, 48:2 (1975), pp. 215–229, 223; Geok Boi Lee, *The Syonan Years: Singapore under Japanese Rule 1942–1945* (Singapore, 2005), p. 255.
49. Only a few publications about the *heiho* mobilization are in Western languages. For an introduction to the subject see Kaori Maekawa, "The Heiho during the Japanese Occupation of Indonesia", in Kratoska, *Asian Labor in the Wartime Japanese Empire*, pp. 179–196.

"coerced labour during the Japanese occupation in South East Asia" in terms of labour relations. The spectrum of forced labour was most likely wide-ranging – for example from manual to non-manual work, or from those who worked for the occupying power to those who worked for private Japanese employers. Many more case studies are required to allow us a usefully closer view of the subject. That said, a first attempt at an interpretation of *rōmusha* labour relations might read as follows. It is based on what is known so far about the forced recruitment of local inhabitants for manual work conducted "in the name of the state", meaning, of course, Japan, as the occupying power.

With reference to the construction of the Burma-Siam Railway, it becomes obvious that, initially, the Japanese meant to recruit volunteers as manual labourers, but that soon after the recruitment process had started it became clear to them that too few of the local inhabitants were prepared to volunteer to do that type of work. The Japanese were therefore obliged to adopt other methods to acquire a large enough workforce, and the recruitment of locals by force increased. The taxonomy of the *rōmusha*'s labour relation is in accordance with the development of the recruitment process, in that generally speaking the *rōmusha* of the Burma-Siam Railway and most other construction projects worked for the polity, under a new system that was propagated with the catchphrase "Greater East Asia" (*Daitōa*). Those *rōmusha* were tributary labourers and their labour was not commodified. Upon closer examination, however, we can see clearly that the first labourers working on the Burma-Siam Railway were, in principle, wage labourers for the polity (labour relation 18) and at least some of them were able to return home. Once home, the returnees reported on the real working conditions along the railway, which unsurprisingly had a dramatic impact on the recruitment process. From then on – and with good reason – almost no one volunteered and so the occupying power saw no option but to intensify its coercive recruiting. In conclusion, local inhabitants recruited by force to work as *rōmusha*, for example on the Burma-Siam Railway, which was the greatest construction project of the Japanese occupation period in South East Asia, may be described generally – and in reference to the categories of labour relations defined by Karin Hofmeester *et al.* – as "tributary slaves" (labour relation 11). The *rōmusha* of the "Death Railway" were owned by and worked indefinitely for the polity; they were deprived of the right to leave the railway and could not return home. Many died along the railway either as a consequence of the cruel working conditions or in attempts to escape to their homes.[50]

50. Karin Hofmeester *et al.*, "The Global Collaboratory on the History of Labour Relations, 1500–2000: Background, Set-Up, Taxonomy, and Applications", available at http://hdl.handle. net/10622/4OGRAD, last accessed 25 April 2016.

CONTINUITY OF LABOUR RELATIONS IN PRE-WAR AND
WARTIME SOUTH EAST ASIA

The Japanese were the last major group to enter the labour market of South
East Asia at the end of the nineteenth century. At the beginning of the
twentieth century, thousands of Japanese immigrants worked not as colonial entrepreneurs, but also as "coolies", for instance on the construction of
the Baguio road in the Philippines. But after its opening up to the West from
the mid-nineteenth century, the Japanese empire modernized and indus-
trialized rapidly and Japan's economy grew. The result was that the Japanese
empire's role in Asia shifted in economic terms. The islands of Japan itself,
which had so far exported mainly cheap labour to neighbouring countries,
were now increasingly represented in South East Asia by mercantile people.
However, in comparison with the period of Japan's occupation of South
East Asia its prior economic involvement had been marginal. During the
first half of the twentieth century, Japanese manufacturers primarily
exported their own products, for example textiles, and Japanese companies
acted as importers of local raw materials.[51]

Until the beginning of the 1940s, the natural resources of South East Asia
(raw materials, but mainly also oil for petroleum products) were in
increasingly high demand in Japan, until, in the end, demand for those
natural resources became one of the main reasons for Japan's decision to
occupy the South East Asian territories. But Japan's mobilization of labour
changed as the war went on. Immediately after the seizure of the Asian
territories the new occupying power began to mobilize labourers for
restoration work, such as the reconstruction of bridges, harbour facilities,
or strategically important factories. That phase of restoration continued
until around autumn 1943, but from the second half of 1943 the likely
course of the war, with its inevitable consequences, became increasingly
impossible to ignore. Japan could obviously expect an Allied invasion of
South East Asian territories, so labourers were mobilized for defence
projects such as the construction of military airbases or fortifications.
In addition to "defence", "production" now became a key word in Japanese
propaganda. As a consequence of the Battle of Midway and its subsequent
mounting loss of maritime control, which had brought with it the pervasive
shortage of food, clothing, and other daily necessities, from summer 1943
onwards Japan began a campaign to increase local self-sufficiency, especially
in food, in all areas under the direct control of its empire, such as the territories of the former Dutch East Indies, Malaya, and the Philippines. Pure
pragmatism had by now replaced the original Japanese idea of establishing
a "Greater East Asia Co-Prosperity Sphere" with Japan at its centre.

---

51. Norman G. Owen (ed.), *The Emergence of Modern Southeast Asia: A New History*
(Honolulu, HI, 2005), p. 177f.

The extensive mobilization of the workforce, and especially the so-called Grow More Food Campaign, was a "total mobilization" not only of skilled, but also of unskilled workers. Simply put, it was nothing less than the mobilization of the entire society of South East Asia, owing to pragmatic reasons in wartime. "The Japanese conducted a series of campaigns for a 'total mobilization' of manpower under the slogan of 'defence and production.' These campaigns involved virtually the entire workforce in the occupied land, including many women and children."[52] "Production" referred to, among other things, strategic resources such as oil, minerals, or ammunition, clothing both for the troops and local inhabitants, as well as construction work for the transport sector. Food production, especially of staples such as rice became much more important on the plantations than the production of export crops, which had lost their markets anyway because of Japan's economic isolation. One consequence was, therefore, the continuous deterioration of the plantation economy during the Japanese occupation.[53] It is worth pointing out that, in the context of total labour mobilization, the experiences of the people mobilized varied greatly, but the fate of indigenous forced labourers was the most extreme of course.[54]

However, it was not the Japanese occupying power that was the first to introduce coercive labour into South East Asia as a mode of production, for the preceding Western colonial governments had used state power to draft corvée labour or to force the inhabitants to grow food for local consumption. For example, in Java as early as the mid-nineteenth century local peasants had been forced by the colonial power to produce food, while in 1830 the colonial government of the Dutch East Indies established a cultivation system under which the local peasants had to provide clearly determined quantities of foodstuffs to the government. Sugar as well as coffee became typical Javanese products, the export of which was based on a modern tribute system. Even if that cultivation system had been abolished by about 1870, nevertheless "[...] the Javanese were no longer compelled to work by the state, [...] in practice most of them kept growing the same crops under very similar conditions. By the late nineteenth century the use of direct coercion in export production was generally disappearing in South East Asia, less because it violated principles of human rights and dignity than because it was inefficient."[55]

---

52. Satō, "Relocation of Labor", p. 245.
53. Aiko Kurasawa, "Social Change", in Post, *The Encyclopedia of Indonesia in the Pacific War*, pp. 282–289, 289.
54. Satō, "Relocation of Labor", p. 248f.
55. Owen, *The Emergence of Modern Southeast Asia*, p. 180ff. See also Elise Nederveen van Meerkerk's contribution to the present Special Issue, "Grammar of Difference? The Dutch Colonial State, Labour Policies, and Social Norms on Work and Gender, c.1800–1940". Concerning the quote, see Owen, *The Emergence of Modern Southeast Asia*, p. 182.

By the beginning of the twentieth century the industrial revolution had entered a new stage. Among other things, the motor industry was developing at a great pace, which led to increasing demand worldwide for oil and rubber. Until the outbreak of World War II, more than ninety per cent of the world's rubber came from South East Asia, and the Dutch East Indies and Malaya were teeming with rubber plantations, where the "[working] conditions were terrible […], with long hours, poor food, inadequate medicine, and strict discipline leading to high desertion and mortality rates."[56] At the outbreak of the war, South East Asia as a workplace was dominated by a plantation economy with harsh working conditions.

In conclusion, Japanese administrators found themselves able to use the harsh working conditions of earlier colonial systems as a springboard for their own approach. Under Japanese rule, forced labour therefore experienced a renewal, although to a much greater extent and under much harsher conditions. Japan was at war, so this was a war economy, and the unfavourable course of the war for Japan served as a catalyst for the exploitation of the indigenous people as forced labourers.

Even the transport and relocation of labourers was not unique to the Japanese occupation period. The system of plantations, which prevailed in the period of the early industrialization of South East Asia, had always been based on the import of human labour. Plantations (rubber, tea, coffee, tobacco, palm oil, etc.) were in general established in "empty" regions where suitable land was both cheap and abundant and the population was comparatively sparse, such as in areas of Sumatra or Malaya. Because

> […] the locals had no need or desire for wage labor – their eventual response to the rubber boom [in the first half of the twentieth century] was smallholding rather than working on the estates – so plantation managers imported immigrant labor to work the fields. […] Over time many immigrant workers settled in, local peasants began to change their economic outlook and accept wage labor […].[57]

When the Chinese, as the first "batch" of imported labourers, began increasingly to work as tradesmen or shop owners in the cities, from about 1890, the Javanese became the main source of imported labour on plantations in South East Asia.[58] Of course, the main difference from the time of the Japanese occupation came from below. At the turn of the century, the need for plantation workers attracted migration into South East Asia, and immigrants themselves took the initiative in their own movement.

---

56. Owen, *The Emergence of Modern Southeast Asia*, p. 184.
57. *Ibid.*, p. 183. Even "in sparsely populated Malaya, much of the labour the plantations needed came from Indian and Chinese immigrants". Nicholas Tarling, *Southeast Asia: A Modern History* (South Melbourne and Oxford, 2001), p. 192.
58. Owen, *The Emergence of Modern Southeast Asia*, p. 186.

By contrast, during World War II it was the Japanese occupying power acting from above that forced Javanese or Malayans to leave their homes and go to work as labourers in other parts of the "Greater East Asia Co-Prosperity Sphere".

Although the war economy in Japanese-occupied South East Asia is a comparatively under-researched topic, it is well known that, in general, the economies of the occupied territories, for example that of the former Dutch East Indies, deteriorated during the war. Living conditions became worse for many reasons, such as disorderly production, inflation, and corruption.[59] Before the war, most South East Asian territories were fully integrated into the world economy and some, such as the Malay Peninsula with its rubber production, were economically significant. However, labour relations were greatly affected when production decreased at the beginning of the occupation for the simple reason that Japan and its occupied zones were cut off from the world market. Unemployment, especially in urban areas, was one consequence during the initial stage of the occupation, although joblessness and general destitution had already become serious problems before the war. For example, during the first half of the twentieth century, many thousands of inhabitants worked full time or seasonally on Java's plantations, producing crops such as tea, coffee, rubber, or sugar for export. Because of the worldwide economic crisis and because of the outbreak of World War II in Europe in 1939, the production and export of crops in Java were drastically reduced, causing large-scale unemployment that, in turn, led to begging and prostitution.[60]

Many historically interesting sources from the occupation period were systemically destroyed, among them information on the "recruiting" of *rōmusha*, while some of those that survived the war are inaccessible for various reasons. Thus, it is rather difficult to answer the question of exactly what kind of work people did before their recruitment as *rōmusha*. Concerning Java at least, it is known that in the 1930s most people worked in the agrarian sector as peasant smallholders or on the plantations and in the import-export market. At the outbreak of World War II in Europe, the Indonesian territories lost their export markets – with the exception of that for rubber, which was now in great demand in the United States. Nevertheless, a great many plantation workers were dismissed and no-income areas like the northern territories of Java became real hunger zones. Although Japan tried to replace the European factories with Japanese ones, Java's industry collapsed during the war years from lack of resources and transport problems. Not much data is available about the employment

---

59. Shigeru Satō, "Introduction", in Post, *The Encyclopedia of Indonesia in the Pacific War*, p. 218.
60. Satō, "Relocation of Labor", p. 250.

situation immediately before Japan invaded Java, but according to the Japanese historian Satō Shigeru, "a regional difference was observed between the western half and eastern half of the island [Java]. [...] unemployment and destitution became markedly more serious in the eastern half".[61] On the one hand, local inhabitants who had already lost or were losing their work on plantations or in cities returned to the rural areas. On the other, those who had lost their livelihoods in the countryside migrated to urban areas. In the cities of, in particular, eastern Java, more beggars and prostitutes were noted,[62] a tendency, already visible at the end of the Dutch era, now intensified by the nascent international economic isolation of the Japanese-occupied South East Asian territories and which caused workers in export-import industries, for example, or military personnel of the former colonial forces to lose their jobs too. Japan as the "new power" was unable to generate enough jobs for those newly unemployed. It is notable that the development of the employment situation on the Malay Peninsula and in Singapore seems to bear a resemblance to that in Indonesia. As a result, the Japanese were able to draw on a large pool of the unemployed when it began to draft *rōmusha* from spring 1943 onwards. As Satō says, "The Japanese inherited Dutch policies in broad outlines but the manner in which they enforced the policies, such as [...] forced mobilization of labour, were obviously inappropriate and worsened the economic conditions."[63]

While at the beginning of the Japanese occupation the mass of the unemployed, especially from export industries, increased because of Japan's worldwide economic isolation, by the end of the occupation there were actually shortages of labour in places after the Japanese had mobilized and transported local inhabitants as forced labourers. Concerning this phenomenon Satō states:

> If the Japanese had needed labor solely for their military operations, this surplus population would have been more than enough, and Java would have continued to suffer from serious unemployment throughout the occupation. The mobilization campaigns from late 1943 soon eradicated unemployment, however, and created labor shortages in many villages from around mid-1944. The labor mobilization for the Japanese defense endeavor was substantial, but their economic endeavors also absorbed much labor. The transformation from a surplus to a shortage of labor can be explained to an extent in terms of a decline in production efficiency in an isolated economy.[64]

61. Shigeru Satō, "Indonesia 1939–1942: Prelude to the Japanese Occupation", *Journal of Southeast Asian Studies*, 37:2 (2006), pp. 225–248, 242.
62. *Ibid.*
63. *Ibid.*, p. 248.
64. Satō, "Relocation of Labor", p. 247. Concerning the inefficiency of production, Satō gives the example of coal mining in Java. The Japanese authorities tried to recommence the import of coal, but it was impossible because of the lack of cargo ships. The main body of these ships (before the war around seventy per cent of them were British or Dutch) had left the area prior to the Japanese

However, unemployment in Japanese-occupied South East Asia had its roots in pre-war times, and its development was clearly continuous. Not only in Java, but in other occupied territories, too, Japan encountered a system of labour relations that was already unstable and suffering from the prevailing economic crisis and the consequences of the outbreak of the war in Europe.

Finally, with regard to Java, one parallel between the pre-war Dutch and the Japanese economic systems is striking. Neither the Dutch colonial authorities, nor the Japanese administrators were really interested in industrializing Java. Because of the worldwide depression and the outbreak of World War II in Europe, the Dutch were, on the one hand, more or less forced to introduce basic industries such as metal, chemical, textile, or paper industries in its colony. But in reality, even the Dutch had hitherto considered Java as a source of resources, meaning raw materials, export crops, and cheap labour. For Japan, it was the course of the Pacific War that forced the imperialist state to change its initial plan of building an "Asian economic bloc" and establishing a system of economic "self-sufficiency" in South East Asia. Consequently, in certain fields industrial efforts had to be intensified.[65] In fact, the real industrialization of the region began only after the war, when a process of recovery and economic modernization accompanied the return of the pre-war colonial powers to their former South East Asian territories. In the end, the targeted restoration of pre-war political and economic patterns was partly successful. Finally, with the liberation movements, the shaking off of the yoke of colonial rule, and the founding of independent nation states, forced labour disappeared from South East Asia.

CONCLUSION

Japanese historians such as Kurasawa Aiko, Gotō Kenichi, and Satō Shigeru are pioneers of research on *rōmusha*. Nevertheless, they have focused largely exclusively on Indonesia and in particular on Java, because Java was Japan's main source of forced labourers in South East Asia. Javanese *rōmusha* were shipped from Java, mostly via Sumatra, to neighbouring regions, or used on the spot, including, notoriously, as forced labourers on the Burma-Siam Railway. The majority of the labourers on the "Death Railway" were not, in fact, the Allied POWs, but people from Burma or Malaya. It should also not be forgotten that the *rōmusha* of the Burma-Siam Railway project were themselves not the only forced labourers in the

---

invasion. The Japanese authorities were therefore forced to begin coal mining, mainly in the western part of Java. But even if labour was mobilized for the mining and for the construction of a railroad to transport the coal on the island, the effect was minimal and the coal shortage increased, although there was an enormous amount of coal on the neighbouring islands.

65. *Ibid.*, p. 253.

"Greater East Asia Co-Prosperity Sphere". Forced labour was used in various sectors, but not all of it was manual labour. Besides, the conditions of forced labourers could differ considerably, even on the Burma-Siam Railway.

Indeed, the prospect of recruitment for the construction work on the Burma-Siam Railway was without doubt greatly feared by all of Malaya's local populations, their fear prompted chiefly by the reports of returnees about the appalling working conditions on the "Death Railway". Ironically, many of those returnees had volunteered to work on the railway, but fled when they realized the truth of the situation in Siam.

At the same time as the Japanese increasingly used force to recruit labour, the local population found ways to develop avoidance strategies. For example, to escape *rōmusha*, some locals took to specializing in the production of certain goods necessary for the Japanese troops in the region. Others collaborated with the occupying force in other ways, such as the young men who were confronted with the choice of being frogmarched into a batch of *rōmusha* or volunteering to join paramilitary outfits like the *heiho*. Some locals did construction work other than that on the Burma-Siam Railway, perhaps working on other railway projects, or building airfields and other kinds of construction works. They were, in turn, guarded and overseen by other locals who had joined a collaborating paramilitary unit, an aspect of *rōmusha* that is only one "irony of the history" of the Japanese occupation of South East Asia. Further, it illustrates an unintended consequence of the actions of the occupying power, whose aim had been to recruit labour for the Burma-Siam Railway, by coercion, if necessary. Yet, the ultimate effect was that members of the labour force chose less coercive labour relations, and even if their agency led them into collaboration rather than open resistance, the imposition of particular labour relations could sometimes be eluded.

IRSH 61 (2016), Special Issue, pp. 187–211 doi:10.1017/S0020859016000407
© 2016 Internationaal Instituut voor Sociale Geschiedenis

The Role of Unfree Labour in Capitalist Development: Spain and Its Empire, Nineteenth to the Twenty-First Centuries*

FERNANDO MENDIOLA

*Department of Economics, Public University of Navarre
Campus Arrosadia, Edificio Departamental Los Madroños,
31006 Iruñea-Pamplona, Spain*

E-mail: fernando.mendiola@unavarra.es

ABSTRACT: This article contributes to the debate on the persistence of forced labour within capitalist development. It focuses on Spain, which has been deeply rooted in the global economy, firstly as a colonial metropolis, and later as part of the European Union. In the first place, I analyse the different modalities of unfree labour that are included in the taxonomy established by the Global Collaboratory on the History of Labour Relations, taking into account the different political regimes in which they are inserted. Therefore, the legal framework regarding unfree labour is analysed for four different political contexts: liberal revolution with colonial empire (1812–1874); liberal parliamentarism with colonial empire (1874–1936); civil war and fascist dictatorship, with decolonization (1936–1975); and parliamentary democracy within globalization (1975–2014). The article goes on to deal with the importance of the main economic reasons driving the demand for forced labour: relative labour shortage and the search for increasing profits. In the conclusion, and taking the Spanish case as a basis, I suggest a series of challenges for furthering the global debate on the role of forced labour under capitalism.

INTRODUCTION

Forced labour is still an important problem today, not only in developing countries, but also in developed ones, as recent reports by the ILO point out.[1] As a result, economic debate on unfree labour is open, and much

* The article is part of the research project "Crime Control in Modern Spain: Security Discourses, Punitive Institutions and Emergency Practices" (HAR2013–40621–P), directed by Pedro Oliver Olmo (Universidad de Castilla–La Mancha) and funded by the Spanish Ministry of Science and Innovation. I want to thank the anonymous referees and the editors of this Special Issue for their helpful comments and Robert Curwen for his help with the translation into English.
1. ILO, *The Cost of Coercion* (Geneva, 2009); *idem, Profits and Poverty: The Economics of Forced Labour* (Geneva, 2014).

of the argument concerns not only the measures to be taken in order to put an end to such labour exploitation,[2] but also the theoretical implications of its persistence in our understanding of capitalism. This debate, moreover, is not only related to contemporary reality, but also to historical dynamics, being a source of important controversies within the literature on development and labour relations.[3] In fact, economists and historians have underlined the persistence of different modalities of unfree labour relationships during the past two centuries, closely related to the historical dynamics of capitalism.[4] As a result, historiography focusing on the importance of forced and unfree labour for economic development has faced two main, complementary and almost always overlapping challenges: the first, mainly related to public policies and to the role of the state, is to identify the legal framework of the different modalities of unfree labour, while the second draws our attention to explaining its economic logic.

The first challenge, analysed below, is closely linked to the difficulty of giving a definition of forced labour valid for different times and places. Although coercion, both for entering into such work or to prevent workers leaving it, has long been regarded as the main factor in defining forced labour,[5] several historians have pointed out the necessity of broader approaches to understand the history of labour relations.[6] Recently, the

---

2. Nicola Phillips and Fabiola Mieres, "The Governance of Forced Labour in the Global Economy", *Globalizations*, 12:2 (2015), pp. 244–260.

3. *Ibid.;* Jairus Banaji, "The Fictions of Free Labour: Contract, Coercion, and So-Called Unfree Labour", *Historical Materialism*, 11:3 (2003), pp. 69–95; Yann Moulier Boutang, *De l'esclavage au salariat. Économie historique du salariat bridé* (Paris, 1998); Marcel van der Linden, *Workers of the World: Essays Toward a Global Labor History* (Leiden [etc.], 2008); Tom Brass, *Labour Regime Change in the Twenty-First Century: Unfreedom, Capitalism and Primitive Accumulation* (Chicago, IL, 2011); Stephanie W. Barrientos, "'Labour Chains': Analysing the Role of Labour Contractors in Global Production Networks", *Journal of Development Studies*, 49:8 (2013), pp. 1058–1071; Stephanie Barrientos, Uma Kothari, and Nicola Phillips, "Dynamics of Unfree Labour in the Contemporary Global Economy", *Journal of Development Studies*, 49:8 (2013), pp. 1037–1041; Tom Brass, "Debating Capitalist Dynamics and Unfree Labour: A Missing Link?", *Journal of Development Studies*, 50:4 (2014), pp. 570–582.

4. Tom Brass and Marcel van der Linden (eds), *Free and Unfree Labour: The Debate Continues* (Berne, 1997); Marcel van der Linden (ed.), *Humanitarian Intervention and Changing Labor Relations: The Long-Term Consequences of the Abolition of the Slave Trade* (Leiden [etc.], 2012); Alessandro Stanziani (ed.), *Labour, Coercion, and Economic Growth in Eurasia, 17th–20th Centuries* (Leiden [etc.], 2013).

5. Tom Brass, "Some Observations on Unfree Labour, Capitalist Restructuring and Deproletarianization", in *idem* and Van der Linden, *Free and Unfree Labour*, pp. 57–75, 58–59; Robert J. Steinfeld, *Coercion, Contract, and Free Labor in the Nineteenth Century* (Cambridge, 2001).

6. Moulier Boutang, *De l'esclavage au salariat*; Marcel van der Linden, "Introduction", in Van der Linden, *Humanitarian Intervention and Changing Labor Relations*, pp. 1–45; Alessandro Stanziani, "Introduction: Labour, Coercion, and Economic Growth in Eurasia, Seventeenth – Early Twentieth Centuries", in Stanziani, *Labour, Coercion, and Economic Growth in Eurasia*, pp. 1–28.

taxonomy established by the Global Collaboratory on the History of Labour Relations at the International Institute of Social History has given us a very useful tool for furthering comparative studies on forced labour.[7]

This project, where the state plays an important role in shaping labour relations, as conqueror, employer, or redistributor, enables us to approach the history of labour relations by taking into account political factors. These factors include the structure of political domination over the colonies, the penitentiary system, policies towards the dissident population in the framework of a civil war, or the regulation of migratory flows. They are also essential to understanding the mechanisms shaping forced labour supply; that is, the creation of social groups susceptible to being employed in work on the margins of mercantile mechanisms. With that purpose in mind, and in order to better understand the role of the state and the global implications of imperialism for labour relations, we will analyse forced labour within Spain's legal borders during each period, including the empire.

In section three, we will deal with the second challenge, focused on two driving factors encouraging the demand for unfree labour. The first is the relative shortage of labour, something that was pointed out by Domar in his seminal article and that has been the source of several debates.[8] The second relates to the possibility of increasing profits thanks to changes in the labour market that reduce the cost of labour, always keeping in mind that the margins of such profit, their relation to the levels of productivity, and their centrality in the cycles of capital accumulation remain open questions that are the subject of debate.[9] Thus, what is set out here should be understood as a contribution to ongoing global debates that must necessarily be revised or enriched in the future as new studies are carried out.

---

7. Karin Hofmeester, Jan Lucassen, Leo Lucassen, Rombert Stapel, and Richard Zijdeman, 2016, "The Global Collaboratory on the History of Labour Relations, 1500–2000: Background, Set-Up, Taxonomy, and Applications", http://hdl.handle.net/10622/4OGRAD, IISH Dataverse, V1 (access subject to registration), last accessed 22 August 2016. For new directions in labour history based on the taxonomy, see Leo Lucassen, "Working Together: New Directions in Global Labour History", *Journal of Global History*, 11 (2016), pp. 66–87. For some critical reflections on this taxonomy and the need to integrate different kinds of subaltern worker, following Van der Linden's concept of "coerced commodification of labour power", see Christian G. De Vito and Alex Lichtenstein, "Writing a Global History of Convict Labour", in Christian G. De Vito and Alex Lichtenstein (eds), *Global Convict Labour* (Leiden [etc.], 2015), pp. 2–10. These authors also present us with an overall evaluation of the work of prisoners in modern history and of how it fits in with the taxonomy of the Global Collaboratory.
8. Evsey D. Domar, "The Causes of Slavery or Serfdom: A Hypothesis", *The Journal of Economic History*, 30:1 (1970), pp. 18–32.
9. For a theoretical analysis of the role of primitive accumulation and its relation to forced labour, see Brass, *Labour Regime Change*, pp. 136–166. This author also offers a critical reading of the usefulness of the concept of accumulation by dispossession, proposed by Harvey, when explaining the recourse to forced labour in the neoliberal contexts of the present. David Harvey, *A Brief History of Neoliberalism* (Oxford, 2005), pp. 160–165. See also Brass, "Debating Capitalist Dynamics".

POLITICAL REGIMES AND MAIN MODALITIES OF FORCED LABOUR IN SPAIN (1812–2014)

In spite of recent research, we still lack an overall view of the persistence of forced labour in Spanish economic development. The only attempt to estimate the relative importance of the different categories of labour relations established by the Global Collaboratory on the History of Labour Relations has been made by Lana for 1797, 1900, and 2001.[10] However, Lana takes today's territory as a reference, and so labour relations in the colonial sphere are not included. Moreover, category 11 (tributary slaves, in this case prisoners of war in concentration camps) does not figure, as the opening and closure of concentration camps in the twentieth century falls outside these temporal cross sections; nor is today's debt bondage (category 15) included, as Lana uses official data that do not reflect these illegal situations.[11]

For the purposes of this article, and in order to identify different modalities of forced or unfree labour, we will take as a basis the taxonomy established by the Global Collaboratory on the History of Labour Relations and consider categories 8 (obligatory labourers),[12] 11 (tributary slaves),[13] 15 (indentured labourers),[14] and 17 (slaves who produce for the market)[15] in our analysis of forced labour, as seen in Table 1.

Liberal revolution and the golden age of colonial slavery (1812–1874)

From 1812, when the first liberal constitution was passed in Cádiz, to 1874, when a coup restored the monarchy, liberal reforms were progressively passed in Spain. Regarding labour relations, serfdom and slavery were under discussion, but while the former had disappeared during the

10. José-Miguel Lana-Berasain, 2016, "Spain 1800,1900,2000 [Global Collaboratory on the History of Labour Relations 1500–2000 Dataset]", http://hdl.handle.net/10622/CH6ZP5, IISH Dataverse, V1 (access subject to registration), last accessed 22 August 2016.

11. With respect to convict labour included in category 8, I will detail my disagreements with Lana's figures for the cross sections for 1900 and 2001 in the corresponding chronological parts.

12. "Those who have to work for the polity, and are remunerated mainly in kind. This category includes those subject to civil obligations (corvée labourers, conscripted soldiers and sailors), and work as punishment, i.e. convicts. Hofmeester, Lucassen, Lucassen, Stapel and Zijdeman "The Global Collaboratory", p. 19.

13. "Those who are owned by and work for the polity indefinitely (deprived of the right to leave, to refuse to work, or to receive compensation for their labour). One example is forced labourers in concentration camps". *Ibid.*

14. "Those contracted to work as unfree labourers for an employer for a specific period of time to pay off a private debt". *Ibid.*, p. 20.

15. "Those owned by their employers (masters). They are deprived of the right to leave, to refuse to work or to receive compensation for their labour". *Ibid.*

Table 1. *Modalities of forced labour in Spain (1812–2014) in different political and global contexts.*

		1812–1874 Liberal Revolution Colonial Power / Decolonization	1875–1936 Liberal Parliamentarism Colonial Power / Decolonization	1936–1975 Civil War / Fascist Dictatorship Colonial Power / Decolonization	1975–2014 Parliamentary Democracy / Globalization
Tributary labour	8. Obligatory labourers (State as conqueror)	– Prisoners in penitentiary workshops – Prisoners in the exterior (public works and navy arsenals) – Prisoners in North African prisons – Military service* – *Prestaciones* for rural roads	– Prisoners in penitentiary workshops – Prisoners in North African prisons (until 1911) – Provision of labour (labour tax in Guinea) – Prisoners in Cuba on sugar plantations (until 1898) – Military service* – *Prestaciones* for rural roads	– Prisoners in prison – Prisoners outside prison (until 1970) – Provision of labour: labour tax in Guinea (gradually disappeared, until 1968) – Military service*	– Prisoners in penitentiary workshops – Military service and alternative social service* (until 2001) – Community service work*
	11. Tributary slaves (State as conqueror)			– Prisoners of war (POWs) in concentration camps (until 1945) – POWs in labour battalions depending on the concentration camp structure (until 1945)	

Table 1. (*Continued*)

		1812–1874 Liberal Revolution Colonial Power / Decolonization	1875–1936 Liberal Parliamentarism Colonial Power / Decolonization	1936–1975 Civil War / Fascist Dictatorship Colonial Power / Decolonization	1975–2014 Parliamentary Democracy / Globalization
Commodified labour	15. Indentured labourers for the market (State as redistributor)	– Indigenous Latin Americans in Cuba – Chinese coolies in Cuba	– Plantations in Fernando Poo – Coolies in Cuba – Tobacco plantations in Philippines (until 1898)	– Plantations in Fernando Poo (until 1968)	– Trafficking and indebted migrant labourers – Subcontracting abroad by companies working with indebted migrants**
	17. Slaves producing for the market (State as conqueror)	– Slavery and slave trade in Cuba and Puerto Rico	– Slavery in Puerto Rico and Cuba (until 1873 and 1886 respectively)		

* Neither analysed, nor calculated in this article.
** This kind of labour contract should not be included in this article if we apply the territorial criterion mentioned previously. Nevertheless, we mention it due to its importance in understanding the new accumulation cycle linked to contemporary globalization.

eighteenth century slavery continued in these decades, during which Spain lost most of its American colonial empire.

In spite of this colonial decline, slavery became more widespread during the first half of the nineteenth century, linked to the expansion of sugar production in the framework of what Tomich has termed the "second slavery".[16] For Spanish colonies, the Cuban case is the most important and well documented, owing to its role in Spanish capital accumulation.[17] In spite of the agreement between England and Spain, which made the slave trade illegal after 1817, slavery in Cuba was carried out in conditions of consensual secrecy. This agreement was no obstacle to over 500,000 Africans being landed on the island in the first half of the nineteenth century and a further 163,947 being landed in the following sixteen years, with the result that, at the end of the 1860s, there were about 400,000 slaves on the island,[18] while the island's economy depended on their work in the flourishing sugar industry.[19]

Within the framework of that process of economic growth, immigration through contract and the indenture of settlers from China, the so-called coolies, was also set in motion; their number reached 120,000 between 1847 and 1874.[20] These were workers who remained tied to their employers for a fixed period until they managed to meet the debt contracted for the journey, as well as the costs of their upkeep.[21]

---

16. Dale Tomich, *Through the Prism of Slavery, Labor, Capital, and World Economy* (Lanham, MD, 2004).

17. For a comparison between plantation systems in Cuba and Puerto Rico, see Antonio Santamaría García, "Las islas españolas del azúcar (1760–1898). Grandes debates en perspectiva comparada y caribeña", *América Latina en la Historia Económica*, 35 (2011), pp. 147–176.

18. *Trans-Atlantic Slave Trade Database* (http://www.slavevoyages.org), directed by David Eltis and Martin Halbert, last accessed 22 August 2016. For further details, see Imilcy Balboa Navarro, *Los brazos necesarios. Inmigración, colonización y trabajo libre en Cuba, 1878–1898* (Valencia, 2000), Imilcy Balboa Navarro, "Brazos para el azúcar. Reformas, centralización e inmigración. Cuba, 1820–1886", in José Antonio Piqueras (ed.), *Azúcar y esclavitud en el final del trabajo forzado* (Madrid, 2002), pp. 50–75; Reinaldo Funes Monzote and Dale Tomich, "Naturaleza, tecnología esclavitud en Cuba. Frontera azucarera y revolución industrial", in José Antonio Piqueras (ed.), *Trabajo libre y coactivo en sociedades de plantación* (Madrid, 2009), pp. 75–120; José Antonio Piqueras, "Censos *lato sensu*. La abolición de la esclavitud y el número de esclavos en Cuba", *Revista de Indias*, 71:251 (2011), pp. 193–230.

19. Slavery was also a feature in other sectors of the Cuban economy, such as laying railway lines, for which Asian coolies were also deployed: Oscar Zanetti and Alejandro García, *Sugar and Railroads: A Cuban History, 1837–1959* (Chapel Hill, NC, 1996).

20. Balboa Navarro, *Los brazos necesarios*, p. 28.

21. Evelyn Hu-Dehart, "Chinese Coolie Labor in Cuba in the Nineteenth Century: Free Labor of Neoslavery", *Contributions in Black Studies*, 12 (1994), pp. 38–54; Consuelo Naranjo Orovio and Imilcy Balboa Navarro, "Colonos asiáticos para una economía en expansión: Cuba, 1847–1880", *Revista Mexicana del Caribe*, 8 (1999), pp. 32–65; Benjamin N. Narvaez, "Chinese Coolies in Cuba and Peru: Race, Labor, and Immigration, 1839–1886" (Ph.D. dissertation, University of Texas, 2010). Moreover, some 2,000 Yucatan Indians were also transported under an analogous

With respect to convict labour, the liberal revolution meant that deprivation of liberty was established as a fundamental punishment and prison as the place for its fulfilment. There was thus a progressive elimination of sentencing to forced labour that was more typical of the *ancien régime*, such as sentencing to the galleys (abolished in 1803), work in the navy's arsenals (abolished in 1835, when this was reserved for military prisoners), or work in the mercury mines of Almadén (terminated in 1800).[22] So, although in the peninsula there were cases in which convicts continued to be used in public works, this practice was eliminated in the Penal Code of 1870. As a result, throughout the century, the main experiment in captive labour took place inside the prisons, in workshops.[23] The reality was quite different in the colonial territories,[24] since outdoor work continued in Cuba[25] and in northern Morocco, mainly in the special prisons, the so called *presidios*, where such work generally involved constructing and maintaining military buildings and defence infrastructures.[26]

system: Balboa Navarro, *Los brazos necesarios*, p. 29. Izaskun Álvarez Cuartero, "De Tihosuco a La Habana. La venta de indios yucatecos a Cuba durante la Guerra de Castas", *Studia historica. Historia antigua*, 25 (2007), pp. 559–576. On the contrary, and despite the labour problems in Puerto Rico, indentured migration was not practiced on that island. Santamaría García, "Las islas españolas", pp. 164–165.

22. Pedro A. Llorente de Pedro, "Modalidades de la ejecución penitenciaria en España hasta el siglo XIX", *Anuario de Derecho Penal y Ciencias Penales*, 57 (1998), pp. 311–386.

23. Prison workshops, however, were always few in number and never met the expectations of one of their main promoters, Manuel Montesinos, who was governor of several prisons and played a key role in the liberal reforms of the prison system. For labour in Spanish liberal prisons, see Pedro Trinidad Fernández, *La defensa de la sociedad. Cárcel y delincuencia en España (siglos XVIII–XX)* (Madrid, 1991); Justo Serna Alonso, *Presos y pobres en la España del XIX* (Barcelona, 1988); Fernando Burillo Albacete, *El nacimiento de la pena privativa de libertad* (Madrid, 1999). See also Pedro Oliver Olmo, "Historia y reinvención del utilitarismo punitivo", in José M. Gastón Aguas and Fernando Mendiola Gonzalo (eds), *Los trabajos forzados en la dictadura franquista* (Iruñea-Pamplona, 2007), pp. 18–29; Dario Melossi and Massimo Pavarini, *The Prison and the Factory: Origins of the Penitentiary System* (London, 1981).

24. Recent research has shown that unfree and convict labour have played different and important roles in shaping colonial empires. See John Donoghue and Evelyn P. Jennings, "Introduction", in *idem* (eds), *Building the Atlantic Empires: Unfree Labor and Imperial States in the Political Economy of Capitalism, ca. 1500–1914* (Leiden [etc.], 2016), pp. 1–24; De Vito and Lichtenstein, "Writing a Global History", pp. 10–29.

25. Yolanda Diaz Martínez, "De marginados a trabajadores. Usos y destinos de la población penal en La Habana", *Millars*, XXXV (2012), pp. 129–149.

26. Fernando Burillo Albacete, *La cuestión penitenciaria. Del Sexenio a la Restauración (1868–1913)* (Zaragoza, 2011). This role has similarities with that of Portuguese-African prisons, mainly oriented to infrastructure tasks during the nineteenth century, and was somehow different to British convict labour in Africa, where agricultural work played an important role: Timothy J. Coates, "The Long View of Convict Labour in the Portuguese Empire, 1415–1932", in De Vito and Lichtenstein, *Global Convict Labour*, pp. 151–165; Stacey Hynd, "'… a Weapon of Immense Value'? Convict Labour in British Colonial Africa, c. 1850–1950s", in De Vito and Lichtenstein, *Global Convict Labour*, pp. 249–272, 257–267.

Finally, we also should take into account the survival of some labour-tax systems for different communities during the transition to the liberal regime. One of these systems, the *mita*, was essential for the exploitation of silver mines in Potosí during colonial rule.[27] But it should be remembered that such work was not only a colonial practice; in Spain's rural mainland, much of the work involved in repairing roads was carried out under a system of obligatory community work (the *prestaciones*), which was avoided by medium and large landowners who could afford to pay the corresponding daily wage. This system, created in 1845, was continued in some localities until the first half of the twentieth century.[28]

Industrialization, empire, and liberal parliamentarism (1875–1936)

The period between the signing of the law that outlawed the slave trade in Cuba in 1867 and the abolition of slavery in 1886 was marked by anxiety among landowners, which led to the promotion of other modalities of forced labour, including the indebted immigration of Asians, American Indians, and even Africans under a system of contracts. Despite the attempts of public authorities, that strategy ended in failure as a global solution for labour shortages owing to the inadequate number of workers who finally arrived on the island and to the political instability prior to independence in 1898.[29]

Subsequently, the sugar cycle was somehow replaced in the colonies by another much more limited one, also dependent on forced forms of labour, that of cocoa, cultivated on the island of Bioko (Fernando Poo), in the Gulf of Guinea. In this case, there was considerable pressure from plantation owners to establish mechanisms to force the local population to provide labour.[30] These mechanisms consisted of a labour tax, the *prestaciones*,[31] on the communities,

27. Rossana Barragán, "Dynamics of Continuity and Change: Shifts in Labour Relations in the Potosí Mines (1680–1812)", in the present Special Issue.

28. Francesc-Andreu Martínez Gallego, "La fuerza y la obligación: condenados, asilados y pre-statarios en la obra pública española (1834–1900)", in Santiago Castillo (ed.), *El trabajo a través de la historia* (Madrid, 1996), pp. 313–320.

29. Balboa Navarro, *Los brazos necesarios*, pp. 123–134. In the Philippines, indentured migrants were also deployed on tobacco plantations towards the end of the nineteenth century: Martín Rodrigo y Alharilla, "Del desestanco del tabaco a la puesta en marcha de la Compañía General de Tabacos de Filipinas (1879–1890)", *Boletín Americanista*, 59 (2009), pp. 199–221.

30. One of them is the request of the Agriculture Chamber of Fernando Poo to the colonial governor of the island in 1910 urging him to enforce the *prestaciones* on the Bubi people; although a royal decree issued in 1906 had exempted the Bubi from that kind of labour tax, the governor passed a number of decrees obliging the Bubi to work. Alicia Campos Serrano, "Colonia, derecho y territorio en el Golfo de Guinea. Tensiones del colonialismo español en el siglo XX", *Quaderni Fiorentini*, 33/34 (2004/2005), pp. 865–898.

31. Labour tax was one of the most common ways for the authorities to ensure a labour supply from native populations and one of the basic forms of colonial state income: Marlous van Waijenburg, "Financing the African Colonial State: The Revenue Imperative and Forced Labour", *African Economic History Working Paper*, 20 (2015). See also Julia Seibert, "More Continuity than

and various private contractual formulas through which workers transferred from the continent to the island were left in the hands of the landowners.[32] According to Nerín, in 1917 the number of workers sent to the island was 7,233, the majority of them transferred or held against their will.[33]

With respect to convict labour, it is necessary to analyse the case of colonial Cuba in the context of the abolition of slavery. Here, besides their direct use in quarries and public works benefiting the state, the *leasing* system, through which the state "rented" prisoners to landowners, was adopted through a decree signed in 1883 that accepted the work of prisoners on plantations, thus setting in motion their use in the sugar mills. In fact, in 1886 over half of the 393 convicts working outside the prison of La Habana did so in mills.[34]

On the other side of the Atlantic at the end of the century, the dismantling of the northern African prisons was the subject of a debate, in which concern was raised over what was to be done with some 3,000 prisoners who had been used for fortification and infrastructure in the north of Africa.[35] The reality was that, in spite of plans to use convicts for internal colonization,[36] convict labour was carried out indoors, with around a third of prisoners working in the first few years of the twentieth century and around fifty per cent in the early 1920s (accounting for 0.06 per cent of the active population in 1901).[37] The last attempt to promote work as

Change? New Forms of Unfree Labor in the Belgian Congo, 1908–1930", in Van der Linden, *Humanitarian Intervention and Changing Labor Relations*, pp. 369–386; Kwabena O. Akurang-Parry, "Colonial Forced Labor Policies for Road-Building in Southern Ghana and International Anti-Forced Labor Pressures: 1900–1940", *African Economic History*, 28 (2000), pp. 1–25; De Vito and Lichtenstein, "Writing a Global History", pp. 301–305.

32. Gustau Nerín i Abad, "Els inversors catalans i la conquesta del Muni (1900–1926)", *Illes i imperis*, 8 (2006), pp. 113–131; idem, *La última selva de España. Antropófagos, misioneros y guardias civiles* (Madrid, 2010); Enrique Martino, "Clandestine Recruitment Networks in the Bight of Biafra: Fernando Pó's Answer to the Labour Question, 1926–1945", *International Review of Social History*, 57, Special Issue 20, *Mediating Labour: Worldwide Labour Intermediation in the Nineteenth and Twentieth Centuries* (2012), pp. 39–72.

33. Nerín I Abad, "Els inversors catalans", p. 119.

34. Imilcy Balboa Navarro, "Presidiarios por esclavos. Mano de obra cautiva en la transición al trabajo libre", in Piqueras, *Trabajo libre y coactivo en sociedades de plantación*, pp. 253–282, 260–261.

35. Burillo Albacete, *La cuestión penitenciaria*.

36. The Spanish authorities had rejected deportation and penal colonization in 1875 and later on again in the early twentieth century: Pere Gabriel, "Más allá de los exilios políticos: proscritos y deportados en el siglo XIX", in Santiago Castillo and Pedro Oliver (eds), *Las figuras del desorden. Heterodoxos, proscritos y marginados* (Madrid, 2006), pp. 197–221; Juan José Díaz Matarranz, *De la trata de negros al cultivo del cacao. Evolución del modelo colonial español en Guinea Ecuatorial de 1778 a 1914* (Barcelona, 2005).

37. I must, therefore, disagree with the estimate provided for category 8 in 1900 (treating the whole prison population as workers: 24,690): Lana, "Spain 1800, 1900, 2000", p. 28. The Director General of Prisons stated in 1904 that "the majority of the approximately 17,000 inmates held by our prisons remain in sterile and injurious idleness" (cited by Burillo Albacete, *La cuestión penitenciaria*, p. 192), and the latest estimates by Gargallo show that in 1906 only thirty-five per cent of prisoners were

punishment was the Vagrancy Act of 1933, but it did not result in the development of a specific system of forced labour.[38]

Spanish Civil War and Francoist dictatorship

After the failed *coup d'etat* of 1936, the ensuing civil war made possible extensive mobilization and the capture of an enormous number of prisoners of war, who had started to be used as cheap labour in non-frontline parts of Europe since World War I.[39] In the zone loyal to the Republic, three modalities of forced labour were implanted at the same time as the breakdown of the penitentiary reforms guaranteeing more rights for prisoners, which had been promoted in the early 1930s.[40] In December 1936, the Ministry of Justice opened the first of a series of labour camps for right-wing prisoners, to which would be added the creation of disciplinary battalions in the army itself and the opening in 1938 of six labour camps in Catalonia run under the auspices of the Military Intelligence Service (SIM – Servicio de Inteligencia Militar), in which captives of various origins were incarcerated.[41] In total, the number of people working in captivity on the Republican side can be estimated at between 20,000 and 25,000.[42]

In contrast, much more important in number and economic impact was the implementation by the Francoist side of the largest system of work in

working with a much lower percentage for women: Luis Gargallo Vaamonde, "Desarrollo y destrucción del sistema liberal de prisiones en España. De la Restauración a la Guerra Civil" (Ph.D. dissertation, Universidad de Castilla-La Mancha, 2015), pp. 627–635. In my opinion, of those included in the 1900 data the tens of thousands of conscript soldiers who were doing military service should be included in category 8. Lana puts them in category 18.3 (commodified labour working for non-market institutions): Lana, "Labour Relations in Spain", p. 33.

38. Iván Heredia Urzaiz, "La defensa de la sociedad: uso y abuso de la Ley de Vagos y Maleantes", in Castillo and Oliver, *Las figuras del desorden*.

39. Gerald H. Davis, "Prisoners of War in Twentieth-Century War Economies", *Journal of Contemporary History*, 12:4 (1977), pp. 623–634, 628–630. For World War II in Germany, see Mark Spoerer, *Forced Labor in the Third Reich* (Frankfurt am Main, 2010); Mark Spoerer and Jochen Fleischhacker, "Forced Laborers in Nazi Germany: Categories, Numbers, and Survivors", *Journal of Interdisciplinary History*, XXIII:2 (2002), pp. 169–204; Marc Buggeln, *Slave Labor in Nazi Concentration Camps* (Oxford, 2014). For the USSR, see Paul Gregory and Valery Lazarev (eds), *The Economics of Forced Labor: The Soviet Gulag* (Stanford, CA, 2003). For a comparison of the use of forced labour between Japan and Germany in the two world wars, see Mark Spoerer, "Zwangsarbeitsregimes im Vergleich. Deutschland und Japan im Ersten und Zweiten Weltkrieg", in Hans-Christoph Seidel and Klaus Tenfelde (eds), *Zwangsarbeit im Europa des 20. Jahrhunderts. Bewältigung und vergleichende Aspekte* (Essen, 2007), pp. 187–226.

40. Luis Gargallo Vaamonde, *El sistema penitenciario de la Segunda República. Antes y después de Victoria Kent (1931–1936)* (Madrid, 2011).

41. Francesc Badia, *Els camps de treball a Catalunya durant la Guerra Civil (1936–1939)* (Barcelona, 2001).

42. Julius Ruiz, "'Work and Don't Lose Hope': Republican Forced Labour Camps during the Spanish Civil War", *Contemporary European History*, 18:4 (2009), pp. 419–441.

captivity seen in twentieth-century Spain, starting in spring 1937 with the creation of the Concentration Camp Inspectorate for Prisoners of War (ICCP – Inspección de Campos de Concentración de Prisioneros) and the publication of the Decree on the Concession of the Right to Work to Prisoners and Prisoners of War, which heralded the two great modalities of forced labour during the dictatorship.[43]

The first of these, numerically more significant although more short-lived, was structured on the basis of battalions depending on the ICCP and comprising POWs classified as being opposed to the regime or of doubtful loyalty. These were named Workers' Battalions (BBTT – *Batallones de Trabajadores*) between 1938 and 1940, and Disciplinary Battalions of Worker Soldiers (BDST – *Batallones Disciplinarios de Soldados Trabajadores*) from 1940 until they were disbanded, the majority in 1942 and the rest in 1945. At their highpoint, at the end of the war, the BBTT included some 90,000 POWs, although the number fell to about 40,000 between 1939 and 1942.[44]

The second modality began to be constituted in 1938, with the System of Punishment Redemption through Work for prisoners who had previously been tried. This system encompassed not only the new prison workshops, but also modalities of extramural work, such as the Militarized Penitentiary Colonies[45] or the Penal Detachments.[46] The number of convict workers

43. The text of the decree is very explicit about the obligation to work: "Such a right to work is preceded by the idea of right-function, or right-duty, and, if necessary, right-obligation". *Boletín Oficial del Estado*, 1 June 1937.
44. Fernando Mendiola Gonzalo, "Forced Labor, Public Policies, and Business Strategies During Franco's Dictatorship: An Interim Report", *Enterprise & Society*, 14:1 (2013), pp. 182–213. For further information, see Javier Rodrigo, *Cautivos, campos de concentración en la España franquista, 1936–1947* (Barcelona, 2005); Fernando Mendiola Gonzalo, "Reeducation Through Work? Mountain Roads in the Spanish Concentration Universe (Western Pyrenees, 1939–1942)", *Labor History*, 55:1 (2014), pp. 97–116. The classification of concentration camp POWs as slaves has also been a subject of historiographical debate: Cord Pagenstecher, "'We Were Treated Like Slaves': Remembering Forced Labor for Nazi Germany", in R. Hörmann and G. Mackenthun (eds), *Human Bondage in the Cultural Contact Zone: Transdisciplinary Perspectives on Slavery and Its Discourses* (Münster, 2010), pp. 275–291; Marc Buggeln, "Were Concentration Camp Prisoners Slaves? The Possibilities and Limits of Comparative History and Global Historical Perspectives", *International Review of Social History*, 53:1 (2008), pp. 101–129; Alexander von Plato, "'It was Modern Slavery': First Results of the Documentation Project on Forced and Slave Labour", in Alexander von Plato, Almut Leh, and Christoph Thonfeld (eds), *Hitler's Slaves: Life Stories of Forced Labourers in Nazi-Occupied Europe* (New York and Oxford, 2010), pp. 441–484; Spoerer and Fleischhacker, "Forced Laborers in Nazi Germany", pp. 172–176.
45. These colonies where under public control: Gonzalo Acosta Bono *et al.*, *El Canal de los Presos (1940–1962). Trabajos forzados. De la represión política a la explotación económica* (Barcelona, 2004), pp. 81–101.
46. These detachments were placed with private companies, to which the state "leased" the prisoners: Alicia Quintero, "Sistema penitenciario durante el primer franquismo. Los destacamentos penales", paper presented at II Encuentro de Jóvenes Investigadores en Historia Contemporánea de la AHC, Granada, 2009.

peaked at 24,844 in 1943, from when it started to fall in line with the decline in the size of the prison population, remaining below 10,000 in the 1950s. Following a boom in exterior work in the early years after the civil war, under Francoism forced labour was progressively withdrawn to the interior of the prisons. As noted, the system regulating this work was basically Punishment Redemption, but the 1946 Regulation on Penitentiary Work nonetheless left the door open to work of a compulsory character, with the result that the Francoist prisons housed a growing percentage of working captives.[47]

If we analyse these figures in terms of the long-term evolution of captive labour in Spain, we must emphasize that it was in the immediate aftermath of the civil war, in 1940, that convict labour was at its most important, with 108,781 prisoners and POWs working, 1.16 per cent of the total active population.[48]

Finally, and in relation to imperial policies prior to decolonization, we must note that, although declining in importance, the labour-tax system of *prestaciones* was maintained by the dictatorship, while the main efforts of colonial rulers focused on encouraging indentured and contract migration networks.[49]

Unfree labour in parliamentary democracy within a globalizing context

For post-Francoist Spain, we must take account of contemporary forms of unfree labour in the framework of globalization and the formation of global supply and value networks.[50] These forms, which some authors have conceptualized as "new slavery",[51] involve millions of workers all over the

---

47. Acosta Bono *et al.*, *El Canal de los Presos*; Domingo Rodríguez Teijeiro, *Las cárceles de Franco* (Madrid, 2011); Mendiola Gonzalo, "Forced Labor", pp. 211–212; José R. González Cortés, "Bibliografía de lo punitivo. Los estudios sobre los trabajos forzados del franquismo", in Pedro Oliver Olmo and Jesús C. Urda Lozano (eds), *La prisión y las instituciones punitivas en la investigación histórica* (Cuenca, 2014), pp. 597–614. Under the Vagrancy Act of 1933, during the dictatorship captives, many of them homosexuals, were also forced to work in the Penitentiary Colony of Tefía, in the Canary Islands.

48. For further details, see Mendiola Gonzalo, "Forced Labor". This average percentage does not indicate the importance of forced labour in some specific sectors. In Basque iron-mining, an economically strategic sector, the proportion reached 19.4 per cent in 1938: Fernando Mendiola Gonzalo, "El impacto de los trabajos forzados en la economía Vasconavarra (1937–1945)", *Investigaciones de Historia Económica*, 8:5 (2012), pp. 104–116, 107.

49. Alicia Campos Serrano, "El régimen colonial franquista en el Golfo de Guinea", *Revista Jurídica Universidad Autónoma de Madrid*, 3 (2000), pp. 79–108, 98–102; Martino, "Clandestine Recruitment Networks".

50. For value and supply chains, see Jean Allain *et al.*, *Forced Labour's Business Models and Supply Chains* (York, 2013), pp. 39–53; Nicola Phillips, "Unfree Labour and Adverse Incorporation in the Global Economy: Comparative Perspectives on Brazil and India", *Economy and Society*, 42:2 (2013) pp. 171–196.

51. Kevin Bales, *Disposable People: New Slavery in the Global Economy* (Berkeley, CA, 1999); *idem*, *Understanding Global Slavery* (Berkeley, CA, and London, 2005). Recent estimates for Europe can be found in *idem*, "Slavery in Europe: Part 1, Estimating the Dark Figure", *Human Rights Quarterly*, 35:4 (2013), pp. 817–829.

world, many of them in situations of indentured labour, often as a result of clandestine migratory movements.[52]

Within the previously explained category 8 of the Collaboratory's taxonomy, the end of compulsory military service in 2001 meant that work in prisons was the only type of labour relationship. In fact, it was not completely compulsory, but different testimonies and research have pointed out that refusing work in prison adversely affected a prisoner's chances of being granted parole.[53] Thus, what should be included in the totals provided by Lana[54] for category 8 in 2001 is the total number of prisoners working in the prisons, which that year totalled 9,566, accounting for 0.05 per cent of the active population.[55] The majority of the 16,246 prisoners working in Spanish prisons in 2013 were doing so in the maintenance services of the prison itself, although over 3,000 did so in workshops of private companies established within the prisons.[56] One of the great methodological difficulties and challenges facing researchers is having precise data on company participation in penitentiary workshops, since the official memoranda do not provide them, and we have only partial information through the denunciations of prisoners and solidarity collectives, for both the 1970s[57] and the present.[58]

52. For overall figures: ILO, *Profits and Poverty*. For structural coercion as one of the keys to understanding migrants' debt bondage, see Genevieve LeBaron, "Reconceptualizing Debt Bondage: Debt as a Class-Based Form of Labor Discipline", *Critical Sociology*, 40:5 (2014), pp. 763–780.

53. See, for example, this prisoner's answer to a research questionnaire: "If you refuse to work, reprisals are immediate: they won't give you permissions": Observatori del Sistema Penal i els Drets Humans, *L'empresonament a Catalunya* (Barcelona, 2004), p. 261. This other prisoner, J. Solis, recently declared that "You had to sign that labour contract to have some rights; therefore, it was a complete coercion": Víscera, "Contra los muros. Diálogo visceral con Amadeu Casellas y José Solís", *Víscera*, 4 (2010), p. 8.

54. Lana, "Spain 1800, 1900, 2000", p. 43.

55. Data on prisoners' work are available separately for Catalonia and the rest of Spain. For Catalonia: Departament de Justícia, *Memòria del Departament de Justícia 2001* (Barcelona, 2001), p. 278, available at http://justicia.gencat.cat/web/.content/documents/arxius/doc_43044028_1.pdf, last accessed 22 August 2016; for the rest of Spain: Ministerio del Interior, *Informe General 2001, Dirección General de Instituciones Penitenciarias* (Madrid, 2001), p. 218, available at http://www.institucionpenitenciaria.es/web/export/sites/default/datos/descargables/publicaciones/IFNORME_2001.pdf, last accessed 22 August 2016.

56. For Catalonia: Departament de Justícia, *Memòria del Departament de Justícia 2013* (Barcelona, 2013), p. 180, available at http://justicia.gencat.cat/web/.content/documents/publicacions/memoria_2013/memoria_justicia_2013.pdf, last accessed 22 August 2016; for the rest of Spain: OATPFE, *Memoria 2013 del Organismo Autónomo Trabajo Penitenciario y Formación para el Empleo* (Madrid, 2013), p.10, available at http://www.oatpfe.es/docs/2014/07/24/12330001_4_2_0.pdf, last accessed 22 August 2016. For the evolution of Spanish prisons after Franco's dictatorship, see César Lorenzo Rubio, "Modernización y segregación en las prisiones de la democracia", in Pedro Oliver Olmo (ed.), *El siglo de los castigos. Prisión y formas carcelarias en la España del siglo XX* (Barcelona, 2013), pp. 101–143. The rise between 2001 and 2013 is due mainly to the efforts of prisons to involve more and more prisoners in daily work.

57. Colectiu Arrán, "La lucha en la cárcel en la España de los años 70. Trabajos penitenciarios / Talleres penitenciarios de Carabanchel", *Panóptico*, 5 (2003), pp. 178–186, 182–184.

58. Amadeu Casellas Ramón, *Un reflejo de la sociedad. Crónica de una experiencia en las cárceles de la democracia* (Barcelona, 2014), pp. 337–339.

Outside the prisons, in the Spanish case situations of "new slavery" are basically linked to processes of indebtedness of migrants, the number of which Bales estimates at around 6,116 in 2009.[59] With respect to sectors of work, there are no monographic studies, but there is information on forced labour practices in agriculture,[60] in the building industry,[61] in domestic service,[62] and in prostitution.[63]

Finally, although the deployment of forced labourers is today generally considered only within the context of Spain's borders, we must also consider the use of forced labour by Spanish companies operating internationally – and which is therefore beyond the scope of Spanish legislation. There are, once again, methodological difficulties in clarifying this question owing to the opacity of subcontracting systems and the lack of validity of commitments made, as in the case of Inditex,[64] a company publicly accused of using immigrant workers under debt bondage in workshops in Argentina[65] and Brazil.[66] Moreover, cases have also been confirmed in

---

59. Bales, "Slavery in Europe", p. 827. Due to the clandestine character of this situation, it is impossible to quantify this exactly. Bales has continued to refine this quantification, resulting in this new estimate for 2009, lower than the previous one, of between 10,000 and 15,000, for the early years of the twenty-first century, prior to the economic crisis that started in 2008. In any case, the still unknown number of workers included in category 15 should be added to the figures provided by Lana ("Spain 1800, 1900, 2000", p. 43) on labour relations in 2001, based on the 2001 Census in which, obviously, these workers are not recorded.

60. Rodrigo García Schwarz, *Rompiendo las cadenas de una ciudadanía cautiva* (Madrid, 2011), pp. 241–242; one recent article in *The Guardian* reported that Spanish police had information about this situation, their only concern being to avoid migrants reaching tourist locations: Felicity Lawrence, "Spain's Salad Growers are Modern-Day Slaves, Say Charities", *The Guardian*, 7 February 2011, available at http://www.theguardian.com/business/2011/feb/07/spain-salad-growers-slaves-charities, last accessed 22 August 2016.

61. García Schwarz, *Rompiendo las cadenas*.

62. Office of the Special Representative and Coordinator for Combating Trafficking in Human Beings, "Unprotected Work, Invisible Exploitation: Trafficking for the Purpose of Domestic Servitude", *OSCE Occasional Paper Series*, 4 (2010), p. 10.

63. Luis Gargallo Vaamonde and María Sánchez Fernández, "El tráfico de mujeres para su explotación sexual. Una esclavitud invisible", *Revista General de Derecho Penal*, 16 (2011); ILO, *Profits and Poverty*, p. 17.

64. For the agreement between Inditex and the International Textile, Garment and Leather Workers' Federation (ITGLWF), see ILO, *The Cost of Coercion*, p. 58.

65. Ana Delicado, "Zara recurre al trabajo esclavo en Argentina", *Público*, 8 April 2013, available at http://www.publico.es/internacional/453287/zara-recurre-al-trabajo-esclavo-en-argentina, last accessed 22 August 2016.

66. Agencia EFE, "Brasil expedienta a Zara por un escándalo de esclavitud en Sao Paulo", *La Vanguardia*, 18 August 2011, available at http://www.lavanguardia.com/internacional/20110818/54201597972/brasil-expedienta-a-zara-por-un-escandalo-de-esclavitud-en-sao-paulo.html, last accessed 22 August 2016; José Manuel Rambla, "Brasil amenaza con sancionar a Zara por utilizar mano de obra esclava", *Nueva Tribuna*, 15 May 2015, available at http://www.nuevatribuna.es/articulo/america-latina/brasil-amenaza-sancionar-zara-75-millones-euros-utilizar-mano-obra-esclava/20150513184608115934.html, last accessed 15 November 2016.

fishing companies,[67] and in the building sector by one of the subcontractors for the Spanish company OHL, which is involved in construction work on the stadiums being used for the Football World Cup in Qatar.[68] Clearly, these are all isolated cases, but they reveal the existence of a submerged global economy that Spanish multinational companies are also taking advantage of, in the framework of the new global value and supply chains.[69]

THE DRIVING FORCES BEHIND DEMAND: RELATIVE SCARCITY AND ACCUMULATION CYCLES

The relative scarcity of labour power

Labour scarcity is considered a key factor for understanding the recourse to forced labour.[70] Nonetheless, this has also been questioned by many authors, not only because in some specific situations labour shortage does not serve as an explanatory factor,[71] but also because on occasions it is precisely an element that facilitates a dissolution of coercive bonds specific to labour because of the effects of the option to abandon the work, the so-called *outside option effect.*[72] In any case, all these approaches stress that scarcity must be understood in a relative way, something that is confirmed, too, in the Spanish case.

In the case of the so-called *second slavery* in colonial Cuba, it is beyond dispute that this recourse to slavery was the way to implement a process of expansion that required – in keeping with the process of sugar-mill mechanization and the logic of economies of scale – an extensive use of labour that was not available on the island at that time.[73] We must consider,

---

67. "¿Somos marinos o esclavos?", *Boletín de los Marinos*, Federación Internacional de los Trabajadores del Transporte, 22 (2008).

68. Amnesty International, *The Dark Side of Migration: Spotlight on Qatar's Construction Sector Ahead of the World Cup* (London, 2013), pp. 79–82.

69. Since labour relationships lie within the legal framework of the country where they take place, and, moreover, most of the supplier enterprises are independent of the main one, the Spanish government and the courts have kept themselves apart from this reality.

70. Domar, "The Causes of Slavery". More recently, and in a broader sense, transaction-costs economists have remarked that "hierarchy is favored as asset specificity builds up": Oliver E. Williamson, "The Theory of the Firm as Governance Structure: From Choice to Contract", *Journal of Economic Perspectives*, 16:3 (2002), pp. 171–195, 181.

71. Linden, *Workers of the World*, pp. 39–54; Moulier Boutang, *De l'esclavage au salariat*, pp. 661–672; Erik Green, "The Economics of Slavery in the Eighteenth-Century Cape Colony: Revising the Nieboer-Domar Hypothesis", *International Review of Social History*, 59:1 (2014), pp. 39–70.

72. This is the case, for example, with the crisis in the Low Middle Ages, when labour shortage related to demographic collapse resulted in very different labour regimes depending on the political situation: Daron Acemoglu and Alexander Wolitzky, "The Economics of Labor Coercion", *Econometrica*, 79:2 (2011), pp. 555–600, 587–588.

73. Balboa Navarro, *Los brazos necesarios*; Funes and Tomich, "Naturaleza, tecnología esclavitud en Cuba".

as we shall see later when analysing accumulation strategies, that other types of alternative were ruled out, due precisely to their greater cost. A similar situation took place on the cocoa plantations of Fernando Pó at the end of the nineteenth century, although on a much smaller scale. Here, too, recourse to the imposition of forced labour was linked to complaints on the part of plantation owners about the need for labourers for the cocoa harvest; those plantation owners formed a pressure group, which pushed the Spanish government to retain the continental territory of Muni as a labour reserve for the island.[74]

Secondly, attention must be paid to the only period of modern Spanish history when it is possible to speak of a shortage of labour in a strict sense: the period of the Spanish Civil War, in the framework of global mobilization, repression, and exile, when the Spanish economy suffered a great loss of human capital.[75] There was a very different intensity in the use of forced labour on the two sides during the war, which once again leads us to diminish the significance of this factor. Recent research has shown that in specific situations a scarcity of labour acted as a key element in the demand for forced workers while, in an opposite sense, the end of such scarcity led some companies to actually request that forced workers be replaced by other, free workers. Examples include some mining companies in Biscay and the MZA railway company. The latter initially justified its request for prisoners as being due to the "scarcity of our own workers", while months later, once the war had ended, it requested the replacement of a Workers' Battalion by free workers, arguing that the latter were more productive.[76] This overall shortage of labour ended with the war, not so much because losses in terms of demography or human capital were recovered, but because of the lack of economic dynamism and the slow pace of economic recovery.[77]

Thirdly, account must be taken of the spectacular demand for labour in the last expansive cycle of the Spanish economy, between 1996 and 2007. This was a period when new jobs were created at a much higher pace in

74. Nerín I Abad, *La última selva*.

75. Clara E. Núñez Romero Balmas, "El capital humano en el primer franquismo", in Carlos Barciela López (ed.), *Autarquía y mercado negro. El fracaso económico del primer franquismo, 1939–1959* (Barcelona, 2003), pp. 27–54.

76. Fernando Mendiola, "Of Firms and Captives: Railway Infrastructures and the Economics of Forced Labour (Spain, 1937–1957)", *Revista de Historia Industrial* (forthcoming, 2017). On Basque mining see Fátima Pastor Ruiz, *El Batallón Minero nº 1 en las minas de Vizcaya* (Bilbao, 2010); Mendiola Gonzalo, "El impacto".

77. Jordi Catalán, "La reconstrucción franquista y la experiencia de Europa occidental, 1934–1949", in Barciela López (ed.), *Autarquía y mercado negro*, pp. 123–168; for labour deployment during these years, see Leandro Prados de la Escosura and Joan R. Rosés, "Human Capital and Economic Growth in Spain, 1850–2000", *Explorations in Economic History*, 47:4 (2010), pp. 520–532, 528.

Spain than in Europe as a whole, due to the labour-intensive and natural resource-intensive character of the country's economic growth, which was linked to property expansion and construction work.[78] In this context, the growing demand for labour, concentrated in more precarious and less well-paid jobs, was largely satisfied thanks to one of the spaces most favourable to forced labour: illegal immigration.[79]

These cases show us that, in reality, scarcity must be analysed in relative rather than absolute terms, in terms of the elasticity of demand for labour being higher than the elasticity of supply, while other options that could clearly be costlier to employers must also be analysed. This applies not only to the three situations set out, but also to others in which relative scarcity must be understood according to seasonal, sectoral, territorial, or legal criteria.

The scarce population of certain regions has also been used as a factor explaining the recourse to forced labour, due to the extra costs that could be involved for companies or the state in transferring population to those zones. Internal colonization in areas with a low population density was one option considered at the start of the twentieth century for relocating convicts in African prisons,[80] and it appears subsequently as one reason for deploying forced labour during the Spanish Civil War.[81] Moreover, the opening up of transport infrastructures in sparsely populated regions was a significant problem during the Francoist dictatorship, so recourse was made to Workers' Battalions to open up roads in parts of the Pyrenees, and also to prisoners to open up railway lines.[82]

---

78. Isidro López and Emmanuel Rodríguez, "The Spanish Model", *New Left Review*, 69 (2011), pp. 5–28. The centrality of migration for the expansion of labour force is clear: from 1994 to 2008 Spain's active population increased 40.9 per cent, and this growth was due more to migrants (3,347,400) than to Spanish workers (3,207,500). The former accounted for 0.61 per cent of the active population in 1994 and 15.26 per cent in 2008. Miguel Pajares, *Inmigración y mercado de trabajo. Informe 2009* (Madrid, 2009), pp. 26–27. It should also be noted that unemployment fell sharply between 1994 (22 per cent) and 2007 (8.2 per cent), the year before the crisis, a rate quite similar to that for the eurozone as a whole (7.5 per cent): available at http://ec.europa.eu/eurostat, last accessed 22 August 2016.

79. In 2009, there were 1,449,968 immigrants with a temporary residence permit and about 900,000 in a situation of illegality: Eduardo Romero, *Un deseo apasionado de trabajo más barato y servicial* (Oviedo, 2010), pp. 134–135. See also Pajares, *Inmigración y mercado de trabajo*.

80. The only practical result of this was the opening of the "El Dueso" penitentiary colony in Santoña: Burillo Albacete, *La cuestión penitenciaria*.

81. The labour camps created by the Republican Ministry of Justice in 1936 were essentially agricultural, while in the Francoist zone internal colonization was already the goal of forced labour policies, as can be seen in ICCP memoranda, and also in the case of La Cabrera in León: Juan Carlos García-Funes, *"A recoger bombas". Batallones de trabajo forzado en Castilla y León* (Seville, 2016).

82. On mountain roads: Fernando Mendiola and Edurne Beaumont, *Esclavos del franquismo en el Pirineo* (Tafalla, 2006), and Mendiola Gonzalo, "Reeducation Through Work?". On railway infrastructures: Mendiola, "Of Firms and Captives".

Relative scarcity combined with seasonality is another factor that must be taken into account when explaining the recourse to coercion. Agriculture has always been a sector strongly marked by seasonality in the distribution of labour, and that continues to be the case today. This means that it is a sector conducive to the use of *labour supply chains* for ensuring the presence of workers at the required time owing to its particular characteristics and the existence of highly labour-intensive tasks for short periods of time.[83] It is precisely in special situations, like the harvest, that cases of exploitation of immigrants have been found to border on forced labour.[84] The influence of the greater demand for labour in summer has historically meant that during this season other sectors can be negatively affected by a scarcity of labour or a rise in wages. In fact, in the account of the virtues of work in the Memorandum of the General Directorate of Prisons (DGP) it is explained that recourse to convict labour also served to stabilize the number of workers in the construction sector "at critical seasonal times".[85]

Finally, regarding labour shortage we must consider the relationships between qualification levels and the intensity of work. Indeed, the case of one Basque province, Bizkaia, shows, as in most of the cases that appear in Table 1, that forced labourers were deployed mainly in low-qualification and effort-intensive tasks,[86] such as mining and construction, where the presence of captive workers in industry was much lower. Nevertheless, when necessary those industries requested prisoners or POWs with very specific skills.[87]

Another peculiarity, in this case related to the low elasticity of supply for labour, is that of illegal activities, where forced labour provides an easy

83. Allain *et al.*, *Forced Labour's Business Models*, pp. 42–43 and 47–49.

84. García Schwarz, *Rompiendo las cadenas*. Barrientos has confirmed the presence today of supply chains bringing workers from Africa to English agriculture, through which farmers have access to labourers subjected to debt bondage: Barrientos, "Labor Chains", p. 1063. The importance of seasonality, of course, must also be understood in its political and legal framework.

85. Dirección General de Prisiones, *Memoria de la Dirección General de Prisiones* (Madrid, 1956), p. 73. A similar logic has been found in the post-slavery southern USA and in colonial India: Alex Lichtenstein, *Twice the Work of Free Labor: The Political Economy of Convict Labor in the New South* (London and New York, NY, 1996), pp. 46–47; Chitra Joshi, "Public Works and the Question of Unfree Labour", in Stanziani, *Labour, Coercion, and Economic Growth in Eurasia*, pp. 273–287, 285–287.

86. This positive correlation between effort and coercion was underlined long ago by Fenoaltea: Stefano Fenoaltea, "Slavery and Supervision in Comparative Perspective: A Model", *Journal of Economic History*, 44:3 (1984), pp. 635–668. It has been widely accepted in the literature: Acemoglu and Wolitzki, "The Economics of Labor Coercion". Historical research has proved that coercion and forced labour have also been present in skilled tasks, mainly through incentives: Van der Linden, *Workers of the World*, p. 50.

87. Mendiola Gonzalo, "Forced Labor"; *idem*, "El impacto".

solution to variations in demand.[88] Therefore, we must again emphasize that scarcity, though central to understanding the demand for forced labour, must be analysed also taking into account a number of other economic and political factors.

Forced labour and cycles of capital accumulation

As we have seen in the previous section, the option of forced labour must not be seen as something necessary, but as arising from the balance of forces between labour and capital in different legal frameworks that make it easier for the latter to impose a modality of forced labour, yielding it greater profits or ensuring labourers that would otherwise have been more difficult, or more expensive, to find.[89] Put another way, it is necessary to consider these coercive mechanisms of labour recruitment not only as something characteristic of primitive accumulation prior to capitalism, but also as one of the options used intermittently over the course of its historical development in new cycles of accumulation, as proposed by Brass in the concept of "deproletarianization".[90]

With respect to the Spanish case, I believe that there were three great cycles of capital accumulation during the past two centuries that were based to a certain (and different) extent on the utilization of forced labour: colonial slavery, forced labour under Francoism, and the appearance of new forms of forced labour within the framework of the upward cycle of 1996–2008.

In the case of slavery, the Cuban experience provides a good example of how relations of slavery can be immersed within the cycle of production and accumulation linked to a new world division of labour, not only in the stages prior to capitalist industrialization, as proposed by Williams, but also during the process of industrialization.[91] Moreover, profits generated by slave labour were not only reinvested in the sugar economy, but also used to further the industrializing process in the metropolis, especially in Catalonia.

---

88. Andrew Crane, "Modern Slavery as a Management Practice: Exploring the Conditions and Capabilities for Human Exploitation", *Academy of Management Review*, 38:1 (2013), pp. 49–69, 54.
89. Of course, coercion costs (police, frontier controls, prisons, concentration camps) linked to unfree labour are often paid by the state, and not by the employers.
90. Brass, "Some Observations on Unfree Labour", pp. 71–74; *idem*, "Debating Capitalist Dynamics".
91. Williams holds that commercial capitalism promoted and benefited from slavery, while industrial capitalism destroyed it: Eric Williams, *Capitalism and Slavery* (Chapel Hill, NC, 1944). Taking a different approach, Tomich, *Through the Prism of Slavery*, pp. 17–27 and 56–71, has pointed out that it is necessary to insert this "second slavery" into the capitalist expansion of the early nineteenth century. See also Michael Zeuske, "Historiography and Research Problems of Slavery and the Slave Trade in a Global-Historical Perspective", *International Review of Social History*, 57:1 (2012), pp. 87–111.

This was the case both during the central decades of the nineteenth century and after 1898, when Spain underwent a great investment cycle principally motivated by the arrival of capital from Cuba and other areas of Latin America.[92] The central role of forced labour with respect to capital accumulation was such that the Cuban elites made an effort to extract the greatest possible output from the system, even when slavery was about to be abolished.[93]

The second cycle in which we can relate capital accumulation and forced labour is the Spanish Civil War and the initial period of Francoism. While capital accumulation and the fall in wages must be framed in terms of the transformation of the labour market and the political repression of the time,[94] forced labour, in spite of the productivity problems it entailed, also contributed to that capital accumulation,[95] while functioning at the same time as a key tool to discipline the working population.[96] With respect to

92. Ángel Bahamonde Magro and José Cayuela Fernández, "Traficantes, armadores y hacendados. Elite colonial hispano-cubana y trasvase de capitales a finales del siglo XIX", *Studia Historica*, 15 (1997), pp. 9–20; Luis Alonso Álvarez, "Comercio exterior y formación de capital financiero: el tráfico de negros hispano-cubano, 1821–1868", *Anuario de Estudios Americanos*, 51:2 (1994), pp. 75–92; Michael Zeuske and Orlando García Martínez, "*La Amistad* de Cuba: Ramón Ferrer, contrabando de esclavos, captividad y modernidad atlántica", *Caribbean Studies*, 37 (2009), pp. 97–170; Martín Rodrigo y Alharilla, "Los Goytisolo. De hacendados en Cienfuegos a inversores en Barcelona", *Revista de Historia Industrial*, 23 (2003), pp. 11–37; Martín Rodrigo y Alharilla, "Los amargos beneficios del dulce. Azúcar, Cuba y deuda ecológica", *Anuario de Estudios Americanos*, 63:1 (2006), pp. 211–232.

93. José Antonio Piqueras, "El capital emancipado. Esclavitud, industria azucarera y abolición en Cuba", in Piqueras, *Azúcar y esclavitud*, pp. 214–251. To replace increasingly expensive and scarce slaves, landowners opted for Asian indentured immigrants, rejecting government attempts to encourage the immigration of free Spanish workers who would be more politically loyal, but more expensive as labour: Balboa Navarro, *Los brazos necesarios*, pp. 165–176. Highly illustrative is the complaint of the Plenipotentiary Minister of Spain in Peking in 1878, who stated that "The Cuban landowners did not want to understand that they had to make a brusque but essential conversion from the work of slaves to that of labourers, and on becoming convinced that they could no longer extract blacks from Africa, they have gone to Asia for yellow men, reducing the whole transition to one of colour" (Balboa Navarro, *Los brazos necesarios*, p. 124).

94. Margarita Vilar Rodríguez, *Los salarios del miedo. Mercado de trabajo y crecimiento económico en España durante el franquismo* (Santiago de Compostela, 2009). See also Margarita Vilar, "'The Labour Market under the Iron Fist of the State': The Franco Dictatorship in the Mirror of Hitler, Mussolini and Stalin", *European Review of History: Revue europeenne d'histoire*, 20:3 (2013), pp. 427–443.

95. Lower productivity among POWs with respect to prisoners has been demonstrated for Franco's Spain: Mendiola Gonzalo, "Forced Labor", pp. 198–203. In Nazi Germany, the lower productivity of forced labourers has been proved to be compatible with higher profits for enterprises, due to the extremely low costs of labour: Mark Spoerer, "Profitierten Unternehmen von KZ-Arbeit? Eine kritische Analyse der Literatur", *Historische Zeitschrift*, 268:1 (1999), pp. 61–95.

96. Rodrigo, *Cautivos*; Acosta Bono *et al.*, *El Canal de los Presos*; Gutmaro Gómez Bravo, *La redención de penas. La formación del sistema penitenciario franquista* (Madrid, 2008); Mendiola Gonzalo, "Reeducation through Work?" This political function of forced labour, with clear repercussions on the transformation of the labour market and the evolution of wages, has been

the private sector, forced labour made possible direct profits for the companies that used it, and this has also been conceptualized by Sánchez Albornoz as being similar in a certain sense to primitive accumulation.[97] While, in principle, companies had to pay the state the same wage as that stipulated for free workers in each locality, there were different mechanisms for drawing additional profit from convict workers: paying a lower salary than that paid to free workers in remote areas; the possibility of redirecting foodstuffs intended for the prisoners to the black market; lengthening the working day; or even, in some cases, refusing to pay the state for the use of captive workers.[98] In addition, it is necessary to include as private profit the irrigation of substantial areas of land belonging to large landowners by means of forced labour, as was the case with the Guadalquivir Canal.[99] For its part, the public sector also obtained significant profits as the main employer of forced workers. On the one hand, due to work on public infrastructure such as roads and railways, which involved the work of thousands of POWs and, on the other, due to the money the state Treasury received from the companies that used prisoners. In the case of the Biscayan mining companies, Pastor[100] has calculated that the state made a profit of 55.3 per cent on company payments, while the memoranda of the DGP in 1939 raised this figure to 76 per cent.[101]

The third cycle of Spanish accumulation in which unfree labour has played a significant role is linked to the property and construction expansion of recent decades. While new studies are still needed that could confirm what was indicated by Romero,[102] immigration involving debt and the situation of illegality have enabled a substantial accumulation of profits thanks to the existence of a pocket of workers in a precarious, irregular, or illegal situation. They have been willing to work in conditions worse than those stipulated by law, and also, in some cases, in a situation of provisional servitude until the contracted debt is paid off. With respect to work in prison, it is once again necessary to refer to a double type of profit. On the one hand, public, as the tendency to replace free work by captive work in

underscored by Roth for the case of Nazi Germany: Karl H. Roth, "Unfree Labour in the Area under German Hegemony, 1930–1945: Some Historical and Methodological Questions", in Brass and Van der Linden, *Free and Unfree Labour*, pp. 127–143.

97. Nicolás Sánchez-Albornoz, *Cárceles y exilios* (Barcelona, 2012), p. 165.

98. Mendiola Gonzalo, "Forced Labor". For construction enterprises see Sánchez-Albornoz, *Cárceles y exilios*, pp. 165–171; for railways see Mendiola, "Of Firms and Captives".

99. Antonio M. Bernal, "Los beneficiarios del Canal. Latifundios de regadío", in Acosta *et al.*, *El Canal de los Presos*, pp. xxvii–xxxvi.

100. Pastor Ruiz, *El Batallón Minero n° 1*, p. 74.

101. Mendiola Gonzalo, "Forced Labor", p. 197.

102. Romero, *Un deseo apasionado*. Leonidas K. Cheliotis, "Punitive Inclusion: A Political Economy of Irregular Migration in the Margins of Europe", *European Journal of Criminology* (2016, in press).

maintaining prisons has demonstrated,[103] and on the other, private, in the search for especially cheap labour. In fact, the administration itself underscores the advantages that prison workshops offer companies, as recently pointed out by the manager of CIRE:[104] "in many cases we are an alternative to delocalization" of manufacturing to other places with lower wages.[105] Although in the Spanish case it makes no sense to speak of what has been defined – not without controversy – in the USA as the prison industrial complex,[106] some trade unions and parliamentary groups are starting to criticize prison work as unfair competition based on dumping.[107] To conclude, it is even more difficult to estimate the role that might be played in the already mentioned global value chains by the utilization of subcontracting that uses forced labour in the Global South. Such difficulty is due to the illegality of such practices and the company fragmentation within which global production networks move. The implication of Inditex, one of the fastest-growing Spanish companies in recent years, leads me to think that this is not an unusual practice, and the denunciations made in Brazil and Argentina indicate that this practice was well known to company managers.[108]

103. One of the strategies considered by Wacquant for dealing with the increase in costs inside the prisons: Loïc Wacquant, "Four Strategies to Curb Carceral Costs: On Managing Mass Imprisonment in the United States", *Studies in Political Economy*, 69 (2002), pp. 19–30, 25–28. LeBaron frames the work of prisoners in terms of present-day accumulation through dispossession: Genevieve LeBaron, "Rethinking Prison Labor: Social Discipline and the State in Historical Perspective", *Working USA. The Journal of Labor & Society*, 15:3 (2012), pp. 327–351.

104. CIRE (Centre d'Iniciatives per a la Reinserció / Centre of Initiatives for Inclusion) is the public institution that regulates prison labour in Catalonia.

105. Antoni López, "Los talleres de las cárceles catalanas facturarán 20 millones este año", *La Vanguardia*, 13 November 2008, available at www.derechopenitenciario.com/noticias/noticia. asp?id=1870, last accessed 22 August 2016. See also Jesús García, "Los presos sustituyen a empleados en los servicios de las cárceles catalanas", *El País*, 27 April 2014, available at http://ccaa. elpais.com/ccaa/2014/04/27/catalunya/1398623340_711633.html, last accessed 22 August 2016. Similarly, in the conservative media COPE, penitentiary workshops have been described as "a national substitute for Asian factories specializing in intensive work"; COPE, "Talleres 'low cost' entre rejas", 3 May 2009, available at http://www.derechopenitenciario.com/noticias/noticia.asp? id=2293, last accessed 22 August 2016.

106. For a position critical of this concept, see Loïc Wacquant, "Prisoner Reentry as Myth and Ceremony", *Dialect Anthropol*, 34 (2010), pp. 605–620, 606–611. In the USA, LeBaron has documented the effect of captive labour on the free labour market, with a fall in wages and its use during strikes: LeBaron, "Rethinking Prison Labor", pp. 345–347.

107. For trade union complaints: "La Sección Estatal de FSC-CCOO presenta un escrito de queja respecto a la actividad desarrollada por los internos en los talleres de producción con empresas externas", available at http://www.derechopenitenciario.com/noticias/noticia.asp?id=5622, last accessed 22 August 2016. In the Spanish Congress, the left-wing Izquierda Plural group presented a proposal that would prohibit enterprises that had previously dismissed workers from concluding labour agreements with prisons. The proposal is available in *Boletín Oficial de las Cortes Generales, Congreso de los Diputados*. Serie D, 511 (2014), pp. 13-14, available at http://www.congreso.es/ public_oficiales/L10/CONG/BOCG/D/BOCG-10-D-511.PDF, last accessed 22 August 2016.

108. Ana Delicado, "Zara recurre al trabajo esclavo"; Agencia EFE, "Brasil expedienta a Zara".

CONCLUSION: THE COMPLEMENTARITY OF SUPPLY- AND DEMAND-SIDE APPROACHES

Throughout these pages we have been able to confirm that in Spain, like in most regions in the world, the development of capitalism did not mean the total triumph of free wage labour; instead, its spread was compatible with the maintenance or creation of modalities of unfree labour.

Taking as a basis the categories established by the Global Collaboratory on the History of Labour Relations, we have been able to see how these modalities show clearly the centrality of the institutional and political framework when it comes to understanding the persistence of forced labour. There is a very evident shift from one period to the next regarding the main categories of unfree labour relations deployed during each of them. First, we must underline the centrality of slavery (category 17) for the decades of liberal revolution and colonial empire until 1874. During the next period, that of liberal parliamentarism, labour relations included in category 8, such as labour taxes for colonial ethnic groups and obligatory work for convicts in African prisons, predominated, with unfree labour being much more important for colonial political and economic control than for the mainland, where unfree labour experienced a clear decline. This reality changed with the civil war and the fascist dictatorship, when political repression enabled the deployment of thousands of prisoners and mostly POWs (category 11). The civil war and its aftermath is precisely the period when forced labour as a proportion of the active population peaked in mainland Spain. Finally, we must remark that during neoliberal globalization unfree labour was found mainly in prisons (category 8) and in the form of indentured migration (category 15).

Moreover, the research so far suggests that the demand for forced labour was also linked in different ways to the two main reasons identified in the historiography: on the one hand, the relative scarcity of workers, and on the other the pressure to increase profits by cutting labour costs. Nevertheless, historical research has shown that those demand-side factors do not operate in a simple or unilateral way, and that several other elements, such as variations in productivity, level of qualification, living conditions, as well as questions related to the agency of workers (resistance, response to incentives, for example), were essential for explaining why enterprises had recourse to, or rejected, forced labour. Moreover, it is still a challenge for research to be able to determine more precisely the exact contribution of this modality of labour relations to the cycles of capital accumulation and economic growth, as well as the exact proportion of free/unfree labour in different sectors and situations. In addition, one of the main conclusions of this article is that none of these economic factors that help us understand the demand side of forced labour can be correctly understood if we do not also take into account supply-side explanations, those related to public policies.

We will need more micro-level research in order to better understand the political and economic reasons that explain the survival of unfree labour, not only within historical capitalist development, but also for the disturbing contemporary reality, when unfree labour remains one of the mechanisms underpinning the growing inequality in most parts of the world.

IRSH 61 (2016), Special Issue, pp. 213–241 doi:10.1017/S002085901600047X
© 2016 Internationaal Instituut voor Sociale Geschiedenis

Working for the State in the Urban Economies of Ankara, Bursa, and Salonica: From Empire to Nation State, 1840s–1940s*

M . E R D E M K A B A D A Y I

Koç University
Rumelifeneri Yolu 34450 Sarıyer, Istanbul, Turkey

E-mail: mkabadayi@ku.edu.tr

ABSTRACT: In most cases, and particularly in the cases of Greece and Turkey, political transformation from multinational empire to nation state has been experienced to a great extent in urban centres. In Ankara, Bursa, and Salonica, the cities selected for this article, the consequences of state-making were drastic for all their inhabitants; Ankara and Bursa had strong Greek communities, while in the 1840s Salonica was the Jewish metropolis of the eastern Mediterranean, with a lively Muslim community. However, by the 1940s, Ankara and Bursa had lost almost all their non-Muslim inhabitants and Salonica had lost almost all its Muslims. This article analyses the occupational structures of those three cities in the mid-nineteenth century and the first half of the twentieth, tracing the role of the state as an employer and the effects of radical political change on the city-level historical dynamics of labour relations.

INTRODUCTION

The aim of this article is to examine the effect of political change on labour relations. In this case study we encounter the state both as an actor and implementer of political change as well as being itself the product of a process of political change. It covers approximately a hundred years between 1840 and 1940 and examines three cities: Ankara, Bursa, and Salonica. The primary focus throughout will be the state, or polities in general, as employers, and their role in constituting labour relations. However, the

* This study is based upon the findings of a research project "An Introduction to the Occupational History of Turkey via New Methods and New Approaches (1840–1940)", funded by the Scientific and Technological Research Council of Turkey (TUBITAK, Project No. 112K271), which ended in October 2015. As the principal investigator for the project I would like to thank the other members, Zeynep Akan, Berkay Küçükbaşlar, Esin Uyar, and Fatih Yücel. I am very grateful to the editors of this special issue, especially to Gijs Kessler, for their helpful and detailed comments and suggestions.

disintegration of the Ottoman Empire and the nation-building processes that led to the formation of the Greek and Turkish nation states are the historical common ground upon which imperial polities or nation states not only facilitated labour relations as employers within their respective populaces, but also actually crafted their national populations.

It is essential from the outset to explain the limitations of the available data and concomitantly narrow scope of this undertaking. While the labour relations categories of the Global Collaboratory on the History of Labour Relations are powerful tools for comparing shifts in labour relations across time and space, the limitations of the occupational data used for this study mean that those tools are unsuitable and so will not be used. Later in this introduction I will delineate the data sources and the methodology developed for their use, before doing so I must explain what I could *not* do. For this article I used three sets of sources: an Ottoman tax survey from the mid-nineteenth century, and one Turkish and one Greek census from the twentieth century. The Ottoman survey has the advantage of providing individual occupational titles, but unfortunately those titles are difficult to code into the Collaboratory's categories of labour relations. The chief problem is that for most occupations it is impossible to differentiate between self-employed individuals, employers, and sometimes employed; this creates such a high level of ambiguity that the precise labour relations must remain unclear. The explanatory capability of the taxonomy of labour relations cannot therefore be fully utilized in this case. The rare and invaluable detail of the uncoded individual occupational titles can thus be both a blessing and a curse.[1] Finally, I opted to code the occupational titles into a customized version of the 1935 Turkish population census for the purposes of compatibility. More importantly, it is a more efficient methodology for reaching the main goal of this study, which is to detect shifts in the employment of people working for the polities of the cities chosen as they changed from being part of the Ottoman Empire to being part of the separate Greek and Turkish states during the period from the 1840s to the 1940s.

The occupational data to be found in the early twentieth-century Greek and Turkish national censuses are coded into generic categories, so it is not possible to extract individual occupational titles or labour relations in order to compare them with the mid-nineteenth century data. Until the 1950s, categories of occupations in Turkish censuses did not differentiate labour relations, with occupations instead grouped into broad categories according to fields of economic activity. Among the categories, we see that "public services" stands out, since it records the specific labour relation of "working

---

1. The possibilities and limitations of working with uncoded occupational titles have been fully discussed in Bart Van De Putte and Erik Buyst, "Occupational Titles? Hard to Eat, Easy to Catch", *Belgisch Tijdschrift voor Nieuwste Geschiedenis*, 40:1–2 (2010), pp. 7–31.

for the state". All other categories are ambiguous about labour relations in general and about working for the state in particular, and it is because of that limitation of the sources that the focus here will be on public service occupations. However, "public services" must then be reinterpreted and extended to create a more inclusive category for the mid-nineteenth century Ottoman urban setting. That is why I have used the category "public utility services" as a proxy to examine inclusion of Ottoman urban dwellers in such employment – or their exclusion from it. For the first half of the twentieth century, Greek and Turkish census data on occupations are also suitable to use for the same categories of public utility services; this enabled me to compare not only urban settings in the mid-nineteenth century, but also the effects of nation-state-building policies. That was possible because the data cover not only occupations, but also the people in them within public utility services in the same cities in the mid-twentieth century. What the data reveal are the especially profound effects on employment chances of religion and gender combined, as well as the effects of *national* differences on chances of occupational advancement and exclusion in these two examples of state-making.

This article focuses on occupational changes in the urban economies of three cities, Ankara, Bursa, and Salonica, between the 1840s and the 1940s. During that century, each of these cities experienced extreme social and demographic change resulting from radical political transformations. In the 1840s, the inhabitants of these cities had diverse ethno-religious affiliations and lived under the political rule of the Ottoman central authority. In the 1940s, Ankara was the capital of Turkey and Bursa an important urban industrial centre; by then, the populations of the two cities had almost entirely lost their non-Muslim and non-Turkish elements. Ankara's state apparatus has employed large numbers of both civilian and military personnel ever since. Salonica in the late 1920s still had a very large Jewish community, yet all other non-Christian and, to a great extent, non-Greek elements of the urban population did not survive the political shift from the Ottoman Empire to the Greek state in 1913. After the Greco-Turkish War of 1919–1922,[2] both Salonica and Athens saw a huge influx of Orthodox Christian[3] immigrants from Turkey, as a result of the compulsory

---

2. The Asia Minor Catastrophe or the Turkish War of Independence, depending on national historiography.
3. In this study, instead of Greeks the Orthodox Christians will be used for the mainly Greek Orthodox Christian populations of the cities. At the complex intersection of ethnic and religious affiliations in the late Ottoman Empire and Turkish and Greek states in the twentieth century I opted for the Orthodox Christians as the denominator. For a detailed discussion of the terminology see Ayse Ozil, *Orthodox Christians in the Late Ottoman Empire: A Study of Communal Relations in Anatolia*, SOAS/Routledge Studies on the Middle East, 19 (London, 2013), pp. 11–14.

population exchange between Greece and Turkey in 1923. The Greek capital, Athens, was the final destination of most of those migrating to Greece and was where the state apparatus employed most of its servants. In the following sections, therefore, Athens, too, has been included in the analysis for 1928. There is, therefore, a comparative perspective on the respective capacities of the Turkish and Greek bureaucracies to create employment shortly after the 1923 population exchange. However, the rest of the study will be focused on Ankara, Bursa, and Salonica, for which purpose public-sector employment will have a broader meaning to refer to more than just the group of civil servants working for the apparatus of the national state or the municipality. It will, in fact, include the men and women living in the cities who actually provided the public utility services, such as religious, educational, and health services, and served in the administration at local and neighbourhood level. That includes the job of neighbourhood headman, security agents in the neighbourhoods and marketplaces, and membership of military units or the fire brigade. I believe that this categorization is more useful when applied to the mid-nineteenth century Ottoman polity as well as to the Greek and Turkish nation states of the 1930s.

Two sources were used. First, a detailed Ottoman tax survey, the *temettuat*,[4] conducted in 1844 and 1845,[5] for Ankara, Bursa, and Salonica, and secondly the national censuses of Greece, for 1928, and of Turkey, for 1927, 1935, and 1945. There are two parts to the study. The first examines the occupational data and ethno-religious characteristics of the inhabitants of the same three cities in 1845 and tries to compare the dynamics behind employment in the public utility services in those cities by taking into consideration occupational choices as well as residential patterns at the neighbourhood level. The results of that investigation were then mapped. Meanwhile, the second part focuses on the drastic demographic changes that followed the 1923 population exchange[6] and how those changes affected employment in general and public utility services in particular for men and women living in Ankara/Bursa and Salonica/Athens.

---

4. *Temettuat* can be translated as income-yielding assets. These registers are very rich sources for Ottoman economic history. For a general evaluation of their uses and limitations see Kayoko Hayashi and Mahir Aydin (eds), *The Ottoman State and Societies in Change: A Study of the Nineteenth Century Temettuat Registers*, vol. 5, Islamic Area Studies (London, 2004).

5. The first attempt to compile *temettuat* registers failed to reach an empire-wide coverage. A second and more successful attempt was made in 1844/1845. Since the Ottoman administration used the Islamic lunar calendar, the year of the register corresponds to 1844/1845. For the sake of simplicity this date has been abbreviated to 1845 in this study.

6. This study will not explain the reasons for and effects of the compulsory population exchange. For a good introduction to the subject see Renee Hirschon (ed.), *Crossing the Aegean: An Appraisal of the 1923 Compulsory Population Exchange between Greece and Turkey*, Studies in Forced Migration, vol. 12 (New York, 2003).

A TALE OF THREE CITIES, 1845–1945

In the nineteenth century, the Ottoman state had a pluralistic structure and in both the capital, Istanbul, and in other urban centres religious and communal authorities were part and parcel of the diverse polity of what was a multi-ethnic and multi-religious empire. The Ottoman Empire achieved extraordinary longevity and through the centuries its polity went through enormous changes and successfully absorbed major crises. The Ottoman dynasty and the central state authority maintained control for more than 500 years between the end of a short interregnum in 1413 and the end of its empire after World War I. As for the three cities selected for examination here, they were integrated into the Ottoman Empire quite early, with Bursa actually the birthplace of the Ottoman state structure. The Byzantine city of Prousa (modern-day Bursa) became the first capital of the newly created Ottoman state in the fourteenth century and Ankara did not acquire its socio-economic urban qualities as early as Bursa, although it was central to the Anatolian core region of the empire throughout its existence. Ankara developed into an important urban centre in the nineteenth century, and then, in 1923, after the end of the Ottoman Empire, it became the capital of the successor state, the Turkish Republic. Salonica had been incorporated into the empire in 1430 and remained an Ottoman city until 1913. By the 1840s, all these cities, with their long histories in the empire, were important constituting urban centres of Ottoman social and economic life. An important point to note here is that all three of the cities suffered catastrophic events in the early twentieth century that tore apart their urban socio-economic fabric, something especially true for the Jews of Salonica under German occupation during World War II. These calamities involved fires, earthquakes, and man-made disasters, such as deportations, forced migration, and ethnic cleansing, and there were other social-engineering projects implemented by new nation states and occupying forces. The table below lists some indicators of economic development for the second half of the nineteenth century, and important dates of destruction from the twentieth century, for all three cities.

OCCUPATIONS AND ETHNO-RELIGIOUS CHARACTERISTICS OF THE CITIES IN THE MID-NINETEENTH CENTURY

The micro data on occupational titles derived from the 1845 Ottoman tax survey are very rich in detail but are not coded and so not aggregated, which is a major limitation. However, the fact that the data are available at all can be seen as an advantage, for two reasons. First, it is, of course, still possible to make comparisons across time for Ottoman or Turkish

Table 1. *Turning points and demographic shocks in the history of the cities.*

Connections	Salonica	Bursa	Ankara
Opening of a branch of the Ottoman Bank	1862	1875	1893
Railway connection/ Modern port facilities	1888/1896– 1904	1890s Marseilles-Mudanya regular ferry connection	1892
Disasters and Deportations			
Great Fire	1917	1855 following a devastating earthquake	1916
The Balkan Wars	Muslims, Bulgarians		
The Extermination of Armenians		1915	1915
Compulsory Population Exchange	Muslims	Orthodox Christians	Orthodox Christians
World War II	Jews		

cities by coding the Ottoman data into the occupational categories of the Turkish national censuses from the twentieth century. Secondly, the Ottoman data can likewise be coded into internationally accepted and utilized schemes of occupational classifications, specifically HISCO (Historical International Standard Classification of Occupations), developed by the International Institute of Social History, Amsterdam,[7] and PSTI (Primary-Secondary-Tertiary International), originally developed by the Cambridge Group for the History of Population and Social Structure and subsequently adopted by INCHOS, the International Network for the Comparative History of Occupational Structure.[8]

However, it is unfortunate that for the twentieth century the occupational data contained in the 1928 Greek census are unsuitable for conversion into either HISCO or PSTI. More importantly, no uncoded individual micro data are available for either Greek or Turkish cases, and those data are available only as aggregated cross-tabulations. As a result, for the comparative purposes of this study neither HISCO, nor PSTI but the coding scheme for the 1935 Turkish national census was used to convert the occupational data from the 1845 Ottoman survey and the data given in the 1928 Greek census.

7. Marco H.D. van Leeuwen, Ineke Maas, and Andrew Miles, *HISCO: Historical International Standard Classification of Occupations* (Leuven, 2002).
8. Available at: http://www.geog.cam.ac.uk/research/projects/occupations/britain19c/inchos. html, last accessed 3 August 2016.

As can be traced in the table above, the inhabitants of the cities experienced drastic social-engineering projects. We can conclude that Salonica's population went through Hellenization and that the inhabitants of Ankara and Bursa experienced Turkification and Islamification. In the 1840s, the populations of the cities had diverse ethno-religious characteristics, and nation-state-making was not then in operation. The Ottoman tax survey of 1845 used the household as its data collection unit, and it gives detailed information about both the ethno-religious characteristics and the occupations of heads of households for each of the three cities. In numerous cases, more than one gainfully employed male (including brothers or sons of household heads) was registered per household along with their occupations and income-yielding assets. Nevertheless, a lack of regularity and uniformity means it is impossible to conclude that every man with an income or an occupation was included in the survey. In that sense, 1845 is a pre-census survey, for it did not achieve universal coverage. As a result, there is a mismatch in the units of data collection between the 1845 survey and the twentieth-century Greek and Turkish national censuses, which were based on personal data from individuals rather than households. However, for our purposes – a two-stage comparison among the three cities in 1845 and then in the twentieth century – that change in the unit of comparison is not problematic. Real incompatibility would arise only if one wished to treat the datasets as if they constituted a unified panel dataset and make percentual or distributional comparisons of occupations across time among cities between the 1840s and the 1940s; that is not the intention of this paper.

The figures below in Figure 1 were extracted from the survey. They require explanation and they should not be considered exhaustive. The total number of households was calculated from the numbers in available registers in the Ottoman state archives; therefore, the data used and categorized above might be far from being fully comprehensive. There is the double risk of incompleteness, both when the original surveys were conducted in the individual cities and then collated in Istanbul in 1845, to say nothing of the 150 years the registers were kept in the archives until they were catalogued in the 1990s. That said, the registered household numbers match mid-nineteenth century population figures for the cities. Ottoman population registers contemporaneous with the 1845 survey are structured differently. They provide figures for the number of dwellings and the total number of males of any age, including infants, living in them per neighbourhood, but they give no city total. If the neighbourhood totals are added together we reach figures similar to those obtained from the 1845 survey. Although logically, and concomitantly, units of registration differ between the 1845 tax survey and the population registers, comparing the total number of males in households (extracted from the 1845 survey) with the number of dwellings and the total number of males given in the

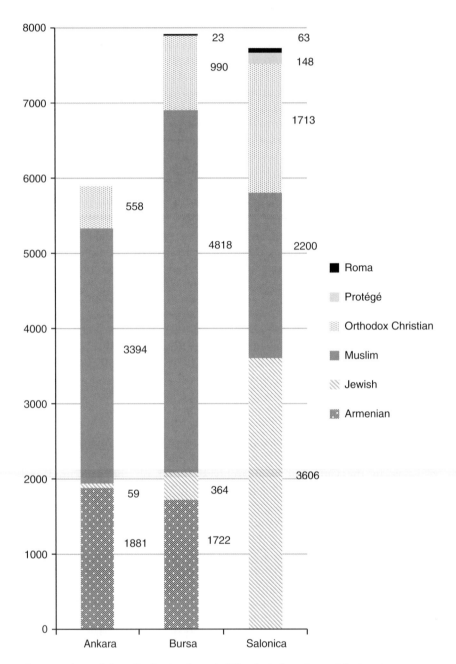

Figure 1. Ethno-religious distribution, household heads, Ankara, Bursa, Salonica, 1845.

population registers, it is clear that the 1845 tax survey covers a very large proportion of working males in the three cities.[9] The ethno-religious categories are based on the categories used by the Ottomans themselves for their survey.

The ethno-religious categories given above also need clarification. In the Ottoman Empire of 1845 "Muslims" referred to a religious category almost irrespective of ethnicity. For the 1845 survey, all Turks, Kurds, and Arabs were counted and categorized as Muslims with no differentiation of their ethnic characteristics, and for the Ottomans only Roma was a primarily ethnic category. Ottoman Roma and Sinti alike were generally registered simply as Roma (*kıptiyan* in Ottoman Turkish), with no mention being made of their religious affiliations. Roma in the Ottoman Empire might have been either Muslim or non-Muslim. Figure 1 above shows that no Roma were registered in Ankara and their numbers in Bursa and Salonica were rather modest. By contrast, Orthodox Christians, or *rum* in the original Ottoman category, were categorized by religion. Like the Muslims, Christians, too, comprised different ethnic origins, including Greeks, Bulgarians, and other Slavic populations. Lastly, there were "Armenians", whose category was ethno-religious, with the emphasis on ethnicity. This category included mainly Apostolic and Catholic Armenians, who belonged not to the Roman Catholic community but to the Armenian Catholic Church. In Ankara, the registers used "Catholic" as a category for Armenians belonging to the Armenian Catholic Church, but in the empire-wide taxonomy of the nineteenth century other confessions were included as "Armenians". One specific category, the "protégés" (*müstemin* in Ottoman Turkish), had, until then, only been seen in Salonica. The heads of those households were mainly Orthodox Christians in possession of European passports, and in 1845 they generally belonged to the Greek clergy, although by the second half of the nineteenth century a new, wealthy group had emerged with closer ties to Western European economic centres. Although similar developments could be seen in most of the port cities of the Ottoman Empire, late-nineteenth century "protégé" status had a more significant role in Salonica. In the 1880s and the 1890s, in particular, protégés were local honorary Europeans, most of whom were wealthy Greek or Jewish merchants,[10] and the fact that no

9. NFS.d. is the catalogue code for the population registers in the Ottoman State Archives. For Ankara, the registers NFS.d. 1741, 1748, and 1749 give 4,865 as the total number of dwellings and 10,505 as the total male population including infants. For Bursa, the registers NFS.d. 1396 and 1398 record 6,335 dwellings and 13,221 males. For Salonica, Akyalçın Kaya used NFS.d. 4971, 4973, and 4974 and gives 14,028 as the total male population for the year 1843/1844. See Dilek Akyalçın Kaya, "Les conditions économiques et les caractéristiques démographiques des Juifs saloniciens au milieu du XIXe siècle", in Esther Benbassa (ed.), *Salonique. Ville juive, ville ottomane, ville grecque* (Paris, 2014), pp. 19–48, 43, Table 7.
10. For a brief account of the protégés of Salonica, see Mark Mazower, *Salonica: City of Ghosts: Christians, Muslims and Jews 1430-1950* (London, 2004), ch. 11, pp. 204–252.

Armenian household was registered in Salonica is suspicious, although it is also known that there was never a strong Armenian community there.

As the next step for this research, the occupational titles of the household heads were coded according to the occupational classification and field of economic activity taxonomies found in the 1935 census.[11] The differences between occupations and fields of economic activity are important, albeit not clearly defined in the censuses. In fact, the categories listed below are fields of economic activity rather than occupational ones.[12] The 1935 Turkish National Census had seven broad fields of economic activity, with descriptions given in Turkish and French:

Table 2. *Broad categories of fields of economic activity/occupations given in the 1935 Turkish National 'Census'*

Code	Occupations (English translations)[13]	*Meslekler* (in Turkish)	*Professions* (in French)
A	Agriculture	Toprak mahsulleri	Production du sol
B	Industry	Sanayi ve küçük san'atler	Industries et métiers
C	Commerce	Ticaret	Commerce
Ç	Communication and Transport	Nakliye ve muvasala	Transport et communications
D	Public Services	Umumî idare ve hizmetler, serbest meslekler	Administration et services publics, profession libérales
E	Private Services	Ev iktısadiyatı, şahsî hizmetler	Economie domestique, services personnels
F	No or Unknown Profession	Mesleksiz, mesleği meçhul veya gayri muayyen olanlar	Sans professions, professions inconnues ou indéterminées

The category *D. Public Services* does not correspond with my preferred category for this study of *working for the state or polity*, since it contains fields of economic activity that cannot be seen as public services, for example communal or religious services offered at the neighbourhood level. Moreover, some of the public utility services, such as postal services, are

11. The 1935 Turkish National Census was the second, the first being in 1927. Cross-tabulations from national censuses are available as PDF files for download via the webpage of the Turkish Statistics Institute Library (http://kutuphane.tuik.gov.tr/), Présidence du Conseil Office Central du Statistique, *Genel Nüfus Sayımı, 1935 = Recensement Général de La Population, 1935* (Ankara, 1937).
12. For a full discussion of the taxonomy of occupations and fields of economic activity in the early Turkish censuses see Haluk Cillov, *Meslek istatistikleri: metodolojide yeni meseleler* (Istanbul, 1956).
13. Author's translation.

included in category *Ç. Communication and Transport*. That therefore meant a mismatch and categorical ambiguity, forcing me to create a new category of public services by using sub-categories of two broad categories: Public Services, and Communication and Transport. After these adjustments, new broad categories appear as below:

Table 3. *Adjusted six broad categories of fields of economic activity.*

1	Agriculture
2	Industry
3	Commerce
4	Communication & Transport/Private Services/Liberal Professions
5	Public Services
6	No or Unknown Profession

The adjustment means that for each of the selected cities it was now possible to code the micro data of individual occupational titles of heads of households from the 1845 survey into the broad categories above. Obviously, the aim of that exercise was to filter out heads of households who were working for public utility services and to compare their respective proportions among all occupations in the three locations.

Table 4. *Distributions of occupational categories, household heads, 1845.*

Occupational Categories	Ankara	Bursa	Salonica
Agriculture	469	768	427
Industry	2460	3034	2170
Commerce	595	858	1160
Communication & Transport/Private Services/Liberal Professions	243	481	1022
Public Services	309	491	262
No or Unknown Profession	1816	2285	2689
Total	5892	7917	7730

In order to make public services as a share of urban occupations more visible, we can omit the category *No or Unknown Professions* and redraw the chart using percentages.

How can we interpret the chart below? What we should *not* do is use the percentages of heads of households with occupations in public service for any further detailed statistical analysis. The reason for this is, firstly, the aforementioned non-exhaustive nature of the data, and, secondly, and methodologically more importantly, that the chart is based on calculations using data that, although extracted, coded, and recoded from an 1845

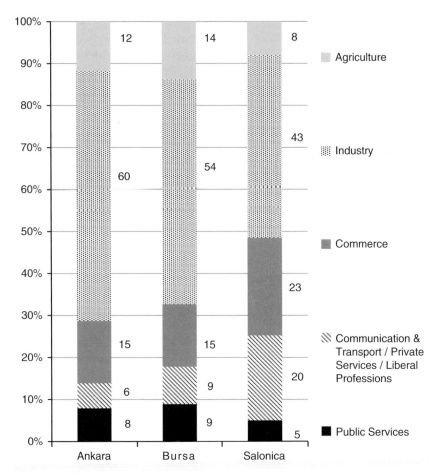

Figure 2. Distributions of occupations in five categories, household heads, Ankara, Bursa, Salonica, 1845 (%).

Ottoman tax survey, are nevertheless arranged according to the taxonomy of the 1935 Turkish National Census. The numerical values should therefore be used only to analyse the relative importance of occupations in the public services in given locations. However, within the limitations of the model we can still see that the total numbers of occupations in the public services are close for each city, both in terms of their total number and their share of the overall occupational distribution. The same assessment applies for other broad categories of occupations of household heads. Thanks to the quality of the data, we can go further into the category of households with occupations in the public services and break the figures down according to registered ethno-religious affiliations. We can then compare

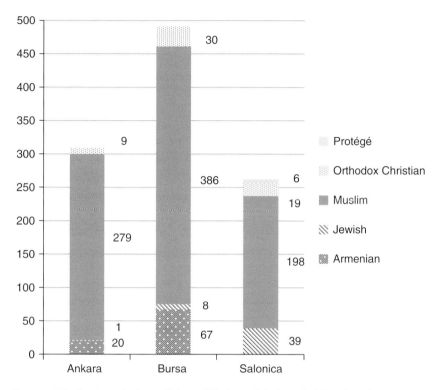

Figure 3. Distributions of ethno-religious affiliations of the household heads with occupations in the public service, Ankara, Bursa, Salonica, 1845.

this data with the general ethno-religious distribution of all the city's households, as shown in Figure 1 above.

It is no surprise to see that Muslim households are overrepresented among occupations in public services. Nor is it surprising to see Armenian, Orthodox Christian and Jewish subjects also involved in them, given what we learned earlier of the diverse and pluralistic nature of public utility services provided by the Ottomans. Nevertheless, non-Muslim households are greatly underrepresented in Ankara. Why, then, should fewer non-Muslim households have worked in public utility services in Ankara than did non-Muslims in Bursa or Salonica? After all, at 2,498 out of a total of 5,892, non-Muslim households comprised almost half of all households in Ankara in 1845. To answer the question, we need to consider spatial demarcation and try to draw dividing lines appropriate to the social and economic life of mid-nineteenth century Ottoman cities, and, specifically for this exercise, along ethno-religious lines for Ankara, Bursa, and Salonica.

MAPPING RESIDENTIAL PATTERNS AT NEIGHBOURHOOD LEVEL ACCORDING TO ETHNO-RELIGIOUS CHARACTERISTICS

The ethno-religious composition of Ottoman neighbourhoods is a subject of ongoing and unresolved debate in the historiography. Satisfactory comprehensive data on the ethno-religious characteristics of Ottoman neighbourhoods are lacking for suitable levels of numerous cities. There are varying claims about the urban fabric and spatial organization of Ottoman cities, with views in the literature oscillating between visions of peacefully shared urban life and a belief in strict residential segregation along ethno-religious lines. One of the major assets of the *temettuat* registers is that the unit of record-keeping in urban settings was the neighbourhood, so the registers reveal the ethno-religious affiliations of each neighbourhood's inhabitants. Since the registers are from 1845, and the earliest detailed modern maps and plans of Ottoman cities are also from the second half of the nineteenth and the early twentieth century, it is technically possible to map the information in the *temettuat* registers to show the occupational and ethno-religious composition of neighbourhoods in Ankara, Bursa, and Salonica,[14] although that was not done on those early maps. It is not an easy matter to draw exact borders for all neighbourhoods, especially not for the mid-nineteenth century Ottoman urban spaces, and since not all the neighbourhoods in the 1845 registers could be located on available maps there are blank spaces. All three of the maps are works in progress and I must emphasize that these are preliminary attempts to visualize the information at the neighbourhood level contained in the 1845 registers. So what, then, is the value of these maps for the purposes of this study?

My wish is to question the relationship between the level of ethno-religious heterogeneity and the role of religion in finding occupations in public utility services in Ottoman cities in the mid-nineteenth century. We may presume that before municipal administrations were established most public utility services were provided by ethno-religious communities. To test that presumption, I selected the three cities and compared the ethno-religious composition of their neighbourhoods. I believe that instead of comparing the proportions of the ethno-religious affiliations of registered inhabitants in neighbourhoods as alphabetical lists, showing them on a map – as far as possible – has more explanatory power for the levels and concentrations of ethno-religious heterogeneity in the cities chosen. As part of an atomistic list a neighbourhood would be

---

14. The maps are inconsistent, with Greeks used instead of Orthodox Christians, and in Salonica very few protégés were added to the Greeks since all were Orthodox Christians with European passports. My thanks to Berkay Küçükbaşlar, who prepared all of the maps used in this article.

separated from its place in the spatial organization of a city, which is what constitutes its urban fabric. Therefore, ethno-religious heterogeneity can be more holistically assessed and visualized on a map.

For Ankara, the earliest detailed plan on which the neighbourhoods of 1845 Ankara can be detected is that by Carl Christoph Lörcher from 1924.[15] We used the Lörcher plan as the template to position the neighbourhoods of the 1845 Ankara *temettuat* registers. In doing so, we were able to locate sixty-nine out of ninety neighbourhoods on this map.[16]

The earliest detailed cadastral plan of Bursa is from 1855, and there is also a detailed insurance map of the city from the 1880s that shows neighbourhoods. Using these two maps we were able to locate 129 neighbourhoods out of 142 listed in the *temettuat* registers for Bursa.[17]

Lastly, the picture of Salonica's neighbourhoods in 1845 is based on a map by Vassilis Dimitriadis.[18] In the preparation of our map we were supported by Dilek Akyalçın Kaya,[19] and we were able to locate all sixty-eight neighbourhoods in the *temettuat* registers.

Comparing the residential patterns of the neighbourhoods in the three cities, it is remarkable to see that Salonica's spatial organization came close to amounting to an ethno-religious segregation of its urban life. In fact, we see a strictly divided city, with not a single mixed neighbourhood. There are only five Orthodox Christian residential units in Muslim or Jewish parts of the city: Çavuş Manastırı, Tavşan Manastırı, Yanık Manastır, Kızlar Manastırı, and Metropolid, all of which were either monasteries with few inhabitants or the Metropolitan residential unit. There were only four Muslim neighbourhoods on the border between the Jewish and Orthodox Christian parts of the city.

Among the three cities selected Bursa lies in the middle as far as ethno-religious segregation is concerned. There are mixed neighbourhoods there, but only one Jewish quarter and no neighbourhood of mixed Orthodox

15. For a very detailed study of this plan see Ali Cengizkan, *Ankara'nın ilk planı: 1924–25 Lörcher planı, kentsel mekan özellikleri, 1932 Jansen Planı'na ve bugüne katkıları, etki ve kalıntıları* (Ankara, 2004).

16. I would like to thank a group of local historians from Ankara, especially Gökçe Günel, Erman Tamur, and the antiquarian Ahmet Yüksel, for their generosity in sharing their knowledge and maps of Ankara.

17. I would like to record my thanks to Raif Kaplanoğlu, who is an expert on the urban history of Bursa, for his generous support. His numerous publications, and especially Raif Kaplanoğlu, *Bursa Yer Adları Ansiklopedisi: Bursa Ticaret Borsası Kültür Yayınları* (Bursa, 1996) and the maps therein, were extremely helpful in the preparation of our map.

18. Vassilis Dimitriadis, *Topographia tis Thessalonikis kata tin epohi tis Tourkokratias, 1430–1912* [Topography of Thessaloniki during the Period of Turkish Rule, 1430–1912] (Thessaloniki, 1983).

19. Dilek Akyalçın Kaya, *Les Sabbatéens saloniciens (1845–1912): des individus pluriels dans une société urbaine en transition* (Ph.D., École des Hautes Études en Sciences Sociales, Paris, 2013).

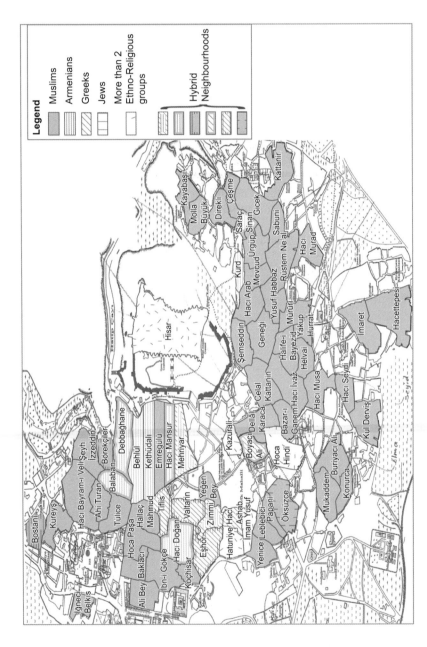

Figure 4. Ankara, 1845, ethno-religious division of neighbourhoods.

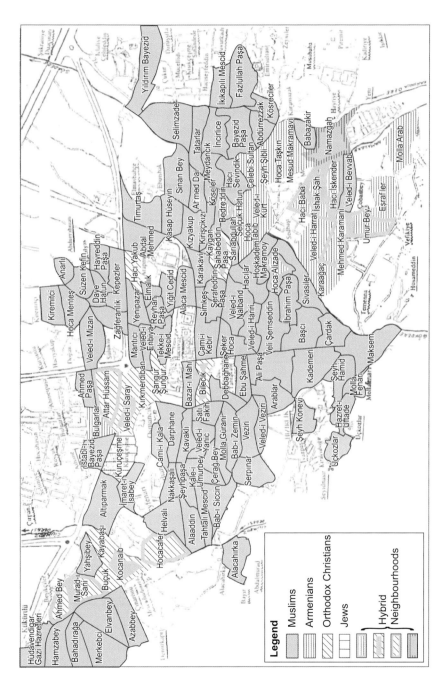

Figure 5. Bursa, 1845, ethno-religious division of neighbourhoods.

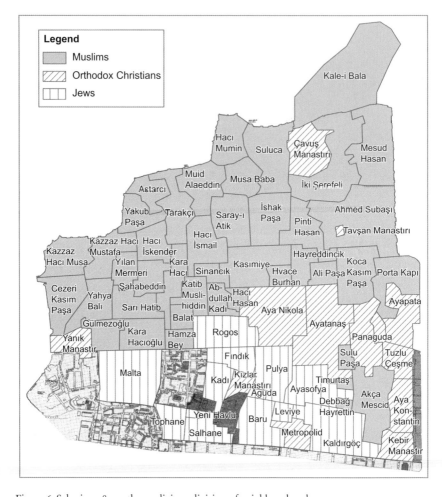

Figure 6. Salonica, 1845, ethno-religious division of neighbourhoods.

Christians and Armenians. Apart from a single Armenian neighbourhood in the north-west, all the Armenian neighbourhoods are in the south-east of the city. We should not forget that thirteen of Bursa's neighbourhoods could not be located on the map, but none of them had mixed Armenian and Orthodox Christian inhabitants, and no Jewish household was registered there. As a result, Bursa was still deeply segregated along ethno-religious lines, albeit to a lesser degree than in Salonica.

Ankara's pattern of neighbourhoods shows the least ethno-religious segregation. There were mixed neighbourhoods shared by Muslims, Armenians, and Orthodox Christians, and the citadel, *hisar*, along with three other neighbourhoods had more than two ethno-religious groups. There was no homogenous Jewish quarter. Twenty-one neighbourhoods could not be located on the map of Ankara, but sixty-nine of them are present and those missing would not decrease the overall diversity of the ethno-religious groups in all the neighbourhoods. There is even potential for more diversity to be revealed because the largest neighbourhood not yet mapped, Bölücek-i Atik, was another mixed neighbourhood.

Comparison of the residential patterns and the ethno-religious characteristics of public utility sector occupations suggests a correlation between the level of residential segregation and the proportion of non-Muslims in the public utility sector in the city. For example, in Salonica, where we have the most segregated urban fabric, we see the largest proportion (64 out of 262) of non-Muslims with occupations in public services compared with Ankara and Bursa. Again, not surprisingly, Salonica had the highest number of Jewish households with occupations in public services. In a similar vein, the high concentration of Armenians in Bursa is also reflected in the large proportion of Armenian households with occupations in the public sector (67 out of 386). My own interpretation of the situation is twofold. First, before the emergence of central urban municipal organizations,[20] public services were organized and provided at the communal level, in the neighbourhoods. Secondly, in mixed neighbourhoods, with Muslim and non-Muslim inhabitants, non-Muslims had proportionately fewer occupations in the public utility sector. That claim must, of course, be tested for other locations in the mid-nineteenth century Ottoman Empire, especially from the perspective of the administrative autonomy of communities. Nonetheless, I am confident that given the Islamic ideological base of the Ottoman Empire it is fair to say that in urban locations where their communities were neither building a majority, nor strongly represented, the relative share of public utility service work done by non-Muslims would have been smaller than that done by Muslims.

In the second part of this study the role of the 1923 population exchange and its repercussions on the ethno-religious homogenization and occupational structure will be assessed.

WORKING FOR THE STATE IN TWENTIETH-CENTURY GREECE AND TURKEY

The compulsory exchange of population between Greece and Turkey in 1923 had devastating effects on the urban populations in both countries, for

---

20. The first municipality in the Ottoman Empire was established in Istanbul in 1857. See Steven Rosenthal, "Foreigners and Municipal Reform in Istanbul: 1855–1865", *International Journal of Middle East Studies*, 11:2 (1980), pp. 227–245.

each of which it can be seen as the last and most decisive instance of forced deportations and ethno-religious homogenization. The tables below show the end results of the respective Hellenization and Turkification of the urban populace of the selected cities.

Table 5. *Religious affiliations of city population in Athens and Salonica, 1928.*

	Athens	Salonica	Athens	Salonica
Orthodox	448161	184784	97.6%	75.5%
Jewish	1578	55250	0.3%	22.6%
Muslim	247	1024	0.1%	0.4%
Catholic	6815	2654	1.5%	1.1%
Protestant	2316	968	0.5%	0.4%
Other	12	0	0.0%	0.0%
No Religion	82	0	0.0%	0.0%
Total	459211	244680	100%	100%

Source: *Résultats Statistiques du Recensement de la Population de la Grèce du 15–16 Mai 1928. IV. Lieu de Naissance – Religion et Langue – Sujétion* (Athens, 1937).

The demographic impact was greater on the Greek side and was felt mainly in Athens and Salonica. Between 1920 and 1928, the population of Athens soared from 293,000 to 453,000, a fifty-four per cent increase; and Salonica's rose from 170,000 to 251,000, a thirty-nine per cent increase in only eight years.[21] That increase was mainly the result of the arrival of Orthodox Christian immigrants deported from Turkey. In the immediate aftermath of the population exchange, the general demographic outcome for Greece was the loss of non-Orthodox-Christian elements of the population, though with the exception of the Jews of Salonica.[22] Meanwhile, in Turkey, a similarly radical religious homogenization took place, caused both by the extermination of the Armenian population and by the population exchange.

As can be seen in the above table, by 1927 the male populations of Ankara and Bursa were ninety-five and ninety-seven per cent Muslim, respectively. Both those cities grew rapidly between 1927 and 1945, but percentages of non-Muslim males fell even further as male Muslim populations rose to ninety-eight per cent in Ankara and ninety-nine per cent in Bursa. Such extremely radical demographic shifts were purposely planned and executed as the policies of relatively late, brutal, and militaristic nation-state builders. The newly created Turkish and post-Greco-Turkish-War Greek national states each carved out their nations by implementing drastic social

21. A.A. Pallis, "The Greek Census of 1928", *The Geographical Journal*, 73:6 (1929), pp. 543–548. The figures provided by Pallis in 1929 are very close but not exactly in accordance with the census of 1928 published in 1937.
22. It is well known that the Jews of Salonica did not survive the Nazi occupation during World War II. In this regard, World War II marks the final stage of Hellenization for Salonica.

Table 6. *Religious affiliations of city population in Ankara and Bursa, 1927, 1935, 1945.*

		Ankara Male	Ankara Female	Bursa Male	Bursa Female
1927	Muslim	47032	23646	29561	30147
1927	Christian	1828	1173	69	44
1927	Jewish	330	328	921	941
1927	Miscellaneous	158	58	6	1
1935	Muslim	72803	45900	34359	35781
1935	Christian	1366	1445	72	71
1935	Jewish	496	501	880	1020
1935	Miscellaneous	144	65	3	1
1945	Muslim	133939	87413	42427	42318
1945	Christian	2067	1599	48	37
1945	Jewish	939	575	451	636
1945	Miscellaneous	108	67	1	1
1927	Muslim	95.3%	93.8%	96.7%	96.8%
1927	Christian	3.7%	4.7%	0.2%	0.1%
1927	Jewish	0.7%	1.3%	3.0%	3.0%
1927	Miscellaneous	0.3%	0.2%	0.0%	0.0%
1935	Muslim	97.3%	95.8%	97.3%	97.0%
1935	Christian	1.8%	3.0%	0.2%	0.2%
1935	Jewish	0.7%	1.0%	2.5%	2.8%
1935	Miscellaneous	0.2%	0.1%	0.0%	0.0%
1945	Muslim	97.7%	97.5%	98.8%	98.4%
1945	Christian	1.5%	1.8%	0.1%	0.1%
1945	Jewish	0.7%	0.6%	1.1%	1.5%
1945	Miscellaneous	0.1%	0.1%	0.0%	0.0%

Sources: Turkish national censuses.

engineering projects, defined along religious lines, rather than the more blurred ethnic ones. As an influential author succinctly commented on the 1923 Greek-Turkish population exchange: "A Western observer, accustomed to a different system of social and national classification, might even conclude that this was no repatriation at all, but two deportations into exile – of Christian Turks to Greece, and of Muslim Greeks to Turkey."[23]

There is limited literature[24] on the impact of the population exchange on the Greek and Turkish economies, and, although no detailed analysis of the

23. Bernard Lewis, *The Emergence of Modern Turkey*, 2nd ed. (Oxford, 1968), p. 355, quoted in Ayhan Aktar, "Homogenizing the Nation, Turkifying the Economy: The Turkish Experience of Population Exchange Reconsidered", in Hirschon, *Crossing the Aegean*, pp. 79–95, 88.
24. For a pioneering study of the impact of the exchange on the Turkish economy, see Aytek Soner Alpan, "The Economic Impact of the 1923 Greco-Turkish Population Exchange upon Turkey" (MA thesis, Middle East Technical University, 2008).

effects of the exchange on the occupational structure has yet been conducted, what follows is not an attempt to do that. Instead, I have compared occupational structures, with the focus on public services in Ankara, Bursa, and Salonica – as well as in Athens, but only for the joint census year 1927/1928. In what follows, I will attempt to bring a gendered perspective into the comparison and to assess the role gender played in Greece and in Turkey in finding employment in the public sector in the cities selected in 1927/1928.[25]

In order to do this, a last two-stage data conversion was necessary. As mentioned before, the 1935 Turkish census utilized categories of fields of economic activity very similar to the ones in the Greek census of 1928. Therefore, I first converted the 1928 Greek economic categories into the 1935 Turkish ones and then the 1927 Turkish economic activity codes into the 1935 Turkish codes, so that they would be in accordance with the coding scheme of the data extracted from the 1845 tax survey. The result of that comparison is shown below for males and females. One important caveat is necessary before commenting on the results of this comparison. The occupational data extracted from the Turkish 1927 census encompass the entire urban population of Ankara and Bursa irrespective of age and therefore include infants and the elderly, who were not expected to work. Those groups are registered and then coded into the category "No or Unknown Profession". The occupational data from the 1928 Greek census, on the other hand, excludes anyone younger than ten years old.[26] Therefore, the total number of observations varies from the general census used in the preparation of Table 5 above, which gives the total population of Athens as 459,211 and that of Salonica as 244,680. The occupational data from the 1928 Greek census provide information on 387,534 individuals for Athens and on 195,855 for Salonica.

The population exchange and the preceding wars had profound demographic and economic effects. The proportion of the population without an occupation was highest in Athens, at more than twenty-five per cent (57,081 males over ten years old without an occupation out of 193,451 registered males, see Table 8). Salonica had fewer unemployed males but their number was proportionately higher than those in Ankara and Bursa, despite the fact that the Turkish data actually include males under ten years old. Employment in public services could not provide enough jobs to absorb the high level of urban unemployment in either Athens or Salonica. The relative share of occupations in public services is the second lowest,

25. The gender aspect has been necessarily absent in this paper until now, because the 1845 tax survey conveys neither information on the household division of labour, nor on occupations of female members of registered households.

26. *Résultats Statistiques du Recensement de la Population de la Grèce du 15–16 Mai 1928. III. Professions* (Athens, 1937).

Table 7. *Sectoral breakdowns of female occupations, Ankara, Bursa (1927, 1935, 1945), Salonica, Athens (1928).*

Fields of Economic Activity	Ankara 1927	Ankara 1935	Ankara 1945	Bursa 1927	Bursa 1935	Bursa 1945	Athens 1928	Salonica 1928
Agriculture	620	482	171	841	549	303	215	256
Industry	108	865	1216	169	2373	2223	14949	8095
Commerce	106	483	1162	66	128	142	2077	683
Communication & Transport/Private Services/Liberal Professions	243	1587	1900	119	322	161	13354	3675
Public Services	180	1305	5036	19	372	607	4737	1333
No or Unknown Profession	23948	43189	80169	29919	33129	39556	158751	83000
TOTAL	25205	47911	89654	31133	36873	42992	194083	97042
in percentages								
Agriculture	2.5%	1%	0%	2.7%	1%	1%	0.1%	0.3%
Industry	0.4%	2%	1%	0.5%	6%	5%	7.7%	8.3%
Commerce	0.4%	1%	1%	0.2%	0%	0%	1.1%	0.7%
Communication & Transport/Private Services/Liberal Professions	1.0%	3%	2%	0.4%	1%	0%	6.9%	3.8%
Public Services	0.7%	3%	6%	0.1%	1%	1%	2.4%	1.4%
No or Unknown Profession	95.0%	90%	89%	96.1%	90%	92%	81.8%	85.5%
TOTAL	100%	100%	100%	100%	100%	100%	100%	100%

Table 8. *Sectoral breakdowns of male occupations, Ankara, Bursa (1927), Athens, Salonica (1928).*

Fields of Economic Activity	Ankara 1927	Bursa 1927	Athens 1928	Salonica 1928
Agriculture	9799	4172	5458	5111
Industry	6667	5119	50700	27471
Commerce	4707	3938	38640	21103
Communication & Transport/Private Services/ Liberal Professions	1329	673	20041	10441
Public Services	15444	3903	21531	8623
No or Unknown Profession	11402	12572	57081	26064
TOTAL	49348	30377	193451	98813
in percentages				
Agriculture	20%	14%	3%	5%
Industry	14%	17%	26%	28%
Commerce	10%	13%	20%	21%
Communication & Transport/Private Services/ Liberal Professions	3%	2%	10%	11%
Public Services	31%	13%	11%	9%
No or Unknown Profession	23%	41%	30%	26%
TOTAL	100%	100%	100%	100%

after occupations in agriculture. The figure below compare the number of male inhabitants who had occupations and the distribution of males across occupational categories in percentages.

It is clear from the above chart that the Turkish state apparatus provided employment opportunities both in civil and military sectors to the male inhabitants of its capital city; that was not the case in Athens. Yet, the figures should be seen in relation to the proportion of urban unemployed actually registered in the censuses as having occupations. Indeed, it is at exactly this point that the census data and occupational data extracted from them should be handled with extra care. Not only are the ambiguities in the taxonomy, such as professions, occupations, or fields of economic activity, problematic, people who had an occupation may be used only as a proxy for what their employment actually was. For instance, some residents, registered with certain occupations on the day of the census, might have been unemployed for the rest of the census year, or might have worked in different sectors. The numbers presented above are therefore not suitable for further quantitative analysis. That said, I believe the potential of occupational data extracted from the censuses is still untapped, especially for comparative studies.

Another major advantage of occupational data from the modern national censuses is their units of registration. Since, to a great extent, in twentieth-century censuses households were replaced as the unit of registration by

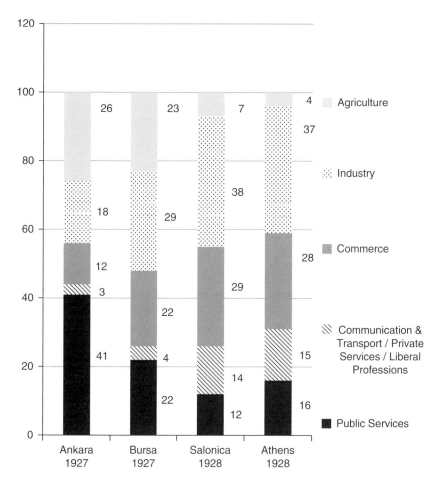

Figure 7. Distribution of occupational categories, males with occupations, Ankara, Bursa, Salonica, Athens, 1927/1928 (in %).

individual citizens, they can be used to avoid a historical and categorical undercount of women and sometimes the direct gender-blind processes of registration practised by earlier surveys. One should be extremely cautious about the gendered technicalities and dynamics of varying methods of census-taking in different locations; even so, the quality of data (and their very presence) on female employment from the national census speaks for itself in comparison with the non-existence of any such data in the 1845 tax survey, which, as we know, registered almost exclusively male members of households. Women were only registered in a negligible number of cases where no male members lived in a household. As a result, very few women appear in the census data, and for most of them no occupation was recorded.

Table 7 shows a severely low degree of participation by females in the labour markets in all the locations selected. The very small number of females with occupations registered in Ankara and Bursa demands explanation; in Ankara in 1927 there were only 180 women with occupations in public service out of a total of 25,205, and the exact breakdown of their occupations is shown. Even the total number of women who had any occupation in any sector was fewer than five per cent in both Ankara and Bursa. I can only conclude that females in Ankara and Bursa were registered as having no or unknown occupations and that their share in the household division of labour went unrecorded.

The situation in Athens and Salonica was different. In Salonica, approximately 100,000 females over the age of ten were registered, around fourteen per cent of them with occupations, while in Athens close to 200,000 females over ten years were registered, eighteen per cent with occupations. Most of those occupations were in industry, followed by the generic category of "Communication & Transport/Private Services/Liberal Professions". Although smaller than the first two sectors, public services nevertheless offered occupations to thousands of women living in Athens and Salonica in 1928.

The extremely small number of females with occupations reported in Ankara and Bursa cannot be explained by the political and economic weakness of the newly established Turkish state in the 1920s, for its policy was at least intended to increase the inclusion of girls in education and to facilitate female participation in the workforce. However, a look at the occupational information extracted from the later censuses shows that the situation did not change very considerably. Even during the interwar period and immediately after World War II only about ten per cent of the women of Ankara were recorded as having occupations, and in Bursa there were even fewer opportunities for women to be employed. In the same cross sections, the total number of women with occupations fell from 3,744 of 36,873 in 1935 to 3,436 of 42,992 in 1945.

The extremely small proportion of women with occupations in Ankara and Bursa gains another dimension from comparison with the figures for Athens and Salonica. The comparison hints at cultural explanations and poses questions about the division of labour within Muslim and non-Muslim households. The figures above should be considered in light of the radical Turkification and Islamification of city dwellers in Ankara and Bursa and the simultaneous Hellenization going on in Athens and Salonica. Even so, the role of religion should be examined in more depth before any premature conclusions are reached. One judicious remark to be made here would be to highlight the importance of the joint effects of gender and religion in Turkified and Islamicized Ankara and Bursa, which, in their interaction, superimposed a double barrier to entry for women's employment in Turkish cities compared with Greek cities.

CONCLUSION

In this study, the occupational structures of Ankara, Bursa, and Salonica have been examined through two cross sections, taken from the mid-nineteenth century, when the cities were major urban centres of the Ottoman Empire, and from the late 1920s, when the same cities were re-inventing themselves as economic and political centres of the new nation states of Greece and Turkey, neighbours interconnected in their making and remaking owing to the population exchange of 1923. The results of these two examinations have highlighted the importance of religion to the organization of public utility services at the neighbourhood level in mid-nineteenth century Ottoman cities, and how the same religion limited female employment in Turkish cities in the late 1920s.

For the Ottoman Empire, ethno-religious population groups and the communities they built were crucial to its functioning as a multi-religious and multi-ethnic polity. The effect of religion on both bringing people together and keeping them apart in neighbourhoods with reference to patterns of residential building and as a determinant of occupational choice is an under-researched topic. I would argue that mapping occupational structures onto residential patterns according to ethnicity and religion can reveal aspects of the spatial organization of urban economic and social life in the late Ottoman Empire. I believe that for non-Muslim Ottoman city dwellers, finding employment in the public utility sector was positively correlated with ethno-religious segregation at neighbourhood level in Ankara, Bursa, and Salonica in 1845. It was especially true in neighbourhoods where non-Muslims lived, where everyone belonged to ethno-religious groups, such as the Jewish community in Salonica. On the other hand, mixed neighbourhoods in Ankara resulted in overrepresentation of Muslims in public service sector employment, which suggests that although the Ottoman Empire was a multi-ethnic and multi-religious polity Muslims had leverage in organizing and finding employment in public services at neighbourhood level. This point should be further analysed by examining the components of the public services provided in neighbourhoods and assessing the importance of religion.

The second finding of the study is related to religion and gender. It argues that in the Turkey of the late 1920s adherence – or not – to the Muslim faith affected women's occupational choices and employment opportunities. Both Greece and Turkey, as successors to the Ottoman Empire, imagined and constructed their nationhood along religious lines, and implemented social-engineering projects to create, respectively, Orthodox Christian and Muslim nations. After 1923, the populations of Ankara, Bursa, and Athens were religiously homogenized, while Salonica, once the metropolis of Mediterranean Jewry under Ottoman rule, with Jews constituting more than half its population, transformed itself into a Greek city with a sizeable Jewish community of around a fifth of its population in 1928. Non-Muslims had disappeared from both Ankara and Bursa by 1928 and hardly any female members of Muslim households were registered as having occupations. Non-Muslim females living in Athens and Salonica, on the other hand, had higher levels of employment, including in the public sector. This finding should also be further developed and the question asked whether Jewish women had equal opportunities for employment, especially in the public sector. In a similar vein, the time span of this examination should be extended to the period after World War II to allow an evaluation of how the loss of Salonica's Jewish population affected the general occupational structure there.

This article has compared the occupational structures of Ankara, Bursa, and Salonica as they were in the mid-nineteenth century and then again in the first half of the twentieth century. The focus was not on shifts in labour relations, but rather on changes in urban occupational structures. Even so, by focusing on the sub-sectoral group of occupations providing public utility services we have been able to trace the changing dynamics of working for a polity in those cities between the 1840s and the 1920s. I have deliberately used the term "polity", rather than "state", because of the wider-ranging and more inclusive nature of the political structures that organized the public utility services for Ankara, Bursa, and Salonica in the mid-nineteenth century. In the 1840s, before the advent of the municipal administrations, several public utility services, including religious, safety, communal, and educational services, were organized and provided in Ottoman urban localities by communities at both town and neighbourhood level. In the second cross section, taken from the 1920s, the three cities had, by then, become important urban centres in two nation states: a consolidating and re-forming Greece and an emerging Turkey. Public utility services were more centrally organized under the new polities and were handed to a newly growing but central occupational category and labour relation, namely public services and public servants. A greater proportion of people in the three cities were employed by the central national state than had been the case in the mid-nineteenth century. In those three towns, the representative bodies of the Ottoman central state changed from provincial administrations with fewer responsibilities for providing public utility services in the 1840s to more centrally organized administrative and municipal structures that acted almost monopolistically as employers of public servants, providing most of the public services in the fields of safety, education, sanitation, and religion.

The political change brought about by the fall of the Ottoman Empire was a drastic one, for it not only dissolved an imperial polity and led to the emergence of, among others, Greek and Turkish nation states, it also led them in their early existence briefly but decisively to war.

The Greco-Turkish War of 1919–1922 resulted in a compulsory exchange of populations between Greece and Turkey. This transformed the ethno-religious composition on both sides of the Aegean, creating a framework of interaction for the people of both states that affected a number of aspects of social and economic life, including labour relations.

IRSH 61 (2016), Special Issue, pp. 243–262 doi:10.1017/S0020859016000419
© 2016 Internationaal Instituut voor Sociale Geschiedenis

The Role of the State in Employment and Welfare Regulation: Sweden in the European Context

MAX KOCH

Lund University, Faculty of Social Sciences,
Socialhögskolan
Box 23, 22100, Lund, Sweden

E-mail: max.koch@soch.lu.se

ABSTRACT: This article examines the changing role of the Swedish state in employment and welfare regulation in an environment that has become more market driven, commodified, and Europeanized. It begins with a theoretical reflection on the role of the state in capitalist development and a review of the recent debate on the spatiality of state regulation: the state as employer, redistributor, and arbiter, and as a shaper of employment relations and welfare. In the latter role, the state is conceptualized as employer, guarantor of employment rights, and procedural regulator, as intermediating neo-corporatist processes, as macroeconomic manager, and as welfare state. From this theoretical basis, the paper identifies changes in state employment and welfare regulation by comparing two periods: the original and mainly nation-state-based founding stage of the Swedish welfare and employment model as it developed after the 1938 Saltsjöbaden Agreement, and the period after Sweden's accession to the European Union in 1995.

INTRODUCTION

The Global Collaboratory on the History of Labour Relations distinguishes four main categories of labour: non-working, reciprocal labour, tributary labour, and commodified labour. Though all of these categories can be empirically found at all times in the past 500 years and across space, attempts to theorize the link between the development of the capitalist mode of production, labour regimes, and employment relations[1] have presupposed a long-term trend towards an increase in commodified and market-oriented labour at the expense of the other types. Empirically referring to capitalist core countries, Hagelstange called this

---

1. Karl Marx, *Capital: A Critique of Political Economy. Volume One: The Process of Production of Capital* (London, 1977).

trend "proletarianization".[2] Throughout much of the nineteenth and twentieth centuries an increasing percentage of the working-age population found itself in a situation in which there was no alternative but to sell their labour power as a commodity to make ends meet. Commodification as "proletarianization" meant that tributary labour, despite its continuously important role in the capitalist peripheries, came to play a marginal role within capitalist centres, that much of the work that used to be carried out within the household became marketized, and that self-employment diminished. Labour in general came to be seen as largely synonymous with market- and profit-oriented labour, devaluing household, care, community, and voluntary work, while the non-working part of the population came to be defined in relation to the working part: as either too old or too young to be "economically active", too affluent to be in need of selling their labour power, or unemployed and unable to do so. However, capitalist "markets" have never in themselves created labour and employment regimes, but rather were always assisted and embedded through more or less far-reaching socio-economic regulation.[3] The degree to which people were actually forced to sell their labour power as a (fictitious) commodity depended on the strength of societal counter movements[4] and particularly the intermediating role of the state. As a result, much of recent capitalist development appears as waves of commodification, decommodification, and recommodification of labour relations, with states playing key roles in the process.

In conceptualizing the concrete roles of the state in shaping labour regimes and relations, this Special Issue of the *International Review of Social History (IRSH)* distinguishes between three capacities of the state (conqueror, employer, and redistributor/arbiter) and between two relationships (vis-à-vis its own subjects and those of other states). Taking the example of the recent history of Sweden, this paper focuses on state capacities as employer, redistributor, and arbiter, and, in terms of relationships, on taxation and welfare as well as on corresponding ideologies. Recent state theories have stressed the shift from demand- to supply-side economics and towards more market-oriented approaches in state strategies.[5] With regard to the European Union (EU), this literature indicates that the state, the welfare state in particular, has moved towards a weaker commitment to collective rights and to a stronger emphasis on

2. Thomas Hagelstange, *Die Entwicklung von Klassenstrukturen in der EG und in Nordamerika* (Frankfurt am Main, 1988).
3. Max Koch, *Roads to Post-Fordism: Labour Markets and Social Structures in Europe* (Aldershot, 2006).
4. Karl Polanyi, *The Great Transformation: The Political and Economic Origins of Our Time* (Boston, 1944).
5. Bob Jessop, *The Future of the Capitalist State* (Cambridge, 2002).

individual rights and duties,[6] particularly after the introduction of the European Employment Strategy (EES). Europeanization has also led to a rescaling of socio-economic regulation in general and state regulation in particular. Against this background, this paper is concerned with the question of how exactly state roles in shaping labour relations, employment, and welfare changed in Sweden after its accession to the EU and the introduction of the EES. It is based upon a theoretical discussion of the role of the state in capitalist development and the spatiality of state regulation. It further suggests several dimensions along which the state shapes employment and welfare and acts as arbiter between capital and labour. From this theoretical perspective, it then discusses transitions in state strategies in Sweden by comparing the post-Saltsjöbaden and post-EU-accession periods.

STATE ROLES IN CAPITALIST DEVELOPMENT, SPATIAL TARGETING, EMPLOYMENT RELATIONS, AND WELFARE

This section discusses three key roles of the state as employer, arbiter, and redistributor. First, it addresses the general relationship of capitalist development and the state; secondly, it considers the different spatial levels or scales on which states may be active in shaping regulation; thirdly, it refers to the state's role in structuring employment relations and welfare.

Capitalist development and the state

In capitalist economies, processes of production and wealth creation are structurally separated from the political processes of exercising coercive power and administrative control. The Marxian tradition, in particular, has linked the autonomous existence of the state to the structural prerequisites of an economy based on the circulation of commodities. In order to exchange goods, individuals must "recognize one another reciprocally as proprietors".[7] This includes a "juridical moment" since exchange relations are possible only if the individuals acting are not prevented from entering into them by, for example, feudal rule.[8] Equally, appropriating commodities through the use of force is not a legal or legitimate course of action. Hence, respect for the principle of equivalence in exchange relations

6. Gøsta Esping-Andersen, "Who is Harmed by Labour Market Regulations? Quantitative Evidence", in *Idem* and Mario Regini (eds), *Why Deregulate Labour Markets?* (Oxford, 2000), pp. 66–98.
7. Karl Marx, *Grundrisse: Foundations of the Critique of Political Economy* (Harmondsworth, 1973), p. 243.
8. Evgeny Pashukanis, *Law and Marxism: A General Theory* (London, 1978).

depends on a formally independent institution that guarantees the legal and economic independence of the owners of commodities: their equality, legal security, and protection. In the case of an advanced division of labour, this guarantee cannot be ensured in accordance with common law but must be institutionalized in an independent third party that, above all, monopolizes the legitimate use of physical force:[9] the modern state. Hence, unlike pre-capitalist societies where monetary exchange relations play a minor role, the first general role of the state in capitalist development under the *rule of law* is to guarantee private property, the principle of equivalence, and the legal security of its economic subjects.

Exchange relations, however, are not reduced to the exchange of material features of use values. They also reproduce social relationships, which involve power asymmetries and social inequalities. The latter originate in different societal domains and take the form of class, race, religion, linguistic, or gender characteristics. In a social structure based on a dynamic plurality of exploitative and exclusionary relationships,[10] the state is the main location for the political regulation of conflicts and for the maintenance of social order.[11] Since, without state regulation, such a society would disintegrate, the second general role of the state is that of an arbiter to maintain a minimum of social cohesion and, at the same time, to legitimize remaining inequalities. Taxation is the main political means by which the state redistributes primary incomes for these purposes.

In its third role in capitalist development, the state has an indispensable capability of temporarily harmonizing conflicting group interests and creating consensus.[12] A key issue in any capitalist society is the degree and the kind of commodification of socio-economic relations. It is far from being taken for granted, and indeed a controversial matter, what kind of private and social services and use values should take commodity form[13] and be sold and bought on markets that states often have to regulate. Childcare, elderly care, education, the regulation of prostitution as well as of carbon emissions are prominent recent examples of this conflict. The state appears here as an autonomous political sphere, where social classes and groups represent their interests in indirect and mediated ways. As political parties and interest groups raise variable issues, such as religion, age, and the environment, these interests and issues sometimes become the focus of government action, only to be superseded by others at later points

---

9. Max Weber, "Politics as a Vocation", in Hans Gerth and C. Wright Mills (eds), *From Max Weber: Essays in Sociology* (London, 1991), pp. 77–128, 78.
10. Koch, *Roads to Post-Fordism*, pp. 13–16.
11. Claus Offe, *Contradictions of the Welfare State* (London, 1984).
12. Alexander Gallas *et al.* (eds), *Reading Poulantzas* (London, 2011).
13. This includes the issue of the conditions under which "non-working" is seen as legitimate.

in time.[14] State policies cannot be reduced to the strategic interests of single actors, but rather develop as a result of the heterogeneity and changing dynamics of social forces that influence state institutions. The nature of the composition of social forces, which are able to influence state policies in particular historical configurations, cannot be defined in general terms but must be explored empirically. Once such a coalition of relatively powerful actors is formed and has managed to influence the general direction of the state's policies, it takes the character of a relatively homogenous social phenomenon and appears to "act" as if it were a single actor: the more socially coherent the coalition of forces that influences the state, the fewer the contradictions across its policies.[15] Hence, the state is an object of agency of the sociopolitical coalition that creates and recreates it, and, at the same time, a powerful actor, whose policies shape a range of societal fields. It is, to borrow Bourdieu's terms, structured *and* structuring at the same time.

State spatiality

The historical development of markets and capital tends to dissolve previously isolated communities and to regroup their inhabitants according to new spatio-temporal structures. In most parts of Europe in the nineteenth and twentieth centuries these largely followed the borders of the developing nation states. Towards the end of the twentieth century, however, this particular state territoriality began to be faced with Europeanization and internationalization, but also with localization processes that undermined this spatial arrangement. As a consequence, scholars ceased to presuppose a static concurrence of nation and state and began to view state spatiality in more dynamic ways. The spatial dimension of state regulation is not seen as a fixed object but as a delicate structure that is permanently subject to rescaling processes in the course of which new, multi-scalar structures of state organization, political authority, and socio-economic regulation emerge.[16] State institutions are foremost in what Brenner calls "spatial targeting": attempts to "enhance territorially specific locational assets, to accelerate the circulation of capital, to reproduce the labour force, to address place-specific socio-economic problems and/or to maintain territorial cohesion".[17] Similarly, the notion of "spatio-temporal

14. Max Koch and Martin Fritz, "Building the Eco-Social State: Do Welfare Regimes Matter?", *Journal of Social Policy*, 43 (2014), pp. 679–703.

15. Nicos Poulantzas, *State, Power, Socialism* (London, 1978).

16. J. Rogers Hollingsworth and Robert Boyer, *Contemporary Capitalism: The Embeddedness of Institutions* (Cambridge, 1997); Yuri Kazepov, *Rescaling Social Policies towards Multilevel Governance in Europe* (Aldershot, 2010).

17. Neil Brenner, "Urban Governance and Production of New State Spaces in Western Europe, 1960–2000", *Review of International Political Economy*, 11 (2004), pp. 447–488, 453.

fixes" has been developed to reflect the fact that particular accumulation regimes correspond with particular scales of regulation or spatial boundaries (national, transnational, local), in which structural coherence is sought. Spatio-temporal fixes are associated with policy frameworks that target specific jurisdictions, places, and scales as focal points for state regulation in particular periods of time. How state strategies at European and national levels, for example, are linked to each other cannot be clarified in general theoretical terms but must be explored empirically.

From the mid-1970s the Fordist growth model, with its focus on the national level, came under pressure not only through various processes of deregulation and re-regulation, but also through rescaling processes that led to ongoing shifts in the sites, scales, and modalities of the delivery of state activities. In what Jessop summarizes as a "Schumpeterian workfare post-national regime", it is the increased importance of scales of intervention and regulation other than at the national level that moves into focus. New forms of statehood correspond to increasingly open economies, for which the creation of systemic or structural competitiveness is the overall goal. The result is a tendency towards the watering down of the national state apparatus whose tasks are reorganized on "sub-national, national, supranational, and translocal levels".[18] At the same time, foreign agents and institutions become more significant as sources of domestic policy ideas, policy design, and implementation. To the extent to which the increasingly transnational processes of accumulation of capital require forms of regulation that extend beyond the borders and the capacities of individual states, governments – somewhat in compensation for the loss of scope for intervention at national level – attempt to create or strengthen international regulatory systems, of which the EU is especially important. Far from being made redundant by the emergent international and European order, national governments belong to its key architects.

Shaping labour relations, employment, and welfare

The Global Collaboratory on the History of Labour Relations has high-lighted key roles of the state in the provision and regulation of labour relations, employment, and welfare: as employer, arbiter, and redistributor. In the modern (welfare) state these roles take somewhat more specific forms:

- State as *employer*: This role can take the form of internal and direct public employment or, in its market-oriented variant, commodified, indirect, and external forms of economic activity. Indeed, in some countries the state continues to be the largest single employer, offering a great deal of job security. However, it often features more restrictive

---

18. Jessop, *The Future of the Capitalist State*, p. 206.

industrial relations than the private sector, partly because parts of the public workforce are not allowed to strike. As indirect and external employer, a lesser or greater number of jobs in the formally private sector is dependent on state strategies. Employment in the infrastructure, education, and health sectors, among others, may be provided by private actors, but it remains nevertheless linked to governments' strategic priorities as well as to spending and outsourcing decisions.

- As *guarantor* of employment rights and *procedural regulator*: Where labour power takes the form of a commodity, representatives of capital and labour need to negotiate its price and the conditions of its use.[19] Since an individual employee can normally not negotiate with an employer on equal terms, in most countries the state sets legally binding minimum standards that must be respected in employment contracts.[20] Governments have interpreted this role differently, emphasizing either collective rights or individual employment rights and obligations. Furthermore, the state normally defines the status, rights, and obligations of the labour market parties (legally defining who may negotiate collective agreements). This may involve compulsory mechanisms for collective employee representation at company and/or workplace level, and the obligation on management to inform and consult representatives on key business and personnel policies. The state may also have a crucial role in handling or avoiding breakdowns in collective bargaining. Most national industrial relations systems contain either voluntary or compulsory mechanisms of conciliation, mediation, and arbitration.
- As *arbiter* in *intermediating corporatist or neo-corporatist processes* and *macroeconomic management*: The state facilitates the political exchange between management and labour at different (local, national, European) levels. This can take "harder" forms of government regulation and/or "softer" forms of governance based on the diffusion of good practice and "steering".[21] Furthermore, the state shapes labour markets and employment regimes through demand and/or supply management;
- As *redistributor* and *welfare state*: The extent to which labour power is "decommodified"[22] and institutional protection of workers from total

19. Marx, *Capital*, ch. 8.

20. Richard Hyman, "The State of Industrial Relations", paper presented at the Industrial Relations in Europe Conference, 31 August 2006 to 2 September 2006, Ljubljana.

21. Mark Stuart and Miguel Martínez Lucio, "A Bridge over Troubled Water: The Role of the British Advisory, Conciliation and Arbitration Service (ACAS) in Facilitating Labour-Management Consultation in Public Sector Transformation" (Cornell University ILR School Working Paper, January 2007), available at http://digitalcommons.ilr.cornell.edu/cgi/viewcontent.cgi?article=1003& context=workingpapers, last accessed 6 September 2016; Paul Marginson and Keith Sisson, *European Integration and Industrial Relations: Multi-Level Governance in the Making* (Basingstoke, 2004).

22. Gøsta Esping-Andersen, *The Three Worlds of Welfare Capitalism* (Cambridge, 1990).

dependence for survival on employers is provided. Welfare regimes take different forms and vary, above all, in terms of the particular division of the private and public provision of labour,[23] to which different forms and extents of taxation correspond. Relatively generous welfare regimes with an accordingly high extent of "decommodification" tend to strengthen the position of workers and facilitate the set up and maintenance of institutionally coordinated industrial relations, while less generous regimes often coincide with weakly coordinated and more "individualized" industrial relations systems. The forms and conditions that frame the relations between the state and individual welfare recipients are likewise subject to change and include top-down government approaches and more recent governance models in which the state is *primus inter pares* in wider networks of public, semi-public, and private actors.

GROWTH STRATEGY, LABOUR REGIMES, WELFARE REGULATION, AND THE STATE: TWO PERIODS COMPARED

How have the interpretations of these state roles, particularly as employer, arbiter, and redistributor, and especially its welfare function changed since the origins of the "Swedish model"? What roles did different scales (European, national, local) play in these shifts? And what were the main consequences of these shifts in state strategies for labour relations, employment, and welfare? This section compares two time periods: the original one following the Saltsjöbaden Agreement and the current one that started to take shape in the wake of the crisis of the early 1990s and with Sweden's accession to the EU in 1995.

Growth strategy, employment, and welfare regulation after Saltsjöbaden

Until the 1980s, Sweden's industrial relations system was based on central- or national-level collective bargaining, which was designed to achieve wider normative goals such as full employment and wage equality. The wage determination process comprised central wage negotiations between employers' organizations (Svenska Arbetsgivareföreningen, SAF) and trade unions (Landsorganisationen i Sverige, LO), sector-level bargaining on the application and adjustment of the central agreements, as well as company- level negotiations on any remaining details.[24] However, the underlying

23. Wil Arts and John Gelissen, "Three Worlds of Welfare Capitalism or More? A State-of-the- Art Report", *Journal of European Social Policy*, 12 (2004), pp. 137–158.
24. Victor A. Pestoff, *Beyond the Market and State: Social Enterprises and Civil Democracy in a Welfare Society* (Aldershot, 2004); Max Koch, "Wage Determination, Socio-Economic Regulation and the State", *European Journal of Industrial Relations*, 11 (2005), pp. 327–346.

notion that economic action should reflect social responsibility and promote social cohesion was not always taken for granted. The first three decades of the twentieth century were characterized by severe conflicts between employers and workers. The frequency of strikes was higher in this period than in most other European countries.[25] In this situation, the state, usually represented by Social Democratic governments, played an active and engaged role in bringing together employers' and employees' representatives. This resulted in the 1938 Saltsjöbaden Agreement, the institutional basis of the new socio-economic model. Subsequently, governments could withdraw from the management of wage bargaining, which was increasingly carried out in the form of bipartite bargaining between strong unions and a highly centralized employer organization. Instead, governments supported the general growth strategy through complementary labour market and welfare policies.

This division of labour between the labour market parties, on the one hand, and the state, on the other, was reflected especially in the 1956 wage agreement that is generally seen as a crucial step in the manifestation of a mode of regulation based on central bargaining between the SAF and LO. The socio-economic background to this was a booming economy, which led to maximum utilization of the workforce. However, serious sectoral and regional inequalities had remained and continued to generate wage competition that was not in the interests of the employers as a whole. The trade unions, on their part, also wanted to avoid excessive wage disparities at the company, regional, and sector levels and therefore favoured central bargaining with the paramount goal of reducing these inequalities.[26] Wage levels were not supposed to reflect the competitive situations of particular companies and sectors, but rather the general balance of power between organized capital and labour. The label "solidaristic" refers to the general goal of wage policies to gradually achieve approximate incomes and to avoid labour market segmentation. Trade unions coordinated their bargaining activities in ways such that "better-earning unions [...] restrained themselves in collective bargaining and wage movements for the benefit of the weakest".[27] Any remaining wage differences were supposed to mainly reflect differences in skills. Complementing state active labour market polices stimulated, *inter alia*, geographical mobility and retraining, and were therefore always "supply-oriented". State policies further

25. Mats Benner, *The Politics of Growth: Economic Regulation in Sweden 1930–1994* (Lund, 1997), p. 42.

26. Rune Åberg, "Wage Control and Cost-Push Inflation in Sweden since 1960", in Ronald Dore, Robert Boyer, and Zoe Mars (eds), *The Return to Incomes Policy* (London, 1994), pp. 71–93.

27. Martin Peterson, "Pathways of the Welfare State", in Bengt Larsson, Martin Letell, and Håkan Thörn (eds), *Transformations of the Swedish Welfare State: From Social Engineering to Governance?* (Basingstoke, 2011), pp. 23–38.

included the replacement of industrial jobs with public employment[28] and wage subsidies for sectors and companies whose survival was under threat as a result of these wage policies.

Many observers emphasized that the *conditio sine qua non* for this socio-economic development model to function was that "most people are working and have enough income for a high living standard in relative terms, and during temporary periods of unemployment, sickness, and so on, income losses should be compensated to keep people out of poverty".[29] Not accidently, in European comparison, Swedish governments upheld Keynesian principles in socio-economic regulation the longest. Even during the unstable period of the 1970s and 1980s, when other European countries changed their policy priorities from fighting unemployment to fighting inflation, Sweden "withheld and even strengthened Keynesian principles by the so-called bridging strategy which, among other things, resulted in state investments in non-profitable industries".[30] As long as priority was given to the creation of employment, shortages within the labour market were to be avoided by supporting the mobility of workers towards key industries and geographical regions in need of development.

The political priority of creating employment is reflected in comparatively high economic activity rates that fluctuated above eighty per cent during the 1970s and 1980s. In 1991, this indicator, which measures the percentage of the economically active in the population capable of working,[31] stood at 83.3 per cent.[32] The unemployment rate stood at 2.9 per cent. Unlike central European countries such as Germany, which mainly recruited male so-called guest workers from southern and south-eastern Europe to meet employers' demands for an increasing workforce during the Fordist upswing while leaving the traditional domestic "male breadwinner" model largely intact, the Swedish state initiated campaigns to recruit women to the workforce as early as the 1960s. As a result, women's activity rate exceeded 70 per cent as early as the 1970s and stood at 81 per cent in 1991.[33] At 2.5 per cent, the rate of female

28. Mattias Bengtsson and Tomas Berglund, "Labour Market Policies in Transition: From Social Engineering to Standby-Ability", in Larsson *et al.*, *Transformations of the Swedish Welfare State*, pp. 86–103, 86–87.

29. Daniel Larsson and Björn Halleröd, "Sweden: The Impact of Policy and Labour Market Transformation", in Neil Fraser, Rudolfo Gutiérrez, and Ramón Peña-Casas (eds), *Working Poverty in Europe* (Basingstoke, 2011), pp. 112–132, 113.

30. *Ibid.*, p. 114.

31. More precisely, it measures the percentage of those in the age range 16–64, who are either self-employed, employed, or unemployed but looking for work. Non-active persons include people who for one reason or other cannot or do not want to seek formal employment (including those incapable of working due to sickness or participation in education).

32. Koch, *Roads to Post-Fordism*, p. 76 (based on International Labour Organization (ILO) data at http://laborsta.ilo.org, last accessed 6 September 2016).

33. *Ibid.*

unemployment was below the overall average. In the same period, the average annual number of hours worked per person in employment remained almost constant, with 1,557 hours worked in 1973 and 1,561 hours in 1990.

The welfare and social protection system has often been characterized as "social democratic" and "universal" in the sense that the whole population, regardless of socio-economic position, is insured against risks such as illness and old age. In addition, benefits were introduced that were made dependent on the previous employment status. The welfare system was based on egalitarian values and policy goals such as the equal distribution of incomes, low poverty rates, and the ambition to secure income maintenance in cases of unemployment, and universal access to health, care, and education services.[34] The funding of the system was based on a combination of contributions paid by employers and employees as well as tax revenues. Its two main pillars were a network of encompassing social insurances and an umbrella of social welfare services. Hence, the state not only played a key organizational role in the creation of commodified employment, it also made labour market participation the necessary condition for eligibility for income-related and non-means-tested benefits, especially from unemployment insurance schemes and from sickness, incapacity, and early retirement schemes. From the beginning, the regulating national state was complemented by an important role of the local level, the municipalities. This is especially obvious in the area of minimum income protection (MIP), which mainly takes the form of social assistance. The latter was designed as a means-tested benefit mainly under the responsibility of the municipalities. It was normally claimed if people were either economically active but not entitled to unemployment benefits or economically inactive, for example due to health reasons. The designers of the Swedish welfare state indeed assumed that social assistance would gradually lose significance within MIP as coverage of employment-related insurance would broaden.[35]

Typical for the Fordist period, which dominated the postwar years (1950–1975),[36] the Swedish growth and welfare model included elements of "social engineering" as well as practices of external control and discipline that reflected modernist ideas of top-down government and management philosophies.

34. Mikko Kautto *et al.*, "Introduction: How Distinct are the Nordic Welfare States?", in *Idem et al.* (eds), *Nordic Welfare States in the European Context* (London, 2001), pp. 1–13; Olli Kangas and Joakim Palme (eds), *Social Policy and Economic Development in the Nordic Countries* (Basingstoke, 2005).
35. Anna Angelin, Håkan Johansson, and Max Koch, "Patterns of Institutional Change in Minimum Income Protection in Sweden and Germany", *Journal of International and Comparative Social Policy*, 30 (2014), pp. 165–179.
36. Max Koch, *Capitalism and Climate Change: Theoretical Discussion, Historical Development and Policy Responses* (Basingstoke, 2012), pp. 68–75.

So-called experts of various kinds – including macroeconomists, sociologists, social psychologists, and pedagogues – played leading roles. The point of view "that 'human problems' needed particular experts [...] was echoed [...] in the idea that the welfare of the new 'people's home' [*folkhemmet*] was to be built through a reconstruction not only of the 'home', but also through an improvement of the 'people'".[37] The ambition was nothing less than to "develop 'a new human type', more mature than previous, by collective socialization and eugenics".[38] For Gunnar and Alva Myrdal, leading "experts" in various societal matters of the time and founding parents of the Swedish welfare state, a "full utilization production capacity required a rationally administered population stock, access to subsidized housing in the vicinity of the production sites, free healthcare, child benefits, and institutional education".[39] What came to be known as "consensus culture" was in crucial parts "engineered" from above and put into practice by the use of a range of disciplining measures. In addition, from the beginning, top-down consensus meant placing emphasis on the "responsibility of the individual" and the ideas that "if society should help, there should be reciprocal obligation to do something in return", thereby addressing the "individual's moral sense of obligation to give something back".[40]

Growth strategy, employment, and welfare regulation after the crisis of the early 1990s and EU entry

Sweden's wage determination and industrial relations model appeared to change dramatically in the early 1990s when a Conservative government came to power whose programme deprioritized full employment in favour of price stability and the reduction of the budget deficit. Policy proposals focused on strengthening the role of company-level wage bargaining and improving the competitive position of the employers. Employers' taxes and contributions were reduced, fixed-term employment contracts were facilitated, and welfare entitlements were cut.[41] The period also saw a brief stage of uncoordinated decentralization of collective bargaining, when the employer organization (SAF) withdrew its representatives from tripartite boards in 1991. However, fears that the "Swedish model" would collapse

---

37. Bengt Larsson, Martin Letell, and Håkan Thörn, "Transformations of the Swedish Welfare State: Social Engineering, Governance and Governmentality", in Larsson *et al.*, *Transformations of the Swedish Welfare State*, pp. 3–22, 13.

38. *Ibid.*

39. *Ibid.*

40. Ulla Björnberg, "Social Policy Reforms in Sweden: New Perspectives on Rights and Obligations", in Larsson *et al.*, *Transformations of the Swedish Welfare State*, pp. 71–85, 72.

41. Jonas Pontusson and Peter Swenson, "Labour Markets, Production Strategies, and Wage Bargaining Institutions: The Swedish Employer Offensive in Comparative Perspective", *Comparative Political Studies*, 29 (1996), pp. 223–250.

completely did not become reality.[42] In 1994, once again it was an engaged state that initiated the reorganization of the wage determination process and wider development strategy. The Social Democratic government, which had been voted back into power, convinced the SAF to return to collective bargaining, which was now to take place mainly at sector level. The Central Bank, which was made formally independent in 1993 but which continued to be linked to the government's positions through the government representatives on the board of the bank, supported sectoral wage developments with a complementary interest rates policy. A further new government method to influence the wage-determination process was the introduction of an "arbitration institute", where all labour market parties were to be represented. This new institution was given the power to intervene in wage bargaining if its outcome was deemed unfavourable for general socio-economic development. Its main function, however, was to create and enforce a common basis for negotiation before actual bargaining rounds began. This new "Alliance for Growth", in which the government had taken the initiative, was geared towards the technological upgrading of Swedish industry.[43] Its main features included state support of sectoral innovation systems in existing areas of industrial specialization and research into promising technologies such as telecommunication, pharmaceuticals, biotechnology, and the information sector. Various policies for upgrading regional industrial and technological capacity were developed. At the same time, the institutional infrastructure was improved by establishing clusters that brought together regional actors and organizations. This was complemented by training and retraining programmes for staff and an expansion of the educational system.

This "high road" of competing within increasingly transnational markets was also the strategy with which Sweden joined the European Union in 1995. Subsequently, the country became subordinated to EU regulations in various policy fields as well as part of European labour market policies, such as the EES. For a long period, and not only in Sweden, the launching of a European employment policy, and indeed a European Social Model, had been regarded as conflicting with national traditions, and it was also seen as an obstacle to the achievement of competitiveness through market liberalization.[44] In the course of the 1990s, however, this perception was reversed and European employment initiatives were no longer perceived as an obstacle to growth and development but, on the contrary, as one of their

---

42. Koch, *Roads to Post-Fordism*, pp. 84–88.
43. Mats Benner, "The Scandinavian Challenge: The Future of Advanced Welfare States in the Knowledge Economy", *Acta Sociologica*, 46 (2003), pp. 136–149.
44. Frank Deppe, Michael Felder, and Stefan Tidow, "Structuring the State – The Case of European Employment Policy", in Beate Kohler-Koch (ed.), *Linking EU and National Governance* (Oxford, 2004), pp. 175–200.

structural preconditions.[45] Domestic employment regimes were opened up to new practices and strategies designed at European level and the link between economic and social policies was tightened, above all, through an integrated "activation" approach to welfare policies. Benchmarking of employment policies became a legal obligation across the EU, with the aim of achieving greater convergence in the goals of employment policy.[46] EU employment policy goals took the form of several "Integrated Guidelines", particularly aiming at the creation of more jobs both as standard and non-standard employment.[47]

Within this rescaled employment regulation, the operation of "soft" governance techniques came to predominate over "hard" laws. The EU applies the Open Method of Coordination (OMC), an iterative procedure, involving a "rolling programme of yearly planning, monitoring, examination and readjustment" whereby, in the case of the EES, "national employment policies are put to the test of cross-country comparison, including peer review".[48] A range of quantitative targets were specified around these pillars that EU member states were supposed to achieve in three-year National Reform Programmes. The European emphasis on "employability" and the corresponding employment guidelines stress the self-responsibility of citizens. In a sort of new social contract, it is the individual's duty to look for work and to improve his or her adaptability to the demands of the labour market, while the state not only encourages the "return to the labour market of those inactive persons willing and able to take up a job"[49] but also cuts or abolishes the unemployment benefits of those who are not willing to do so. This fitted nicely with the Swedish Social Democrats' focus on people's working capacities and motivations to improve their labour market prospects. Coinciding with Sweden's accession to the EU, its employment discourse shifted from "lack of employment" (implying demand-oriented measures) to "lack of employability" (implying supply-oriented measures).[50]

During the 1994–2006, Social Democratic government austerity measures to lower the budget deficit were combined with the ambition to transform Sweden into a "leading knowledge-nation".[51] Accordingly, the

45. Max Koch, "The State in European Employment Regulation", *Journal of European Integration*, 30 (2008), pp. 255–272.
46. Paul Teague, "Deliberative Governance and EU Social Policy", *European Journal of Industrial Relations*, 7 (2001), pp. 7–26.
47. Julia S. O'Connor, "Non-Standard Employment and European Union Employment Regulation", in Max Koch and Martin Fritz (eds), *Non-Standard Employment in Europe: Paradigms, Prevalence and Policy Responses* (Basingstoke, 2013), pp. 46–66.
48. Marginson and Sisson, *European Integration and Industrial Relations*, p. 95.
49. Deppe *et al.*, "Structuring the State", pp. 175–200, 188.
50. Bengtsson and Berglund, "Labour Market Policies in Transition", p. 87.
51. *Ibid.*, p. 90.

"work strategy" (*arbetslinjen*), designed to bring as many people as possible into employment, was complemented with a "competence strategy" (*kompetenslinjen*) and lifelong learning was "championed as necessary to maintain full employment in the future".[52] As a corollary, state investment in higher education expanded in order to increase the employability and competitiveness of the Swedish workforce. The compulsory schooling age was increased to nineteen, and the number of students at university doubled in comparison to the late 1980s. In the same period, however, "activation" policies began to be applied more strictly, mainly in the form of "economic pressures through unemployment insurance", but also through the involvement of the unemployed through "action plans" or, more generally, the contractualization of relations between an unemployed individual and the employment office. Obligations for citizens to take responsibility for supporting themselves were increased both in discourse and policies, while the role of the state as direct employer became less pronounced. However, the fact that the Social Democrats reversed some of the Conservative reforms in labour market and welfare regulation ensured trade union support. While maximum unemployment benefits were reduced twice, active labour market policies were expanded during the crisis of the 1990s, with five per cent of the labour force being temporarily employed in job creation programmes.[53] Further welfare reforms included a reduction in the generosity of the social insurance system (introduction of fees, individual contributions, waiting days as well as a general lowering of replacement rates), a reform of the pension system to reduce costs and to increase the supply of labour by basing pensions on lifelong employment, and also savings in health and social services expenditure.

The Centre–Conservative government, in power from 2006 to late 2014 when it was replaced by a Red–Green minority government, continued the "supply-oriented" growth and employment strategy in many ways but particularly stressed "social exclusion" (*utanförskapet*) within the "work strategy" in order to raise the incentive to work and to increase the labour supply. Hence, "social exclusion" began to be used largely synonymously with "unemployment". Accordingly, labour market programmes were "reduced, shortened and individually adapted", while more of the Public Employment Service's resources were invested in matching and placement.[54] Prime targets of government reforms were sickness and unemployment insurance. Sickness insurance benefits became subject to stricter rules and "work tests", while the duration of eligibility was shortened. The formal replacement rate for unemployment insurance decreased

52. *Ibid.*
53. Anders Björklund, "Going Different Ways: Labour Market Policy in Denmark and Sweden", in Esping-Andersen and Regini, *Why Deregulate Labour Markets?* pp. 148–180, 157.
54. Bengtsson and Berglund, "Labour Market Policies in Transition", pp. 92–93.

to a maximum of seventy-five per cent of the former employment-related income, with direct effects on the actual replacement rate individuals received. Interpretations and applications of the work requirement became generally stricter. Unemployed people had to be "prepared to take a job nationally from the first day of being registered at the employment office",[55] while the receipt of unemployment benefits was reduced to a maximum of 300 days. For Ferrarini _et al._ the overall outcome of these reforms was that the income protection system had fallen from grace.[56] In comparison to other OECD countries, these authors demonstrate that Sweden features slightly higher replacement rates through sickness insurance than the OECD average, yet lower replacement rates through unemployment insurance. A further crucial change concerned the drastic increase (from 99 to 344 kronor in 2007) in the membership fee to the unemployment insurance funds, which are administered by the unions.[57] This led to an increase in the number of people opting out of these funds and of trade union representation in general. Gaps between the employed and unemployed grew further through the Job Tax Deduction (_jobskat-teavdraget_), which increased the income of the employed relative to that of the unemployed.

Arbetslinje as a political priority is reflected in the still high overall economic activity rate of 75.4 per cent in 2000.[58] The decrease since 1991 is mainly down to lower activity rates among younger and older people (31 per cent among people 16–19 and 52 per cent among people 60–64). The unemployment rate stood at 4.1 per cent in 2000. By 2008, the activity rate among people aged 16–64 had increased again to 79.5 per cent, and the unemployment rate had risen to 6.7 per cent. In addition, 17.2 per cent of those aged 65–69 and 6.1 per cent of those 70–74 were economically active. Women's activity rate stood at 73.1 per cent in 2000 and unemployment at 4.3 per cent. Also, the activity rate among women aged 16–64 rose to 77.2 per cent in 2008. About 12.6 per cent of women aged 65–69 and 3.2 per cent of those aged 70–74 were economically active. Unemployment stood at 7 per cent in 2008. The average annual number of hours worked per person in employment was 1,642 in 2000 and 1,617 in 2008, higher than in the 1970s and 1980s. Hence, the long-term trend towards a reduction

---

55. _Ibid._, p. 99.

56. Tommy Ferrarini _et al._, _Sveriges socialförsäkringar i jämförande perspektiv. En institutionell analys av sjuk-, arbetsskade- och arbetslöshetsförsäkringarna i 18 OECD-länder 1930 till 2010_, Underlagsrapport till den parlamentariska socialförsäkringsutredningen (S2010:04) (Stockholm, 2012).

57. In Sweden, it is not obligatory to join an unemployment insurance scheme, unlike, for example, in Germany.

58. All employment-related data in this paragraph are taken from the ILO at http://laborsta. ilo.org. The data on hours worked per person in employment are taken from the OECD at http://stats.oecd.org/index.aspx?DataSetCode=ANHRS.

in the length of the working day that had characterized capitalist development in the core countries since the industrial revolution came to a halt in Sweden.

Respondents in a recent study of the Swedish minimum income system[59] pointed out that the increase from 211,000 in 2007 to 247,000 in 2010[60] in the number of households on social assistance was due not only to the global financial crisis and its employment impacts, but also to retrenchment in sickness and unemployment insurance, as a result of which a significant number of clients were transferred to the social assistance system.[61] Salonen's research report concludes that between 60 and 80 per cent of recipients could be lifted out of social assistance if these neighbouring social security systems were reformed accordingly.[62] Interviewees in Angelin *et al.*[63] pointed out that social assistance would receive excessive significance for the unemployed and those with health impairments and that a substantial proportion of clients should instead be covered by other types of welfare. There is, furthermore, evidence that what was originally thought to be a form of short-term support for people in need is becoming a long-term source of income. The average duration for the receipt of social assistance increased from 4.3 months in 1990 to 6.6 months in 2011.

Reflecting developments in the EU agenda on active inclusion and previous shifts towards an active welfare state, Sweden's MIP system and the social assistance system in particular underwent a transition from an emphasis on collective rights, redistribution, and an understanding of poverty as a structural issue to an emphasis on workfare, employability, and the interpretation of poverty and exclusion as individual and attitudinal problems. Status guarantees, the degree to which an individual's position is determined and safeguarded by past efforts without means testing, have been diminished or suspended in order to trigger swift adaptions to market swings.[64] Indeed, both Social Democrats and Conservatives tend to avoid the term "poverty", including the poverty-related EU 2020 benchmarks, and have instead moved the notion of social exclusion (*utanförskap*) into focus. According to the new discourse, every citizen who was either on benefits or unemployed is considered "excluded". Yet, rather than linking social exclusion to the distribution of income and to address it as a structural

---

59. Anna Angelin *et al.*, *The National Arena for Combating Poverty: National Report Sweden* (Lund, 2013), pp. 17–18.
60. Tapio Salonen, *Det nödvändiga uppbrottet – reformera det ekonomiska biståndet* (Stockholm, 2013).
61. This fourteen per cent increase in social assistance uptake was reflected in municipalities' expenditure.
62. Salonen, *Det nödvändiga uppbrottet*.
63. Angelin *et al.*, *The National Arena for Combating Poverty*, pp. 17–18.
64. Angelin *et al.*, "Patterns of Institutional Change in Minimum Income Protection", pp. 165–179.

phenomenon,[65] the Conservative governments, in particular, began to define exclusion as a matter of labour market participation only. Accordingly, it mixed traditional norms of the welfare state with a redefined work ethic and put stronger emphasis on individual duties, while even mention of the term "poverty" was avoided as much as possible.[66]

CONCLUSION

The state plays indispensable roles in capitalist development, spatial targeting, and in shaping labour relations and welfare. The spatial dimension of state regulation is subject to descaling and rescaling processes, during which new, multi-scalar structures of state organization, political authority, and socio-economic regulation emerge. The state retreats from one sphere (for example, from public ownership and national regulation of labour markets) only to enter and re-regulate other spheres and domains (for example, in its new role as "benchmarking" and "advising state" and as an actor at the European level). The developing steering role of the state constitutes a new form of "intervention" as the state provides support for actors to assimilate some of its roles and to work in partnership with them in novel and strategic ways. Particularly in the context of the EES, it defines criteria in relation to what it sees as good practice. The interpretations of state roles in employment and welfare regulation have changed accordingly.

While the state as employer is important in both periods, its role as direct employer has diminished significantly. At the same time, however, its role as indirect employer, especially as organizer of public-private partnerships, increased. As arbiter in intermediating corporatist/neo-corporatist processes and managing macroeconomic processes, governments combined "demand" and "supply" policies in the form of Keynesian economic and employment policies with active labour market polices in the post-Saltsjöbaden period. In the post-EU-accession period, the demand-supporting role decreased significantly, while governments saw their main *raison d'être* in improving Sweden as a location in European and global competition; that is, the supply side. State welfare policies saw a transition from decommodification of labour power and redistribution in the classical Social Democratic welfare regime,[67] in which inequality, unemployment, and poverty were regarded as structural issues, towards an emphasis on recommodification of labour power and workfare, in which, not unlike the

65. Paul Littlewood *et al.* (eds), *Social Exclusion in Europe* (Aldershot, 1999).
66. A related theme on the government's agenda that interviewees in the above report by Angelin *et al.* from 2013 stressed is the increased focus on "cheating", "scrounging", and benefit misuse and a generally more restrictive attitude towards and increasingly moralizing view on benefit recipients' needs.
67. Esping-Andersen, *The Three Worlds of Welfare Capitalism*.

Table 1. *State roles in economic, employment, and welfare regulation in the post-Saltsjöbaden (1938) and post-EU-accession periods*

	After Saltsjöbaden	After the crisis of the 1990s and EU accession
Policy goals and outcomes	Collective rights and redistribution and an understanding of poverty as a structural issue	Strengthened workfare ethic, employability, and the interpretation of poverty and exclusion as individual problems
Industrial relations/wage bargaining	National level	Sector level
Employment	Full employment plus active labour market policies	Full employment plus workfare
Welfare	Creation of a universal system that insures the population against social risks built on insurance plus social assistance as last resort of MIP	Cuts in unemployment and sickness insurance led to change in role of social assistance towards a permanent (and inadequate) means of MIP
State roles		
Spatial target	National plus local	European, national plus local
Employer	Emphasis on creation of direct employment	Decreasing role as direct employer; greater pervasiveness of state influence, e.g. in the form of public-private partnerships
Arbiter in intermediating corporatist / neo-corporatist processes and managing macroeconomic processes	Active state role in bringing about Saltsjöbaden; support of growth strategy through complementary labour market and welfare policies	Loss of national regulatory power due to EU accession partially compensated through representation in EU bodies; active role in rebuilding industrial relations based on sector-level wage bargaining
Guarantor of employment rights	Emphasis on collective rights	Emphasis on individual rights and duties and disciplinary aspects within the "work strategy"
Redistributor and welfare state	Emphasis on decommodifying labour power; social engineering	Emphasis on recommodifying labour power and creating self-regulating, self-supporting, and self-disciplining employees and welfare recipients

classical liberal regimes, MIP and not income redistribution and the limitation of social inequality is in focus.

Reflecting recent European employment discourses, unemployment, inequality, and poverty are today largely regarded as individual problems, for which individual "solutions" are provided – normally at the local level and in the form of activation contracts. Far from weakening or "withering away", the Swedish state continues to "engineer" socio-economic regulation, labour regimes, and employment, and there is also continuity in its use of coercive traits, particularly in its application of *arbetslinje*. Yet, there has been a transition from clear-cut top-down government towards a governance regime in which the execution of state power is much less obvious and where much of the disciplining work has been shifted from external state authorities to and incorporated by individual employees and welfare recipients – a shift in the governmentality of employment and welfare that scholars such as Goul Anderson et al.[68] and Larsson et al.[69] theorize in Foucauldian terms. Indeed, the individualized, self-regulating, self-supporting, and self-disciplining entrepreneurial employee who typifies the current labour regime makes for a much improved "economy of power" than the collectively organized and class-aware worker of the post-Saltsjöbaden period.

68. Jorgen Goul Andersen *et al.* (eds), *The Changing Face of Welfare: Consequences and Outcomes from a Citizenship Perspective* (Bristol, 2005).
69. Larsson *et al.*, *Transformations of the Swedish Welfare State*.

IRSH 61 (2016), Special Issue, pp. 263–284 doi:10.1017/S0020859016000444
© 2016 Internationaal Instituut voor Sociale Geschiedenis

State Policies Towards Precarious Work: Employment and Unemployment in Contemporary Portugal*

RAQUEL VARELA

Instituto de História Contemporânea, Universidade Nova de Lisboa
Av. Berna, 26 C, 1069–061 Lisbon, Portugal
and
International Institute of Social History

E-mail: raquel_cardeira_varela@yahoo.co.uk

ABSTRACT: In the context of the Global Collaboratory on the History of Labour Relations, in this article, we relate the analysis of precarious work in Portugal to the state, in particular, as a direct participant functioning as both employer and mediator. In the second part, we present a short overview of the evolution of casualization in the context of employment and unemployment in contemporary Portugal (1974–2014). In the third section, we discuss state policies on labour relations, particularly in the context of the welfare state. Finally, we compare this present analysis with Swedish research done from the perspective of the state as a direct participant and mediator over the past four decades.

INTRODUCTION

This article offers an analysis of the historical evolution of labour relations in Portugal from the 1970s until the present, focusing on labour precarity and unemployment, and on the role of the state in dealing with it. We will argue that more often than not the phenomenon of unemployment is

* This paper is based on research carried out within the framework of the global project for the study of labour relations, "Global Collaboratory on the History of Labour Relations, 1500–2000", which incorporates the Portuguese project funded by Fundação para a Ciência e a Tecnologia and being carried out at the Instituto de História Contemporânea of the Universidade Nova de Lisboa, "Relações Laborais em Portugal e no Mundo Lusófono, 1800–2000. Continuidades e rupturas" [Labour Relations in Portugal and the Portuguese-speaking World, 1800–2000: Continuities and Disruptions]. The main sources used for characterizing the workforce in Portugal in the period covered were: population censuses for 1991, 2001, and 2011; published results of the Inquérito ao Emprego (IE) [Employment Survey]; and figures on civil servants published by the Direcção-Geral da Administração e do Emprego Público (DGAEP). The first two sources were made available by the Instituto Nacional de Estatística (INE). The translation of this paper was funded by the Instituto de História Contemporânea.

cyclical, implying that precarity and unemployment are two sides of the same coin in the current mode of production, and lead directly to a decrease in wage bills (direct income) and indirectly to a reduction in social costs (the welfare state). Among the multiple variables open to scrutiny (including education, training, taxation, direct creation of public sector jobs, and legislation), we will focus especially on how workers' social security and welfare state funds were put to use in this period, to mitigate in political as well as social terms the social regression condoned when employment rights were curtailed and labour conditions worsened. The Ministry of Labour and Social Security and its Institute of Employment and Training were responsible, along with legislative changes approved by Portugal's parliament and European Union (EU) regulations, for managing the workforce in that direction. There were legislative changes in 1976 that introduced short-term contracts, which had been illegal in 1974–1975; wholesale redundancies were facilitated in 1987 and early retirement in 1991. Further changes came in 2003, 2009, and 2012, which did not take into consideration piecework wages in calculating income and reduced the value of redundancy payments by more than half.

Portugal once had a policy of universal welfare with no obligation to prove poverty or unemployment to gain access to benefits – maintained by progressive taxation – for things such as health, education, and social provisions, including subsidized canteens for workers. However, since the 1990s, the policy has moved towards focused assistance, meaning it is now necessary to prove poverty to gain access to free healthcare, subsidized canteens or transport, and cheap electricity.[1] The new welfare policy might indeed have been intended to address social inequalities and promote reintegration into the labour market,[2] but our contention is that, first, the increase in compensatory and targeted social measures was actually conducive to increased job insecurity and was closely related to the deregulation of employment; second, the compensatory social programmes were created simultaneously with the abolition of free access to health and education in the 1990s. The new policy simply endorsed the principle of "the user pays". Most remarkable among the legal measures dealing with labour flexibility since 1985–1987 were the facilitation of collective dismissal and the use of the social security fund to compensate for redundancy. Then, especially with further legislative changes in 2003 and 2009, it became easier to dismiss individuals. One of the social outcomes of the changes can be seen in the Gini index, which fell from 0.316 in 1974 to 0.174 in 1978, when it reached its lowest level due to the "employment for all" policy of

---

1. Cleusa Santos, "Rendimento de facto Mínimo? Estado, Assistência e Questão Social", in Raquel Varela (ed.), *A Segurança Social é Sustentável. Trabalho, Estado e Segurança Social em Portugal* (Lisbon, 2013), pp. 315–334, 321–323.
2. AAVV, *Pareceres sobre o Rendimento Mínimo Garantido* (Lisbon, 1997), pp. 1–84.

the 1974–1975 revolution. However, with inequality growing thereafter, the index rose to 0.210 in 1983.[3] Since then it has risen to a figure of 0.338 today, one of the highest in the EU, but caused by the "competitiveness of low wages" according to an analysis by the Bank of Portugal.[4] Over the same period, exports increased exponentially from a total of twenty billion euros in 1995 to sixty billion in 2014. The report by the Governor of the Bank of Portugal declared that the transformation in growth was export-driven.[5]

This article begins with a discussion of the notion of labour precarity, adducing several definitions of what is a controversial concept that, until recently, had remained outside the scope of formal studies. The concept of precarity has been subjected to different definitions within the framework of labour relations studies and projects. Inasmuch as it displays each country's distinct reality, the Global Collaboratory on the History of Labour Relations is likely to make a decisive contribution to the debate on the concept and its history. We will also discuss the concept of real versus official unemployment, and relevant data will be compared with those from the Global Collaboratory on the History of Labour Relations.

Later, we will examine the historical background to the changes in labour relations that have taken place in the past five decades, highlighting the occasions when change was abrupt (1974–1975, 1986–1989, and 2012–2014), but also the gradual transformations that occurred throughout the 1990s and the first decade of the present century. Recognizing gradual change is equally important to understanding the historical development of the state's role as far as precarity and unemployment are concerned. Furthermore, we will point out that, in economia this specific instance, the state acted upon the link between protected, precarious and retired workers, making use of social and welfare state funds (net social income) to do so. In defining those changes affecting the role of the state, reference will be made to the relevance of Portugal's position, both regionally and in the context of globalization (as well as to that of the completion of a global labour market) – namely its joining the European Economic Community (now the European Union) in 1986.

Finally, we will compare developments with those in Sweden in order to highlight the similarities in both processes, albeit at different stages, both in

3. Manuela Silva, "A repartição do rendimento em Portugal no pós 25 de Abril 74", *Revista Crítica de Ciências Sociais*, 15–17 (1985), pp. 269–279, 272.
4. Carlos da Silva Costa, "Competitividade da economia portuguesa. Desafios futuros", available at https://www.bportugal.pt/pt-PT/OBancoeoEurosistema/IntervencoesPublicas/Lists/Folder DeListaComLinks/Attachments/257/App_APGEI_10072014.pdf, slide 26, last accessed 11 March 2016.
5. *Idem*, "O desafio da absorção do desemprego estrutural em Portugal", available at https://www.bportugal.pt/pt-PT/OBancoeoEurosistema/IntervencoesPublicas/Lists/FolderDeListaCom Links/Attachments/242/intervpub20140125.pdf, last accessed 5 May 2016.

terms of economic development and the social conditions and distinctive features of the workforce.

PRECARITY AND UNEMPLOYMENT

Throughout the past two decades, labour market researchers in southern Europe and Latin America have discussed the concept of labour precarity in the light of the exponential increase in the number of workers facing labour precarity since the end of the 1980s. Similarly, the concept of unemployment has aroused academic controversy, so we will underline the major debates related to agreeing definitions of the two social phenomena and examine the data available for both.

In recent decades, many authors, including Callaghan and Hartmann,[6] Farber,[7] Hodson,[8] and Van der Linden,[9] have worked with the idea of precarity. A feature recurring in most of their work is a tendency to conflate precarious labour relations, distinct national legal system features and workforce mobility.

As defined by Charles and Chris Tilly, "work" includes any human effort adding use value to goods and services.[10] Ricardo Antunes, the Brazilian sociologist who coined the concept of a new morphology of the working class as the class-that-works-for-a-living, points out that in Western countries the main dynamic of the labour market has seen decreased regulation of work and increased precarity, which are inextricably linked to subcontracting within a flexible business model.[11]

At the height of the outbreak of the most recent global crisis, that model became broader and induced even greater erosion of contracted and regulated labour of the type that had been most common throughout the twentieth century, namely Taylorist/Fordist labour.[12] Such relatively more formalized work has been replaced by several different kinds of informality and precarization – outsourced work in all its wide diversity, including "cooperativism", "entrepreneurship", and "voluntary work".

6. Polly Callaghan and Heidi Hartmann, *Contingent Work: A Chart Book on Part-Time and Temporary Employment* (Washington, DC, 1991).
7. Henry S. Farber, "Alternative and Part-Time Employment Arrangements as a Response to Job Loss", *Journal of Labor Economics*, 17:4 (1999), pp. 142–169.
8. Randy Hodson (ed.), *Marginal Employment, Research in the Sociology of Work* (Stamford, CA, 2000).
9. Marcel van der Linden, "San Precario: A New Inspiration for Labor Historians", *Labor: Studies in Working-Class History of the Americas*, 11:1 (2014), pp. 9–21.
10. Charles Tilly and Chris Tilly, *Work under Capitalism* (Boulder, CO, 1998), p. 22.
11. Ricardo Antunes, *Os Sentidos do Trabalho. Ensaio sobre a Afirmação e a Negação do Trabalho* (São Paulo, 2009), pp. 16–21.
12. J. Breman and M. van der Linden, "Informalizing the Economy: The Return of the Social Question at a Global Level", *Development and Change*, 45:5 (2014), pp. 920–940.

Antunes has emphasized that the class-that-works-for-a-living is irretrievably interconnected, regardless of type of employment: "[...] by then, the two most noticeable and relevant focal points of the Portuguese working class were surfacing: those who had been forced into precarization and the working class that had inherited the welfare state and Fordism".[13]

The close link between flexible modes of production and precarity, as well as its impact in terms of wrecking the whole workforce, has been pointed out by Castillo,[14] Huws[15] – who applied it to the "cyber proletariat" – and Mészáros,[16] among others. According to Felstead and Jewson, in the USA more than half of net employment growth was related to precarious labour.[17]

Graça Druck has devised a typology of precarization: (i) procedures aimed at commodifying the workforce, resulting in a heterogeneous and segmented labour market, characterized by structural vulnerability and precarious modes of integration, with contracts depriving workers of any social protection whatsoever; (ii) labour planning and management standards that have brought about extremely precarious conditions through increased workloads (setting impossible targets, extending working hours, flexibility, etc.); (iii) labour not legally protected, and unfavourable health and safety conditions – the outcome of management standards that despise vital training, information on hazards, collective preventive measures, etc.; (iv) unemployed status and the constant threat of losing one's job; (v) weakened trade unions, methods of resistance, and workers' representation, because of competition, heterogeneity, and splits, against a background of union obliteration caused chiefly by outsourcing practices.[18]

Several researchers have argued that precarity, or casualization, is a new phenomenon – in Portugal it has been around for about thirty years – involving a historically circumscribed definition: absence of the right to work in the post-revolutionary period 1982–2014, in contrast to 1974–1975, when the right to have a job was legally protected by the Constitution. We argue in this paper that the absence of the right to work, here understood in three ways (no right to work, lack of protection from dismissal, and no compensation for dismissal) is not a new phenomenon in

13. Antunes, *Os Sentidos do Trabalho*, p. 6.

14. Juan J. Castillo, *Sociología del trabajo* (Madrid, 1996).

15. Ursula Huws, *The Making of a Cybertariat: Virtual Work in a Real World* (New York and London, 2003).

16. István Mészáros, *Para além do capital* (São Paulo, 2002).

17. A. Felstead and N. Jewson (eds), *Global Trends in Flexible Labour* (London, 1999).

18. Graça Druck, "Precarização social do trabalho", in Anete B.L. Ivo (ed.), *Dicionário Temático Desenvolvimento e Questão Social – 81 problemáticas contemporâneas* (São Paulo, 2012), pp. 373–380.

Portuguese capitalist development. Historically, since the mid-nineteenth century, it has been the rule rather than the exception.

In our work,[19] we suggest a definition of precarity that differentiates precarization from contingent employment. Contingency, or switching between unprotected work and unemployment, is not the sole qualitative variable distinguishing twenty-first-century from nineteenth-century casual work. The concept of precarity is different today from the forms of lack of employment rights prevailing in the nineteenth and twentieth centuries. Precarity in Portugal is a concept that encapsulates other features besides the lack of any right to work and became very widespread during the period of the social pact (1974–1986). It includes the prospect of social regression (and not only of social immobility), and its management as a social phenomenon is heavily dependent on the workers' savings fund (social security) and the family wage. Today it assumes multiple forms, including false self-employment ("green invoices", the popular term for the invoices sent by autonomous workers on piece rates), small businesses, cooperatives, outsourcing, and piecework.

Thus, the concept of precarity is defined based on its opposite, *protected work*, de facto or de jure. What is involved is an analysis of employment security, which may derive from legal protection or skills training rather than from the conditions under which the work is performed – for instance, working in a mine can be physically precarious, because it is dangerous – but is not necessarily contingent with regard to protection against redundancy. That being so, precarity does not depend on any lack of good hygienic conditions, physical safety, or mental health but is purely a matter of the mobility of a workforce perpetually facing either precarity or unemployment. There is a direct link between precarity and unemployment. However, structural precarization of employment and unemployment are two sides of the same coin, since the same worker is caught in a cycle of precarious employment for part of the year followed by unemployment the rest of the year. For unions and state policy it is essential to understand this point.

In Portugal after the 1974 Carnation Revolution, to work became an absolute right, so that whoever is deprived of that right becomes precarious. It was enshrined in Article 58 of the 1976 Constitution[20] (the social pact),

---

19. Raquel Varela, "Eugenização da Força de Trabalho em Portugal", in *idem, A Segurança Social é Sustentável*, pp. 23–85; *idem et al.*, "Relações Laborais em Portugal 1930–2011", *Revista O Social em Questão*, 18:34 (2015) pp. 41–58.

20. Constitution of the Portuguese Republic, Seventh Revision [2005], available at http://www.tribunalconstitucional.pt/tc/conteudo/files/constituicaoingles.pdf, last accessed 5 May 2016. Article 58 reads: "(Right to work), 1. Everyone has the right to work. 2. In order to ensure the right to work, the state is charged with promoting: a) The implementation of full-employment policies; b) Equal opportunities in the choice of profession or type of work, and the conditions needed to avoid the gender-based preclusion or limitation of access to any position, work or professional category; c) The cultural and technical training and occupational development of

but its actual implementation relied in fact upon employers' concessions and workers' resistance, as well as on how the social pact was operated under the democratic-representative system.[21] The right to work in Portugal was introduced legally and socially as a universal human right (the right to survival) unfolding around three concepts: everyone has the right to work, everyone is entitled to protection from dismissal and, finally, everyone is entitled to protection if they are involuntarily unemployed.[22]

Precarious workers include therefore a wide range of labour relations, quite distinct in their legal outlook but sharing the ease by which workers can be dismissed. The category of precarious workers comprises 1) workers on fixed-term contracts; 2) most workers paid on a piecework basis (freelancer "green invoices", self-employed); 3) those on student grants, interns, and first-job contracts (all funded by the state for a fixed term, assuming the workers are being trained, even though they are actually carrying out paid work); 4) public-sector workers whose contracts are protected, albeit legally subjected to special mobility status (they can be relocated from different cities or jobs within the public sector) or possible dismissal; and 5) workers with permanent contracts whose redundancy pay (compensation for dismissal) was reduced, exposing them to easier dismissal. We have extended the concept of precarity here to include a specific class of small-scale entrepreneurs: in our opinion, in Portugal some precarious workers are labelled self-employed entrepreneurs although they are in essence normally employed workers. Besides "green invoice" workers, those on student grants, and interns, there are more controversial instances such as small business owners who are, in fact, workers. They might technically own a "business", usually founded after a larger company had been dismembered and begun employing its original workers as outsourced labour. The result is, of course, that workers actually remain employed by and are dependent on the same larger companies while themselves bearing all the costs their former employers are no longer obliged to meet: social security, production stoppages, etc. Capital flows through these small companies but does not accumulate in them, so that their income is "barely enough to make ends meet" – often meaning just

workers." Article 59 reads: "(Workers' rights) 1. Regardless of age, sex, race, citizenship, place of origin, religion and political and ideological convictions, every worker has the right: a) To the remuneration of his work in accordance with its volume, nature and quality, with respect for the principle of equal pay for equal work and in such a way as to guarantee a proper living; b) That work be organised under conditions of social dignity and in such a way as to provide personal fulfilment and to make it possible to reconcile work and family life [...]".
21. Raquel Varela, "A persistência do conflito industrial organizado. Greves em Portugal entre 1960 e 2008", *Mundos do Trabalho*, 3:6 (2011), pp. 151–175.
22. For an analysis of the configuration and evolution of the right to work in Portugal, see Manuel Branco, *Economia Política dos Direitos Humanos* (Lisbon, 2012).

barely enough to cover running costs. Some might indeed be true small business proprietors genuinely in competition with others, but a good number are ordinary workers who are really precarious despite being officially labelled as operators of small businesses. Ultimately, the models applied by the Instituto Nacional de Estatística (INE, National Statistical Office) do not go beyond the scope of formal and legal frameworks to allow us to see who really is in labour relationships equivalent to employer and employee, as far as small businesses are concerned. Finally, some contracts, whether fixed-term or even for piecework, imply a workforce that could not easily be replaced – doctors, for instance – and therefore were not precarious because for them neither mobility, nor intensification would lead to unemployment. So it is true that not all mobility is precarious, although there are certain legally protected labour relations, including those of some business holders, that embody precarious work.

Discussing such concepts is paramount to assessing their reality throughout history, as well as their current prevalence, and we shall pinpoint below how deeply methodology affects the data on the general workforce.

If we look at the whole population of Portugal broken down by broad age groups for our period, we notice a substantial variation both in young people and the elderly. The proportion of young people fell steadily, from 29.2 per cent in 1960 to 14.9 per cent in 2011, while the proportion of elderly rose, also steadily, from eight per cent in 1960 to nineteen per cent in 2011. Nevertheless, the age group of people fit for work (aged twelve to sixty-four in 1991 and fifteen to sixty-five in 2001 and 2011) remained noticeably stable. The lowest figure was 61.9 per cent in 1970, with a peak of 67.7 per cent in 2001. Such figures are likely to trigger social repercussions. For instance, from the point of view of social security, spending on younger groups would be replaced by spending on the elderly, but the figures illustrate something else that is rather important. The population available for work has risen from 1960 until today, for the most part because of the number of women joining the labour market. Another change must be stressed, that in education: in 1970 there were about 30,000 university graduates, in 2012 there were 1.3 million.

By 1970, market wage earners represented 14.51 per cent of all labour relations, a figure that had risen to 14.70 per cent by 1981. Those employed outside the market (that is, working for the state, NGOs, the church, or the armed forces, bearing in mind that state and market are of course related spheres) made up only 12.87 per cent of the whole population in 1971. By 1981, however, they accounted for 15.26 per cent, with the nationalizations carried out throughout the revolutionary years of 1974 and 1975 as well as the expansion of state agencies as a result of urbanization being the primary factors behind that rise. In 1981, nationalized sector personnel represented thirteen per cent of those employed (salaried) in companies, and about ninety-six per cent in the electricity-, gas-, and water-supply industries, sixty-nine per cent in communications and transport and fifty-seven per cent in banking and insurance. By 1982, "state-owned enterprises" accounted for over twenty per cent of the whole national economy, the highest figure among all OECD members.[23]

As far as economic activity is concerned, the INE divides the population into two large groups, the working and non-working populations. The "active population" comprises those both employed and unemployed who were older than twelve at the time of the 1991 census or older than fifteen in 2001 and 2011. Everyone else is classed as "inactive", so those younger than twelve or fifteen, depending on the census, domestic workers, students, retired people and pensioners, those incapacitated for work, and others, including anyone available for work regardless of having been out of the workforce for a long time. Nonetheless, it must be stressed that when it comes to those unemployed the concept of active and inactive populations in the census is strictly linked to their status, or lack of it, as effective or potential market producers. The taxonomy of the Global Collaboratory on the History of Labour Relations includes both market and non-market producers as active populations, as long as they effectively produce or perform services. The rest are then labelled inactive. There are then two considerable differences in the methodologies employed by the census and the taxonomy in that the taxonomy regards the unemployed as inactive, whereas domestic workers are labelled active.

Both the INE and EU member states follow the International Labour Organization (ILO) in defining an unemployed person as anyone old but not undertaking paid (or unpaid) work of any kind despite being available and actively seeking employment. The notion of "actively seeking employment" consists of a set of procedures that, according to the INE's employment survey, includes being registered at a job centre, applying to employers and attending job interviews. If a potential worker fails to fulfil such requirements, they will automatically be labelled available but inactive, or despondent. Economist Eugénio Rosa challenges the definition of "available but inactive" and includes it instead as part of the "unemployed" category, to which he adds those visibly under-employed; that is, "the number of individuals aged at least fifteen who, during the reference period, had a job comprising less working time than would be expected for their assigned operating position and declare themselves willing to work longer hours".[24] The gap between inactive and unemployed people led to a clear discrepancy in 2014 between figures

---

23. Maria João Rodrigues, "O mercado de trabalho nos Anos 70. Das tensões aos metabolismos", *Análise Social*, XXI:87–89 (1985), pp. 679–733.
24. Eugénio Rosa, "Dados do Desemprego em Portugal" [Unemployment in Portugal: Data] 2011, available at https://www.eugeniorosa.com/Sites/eugeniorosa.com/Documentos/2011/27-2011-Ataque-Estado-social-em-Portugal.pdf, last accessed 11 March 2016.

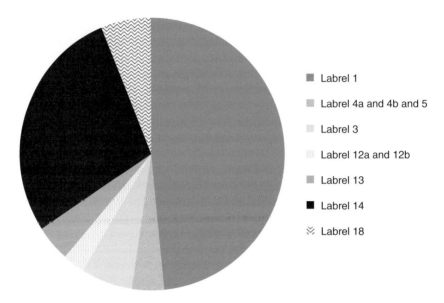

Figure 1. Labour relations, Portugal 2011, according to the taxonomy of the Collaboratory
Source: Ana Rajado, Cátia Teixeira, and Joana Alcântara, "Taxonomia das Relações Laborais em Portugal, 1930–2011", *O Social em Questão*, XVIII:4 (2015), pp. 41–58, 56–57, available at http://osocialemquestao.ser.puc-rio.br/media/OSQ_34_2_Rajado_Teixeira_Alcantara_Varela. pdf, last accessed 12 April 2016.

on official unemployment (thirteen per cent) and real unemployment (23.7 per cent). As we have explained, the Global Collaboratory uses a different definition of unemployment (labour relation 3), according to which unemployment was six per cent in 2011 (see Figure 1).

According to Eurostat, in the fourth quarter of 2012 the proportion of fixed-term workers among employed persons was higher in Portugal (20.3 per cent) than in almost any other country. In absolute terms, this amounted to 900,000 fixed-term workers. In order better to assess the amount of precarious work in Portugal, we should have to include the proportion of workers paid for piecework ("green invoices"). Although there are no such data available for the fourth quarter of 2012, we can estimate it from the 2011 census, which gives a figure of 827,000 precarious "green invoice" workers doing piecework. Those two types of fringe employment covered over 1.5 million precarious workers out of an "active population" of 5,658 million workers. That figure comprises an active population according to the INE of 5,455 million, employed and unemployed, plus 203,000 considered available but inactive, and contrasts with a real unemployment rate of 19.9 per cent (1,126,000) in the fourth quarter of 2012. Thus, in 2012 half the workforce faced either precarity or unemployment (see Figure 2) – precarity having threatened

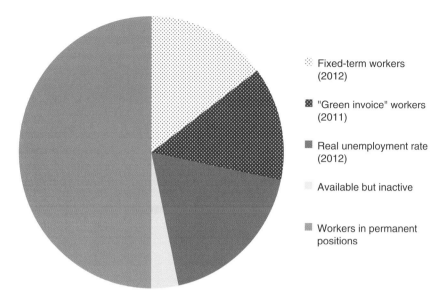

Figure 2. Precarious work in Portugal, 2011 and 2012.

less than half the workforce in previous decades, when unemployment was never higher than seven per cent. In addition, on average, workers on permanent contracts earned sixteen per cent more than those on fixed-term contracts, while in a study published in 2008 Eugénio Rosa estimated that on average a precarious worker earned thirty-seven per cent less than one on an open-ended contract.[25] Furthermore, only twelve per cent of fixed-term contracts were subsequently converted into permanent contracts.[26]

Figure 3 gives official unemployment figures, illustrating the impact in times of economic crisis, and how unemployment has been counter cyclical since the 1980s. The figure for 2012 was unprecedented. It is worth mentioning that this figure, as well as all the others, relates solely to the active population;[27] still, it depicts clearly the impact of the unemployment cycle on the unemployed population, as well as the upward trend on which that cycle is superimposed. Plainly, in the last cycle, triggered by the 2008 crisis, unemployment figures were unprecedentedly high: 16.2 per cent in 2012.

25. Eugénio Rosa, "Emprego a tempo parcial, a prazo e a recibos verdes", available at: http://resistir.info/e_rosa/precariedade.html, last accessed 23 March 2013.
26. Costa, "O desafio da absorção do desemprego estrutural em Portugal".
27. In INE statistics, unemployment is included as part of the active population and thus the active population differs from the employed population.

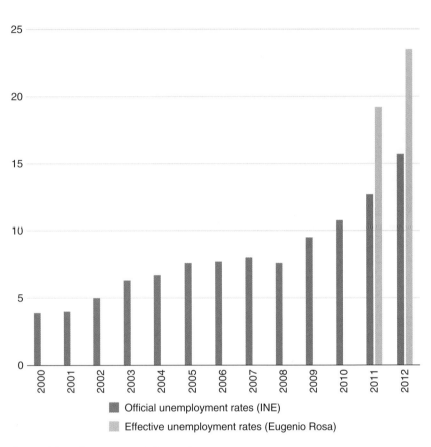

Figure 3. Unemployment rates in Portugal, 2000–2012.

THE ROLE OF THE STATE

Today, neither statistics, nor the legal framework convey the full complexity of the kinds of state intervention that shape labour relations or employment conditions, both directly and indirectly. The Global Collaboratory on the History of Labour Relations is an ambitious attempt to categorize labour relations, which are becoming increasingly complex due to urbanization, education and globalization. Here, we shall focus mainly on the relationship between the state and the workforce. Understandably, this topic does not exhaust the whole multiplicity of variables binding the state to labour relations – for instance, in terms of preserving the health of the workforce (healthcare) or training it (education and vocational training); fiscal policy; public debt and public-sector budgets; public areas and amenities; or transport management. Our research into the management of labour precarity and unemployment and its relationship to the welfare state, especially with respect to social security, is an important part of a wide and complex network of relationships between state and workforce.

Currently prevailing explanations critical of neoliberalism have emphasized the fact that the period since the 1970s has been characterized by increased deregulation of the labour market, along with a decreased role for the state in the economy. In this article, we claim that labour precarity and unemployment amount to direct state intervention, and that it is increasing rather than being reduced. Close attention must be paid to changes in state intervention, instead of taking for granted any explanations presuming a steady decrease in that role.[28] Such changes might be seen in social dialogue mechanisms, including state, union federations, and employers' associations; targeted and non-universal social welfare policies to counterbalance the effects of rising unemployment and low wages; and changes in the legal framework regulating labour precarity. We should mention here our particular insistence that we see labour flexibility as being typified by a type of state regulation that promotes it. We look, too, at the close similarities between Portugal and Sweden, despite slight differences in the years of implementation, with Portugal joining the EU earlier (1986) than Sweden (1995), and the different figures for the cost of consumer goods and the different living standards enjoyed by workers in these two countries.

In the past four decades there has been no reduction in the state's role as a direct employer – in fact, it has increased. In 1979, there were 383,000 civil servants in a total working population of nearly four million people. By 2014, there were 665,620 civil servants out of a total 4.5 million people employed.[29] It should be noted that the country's active population has risen significantly since the 1970s. It was 3.91 million in 1974, peaking at 5,534 million in 2008; in 2015 it was 5,225 million. Concomitantly, unemployment has risen. With 23.7 per cent of the whole population unemployed, the figure for 2015 was the highest in the country's history.[30]

Unemployment is a historical thing, and is derived from choices related to a certain means of accumulation and global competition based on reducing unit labour costs. In Europe, the unemployment of the past four

---

28. Mimi Abramovitz, "Theorising the Neoliberal Welfare State for Social Work", in Mel Gray, James A. Midgley, and Stephen Webb (eds), *The Sage Handbook of Social Work* (London, 2012), pp. 33–50.
29. Civil Service Employment: Central, Regional, Local, and Social Security Funds. Data sources: DGAEP/MEF – Civil Service Human Resources Survey (1979, 1983, 1986) | First and Second Civil Service Public Census (1996, 1999) | Civil Service Database (2005) | Information System on State Organization (SIOE) (from 2007 onwards). Source: Pordata. Last update: 26 June 2015, available at http://www.pordata.pt/Portugal, last accessed 16 January 2016.
30. *Ibid.*

decades must be regarded as a complex phenomenon strictly linked to labour market restructuring and not to the "end of labour".[31] Authors in Portugal from the whole spectrum of economic thinking all agree that unemployment is nowadays the main cause of pressure on wages. We argue that, despite a minority of the workforce who tend to leave the labour market never to return, in most cases the data reveal that unemployment is cyclical and that there is a direct connection between unemployment and labour precarity: they are two sides of the same coin.

SOCIAL ASSISTANCE AND PRECARITY

Organized mutual institutions or solidarity cooperatives have existed since the nineteenth century, but the Portuguese welfare state and the qualitative and quantitative generalization of social rights came late, thirty years after France and Britain in 1945 with the Beveridge Plan of 1942. But such institutions were born partly out of causes similar to those that gave rise to the welfare states in western and northern Europe, from the "concerns of the economic and political system with industrialization (including demographic explosion, social and political conflicts, economic crises)", as pointed out by Luís Graça.[32] Ângelo Ribeiro[33] noted that between 1926 and 1974 "human rights, taken as the civil liberties in their multiple aspects of civil, political, social, economic, and cultural rights that make a country a 'state of law', were practically non-existent in Portugal". All researchers agree that the pension system during the Estado Novo (the forty-eight-year period of dictatorship under Salazar and Caetano) was both restricted and offered little.[34] All other indicators of well-being – life expectancy, health, infant mortality, literacy and education, leisure – were equivalent to those in underdeveloped and backward countries. Total state spending in Portugal on social issues in 1973 was 4.4 per cent of total GDP, while in Britain it was 13.9 per cent, in Italy 10.6 per cent, and 15.4 per cent in Denmark.[35] Portugal was to undergo fundamental changes after the 1974–1975 revolution, which brought to an end the oldest dictatorship in Europe, under which a system of forced labour had persisted in its colonies. Unable

31. For a rebuttal of the "end of labour" thesis, see Antunes, *Os Sentidos do Trabalho*, and *idem*, *Adeus ao Trabalho? Ensaio sobre as Metamorfoses e a Centralidade do Mundo do Trabalho* (São Paulo, 2011).

32. Luís Graça, *Evolução do sistema hospitalar. Uma perspetiva sociológica* (Lisbon, 1996), pp. 1238–1242.

33. Ângelo Ribeiro, "Direitos Humanos", in António Barreto and Maria Filomena Mónica (eds), *Dicionário de História de Portugal* (Oporto, 2000), p. 559.

34. Manuel de Lucena, "Previdência", in Barreto and Mónica, *Dicionário de História de Portugal*, p. 160.

35. Bernardete Maria Fonseca, "Ideologia ou Economia? Evolução da Proteção no Desemprego em Portugal" (MA thesis, Universidade de Aveiro, 2008), p. 78.

to reform itself, the Portuguese regime collapsed on its backbone[36] in a coup d'état led by middle-ranking army officers, but which was followed by social revolution. Then, one-third of the population (three million people) participated in workers' and residents' committees, with state expenditure at a correspondingly high level; today, expenditure on education, health and social security, the state's social functions, is equivalent to 18.1 per cent of GDP.[37]

In the aftermath of 25 April 1974, a huge demonstration forced the dissolution of the Ministry for Guilds and Social Welfare, which was renamed the Ministry for Labour and Social Security,[38] so that in 1974 *welfare* was replaced by *security*. Social security encompasses two main areas, namely pensions, funded by deductions from workers' wages or, for non-contributory pensions, by transfers from the national budget, and so-called social welfare policies, aimed at tackling poverty and involuntary unemployment. The former would not be feasible without the historical rise in wages, while the latter were implemented on a large scale only in the 1980s. Two interdependent ideas form the foundation of the universal social security system created in 1974 and 1975. First was the transfer of income from capital to labour. It was the most thorough instance of this in contemporary Portugal, and according to official data the proportion of income accounted for by labour grew from forty-nine per cent before the revolution to sixty-seven per cent after, while the proportion of income from capital fell, from fifty-two to thirty-three per cent.[39] The second was a public commitment to universal social protection and solidarity, which put an end to discriminatory and discretionary schemes and widened the scope of social protection. Universal protection was established, by means of education, healthcare and pensions, to maintain and train the workforce, and support was given to such things as culture, sport and general leisure. The average annual state pension rose more than fifty per cent between 1973 and 1975.[40]

A look at the figures reveals that due in part to inflation real direct wages actually fell in 1974 and 1975. Nonetheless, for social wages, i.e. the benefits

---

36. Fernando Rosas, *Pensamento e Ação Política. Portugal Século XX (1890–1976)* (Lisbon, 2004).

37. Eurostat. Social protection statistics, available at: http://ec.europa.eu/eurostat/statistics-explained/index.php/Social_protection_statistics_-_main_indicators, last accessed 12 August 2015.

38. Author's interview with Cruz Oliveira, 24 July 2012, Lisbon.

39. Silva, "A repartição do rendimento", pp. 269–279. Manuela Silva was a former State Secretary and Researcher at the Ministry of Labour. She cites figures from an article by the former Minister of Economic Affairs, A. Mateus.

40. Pordata, "Pensões. Total, da Segurança Social e da Caixa Geral de Aposentações – Portugal", available at: http://www.pordata.pt/Portugal/Pens%C3%B5es+total++da+Seguran%C3%A7a+Social+e+da+Caixa+Geral+de+Aposenta%C3%A7%C3%B5es-851, last accessed 16 March 2013.

provided by the welfare state and social security, the advantages were clear. It should be stressed that not only did wages rise, income disparities, too, were reduced, so that the gap between higher and lower incomes narrowed.[41] We must emphasize this point in particular, that the greatest impact of the rise in incomes in this period was not on direct wages, but on *social wages*; that is to say, on the welfare state. That being so, and social contributions aside, wages were therefore lower in 1983 than in 1973.[42] There was precarity in the earlier period, too, but as unemployment remained residual – although still cyclical – between 1970 and 1990 (regardless of a peak following the 1982–1984 crisis), state measures for the management and support of unemployment were similarly residual until 1986.

In the 1980s, the end of the social pact initiated a period of social dialogue. The Conselho Económico Social (Social Economic Committee) was established in 1986, in a tripartite configuration of employees, employers, and the state, similar to the Swedish model. It was therefore a neo-corporative structure, switching company- or factory-based conflicts between employers and employees to a situation in which they were negotiated and prevented, as pointed out by Stoleroff[43] and Stråth.[44] In Sweden, a very similar mechanism of "pre-negotiating" before official negotiations took place was established. Over the past twenty years the new policy has been steadily expanded and extended to include unemployment; this expansion has been financed by funds comprising contributions to retirement pensions. Marques argues that within the EEC (later EU) and the single market framework various measures were taken, such as "unemployment benefits, early retirement due to unemployment, explicit support for restructuring, active labour market policies, and professional training".[45] As mentioned by Hespanha *et al.*, the setting up of the Fundo de Estabilização Financeira (Financial Stabilization Fund) and the amalgamation of the social security and the unemployment funds were measures simply heralding the relationship between "unemployment problems and the need to maximize collected contributions".[46]

In Portugal, such changes took place only because there was a specific historical juncture (the economic crises of 1981–1984) characterized by the

41. Silva, "A repartição do rendimento", p. 271.

42. *Ibid.*, p. 270.

43. Alan Stoleroff, "All's Fair in Love and (Class) War", 26 October 2012, available at: http://www.snesup.pt/htmls/_dlds/All_is_fair_in_love_and_class_war_Stoleroff.pdf, last accessed 15 March 2013.

44. Bo Stråth, *The Politics of De-Industrialization: The Contraction of the West European Shipbuilding Industry* (London [etc.], 1987).

45. F. Marques, *Evolução e Problemas da Segurança Social em Portugal no Após 25 de Abril* (Lisbon, 1997), cited in Fonseca, "Ideologia ou Economia?", pp. 78, 79.

46. Pedro Hespanha *et al.*, *Entre o Estado e o Mercado. As Fragilidades das Instituições de Proteção Social em Portugal* (Coimbra, 2000), cited in Fonseca, "Ideologia ou Economia?", p. 78.

following near simultaneous developments. First, there was widespread social conflict involving some minor trade unions, in steelworking and heavy industry, who were opposed to the social dialogue. Their defeat in the 1984–1986 strikes had a symbolic effect that spread to other sectors, and Stråth[47] notes that a similar effect was felt in Britain, Germany, and Scandinavia. Second, trade unions committed themselves strongly to negotiations instead of to conflict. Unlike during the revolution, they no longer saw the state as an opponent, but – rather than companies – as an arbiter to whom proposals should be addressed.[48] Moreover, the working and middle classes gained wider access to consumer goods as Portuguese markets were opened up to Asian businesses and pressure was applied to wages on a worldwide scale. A fourth factor, and in our opinion pivotal, was the deployment of the social security fund to manage precarity and unemployment, providing a social cushion. This move complied with the World Bank research guidelines on assistance, inflation, and unemployment[49] aimed at preventing extreme poverty, inequality, and social decline. The deployment was negotiated case by case by way of early retirement and was mostly accepted by the unions.[50] The process affected millions of workers throughout Europe, from Britain to Portugal, and Sweden to Spain. In return, "acquired rights" were left unaffected for those who already had them, while recently employed workers were suspended or made subject to precarity schemes. Finally, in southern Europe – and this was not a relevant element in Sweden nor in most developed European countries – young people began to join the labour market at a later stage. That naturally implied a decrease in most parents' disposable income, because they had to support their children for longer. In Portugal nowadays, most unemployed people still rely first on their families for subsistence, with unemployment benefit coming second. All the same, in analysing the restructuring of the labour market since the 1980s we noted another important phenomenon, namely that although youth unemployment was high it was in the older segments of the working population that unemployment was more structural. There was a tendency for people over forty-five with fewer than six years of education to be permanently removed from the labour market, in an age/training selection process we call "workforce eugenics".

47. Stråth, *The Politics of De-Industrialization*.
48. Marinús Pires de Lima, "Transformações das Relações de Trabalho e Ação Operária nas Indústrias Navais (1974–1984)", *Revista Crítica de Ciências Sociais*, 18–20 (1986), p. 541.
49. Elisa Pereira Reis and Simon Schwartzman, *Pobreza e exclusão social. Aspectos sócio políticos* (Rio de Janeiro, 2002).
50. On this topic, see Paulo Jorge Martins Fernandes, "As Relações Sociais de Trabalho na Lisnave, Crise ou Redefinição do Papel dos Sindicatos?" (MA thesis, Instituto Superior de Ciências do Trabalho e da Empresa, 1999).

One of the most relevant events in this interwoven relationship between the social security fund and the management of unemployment[51] was the introduction of unemployment benefit (Decree-Law no. 20/85 of 17 January 1985). Most salaried workers had been entitled to unemployment benefit since 1975 (Decree-Law no. 169–D/75 of 31 March 1975) but in 1985 the EEC forced the establishment of a new benefit combining the social security and unemployment funds (leading to an integrated social security contribution, implemented in 1986) into a single fund for both pensions and unemployment benefits. Moreover, a legal framework for early retirement, also mandatory under EU law (Decree-Law no. 261/91 of 25 July 1991),[52] was implemented, and permission was granted to exempt or reduce interest on social security debts owed by companies "in difficult economic situations or subject to special company rescue or creditor protection schemes" (since 1989, these schemes have taken on a variety of forms).

One aspect of this state management was the setting up of pension funds. Further, under Decree-Law no. 415/91 of 17 October 1991, a minimum income was established by 1996, which was subsequently replaced in 2003 by the social integration income. In the spirit of Scandinavian "flexicurity" or the German Hartz IV welfare reforms, "targeted assistance programmes" are being implemented all over Europe aimed at creating a more politically stable workforce, to avoid political conflicts between capital and labour and to ensure social harmony. In his article on Sweden in the present Special Issue, Max Koch reports a decrease in amounts allocated to individuals not returning to the labour market. Despite forty-seven per cent being in poverty in Portugal in 2014 (according to the UN definition), the number of social integration income beneficiaries fell from 526,382 in 2010 to 320,554 in 2014. Part of that state policy involves the Employment and Social Protection Programme (Decree-Law 84/2003 of 24 April 2003), which allows the period for claiming unemployment benefits to be shortened and gives access to early retirement resulting from unemployment, and access to social unemployment benefits. Another very important aspect of this intervention are the active labour market policies.[53] Since the end

---

51. See Ministério da Solidariedade e Segurança Social, "Evolução do sistema de Segurança Social – conteúdo final", available at: http://www.seg-social.pt/evolucao-do-sistema-de-seguranca-social? p_p_id=56_INSTANCE_R6s5&p_p_lifecycle=1&p_p_state=exclusive&p_p_mode=view&p_p_ col_id=column-1&p_p_col_count=1&_56_INSTANCE_R6s5_struts_action=%2Fjournal_content %2Fexport_article&_56_INSTANCE_R6s5_groupId=10152&_56_INSTANCE_R6s5_articleId= 135838&_56_INSTANCE_R6s5_targetExtension=pdf, last accessed 4 January 2013.

52. See, for instance, Decree-Law no. 119/99 of 14 April 1999; Decree-Law no. 483/99 of 9 November 1999; Decree-Law no. 125/2005 of 3 August 2005. Diários da República, available at https://dre.pt, last accessed 3 March 2016.

53. Mónica Costa Dias and José Varejão, *Estudo da Avaliação das Políticas Ativas de Emprego* (Lisbon, 2012), available at:http://www.igfse.pt/upload/docs/2012/estudopoliticasativasdeem pregoRelFINAL.pdf, pp. 42–60, last accessed 5 April 2016.

of the 1980s, mechanisms have been established whereby businesses can be exempted from making contributions. Initially, companies could be granted exemptions that could be extended for a period of up to three years if a worker were employed permanently. Currently, the PAE (Active Labour Market Policies) programme allows a company to employ a worker for six months on a precarious contract, with wages paid by the social security system. Such an employee may be dismissed at the end of the sixth month.[54] This scheme, along with mini-jobs, is widespread in Austria and Germany. Companies may choose to pay a fraction of the salary, with the remainder paid by partial unemployment benefit. In Portugal there are currently 160,000 workers, including outsourced labour both in private and state employment, affected by policies under which the state, through the social security system, pays up to seventy per cent of their salaries.[55]

Finally, if companies resort to laying-off employees, or in the event of total or partial production stoppages, workers receive social security for up to six months. In many cases they are required to attend official vocational training, which is partially paid for by social security. The number of companies declaring "fake" lay-offs, meaning they file for bankruptcy after six months, is unknown. It is also the responsibility of the social security body to guarantee outstanding remuneration, if certain conditions are met. In 2008, the figure involved was 26 million euros; by 2011 it had risen to nearly 75 million euros.[56] According to Guedes and Pereira's study, by the end of 2011 vocational training and active labour market policies, combined, accounted for 1.4 per cent of Portuguese GDP.[57]

Social security, the densest component of the welfare state, has become a tangle of complex legislation affecting many sectors.[58] In general terms it includes retirement pensions (for workers who have contributed), minimum pensions, and allowances for disability, old age and widowhood; assistance programmes to help the workforce in times of need, such as when they are sick; access to education; subsidized canteens; and a minimum income (later known as social integration income). Nevertheless, there has

---

54. *Ibid.*
55. *Ibid.*
56. Pordata, "Indemnizações compensatórias da Segurança Social por salários em atraso" [Compensatory Allowances for Outstanding Wages], available at: http://www.pordata.pt/Portugal/ Indemniza%C3%A7%C3%B5es+compensat%C3%B3rias+da+Seguran%C3%A7a+Social+por+sal %C3%A1rios+em+atraso-114, last accessed 15 September 2015.
57. Renato Guedes and Rui Viana Pereira, "Quem Paga o Estado Social em Portugal?", in Raquel Varela (ed.), *Quem Paga o Estado Social em Portugal?* (Lisbon, 2012), p. 54.
58. For a detailed analysis of the different contributory schemes and the scope of measures covered by social security, see Lei de Bases da Segurança Social [Social Security Law], Law no. 4/2007 of 16 January 2007.

been a concurrent exponential rise in poverty, and today forty-seven per cent of the Portuguese are poor, before social transfers; despite these transfers, this figure is still as high as eighteen per cent.

To recapitulate, in Portugal there are three parts to the social security system. The first is a contributory pension system based on a repartition system and on social contributions. The system has a surplus – it is the only budget in the overall national budget that has never been in deficit. The second is a non-contributory system designed after 1974–1975 mainly for peasants and domestic workers who had no social security benefits during the dictatorship. That fund had its origins in general taxation. The third is social protection, in principle intended to pay social benefits to impoverished and involuntarily unemployed workers. That fund, too, is financed from general taxation. Unemployment benefits are a statutory contribution, mandatory only for those on a permanent or fixed-term contract. However, some of the workers previously mentioned, including those on student grants, "green invoice" workers, and others, are trapped in forms of precarity and have no access to regular unemployment benefit. In April 2016, the official number of unemployed was 622,000, but just 250,000 received unemployment benefit.[59]

The restructuring of employment, with increased precariousness, unemployment, and labour turnover took place at the same time as universal policies were replaced by targeted policies. After 1974, and during the 1980s, the welfare state was universal. The "unified education system" was free, from primary school to university, and the Portuguese national health service was entirely free for the entire population. Housing rents were "frozen"; by law, rents could not be increased for those tenancies that originated in the 1970s or 1980s. Moreover, such fixed-rent tenancies could be transferred to the tenants' children. However, since the beginning of the 1990s there has been a major shift, with universal policies being replaced by focused ones. Free health care was now means tested, as was university education; and rents were liberalized after 2012–2013, with state subsidies only for those able to provide evidence of inability to pay. During the late 1980s and 1990s a range of unemployment assistance programmes were set up to supplement unemployment benefits. These included a minimum wage and "social unemployment benefit". In theory, all of that should be covered by the tax system, but the contributory system, too, is having to pay for these programmes because the other funding systems are in permanent deficit. Furthermore, with the increase in precarity and unemployment the number of people in the contributory system and the level of their salaries are in dramatic decline. In 1988, the percentage of revenue accounted for by

---

59. *Diário de Notícias*, 18 April 2016, available at: http://www.dn.pt/dinheiro/interior/mais-de-372-mil-desempregados-sem-subsidio-em-marco-5131523.html, last accessed 5 May 2016.

social security contributions was eighty-eight per cent; in 2000 it was 69.8 per cent and in 2012 35.1 per cent.[60]

Ana Elizabete Mota, a professor of social work, has ascertained that targeted assistance policies aimed at those affected by lower wages and unemployment tend to become more prevalent in the exact proportion to that by which the welfare state is curtailed; that is to say, they increase only where universal social solidarity is destroyed.[61] Throughout the 1980s and 1990s the universal solidarity policies that assured the maintenance and training of the workforce were replaced by targeted policies that, while they ensured (biological) social reproduction, resulted in a subsequent fall in wages for all workers, contrary to initial intentions. Poverty and social inequality were the inevitable result. In the words of Pedro Hespanha, in this period the principle of "universality" was jeopardized.[62] Figuratively speaking, it amounts to "using parents' wages to pay for their children's unemployment". Van der Linden adds that "many of the social provisions adopted after the Second World War were *not* supported at the expense of capital. In 1950, the United Nations' *Economic Survey of Europe* stated that 'the whole of the social security system was funded by a huge redistribution of wealth within the working class'".[63]

CONCLUSION

Paradoxically, what had been a historical gain – universal social security won in the revolutionary biennium of 1974–1975 – became, from the end of the 1980s and for political reasons, a social cushion to fund unemployment and precarity. Beforehand, in order to shape these new labour relations, the family wage was legitimized and families took it upon themselves to support their children for longer periods. Then, social security resources, and pension funds in particular, were systematically put to use to follow up the regulation of labour market flexibility by providing support by means of unemployment benefits, subsidies to business, support for lay-offs, and assistance programmes.

Throughout the 1980s and 1990s, universal solidarity policies, which ensured the maintenance (health, social security, and housing) and training (education) of the workforce, were replaced by targeted policies in which

60. Pordata, "Contribuições no total das receitas da Segurança Social", available at http://www.pordata.pt/Portugal/Contribui%C3%A7%C3%B5es+no+total+das+receitas+da+Seguran%C3%A7a+Social+(percentagem)-765, last accessed 5 May 2016.

61. Ana Elizabete Mota, *Cultura da Crise e Seguridade Social* (São Paulo, 1995).

62. Hespanha *et al.*, *Entre o Estado e o Mercado*, cited in Fonseca, "Ideologia ou Economia?", p. 80.

63. Marcel van der Linden, "Prefácio", in Varela (ed.), *A Segurança Social é Sustentável*, p. 9.

only the working poor and unemployed had free access to the social welfare provided by the state.

The process might have left Portuguese society deeply wounded, inasmuch as it resulted in what we believe to be a case of "workforce eugenics". Young people earning low wages see their social (and biological) reproduction being put in jeopardy while their experience of life as adult wage earners is delayed. Scenarios have been proposed centred on an increase in the average lifespan,[64] when, in fact, the pivotal question concerns labour relations. Portugal has an economically active population of roughly 5.5 million people, with 2.5 million pensioners, both contributory and non-contributory. However, because of the state of labour relations and employment conditions, that pyramid has been inverted and half the workforce – there are three million people unemployed or in precarious jobs – has become passive, making little or no material contribution to the economy. This labour market inversion has come about because the state has set up a social cushion, channelling social security funds in a multitude of ways, so that, on the one hand, business is supported while, on the other, unemployment and assistance-based programmes are enacted.

64. The average life expectancy of those over sixty-five in Portugal is one of the lowest in Europe: seven or eight years less than in countries such as Denmark, Sweden, Ireland and the United Kingdom. See Instituto Nacional de Estatística, "Esperança média de vida à nascença e esperança média de vida saudável à nascença", available at: https://www.ine.pt/xportal/xmain?xpid=INE&xpgid=ine_publicacoes&PUBLICACOESpub_boui=275535921&PUBLICACOESmodo=2, last accessed on 15 November 2016.